Water | Mills | Marshes

Life and Work on the Broads

1920 – 2020

EDITORS

Ruth Tolland

Jen Smedley

Teresa Marriott

Olwen Gotts

Published by WISEArchive
admin@wisearchive.co.uk
www.wisearchive.co.uk

Designed and typeset by www.moxiecreative.co.uk

Printed by Biddles Books.

Cover photo: Drainage ditches, Halvergate marshes © Mike Page

ISBN: 978-1-8381087-0-0

Contents

Boats & wherries

Reedham Ferry

CHAPTER 3 | MILLS

CHAPTER 4 | MARSH

Marshmen

Agriculture

Animal health & knackering

Turf Fen Mill

Preface

WISEArchive is an oral history group made up of volunteers. We believe that people make an important contribution to the community in the course of their working lives, and are a valuable resource of knowledge and experience which should be preserved for future generations. We are interested in how things were done and how things change.

The Broads is a unique mix of marshes, fens, rivers and broads which attract over 7 million visitors a year, and it is the marshes and waterways that form the backdrop for this book.

We have recorded almost 100 stories over three years about life, work and change in this remarkable area and we believe that this collection provides a wonderful insight from the perspective of those involved. Unfortunately, not all stories could be included due to lack of space.

Stories relate current thinking and practice, disappearing jobs and skills, restoration of mills and wherries, and conservation initiatives. They offer differing views about the issues and challenges facing this ecologically fragile world. They also highlight the passion and connection so many feel for this special place and how many developed their particular interests as children or young people. The stories have been edited but the words are those of the contributors, as are the opinions.

WISEArchive
www.wisearchive.co.uk

ACKNOWLEDGEMENTS

We are grateful to the Heritage Lottery Fund for funding our heritage project as part of the larger Water, Mills and Marshes Project managed by the Broads Landscape Partnership Scheme. We thank them all for their support.

Many thanks also go to our wonderful contributors for their co-operation and interest and for their generous sharing of memories, knowledge and great anecdotes.

Finally, we have to thank all our hard-working WISEArchive volunteers who have so tirelessly and enthusiastically assisted with this project: Sally Andrews, Cherie Buckland, Ming Cheung, Vicky Fryer, Olwen Gotts, Simon Kettley, Jane Knott, Teresa Marriott, Mary MacMaster, Barbara Milton, Gillian Playford, Geoff Pritchard, Julie Savory, Jen Smedley, Ian Knight Smith, Jan Surtees, Ruth Tolland, Anna Varley, Jo Wood.

WISEArchive
Working Lives

WATER, MILLS & MARSHES
Broads Landscape Partnership Scheme

HERITAGE FUND

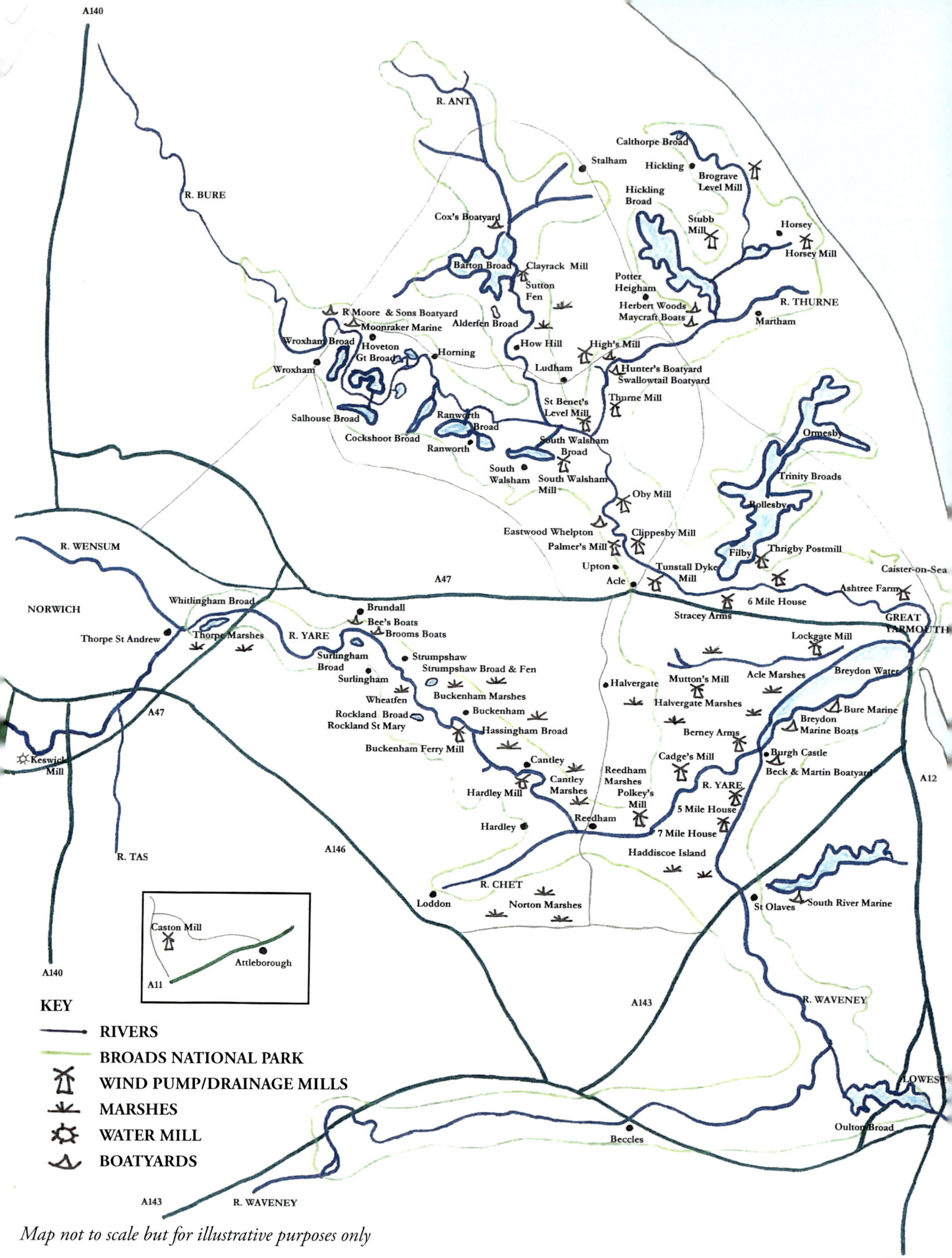

Map not to scale but for illustrative purposes only

Introduction

We know that in Roman times the Broads were full of small islands amidst large areas of wetlands and reed beds. Everywhere it was much more marshy, a nature's paradise for large numbers of fish, eel and birds.

As most of the Broads' rivers were at sea level the remaining dry land was susceptible to tidal changes. It was not an easy area to live in because most of the patchy land was essentially unused by people as it was impassable. Very slowly as the sea fell away the drying marshes became a little more inhabited in terms of crude fishing and local communities. It was really only in the 16th century that drainage of any significance began to happen, mainly due to the influence of the Dutch.

By the end of the 18th century the emergence of wind pump technology improved the drainage systems so the Broads became more agricultural. Nevertheless there were still large areas of fen which were ecologically diverse and internationally recognised as being of very high value. This led to the Broads being seen as a paradise, and in the early part of the 20th century there are many famous pictures of people in boats on crystal clear water with large amounts of water plant life. So the Broads up until about 1930 were unique in terms of wetland ecology.

The history of the discovery of the Broads as an artificial regime was discovered by a geographer called Joyce Lambert who spent her life looking at the ecology and history of the area. She did what I think a really good geographer does: she was as much interested in the history of the area, particularly the parish history and its economy, as she was in the ecology and geomorphology of the land surfaces around and below the Broads. Intriguingly, she found that in some of the Broads, particularly in Barton Broad, there were baulks of peat very close to the surface of the broad which separated two areas of removed sediment and demarcated parish boundaries.

She found that the Broads were artificial, created by peat removal between roughly 1300 and 1500 when this was a primary fuel for medieval England. Boats transferred the peat to London for something like 150 years, so there were large areas of turf removal. Around 1450, there was a subtle change in the use of fuel including the beginnings of coal. The peat areas were not well drained and began to flood as water slowly seeped into them. Over time it became increasingly impossible to cut the peat out and peat cutters would have been

Joyce Lambert

working in watery conditions for many years before actually abandoning them. So the Broads as we know them really became full broads around the latter part of the 15th century.

Although they are considered by a lot of people as not being a natural area they are endemically fascinating because they have this remarkable human history; culturally and historically speaking they are unique. Joyce Lambert's work is a wonderful example of geography at its best and led to a strong interest in the Broads being managed in a special way.

In the 1940s two major reports were published on the future of the national parks in England and Wales. The first was by John Dower, published in 1945 and the second by Arthur Hobhouse which led to the National Parks and Access to the Countryside Act in 1949. The Broads were not included, the main reason being that it was a navigable river system and there was a large amount of commercial boat activity all the way to Norwich and also around Oulton Broad and Lowestoft. So it was not easy to imagine this as being purely a natural area.

As the commercial activity slowed down in the 1960s and 70s there was a greater interest in putting the Broads into a national park context. This was resisted by the boating interests and particularly by the Great Yarmouth Port and Haven Commissioners who were adamant that there would be no such thing as a Broads National Park or anything resembling it.

The Countryside Commission, formed in 1968, set up a review which led to a proposal to make the Broads a special statutory body called the Norfolk and Suffolk Broads. Special legislation, called the Norfolk and Suffolk Broads Act, was passed in 1979 but the Broads did not constitute a national park. This led to the formation of the Broads Authority which was formally recognised under the subsequent Norfolk and Suffolk Broads Act of 1989. But still the Broads did not lie legally within the ambit of the National Parks and Access to the Countryside legislation.

Over time the boating interest has increasingly become recreational with very little commercial activity nowadays. The influence of the Port and Haven Commissioners has subsequently diminished, but the Broads Authority remains legally outside of the national park family. Nevertheless it calls itself the Broads National Park for recreational and tourism purposes.

Last year a further government review chaired by Julian Glover recommended that all national parks in England and Wales become part of a national service as scenic landscapes. This recommendation will cover all of the ten current national parks, the Broads Authority, and the 34 Areas of Outstanding Natural Beauty. This will enable the Broads to be fully part of the scenic landscape family, while also being encouraged to offer the many opportunities for creative and imaginative ways of dealing with the future of sea, land and agriculture, as is being forecast in the forthcoming Agriculture Act. This legislation will provide resources and policies for enhancing nature, for connecting wildlife and scenic corridors, and for funding the capacities of soils, wetlands and vegetation to lock away carbon. The future of the Broads as a safeguard for planetary health is upon us.

Professor Tim O'Riordan
January 2020

CHAPTER 1

Life & childhood on the marshes

Ligger at Repps Level Mill

Cattle in Halvergate

I am part of the marshes

(1934 – 1950s)

Gloria Fagg
(b. 1934)

HALVERGATE

Born and brought up in Halvergate, Gloria describes her childhood during the Second World War, village life and her love of nature and the marshes.

I was born in Halvergate on the edge of the marshes so the marshes are part of my being. I am part of the marshes. As children we spent a lot of time poking about in the dykes which were an absolute paradise of wildlife in those days. The boys used to fish for sticklebacks and there was always a chance of catching a big pike resting in a dyke quite close to land but the boys could never catch it as it was too quick.

There were a lot of big fish in the Fleet Dyke which flowed from springs which emerged beside the Carrs – a wet woodland just on the edge of Halvergate. The water flowed alongside a winding road called Stone Road and it was one of our favourite haunts. There was a turn off which went through to Wickhampton and all sorts of places if you knew the way, and there was a plank bridge, a ligger, which went across the dyke and we used to stand on it and watch the fish. This one was quite special because it had a handrail as Fleet Dyke was quite wide just there – it wasn't the sort where you took two or three steps and then you were over. Because I hadn't a very good sense of balance it was rather disconcerting because I always had the feeling I would be bounced off.

We used to go down to the Stracey Arms after school, a nice old-fashioned pub then and we would go to the back door and buy a bottle of pop and a packet of crisps. We'd sit on the river bank and have our feast and hope the tide would come up while we were still there.

If the water was nice and flat with no wind, a definite doorstep of water, a tidal bore, came up the river as the tide came in. We used to sit with our feet on the flat surface and then as it came up, our feet would be submerged; that was great fun.

I learned later it was because Breydon Water has to fill up before the Bure can fill, so a lot of water in Breydon Water suddenly starts coming up the Bure. We rarely got the right conditions so it was a great treat when it happened.

It would make us late and we had to run a couple of miles to get home. We had a system depending on the time. Either we walked to the first gate along Stracey Road and ran to the next, or we did it the other way round, because the gates were unevenly spaced. There was also a shortcut across the marshes that involved going over the ligger and then around a second marsh with a bull in it, so we would always check that he was safely on the other side. We then ran across the edge of his marsh and into a lane near home; it saved going the long way round.

During the war they mined a bridge which crossed some water on the Branch Road and they tethered some beautiful big barrage balloons on the marshes beside the road. There were sandbags and barbed wire around the bridge and we used to get down on hands and knees to see what was underneath it. There was an Army camp halfway down the Marsh Road with an anti-aircraft gun which fired at German planes which came over in the middle of the night. Once we met some soldiers as we were going home and one very quietly tucked a packet of sweets into my hand, he obviously didn't want his mates to know, so I just whispered, 'Thank you'. Sweets were really something in those days.

Lots of planes crashed on the marshes during the war, usually because they had been damaged on a mission and realised they were not going to make it back. We used to see them fall out of the sky and we always knew what crew should be on which plane, and we would cheer if they all got out. Personnel, mostly American, would come to clear up the mess but one plane was French-Canadian, they stayed with my grandmother so we met them although they couldn't speak English.

Most airmen were Americans and once they gave us a packet of cookies. Because we were barraged with war propaganda we were highly suspicious – it was a case of 'Don't pick up tins, they might be butterfly bombs. Don't say anything that might give information to the enemy…' There were five of us and six cookies so we gave the spare to our friend's dog. The dog survived and we ate the rest!

The Americans were very impressed by a big picture we drew across Chapel Road – there was hardly any traffic as no-one had petrol apart from delivery men. We used lumps of chalk off the fields, bits of broken brick and burnt wood, and we made a picture which depicted children playing down at Stracey Arms: reeds, river, swing, everything. However, when the Americans came along we were terrified of talking to them and dived through the hedge.

I started at the village school in September 1939 when I was five and finished at the end of July 1945 so my school days coincided with the war, exactly. The head teacher wasn't allowed to blow a whistle or bang anything apart from clapping her hands to call us in from play. The school windows had crosses of sticky brown tape to save the glass in case

Channel clearing at Berney Arms

of a bomb blast and we had a special drill for air raid warnings. It was just a two-class school and in the infant room we had to pretend we were bunnies and hop under our tables. The junior room didn't have tables so we would collect our coats, lie down and cover ourselves with the coats. We thought it was fun and didn't realise the implications.

During the war there was less to do so we spent our time wandering on the marshes. They still slubbed out the dykes then, clearing out the surplus mud and dumping it on the side. They used a dydle which was like a giant soup ladle. They also had rakes, including a crome or big rake with curved tines, and cutting implements to cut long vegetation. They wore waders and stood in the dyke and just scooped out the mud so all the dykes had little raised banks around the edges. We liked that because being estuarine mud, it was full of cockleshells which we collected.

Some passageways were left to allow the cattle a way through, preferably where there was a natural slope, because cattle sometimes blundered into the dyke. The Fire Service would be called out and slings used to haul them out. Cattle are rather heavy beasts with small feet which sink into deep mud very easily. Sheep could fall into the dykes as well but there were fewer on the marshes when I was young as they tended to get foot rot in the wet conditions. In winter I can remember seeing the first marsh here as just shining water, with little plants sticking out. It was the same in summer if there was heavy rain.

My grandmother had a little gold ring bought by her mother with the proceeds of wool the sheep had shed or wool that was tangled up in the bushes on the marshes. She had gathered it up to sell and made enough money to buy the ring. I wore it for a long while.

We had rationing during the war but everyone grew their own food. Most houses in the village had a decent-sized garden and usually the fathers worked on them because they were farm labourers in a reserved occupation. People shared what they had. If someone had a good plum tree they would exchange plums, perhaps for some parsnips. So there was an interchange of produce and a bitterly contested flower and produce show.

Half a dozen large Percheron carthorses would clomp through the village and down Marsh Road at the end of the day. They knew where they belonged and the gate was left open so they could go straight onto the marsh and start grazing. A man on his bicycle would follow and shut them in. All the horses wanted was to get to their nice grazing and have a rest but the women in the village were terrified of them.

My father was born on Halvergate and was much more attached to the area than my mother. Father's uncle, Jimmy Banham, was a marshman and my mother had a relative who was a marshman, called Scurrell Youngs. He was a man with immense whiskers, like two long beards either side of his chin, and a huge droopy moustache.

My mother moved to Halvergate from London when she was about 11 and the village school was an awful shock because the old headmaster just taught the 3 Rs and if you got the answer wrong, you got thrashed. Later on when the next teacher was leaving, it was decided that they needed a pupil teacher and Mother got the job. She had to stop work when she married as they didn't employ married women. However, when the war began and the new teacher retired, Mother had a plea from the Education Committee to go back. She agreed on condition that she could have time off when her husband was on leave.

Our relatives had a post office and general store in the village. They also had a smallholding where they kept cows and bottled the milk to take round the village. It was supposed to be on ration but obviously they were not going to waste it so we often got more. The shop also had an old gander that used to strike terror and chase people. One day, the old gander went for an old lady who lived in Tunstall and was tiny and frail-looking. She grabbed him by the neck and spun him round and round and when she sat him down, his head was still going round. He never went after her again!

I'm sure it was growing up on the marshes with their dykes and wildlife that inspired my love of nature: watching water spiders collect a bubble of air and take it down, caddis fly larvae, sticklebacks and frogspawn. There were water hen nests from which the boys took eggs and the hens would go on laying, often in one another's nests, so a nest could have 25 eggs which would never hatch out in the normal way.

We looked for watercress until they began spraying the marshes with weed killer after the war to 'improve' the marshes. They killed off the wildflowers but failed to kill the nettles and thistles; now they know that the natural flora growing in grass is much better for cattle than just plain grass. People in the village were annoyed because the men would gather watercress and mushrooms early in the morning and couldn't do it anymore.

My mother taught me the names of plants, some with Norfolk names, as we sat beside Fleet Dyke. There were King Cups, otherwise known as Marsh Marigolds, a flowering rush which Mother called Apple Pie, and the Greater Hoary Willowherb she called Cherry Pie and had dark pink flowers, and Water Docks.

I remember a plague of goat moths one year. They started as big caterpillars the size of my finger and were beetroot-coloured on top and carrot-coloured underneath, and they were crawling down the road. I gathered up two and took them home, put them in a cardboard box and both pupated and hatched out into fairly dull-coloured, greyish moths. I understand the caterpillars spend three summers growing and eating before pupating. But why there was such a plague of them that particular year, I don't know.

My father's uncle, Jimmy Banham, lived at Lockgate Mill which sent water straight into Breydon Water rather than the river as it was near enough. When it was decided to supply the area with piped water they sank a bore at Strumpshaw and water was carried out to places like Acle and Halvergate, Freethorpe and Wickhampton. My father said, 'They're going to dry the marshes up,' and they did.

He was a bricklayer and had worked on making and repairing a lot of the wells in the village and he knew their depths. When he built our bungalow, he sank a well but didn't like the look of the water so decided to bore further down into the chalk. During the war and in dry summers we were often the only people in the immediate neighbourhood with fresh water, and people would come and pump for drinking water.

The marshes changed a lot after water extraction began because the water table lowered and there was never the same wetness again. The dykes were lower and murkier and much of the greenery was destroyed. I suppose during the war it was felt that the land was being wasted so some farmers started ploughing it up, but there was too much salt in the ground for it to be really successful. Then after the war they tried tulips thinking they'd do alright as they did in Holland, but they didn't. Then a farmer near Yarmouth began keeping cattle intensively and all the effluent from his wretched sheds went into the Fleet Dyke. They sectioned it off but a beautiful flowing stream abruptly came up against boards with foul water on the other side. I'm afraid I rather gave up on Halvergate Marshes after that. When there was a big move to save Halvergate Marshes I said, 'You can't save them; they're ruined.'

Marsh marigolds

In the old days the Acle New Road was lined with willow trees to hold the soil together and keep it reasonably dry, especially at the Acle end, and every year the long straggly bits were harvested in huge quantities and used for basket-making. When the railway line was built they used heaven knows how many faggots and other things to stabilise the ground, particularly near Acle. It was really boggy and they just piled stuff in until they filled up whatever void was at the bottom of the mud and then laid a railway line across.

We had a very bad winter in 1947 and Father went on the dole for the first time because nobody could work and he felt there was no disgrace in it. They would all tramp across the fields through the snow to Acle to collect it and buy some bread because there were no deliveries to the village. I had just started secondary school but had to stay home for six weeks before they got the road between Halvergate and Reedham open. While on the dole Father and other men in the village tried to clear the Branch Road to get through to Acle New Road. It was fine, dry snow with a steady easterly wind. Branch Road ran north-south, so the men would dig their way so far, then turn round and dig their way back again through slightly less snow than when they started. They made a little progress each day but the wind kept blowing the snow back. It wasn't until the weather got a bit milder and there was a slight thaw followed by another freeze that the snow set with a crust on top. Only then could they get on and clear the road. It took a long time.

I was attending art school in 1953 at the time of the flooding. I remember reading 'The Grapes of Wrath' on the train, all about desert dust, and looking up and seeing the marshes at Whitlingham as a sheet of water. I just couldn't get back into the book. My sister worked at the Yarmouth newspaper office and was told to get back home quickly as Breydon Water had burst its banks and water was spreading across the road. She caught the train and got as far as Auntie Kate's in Acle. There was a tremendous gale and trees were coming down. Next day as she biked home in the wind she heard a creaking noise and put on a spurt and a tree crashed on the road behind her. It's a good thing she was a country girl and knew creaking trees could come down.

I can remember taking our dog for walks towards Cantley sugar beet factory and he would run up and down beside the dyke to frighten the cattle and start them stampeding. The ground used to shake, it was like jelly underneath, and it was probably even worse further downstream at Cantley. Apparently they put in a big concrete raft on which to build the factory, but when

Halvergate marshes

they started building one end, it began to tip up. Father told me about it and he thought they were foolish to start at one end but I suppose they put something at the other end to balance it; it wasn't a disaster anyway.

Working at Cantley became an out-of-season job for the farm labourers and I suppose it suited the farmers. Father told me that when they first started growing sugar beet it was treated with kid gloves. Somebody would go round with a steam traction engine and trailer and the sugar beet was laid in carefully with the pointed end inwards. They made a nice, neat pitched-roof shape at the top and then the steam engine trundled down to Cantley where it was unloaded by hand, again very carefully. Of course, they hadn't the quantities then; they were just beginning to grow sugar beet and it was a valuable crop.

The sugar beet lorries used to come through the village during what they called the 'campaign' and the boys would run behind the lorries and try to hang on. The odd beet would drop off and we'd take them home for the rabbits and chickens. I think the whole village fed their pet animals on that sugar beet. The campaign was part of village life; it was a season you went through like the marble season and the skipping season and all the others. It was the sugar beet season – chasing after sugar beet lorries.

A wartime memory

(1940s)

Tom Grapes
(b. 1929)

LUDHAM

Tom and his friends had a great wartime adventure at St Benet's Abbey.

During the war, four of us lads decided to go down to St Benet's Abbey for some fishing and we went down an old track and across the marshes to get there from Ludham. We started fishing but mid-morning it began to rain so we went to the Abbey. At that time there was high steel fencing round it and there was only one place in the corner where you could shin up and get inside.

In the corner I saw a load of old hessian sacking so I pulled one off and found a picture of huntsmen on horseback with their hounds and wearing red jackets. I paraded around with it, not realising what the picture was covering up. There was a box underneath covered with sacking and in the box we found a transmitter. We packed up and went back home and when we saw the village policeman we told him what we'd found. He told us to go to the big army camp in Ludham, the King's Shropshire Light Infantry, and find the adjutant's hut. We found it and paraded in with our muddy boots. The captain was sat at the desk and said, 'What can I do for you lads?' We were told to have our lunch and afterwards we could show the detail exactly what we had found.

We were that excited we were gone and back in less than an hour and when we got to the adjutant's hut there was a lieutenant, in his uniform, with a bike, waiting for us. We set off and everything was alright until we hit the muddy track and mud started to fly up his boots and trousers. We got to the Abbey and climbed over the fencing in the corner but the lieutenant hooked the leg of his trousers on one of the spikes and, of course, his trousers split up the seam, well that did it, he was in a right old state.

We showed him the transmitter under the sacking and he got out his torch and a notebook and wrote down various details, and then covered it all back up and said, 'Now, I don't want you boys to say anything to anybody about what you've found, nothing at all.' And we never said a word.

A week or so later a sergeant from the Home Guard saw us and said, 'You boys found a transmitter down the Abbey didn't yer?' So we told him that we weren't supposed to say anything but he told us that they knew about it. It seems the army had kept a watch and saw two men approach and go into the Abbey, but one of them must have been the look-out because they got away as the army closed in. They had a little rubber dinghy hidden in the reed bed at the back of the Abbey and they managed to get across the river. The army put out a search and caught the men in Wroxham. They turned out to be German spies!

St Benet's Abbey gateway

Story of an Irstead boy

(1930s – 1943)

Alan Cox
(b. 1929)

IRSTEAD

Alan lived with his extended family in a cottage in Irstead. He describes his family home and his very happy childhood.

My grandmother, aunts, uncles and I all lived together in a cottage in Irstead. We didn't have electricity or running water, but we had a lovely coal fire all year round. Let me describe the cottage… You went through the back door into the kitchen with its big brick fireplace and an oven in the wall on the left-hand side. The fire was lit underneath and my grandmother would bake the bread and cook there. On the right-hand side of the fireplace was a copper where my grandmother did the washing. There was a large kitchen table near the window and to the left was a big walk-in pantry which you went through to get to the living room.

In the middle of that room was a big table and on the right was a lovely fireplace with two hobs on the sides and a kettle. There were a couple of cupboards where my grandmother kept the linen and on the left-hand wall was a big chest of drawers and a brown table with a glass case. Inside the case was a stuffed harrier which I thought was fantastic. My favourite chair was a lovely big one next to the fireplace. In the winter we used an oil lamp with a glass globe decorated with flowers. To the left of the fireplace was the door to go upstairs to the two bedrooms. My grandmother and two aunts, Ellen and Nora, slept in the front room and my uncles Tom and Billy and I slept in the other.

We had a massive garden with two big Bramley apple trees beside a water dyke, and on the other side of the dyke there was flat marsh and old reed beds. To do the shopping, my grandmother would write a note to Roys of Wroxham and they would deliver the groceries to the house, they even had a baker's cart which came around with the bread. So we were well looked after.

My Aunt Ellen worked in a big house in Horning. She took me there when I was seven or eight and I remember her taking out a hoover and turning it on. I was so frightened when the big black bag blew up – we had no electricity at home and I had never seen a hoover before. Aunt Ellen bought my first real fishing rod and when she came home with it, I couldn't dig up the worms quick enough and I ran down to the shoals to use it. Most of the summer was spent down by the shoals, swimming and fishing. I learned to swim down there as did everyone else. I had all the freedom in the world.

There were only four or five families in the village and my grandmother's sister, who we called Aunt Sally, lived across the road. I can honestly say I was brought up in that little house with no electricity or water and I was the happiest of kids. I thought the world of my grandmother and they said I was spoilt, but I had a really happy childhood.

When I was five I had to start Neatishead School which was two miles away. It didn't matter if there was rain or snow, there was no excuse for not going. Somebody in the village gave me a little pedal car I thought the world of and I wanted to go to school in it. To keep me quiet my youngest uncle who was still at school said, 'Alright, boy,' and he put a rope on the pedal car and towed me halfway. Then he put it in the hedge at the back of a field and put me on his crossbar for the rest of the way.

Uncle Billy at Hickling Broad 1950s

That only lasted one term as my uncle left school that summer so then I had to go to school on my own, walking both ways. When I got home there was nothing in the house to keep me in so I'd be straight out on the marshes. I left at 14 as back then everyone left school at that age. There was a big garden at the school and because we got the cane whenever we stepped out of line, two of us went into the shed the day before we left and put some spuds in the rockery!

My Uncle Billy was a marshman at How Hill, it was on the other side of the river so he had a boat to get to and from work. He would start reed cutting late in the year and I would hear him talk about a 'fathom' of reed which I discovered was six bundles of reed, 6ft long and he was paid by how many fathoms he cut.

My uncle and a fellow called George were the only marshmen in the area. They worked together at How Hill as estate workers doing the fencing and hedge-clipping as well as reed cutting and clearing out the dykes.

During the war, when eggs were hard to get, I would go to the dykes and collect water hen eggs. I even had a big spoon on the end of a stick, so if they were too far I could bring them in one at a time. Someone once told me that you should get the egg in the palm of your hand and drop it in the water and if it floated, it should go back in the nest as it had young in it, but if it sank it was alright to take. I would go home with a cap full of eggs and my grandmother would put the frying pan on.

My uncle had the boat from work and we used it to go eeling in the evening leaving the eels in the boat overnight. Next morning my uncle slapped their tails against the side of the boat and we would skin them and take them home. My grandmother would put them in a bowl of water with a little bit of salt and leave them until tea time. Then she would drain off the water and chop them into two-inch bits and fry them.

When I left school in 1943 I started work at Irstead Lodge, a massive mansion just down the road. I worked in the garden growing vegetables. The other men had been called up and a lovely old fella called Jack took me under his wing; I think he thought the world of me as a boy. I worked from 8am to 5pm with an hour off for dinner and on Saturday I left off at 12. They put a pound on the table; that was my week's pay and I took it home and gave it to my grandmother. She gave me five bob back. I was chuffed. I had five shillings.

Growing up on the Broads

(1942 – 1950s)

Rex Woods
(b. 1942)

LUDHAM, HORNING

Rex spent his holidays exploring the marshes, rowing a punt on the river and helping in the boatyard.

There were several marshes near Ludham Bridge and I remember wandering through them during the summer holidays. We used to explore the old windpump mills and climb up on them if we could. There were particular marshmen about who didn't like children being there and I remember one old boy called Dick Gibbs, who was good for a chase. We could jump over the dykes more easily than he could.

We also explored the marshes at Horning, down by the River Bure. I had access to a punt so sometimes we rowed up the river and occasionally went across to the Ranworth side. This was part of the Cator Estate and they definitely didn't like us wandering about, so sometimes we'd get shouted at.

We used to ride about on bikes and in the wintertime Horning Ferry could be flooded to a depth of 2ft down the Ferry Road, so when we rode down there, our rubber boots filled up with water.

During the school holidays if we got bored with nothing to do, we'd venture down to the boatyard, Norfolk Broads Yachting Company at Potter Heigham, and we would always be found a job. We'd help launch a boat or pull one out, but bailing them out was usually the thing. We didn't mind because you could play with the pump and spray water about, so we rather enjoyed that task. Sometimes we just ran errands like picking up some bolts from another yard.

I was probably about three or three and a half when the war finished but I do remember my father talking about a Flying Fortress that crash-landed at Repps on the marshes. The crew survived and they posted some sentries but some of the chaps walked across in their lunchtime and were allowed to have a look inside. I also remember that there was an anti-aircraft unit on the playing field at Horning, and a mobile unit in fields which was actually the start of Neatishead radar station.

I remember seeing two fellas come floating down on parachutes after they had bailed out of a B-24 Liberator. Apparently, if it was a war-weary aircraft and a bit knocked about, they used to fly it back to the UK, dump the crew out, turn it round, put it on auto-pilot and send it out to sea. One of the airmen landed in Horning churchyard and he immediately went into the church. The other one landed near Grove Farm at Horning and was taken in by the Tallowins who we were friendly with, so we went to meet him. I was goaded to say, 'Have you got some gum, chum?' But my most vivid memory is seeing him sitting and playing the piano. He looked very much like a musical star of that era, Hoagy Carmichael, and every time I see Hoagy on an old piece of film I think back to this airman sitting at the piano.

A child of the marshes

(1947 – 1963)

Wally Mason
(b. 1947)

ROCKLAND ST MARY

Wally was born in Rockland St Mary and from an early age his life was spent around the water. He remembers life in the village and learning to cut reed.

Before the war my dad was a brickmaker like his dad and after the war he went into brickmaking again. At that time all the little villages had clay on the farmers' fields which brickmakers collected with horses and took down to the brickyard like the one in Rockland. The bricks were red and the clay was brown and you could get some black. There was a bonus system and if they made over 1,000 bricks they got a few more pennies. When I was about age ten I used to help my father wheel the bricks out in my little barrow so they would dry out.

I went to Rockland Primary. My mum grabbed me and took me down to the school gates and said, 'This is where you're going on Monday, and you behave yourself!' Then I moved to Nuneaton, Wales, Framingham Earl, Wales again, and Framingham Earl again. With all the moves my interest went a bit and I left school in 1962 at 14. I should have left at 15 but I had a job and as there was a shortage of jobs they left me alone.

I remember we used to jump off the bridge, have a swim and walk up the beck to see who could catch the most tiddlers using a jam jar. We called them robin redbreasts and we'd set them on the bank to see who had caught the most, and put them back. That was at Hellington, just half a mile down the road. We'd also cycle as a gang to where there was a nice big, horseshoe-shaped green and again we'd have a swim, do a bit of fishing, play in the woods or put a bit of rope up as a swing. We had no money to buy anything but we used to make things like catapults. We'd get a little saw or knife from home, cut out a load of crotch wood, find an old bit of leather and lash it on. We'd pick up some stones and place a tin on a field or chuck it up and that would be a day's fun. Or we'd make a bow and arrow and play cowboys and Indians. That was lovely; we made our own entertainment.

I can remember when the rivers were frozen 3ft deep in 1963 and everything came to a standstill. That was a long drawn out winter.

We had paraffin heaters as there was no central heating and they used to stink, they were horrible. The frost was so severe that the pipes burst and everyone was in trouble. Schools closed, we had to walk everywhere through snow drifts and it was a heck of a job to get bread. We made homemade bread with Mum until we ran out of yeast; the shops were selling out of everything.

I started reed cutting with Dad that year. I had my own section and I did do my best but the ground was just rock hard. And in those days there was no such thing as a thermos flask. Some people took an old tractor and a car on the ice and went skating and I thought, 'I've got to try it'. My first step felt like the man stepping on the moon, even though I knew it was solid and 3ft thick! You expect ponds to freeze over but when you imagine running rivers… that was just solid!

The freeze lasted for weeks and I remember when it did thaw a bit, my dad said, 'Whatever you do, don't take that boat out to go cutting reeds on the river. Leave it till I'm with you.' But when you're young you think you know everything. So one afternoon with the night pulling in quickly, I thought I'd collect some reed already stacked up on trays. I'd only been on the river five minutes when I suddenly heard rumbling under the boat and I couldn't row – there were big lumps of ice underneath. They pushed me across a bend and I was spinning round in the river; big lumps of ice just kept rising up and lifting me up at the same time. That was the most frightening time I've ever had on the river. I didn't know what to do and I just kept spinning round and round. Luckily enough I hit one big bend and I got out and stood on the ice and was able to lift the boat back into the water as the ice had shot out from below it. I was so relieved! I never did tell my dad because he would have given me a good clip on the ear. That was on the River Yare, just past Strumpshaw.

I was always getting it wrong when I used the scythe for reed cutting, you had to toe and heel the scythe. My dad was a big old boy and strong. He'd wet his finger and tell you about the wind, which way to do it and which way to swathe it.

I was a small boy so it was hard for me but once I got the knack of walking and cutting at the same time, it fell into place. I've still got a lot of the hand tools as well as that old scythe.

We were all equal years ago because most people worked on farms and there was seasonal work when we got together. We used to help the farmer and sometimes we played about and the old farmer would say, 'Now come on you boys, behave'. He'd put us right or tell us to clear off. But if you were home early your mum would say, 'What you doing home?' I used to do acorn picking. You'd get a basket and go round the trees and there would be hundreds of them; I think they went towards feeding the pigs. We did it in the holidays when we wanted to earn a few pennies. We also did stone picking for the farmer. He'd say, 'You want a job boy?' And we'd go up and down all day with pails, tipping the stones into a big container – it helped when they were ploughing and when growing plants were coming through. They used the stones for driveways, for the tractors and cars.

We used to go fruit picking: blackcurrants, strawberries, gooseberries. Most days it was mushy blackcurrants and we would bike or walk or mostly run to get to them. That was our pocket money, and the first place we'd go was the village shop to buy some aniseed balls or gobstoppers like golf balls; four for a penny. They would all change colour and last for days.

My father used to take us out on his old 500 Norton motorbike in the sidecar during the school holidays. We'd know that Mum was doing a lot of cooking and then there'd be a knock on the door at five in the morning, 'Come on you guys. You want a day down the beach?' Cor, that was marvellous, a day down the beach! We didn't know what a week's holiday was like, we didn't have the money. Away we'd go, piled into the sidecar. It would be spitting and firing up until we were a few miles up the road and we'd be off for the whole day.

We'd go to Wells and when we got there, Dad would make a little fire in the wood. We'd have some toast and Mum's sandwiches and cakes. When the tide was out there is a lovely channel beside the wood that went down to Wells and out to the sea, and we'd swim and race in it. 'Come on', he'd say, 'feel these on your feet'. You'd think they were stones or pebbles but they were cockles and we'd rake them up and fill a couple of sacks to take home on the sidecar.

There was no such thing as ice creams and fish and chips and if there were, we couldn't afford them. Father had just enough money to get us there for the paddling. Even today it seems like a marvellous day out, just mucking in as a family, putting up a couple of sticks for cricket on the beach and other families joining in. You wouldn't walk past people; you'd all be doing the same thing, just out for the day and we'd all get together, all the kids and parents.

The circus would come to Rockland once a year with their little wooden, colourful caravans and we'd see a sign saying, 'Circus here for a week'. It used to be about sixpence but because we had done jobs to earn money we would have a few pennies. The farmer let them have a bit of meadow for the big marquees and they had a show in the afternoon and another at night. Ponies would run around inside and riders jumped off them into coconut matting. The clowns would get you to join in and pretended to chuck a pail of water over you and then give you a spray. It was exciting and as a child you never forgot.

We used to have the old scissor grinder come down the road with a young lad; he would park his bike and come to the door, 'Any knives or shears for sharpening?' We would watch the sparks fly as he worked away, earning a shilling or two. Another man who came around was the old rag-and-bone man. He'd be shouting, 'Rag n' bone, rag n' bone,' similar to old Steptoe on telly. When we heard the horse's hooves clopping down the road, we would rush out!

I remember the wherries coming through and I knew one of the old boys and sometimes Dad would say, 'Go on, you can go for half an hour'. It wasn't often he'd let me go off but he didn't mind me doing that one, so I used to hop on and go for a little way on the wherry before being chucked off; the old boy would get to the side and I'd jump off, and run back to my dad.

We would get the big coasters coming up and down all the while. They used to draw about 5ft of water and if you were on the river, once you heard them blast their horns on the bends, you'd look up and it was like a tower of flats coming round the trees. If they were in a hurry all you'd see was white foam at the front of the boat and then as they passed you, you'd be bobbing up and down in the swell. They were massive, nearly filling up the whole river and they'd draw you and shove you away, and if you were in a dyke the water would disappear and you'd be sitting on mud holding the oars to keep upright. Then you'd see 2ft of water coming down the dyke and it would sling you about. Afterwards it would all be calm and the water would go back to itself again.

Coaster 'Sonority' on River Yare near Reedham

The water was clear years ago, it's been hit big time by pollution and there is no circulation around the Broads now. The old boys used to cut the sides of the banks when they were reed cutting but that's not allowed now and it's why everything has grown up along the edges and there is more vermin out there than proper wild birdlife. Even in the backyard it's hard to see a thrush. The first thing I used to hear on a summer morning was a tap, tap, tap, and that would be a thrush with a snail, banging it for food. That's gone and there are a lot of little birds that are getting rare now. Young people walk past Mother Nature these days and they don't know about it. It's a bit sad really.

There are not a lot of true villages left and it's sad we are losing the little post offices and shops. We used to have butcher's shops and little delivery vans delivering milk and bread. But it all finished when they just couldn't make a living.

A life in the Reedham marshes

(1947 – 1950s)

Arnold 'Archie' Rednall
(b. 1941)

REEDHAM

Archie was born in London but moved to Reedham aged six. He describes Reedham as it was then and the sense of community and freedom.

Brick Kiln was the old Reedham brickyard which Dad bought in 1947, but because the previous owner had TB we were not allowed to move in straight away, so I lived with my auntie and uncle in Ship Cottages near the river. I can remember the first morning my brother and I woke up at Brick Kiln and we went out through lots of apple trees at the back of the garden and climbed the fence overlooking the school playing field and we watched the kids kicking a football about. In due course we kicked a ball with them.

Reedham was a very sociable community. If someone was ill, my mum used to cook food and take it round on a plate with a dish over the top. People would sit with them and cook for them or take the dogs for a walk. When we walked to school other children would join us and, if needs be, a mum would take maybe five children to school.

I was seven when I started Reedham School in 1947 and being a Cockney kid, I think I was a bit of a novelty. My infant teacher handled me well, blending me in with the class and teaching me to slow down and slowly learn to talk Norfolk. One of the first boys I palled up with was Brian Mace. He and his two sisters used to walk down the railway line every day to go to school from Five Mile House, which is the last house between Reedham and Berney Arms. I used to go down to Berney Arms with him and play on the marshes.

His dad, Reggie Mace, was a marshman and I used to watch him keep the gates in good order and clear the marshes and dykes of harmful plants and thistles so cattle didn't eat them. He also looked after the cattle making sure they were safe and he took them back to the farms for milking. In those days, the marshes were full of cattle. There were also a lot of horses about because it was the very early days of tractors, and horses were still used to pull carts and ploughs. There were marshmen all the way from the rond at Reedham right up to Berney Arms looking after the dykes and caring for the cattle.

A couple of men worked with Reggie slubbing out the dykes using a spade, shovel and fork, all on long poles, and they put the stuff from the bottom of the dyke onto the edge. Then, when the water and the sediment settled you could see the bottom and the fish. Reggie also kept an eye on water levels in the dykes and controlled the water flow from the river into the dykes whenever they got low. Originally they used a water wheel operated by a windmill but that was soon replaced by a big diesel pump house which they could just switch on and off, and they no longer had to worry about the wind. There was also a wrecked, derelict old steam pump which I found interesting.

I was fascinated by the windmill. The steps from the ground floor to the first floor had been taken away to stop us climbing up but we got some six inch nails from the local shop and nailed them into the wooden post that went up the middle, and we climbed up to the first floor. From there we could go up steps to the very top and that was our den where we kept all our Eagle comics. The mill dykes were wide and you could row a rubber dinghy down them. We cut a door off one of the derelict mills and made it into a raft and used that to float down the mill dykes. It was probably a silly thing to do, but we did it.

The normal dykes were about 3ft wide but mill dykes were 6-8ft and were like the main arteries – when the mills were running, water was pumped into the river or vice versa, and all the little dykes fed into the mill dyke. At the back of the mill there was a big chain that pulled the sails into the wind. It was all in operation right up until I was 14, but eventually the windmill seized up and they built the diesel pump house with its big concrete tank outside. It was like a reservoir to prime the pumps and we swam in it.

When I first went down to the marshes, the dykes were all straight, level and clear and we used to go spinning for pike. We would tow a piece of string with a spinning hook through the water and the pike would be attracted by this shining, spinning thing and go after it. We would pull it out, cook it and eat it. We used to go eel babbing in the river on a big rubber dinghy and we cooked those as well. I can't say I was too fond of eels but it was all part of the adventure.

We had the floods in 1953. I was in bed one morning and my mum came in, 'Son come and have a look at this'. She rolled up my blind and I looked down towards Berney Arms and I could see the sea round the edge of Reedham Church. Unbelievable! The marshes were covered in water, and on the high bits the cows were up in the gateways trying to get out of the water. It wasn't deep, about 2ft, but it was an incredible sight. That finished the dykes off and all the fish were killed. They never did recover and fewer people worked on the marshes afterwards.

Mr Rednall

My mum used to play the piano and my dad played the mandolin-banjo down at the Ship or the Nelson on a Saturday night. I can remember when Eddie Calvert came on the scene I decided to learn the trumpet, then when Lonnie Donegan came along with skiffle, I took up the guitar instead and I played at the pubs. People from the boats came in for a drink and sang songs and danced. There could be 40 to 50 people – we used to have incredible times.

Bertie Dawson was a farmer in Reedham and my mum used to cook for him. An elderly lady lived with them and nuns from a Catholic church in Yarmouth helped look after her as she was bedridden. Bertie had the biggest farm in Reedham and was the first to have a tractor – the whole village went to see it. He had three or four people who worked for him with horses and carts and when they ploughed the field or loaded the carts with sugar beet or turnips, they used to let me sit in the cart and I'd pretend I was driving.

At harvest time, we had the old sail binders with a sail on the side that were pulled round by horses.

The horses used to go around in a big circle and as the field got smaller, the whole village stood around the outside with dogs, sticks and guns. When the rabbits eventually ran out they caught them and we had rabbit pie for days afterwards. We had only a few little shops but a lot of people grew their own vegetables, caught rabbits, shot partridges, pigeons, or whatever else was going, and they lived off the land.

There was no piped water in the village. We had a well at the bottom of our garden at Brick Kiln with a bucket on a long piece of rope to bring the water up. It was tipped into another bucket and brought into the kitchen and stored under the sink in a porcelain pail with a lid on top. This was the drinking water, ice cold and lovely.

We didn't have conventional toilets either when we first moved to Reedham, just a shed in the garden which we called the 'thunder box'. Inside was a wooden seat with a big hole for the grownups and a little hole for the children and we had a pail underneath. Then on a Friday night, a man known as Hilton would bring his horse round with a big, square metal cart behind and he tipped in all the night soil and took it down to the allotments. They put in sewage and a water supply in Reedham when I was still a youngish lad and suddenly we had taps and baths!

I think most houses had electricity but it was very primitive with just one plug in the kitchen and a light in each room; when I was very young a lot of people still used candles. We had a little narrow kitchen with a big sink, a pail, a table and a basic electric cooker, but before we had the cooker we cooked on the fire as did many people in the village. The front room had a big black stove with a coal or wood fire on one side, and an oven with a grill on top on the other.

Many people gathered wood for the fire to save money and several people had paraffin stoves to heat the house and paraffin cookers. The Co-Op had a big tank outside and I remember you could go round there and get a gallon of paraffin for ten pence. There was a telephone box at the top of Mill Road which is still there but derelict. As far as I know, nobody had a telephone except for the doctor.

There was a massive field on Church Road which consisted wholly of allotments and nearly every household in the village had one and grew all their potatoes, tomatoes, carrots and the rest. Dad had the last allotment and that's where Hilton spread all the sewage; the joke was that his potatoes were the biggest in Reedham but nobody would eat them! At the bottom of the allotments was the dyke where water radish grew, and they used to take it round and sell to the people on the boats.

There were only a few cars in the village. There was a taxi service next door to the railway station, the vicar had a very old car with a canvas roof and the policeman, schoolmaster and doctor all had them and that was about it. Nearly everybody else had bikes; a few had horses and traps, or they walked. There were no buses so if you went out of the village you got a train for Yarmouth, Lowestoft, or Norwich. If you went to Norwich there was a massive walk up to the marketplace, but you did it.

Once or twice a year, a bus or charabanc would be organised and we would all go off to Gorleston and have a day out on the Pleasure Beach or the circus at Yarmouth. In the summertime we had a carnival on the village green and everybody in the village would go with all the children in fancy dress. There were marquees and big tables to sit round for tea and cakes and in the evenings there were whist drives in the village hall. There was also a concert party in the village once a year and I used to get involved with that.

There were two boatyards in Reedham called Pearson's and Sanderson's which built mainly holiday boats and down at the riverside was a massive shed where the wherry Albion was built; it was used later as a mushroom factory. In the holiday season the boats were two deep and villagers would go round with a basket on their arm selling vegetables and whatever they could.

One of the Albion skippers was a chap called Denny and he lived in Reedham and knew my parents. He would let me go on the Albion and we would sail from Reedham to Berney Arms. The hold would be filled with various goods such as sugar beet and cattle feed. It had a great black sail and it was just incredible. I loved the boats and one of my hobbies in the summer was to go down to the riverside and collect the boat numbers.

Mum and Dad were friendly with Jack Hunt who was a river inspector and had a Yare Y90 boat. We used to call him a river policeman but his proper title was River Commissioner. He was in charge of the river from Berney Arms to Brundall making sure that the holidaymakers drove safely. He was also responsible for dredging the river if anybody drowned; sadly my cousin was playing with his toy boat on a bit of string and leant over the edge of the quay and toppled in, Jack Hunt found him.

Jack would come into the pub when my parents were playing and one day he asked if I would like to go out on his boat. I grabbed the chance and he gave me my ongoing interest in boats. It was tied up under the swing bridge and we crossed the bridge to get to it. After passing Dewhurst Quay where the local GP lived, he would let me drive the boat down to Berney Arms. We used to tie up at the pub and Jack would go in for a beer, and I would walk down the river wall to Breydon Water and just look around and watch the birds.

Learning to swim

(1950s)

My family moved from Freethorpe to Reedham when I was aged four and I've lived there for the past 70 years. I spent my entire school life at Reedham School because the secondary moderns didn't actually open until the year after I finished, so you stayed at your primary school.

The tidal River Yare ran through the village and if you fell off a quay head and couldn't swim you had little chance, but where it was just rough bays and banks and you could walk into the river, it wasn't so dangerous. So Mr Boast, the headmaster, was very keen for all his pupils to swim and he used to take us to Yarmouth swimming pool for swimming lessons.

In the height of summer with nothing else to do we would go to the marshes, down Holly Farm Road, and we would jump into the dykes to cool down and swim. Once we graduated from the dykes we moved on to the river and we regularly swam there in the holidays. Some of the bigger, brave boys used to jump off the swing bridge at Reedham; I can assure you I was not one of them. We thought nothing of it, it was what you did; you learned to swim and you swam in the river. It was accepted as perfectly normal.

Keith Patterson
1942–2018

A Neatishead boy

(1940s – 1950s)

John Horner
(b. 1938)

NEATISHEAD

Neatishead Stores

John spent his childhood in Neatishead where his mother ran the village shop in King Street and his father had a smallholding.

The village shop was an institution for all the farmworkers and locals around. It was open every weekday from 9am until 8pm, and from nine until nine on Saturdays which everyone called 'grocery day'. It was a real meeting place and my mother had that shop for over 40 years. Although it was wartime when I was very young we lived well because of the shop. Father made sure we had enough partridge, pheasant and rabbits and he would bring home other things or 'swopsies', for a rabbit or a pheasant. We also had a big garden out the back and grew all our own veg.

There was an outside loo in the garden. We didn't have any heating only a little fire in the living room and it was nothing to go to bed in the wintertime and wake up with ice ferns on the windows. We didn't seem to take harm, we just jogged along and it was a lovely place to grow up. We were surrounded by good families and everybody knew everybody and looked after everybody. We would walk to school, play out and go home when we felt like it. No-one seemed to worry.

I was too young to remember much about the war but I remember everyone had ration books and had to register with a specific shop to get their rations. My brother and I used to cut the coupons for Mother and the older people often gave us their chocolate or sweet rations and we would accumulate piles of them in the sideboard. Father was in the Home Guard and they met up near Ludham Bridge but I don't think they ever had rifles, although my father had his own shotgun for shooting rabbits.

My grandparents lived just down the road and we could see their little thatched cottage and Grandfather's hut and old barn from the shop. He was a sixth generation horse collar maker and I understand one of his collars is in the Bridewell Museum in Norwich. To make the horse collars he used soft rushes from the river and tied them up in blocks of four to dry out in the meadow just opposite the shop. I was fascinated by his skill in turning the bundles inside out without undoing them; he would pick one up and then sort of flip it. He had a block in his workshop with nails sticking up which he used to shred and soften the rushes, then he sewed leather around them to make the horse collar.

Grandfather also made rush matting and mended bikes; his workshop was full of bike parts. He would do anything for anybody and often he wouldn't charge them. He worshipped bikes and used to get mad if we went down to his workshop with bits of rust on them. Behind his thatched cottage was a little scullery where he charged up accumulators for radios and I would go round to see them all linked up. I have also heard that he kept a black hearse and black horse for funerals. I sometimes wonder whether he could read or write as I never did see him do either.

I went to Neatishead School when I was about five in about 1943. The infant class had a mirror just inside the classroom that looked like a life buoy with the words 'Am I clean and tidy?' written around the edge. There was an open fire and if anybody made a smell, as children do, the teacher would put some brown paper on the hot ash pan and walk around the room with it smoking. After the infants we moved up to the juniors. There was only one big room for juniors and seniors with a curtain in between. It was very difficult to know where to concentrate with two classes running and only a curtain separating them. Mr Challoner was the Headmaster and taught the seniors and up at his end of the room there was another big open fire with a guard all around.

We had a school garden where we had gardening sessions every week. There were apple trees and Mr Challoner used to count the apples because some could go walkabout. He was quite handy with the old cane. He used to cut it out of the hedge and swore blind that if anyone was brave enough to hide his cane or chuck it on the fire, the next one would be thicker and harsher.

I remember when the dentist came to school and they took out the iron rails at the front and pulled in his old caravan. The equipment was all belts and pulleys and ropes which turned at nil miles per hour so Mr Pulham would be working on your teeth and grinding away in there for a long time.

It was just a village school and because I was so keen to get back to the smallholding and get on a tractor or feed some bullocks, I failed my 11 plus, much to Mr Challoner's disgust. I was head boy but all I wanted was to go out and live life. The school is still there but it's a private house now.

Neatishead School, drawn by John

My father ran a smallholding just up the road from the shop. He had meadows, greenhouses, chickens, pigs, bullocks, a Jersey cow for our own milk and some arable for corn and mangolds. We kept the chickens in an old railway carriage with leather straps on the windows – the guy who had the smallholding before us used to live in it with his wife and three children. We made nest boxes out of orange boxes from the shop and it was my job to collect the eggs and look after the chickens. Some of the eggs were sold in the shop and some went to the Egg Man who came every Thursday, so Wednesday nights were spent hand-washing the eggs and putting them into trays.

Once a year, Father had a pig killed by the village butcher and there would be big ham joints hanging behind their bedroom door. Father was a very big bloke but twice a day for years, he would get out his tiny three-legged stool and walk out to the meadow with his pail to milk Trixie, the Jersey cow. He always wore a cap and he would turn it back to front so he could rest up against the cow to milk her; that was just the best milk in the world.

John on the smallholding

We had two meadows for the animals and also a horse called Ginger before Father eventually got a tractor. We had mangolds to feed the bullocks and we would grind them up and mix them with wheat chaff and sugar beet pulp which had little black curly bits and a lovely smell. Even from a young age we were expected to help out on the smallholding. We had two large greenhouses for growing tomatoes and cucumbers, some went to the shop and the rest were sold elsewhere. My job was to pick off the side shoots and water all the plants using a pail: one pail of water for every three plants.

Later on Father decided we needed a proper water supply and he called in a plumber who was also a water diviner. He ambled about at the back of the greenhouses with a hazel twig in his hands and then stuck his heel in and said, 'This is where it is, there's water down there.' Father dug a well and sure enough, he found water. He installed a pipe and a pump leading to a big tank in the middle of the greenhouses and my job became easier.

When the tomatoes were finished, the soil in the greenhouses had to be changed. When I was about 13, Father asked me and my friend Titch to do the job and it took us a fair while. At the end of it, Titch got his first pair of long trousers and all I got was a bar of chocolate! However, when I was about 15 I had to dig the greenhouses out again and this time, Father gave me two tiny pigs straight from the sow to fatten up. I scrimped and scraped everything I could find to feed those pigs and eventually sold them and bought another five little ones. I also kept rabbits on the meadow behind the shop garden which I used to breed and sell off.

I was still at school but all I wanted to do was get home and work on the smallholding. Father had a Standard Fordson tractor by then and I used to run home from school, change, and tear off up the field and he would get off the tractor and go home, and I would carry on. The Standard Fordson was never good at turning, it had iron wheels on the front and rubber tyres on the back and when you turned, it kept ploughing forwards. Mother was certain I was going to finish up in the ditch with the tractor on top of me. I was still at school when Father bought a new Ferguson tractor – the height of luxury! It cost about £350 and he bought it on hire purchase with help from the bank at Wroxham. The bank manager knew everyone and how they worked and he would roll up for a cup of tea or meet in the pub. It was all about local knowledge and people coming together; that has all stopped now.

Swans in the kitchen

(1950 – 2018)

John Crohill
(b. 1944)

BRUNDALL

John grew up in Brundall learning to sail and helping out at a boatyard. Over the years he kept some unusual pets with varying degrees of success before becoming a wildfowler.

I moved from Cambridge to Brundall about 1950 and lived in a little house next to the Lackford Run, a stream that runs from the River Yare and goes up through Braydeston. It was tidal so there were all sorts of fish and swans in it and the end of the garden was just marsh and full of wildlife. I had two sisters and I remember one used to go absolutely mad in the summer because of the mosquitoes. Being near the marsh and water meant the place was seething with them and we were bitten all over quite regularly.

The garden was half marsh and half lawn and I remember the old chap who used to do the garden and how he cut the grass with a scythe. It was amazing to watch as he would get on his knees and cut a beautifully smooth, bowling-green lawn. I also remember waking up one morning to find water all around the house during the big flood of 1953. Luckily it didn't come in but it was quite spectacular. We didn't have mains water or sewage so we had a well in the garden and a soakaway – I remember they were only about 20 yards apart so I'm not quite sure about the quality of the water!

I had two best friends in Brundall and one of their fathers had a boatyard called Tidecraft Cruisers. When I was a bit older, about age 12 or 13, we used to help out at weekends showing people how to drive the boats and generally doing odd jobs. That was quite lucrative as the holidaymakers were fairly generous with their tips so we really enjoyed doing it. We got the use of the boats as well which was quite handy and in winter we would paddle around Surlingham Broad and the rivers. I also learned to sail so it was a lovely childhood apart from the chore of going to school.

I remember the grass snakes; there were hundreds of them basking on piles of reeds in the sunshine but they seem to have all disappeared now. We also had a pair of swans nesting in our garden. They were called Asthma and Jallopy for some reason; I suppose the asthma bit was because they made that coughing noise. They brought up a brood of cygnets and got in the habit of coming into the kitchen to be fed. They would waddle up the lawn and in the back door and demand their slices of bread.

I had some unusual pets. At that time there were quite a few coypu about and I would find them in the garden. I did try and keep them as pets in an aviary in the garden but they generally escaped, I didn't realise how good they were at burrowing. I then tried a bigger version of a cage trap that we had for rats and that seemed to work quite well. I could pick the big ones up by the tail and they couldn't do anything about it, but I learned that the little ones were quite supple and they would climb up and bite you. Later on when they began to do more damage a bounty was put on the tails, so when we saw an advert that a zoo in King's Lynn wanted coypu and would pay £1 each, we

John with his retriever

caught a few and sent them over. I don't know what they did with them. They weighed about 20lb or the size of a medium-sized dog and when my friend's dog dug one out from a burrow, the coypu got it by the throat and if we hadn't been there, I'm sure the dog would have been killed.

I tried to keep grass snakes but that didn't work very well either; I'd put them in a big tin bath but they always escaped. The only thing I had any success with rearing was white mice which were kept in the shed outside. They bred like mad so I used to sell them to the pet shop where I'd got the first pair from, and that made quite a bit of money. I also caught eels and traded them in at the local shop in Brundall, swapping them for packets of sweets. Watercress was another source of income.

After the coypu I became interested in wildfowling. Duck shooting used to be done on a large scale and wildfowl was sold to the markets for extra income. A lot of wildfowlers on Breydon had punt guns and could shoot 20 to 30 birds with one shot. One of my friends moved to Acle and his father had a shotgun and was keen on shooting so Andrew used to shoot as well, and would let me have a go. We would wander over the marshes looking for pigeon or duck for the pot. I was about 15 and boys my age or even younger often started off with airguns.

Having been introduced to wildfowling, I found there was a club in Norwich that organised shooting and I joined in 1970. We used to go after various types of duck, wigeon, teal, mallard and the odd goose if we were lucky, which all went into the pot. This developed and I got involved with the club's committee and eventually became the secretary. It was a lot of work but also meant meeting lots of interesting people like old Ted Ellis, Percy Trett and various other naturalists.

Wildfowling is mainly done in the dark as ducks fly at dawn and dusk so you're actually shooting at shapes – you need a good dog to retrieve as you are never sure where they will fall. Unfortunately, I wasn't too good at training dogs so mine tended to be a bit unruly. One of the retrieves I remember best was actually in daylight when a teal flew over the ronds at Stokesby. I shot it but didn't kill it unfortunately, and it landed in the river. I sent my little spaniel after it and the silly dog ran into the middle of the ronds and not the river, and started digging. I told him to fetch but he carried on digging and pulled the teal out of the hole. There was a coypu burrow under the ronds and he knew the teal was there and he dug it out and brought it to me. That was the most amazing retrieval he ever did.

An unspoiled childhood by the Yare

(1951 – 1960s)

Julia Waters
(b. 1951)

THORPE ST ANDREW

Julia had a simple but lovely childhood growing up on the banks of the River Yare.

When Mum and Dad married their first home was on a houseboat and I remember Mum saying she steered the motorboat, towing the houseboat behind. When he was a toddler, my brother would put things out through the portholes so Mum would look out first thing in the morning to see what was on the bottom of the river, like socks and shoes. Dad had to fix everything down including the clock, so they wouldn't go out as well.

During the Second World War everywhere had to be blacked out because the planes used to follow the glistening river and bomb Norwich. My aunt and uncle lived on the houseboat next door and Mum would invite Auntie round for a cup of tea in the evening and she always tipped the tealeaves out of the porthole. She did this one night and said, 'Oh, I think I've just tipped it over a swan!' As everywhere was in blackout, mum couldn't see it. To get water, Mum had to carry two tin pails from the pump at the top and along the cinder path back down to the houseboat.

After the war Mum and Dad were very happy on the houseboat until Dad sadly lost his leg in a motorbike accident. He did rehab and was given a heavy wooden leg and they stayed on the houseboat. He just about coped and he also continued working as a mechanic at the top of the lane. However, by the time I came along Mum, Dad, my sister and brother had moved into a little wooden hut with a tin roof at the top of the cinder path. The corrugated roof was painted red and the walls were green. Inside was lovely and cosy and painted cream. There were lupins all along the front of the house and on the little path as you went to the front door Mum had two lavender bushes on either side.

Tragically my dad died when I was a few days old so it was 'sink or swim' as my mum said. She had a 'make do and mend' mentality and was very sensible and determined. She was a hard worker and brought us up in a loving, caring home even though she struggled to make ends meet. Because Dad had served in the war, Mum used to get a postal order from the British Legion every Christmas to help us.

The houseboat

The greengrocer delivered every Saturday and because he had children a bit older than us he used to bring clothes which his children had worn and shoes for Mum, so that helped a lot. Mum went to jumble sales and bought woollen jumpers and cardigans which she unpicked and re-knitted as jumpers for us and when our slippers had holes, she embroidered wool daisies over them. Although we were poor we had a lovely childhood. We were

Julia

left on our own a lot. When I was four-and-a-half Mum was told that she had to work, so she worked locally and my brother took me to school.

Mum did her big wash in our wash house in an old copper boiler and used bluebags. She used to boil the white cotton sheets and she let me put them through the mangle while she turned the handle. Because of the steam train line at the back of our house, the sheets used to get covered in smoke smuts, so sometimes she had to wash them all again. When a train went past, I used to wave to the train driver and he'd toot back, and I'd wave to the guard at the back who waved back, a bit like The Railway Children really.

We lived surrounded by dykes and the River Yare and we had no fear of the water but Mum would say not to go near the swans. I remember them hissing. I also remember their lovely cygnets, soft and downy and how they glided through the water so serenely, putting their heads down in the weeds looking for food. There were reeds opposite our house where I made dens and rabbit runs and I remember there was a rope across the dyke with a stick at one end which we sat on, and when we pushed off we would go most of the way across and back again. We did respect the river though.

There was a winch in front of the house and a big boatshed where they built boats and John Fox used to winch up the boats when they had to come out. I remember one of the boats and the wood shavings lying about on the ground. It was absolutely massive and took a long time to build and they named it the Aramajay. John had a lovely wooden motorboat and would offer us a ride in it. We used to row as well and my brother made his own canoes and would take them on the river up near the Postwick bend.

Barges went up the river filled with coal and I'd wave and the men would wave back, and when huge cargo ships went past, they'd wave too. When the floods came we were lucky because our back garden was long enough and there was a ditch and railway bank protecting us. Auntie Ethel wasn't so lucky. Her house opened straight onto two lawns and then the Yare, so she had nothing to stop the river coming in and her hall and kitchen used to flood every year. She got very fed up with it but it was accepted. Then May Gurney built a bank and that stopped the flooding; it wasn't high, but it was wide. Our house was cosy and warm, and despite living near the dykes and river, we never had any damp.

People came past the house to reach their boats and yachts on the river. One gentleman used to come down in a really old, open-top car with a hood on the back and he would say hello and put his hand up. They were the rich people, because they had boats, but they were all very nice.

It was an unspoilt childhood. Not much money, but we were happy and content. Mum left the door open all day long. We'd go off but we knew what time tea was.

A Wheatfen childhood

(1953 – 1970s)

Suzie Hanna
(b. 1953)

WHEATFEN

Suzie is the youngest of five children who grew up at Wheatfen. Her father was the naturalist Ted Ellis and her life was surrounded by nature, music and visitors from around the world.

We think our cottage was built about 1825 as it wasn't on the 1820 map. It was two woodmen's cottages together, poorly built with local bricks which probably came from the brick works in the village; the clay is likely to have been dug from the pit at the top of the field next to the house.

Captain Maurice Cockle and his wife bought the cottages in 1914 as part of a shooting estate which included 140 acres and a wood. My parents knew him and made many visits as he and my father shared an interest in wetland issues and wildlife and also in small things such as mosses and algae. When Captain Cockle died during the war, my parents arranged to rent the property from his widow and then bought it in the 1960s. There was no running water or electricity. We got water from a well that wasn't palatable and had to be boiled, so we drank a vast amount of tea and Mum brewed ginger beer and elderflower champagne; we couldn't have orange squash or anything like that.

Life was quite tough. My sister and I remember sitting on either side of a fallen tree with a two-handed saw, taking turns to pull it. Mum would sell it to us as, 'Oh, it's a bit like a see-saw. It's fun sawing up logs.' I was four at the time.

We would often be in charge of the massive Georgian table with its many leaves which we had to slot in with little bits of brass. As we laid the places we would say the person's name to ensure we got everybody, and remembering names was seen as an exercise. It was Dad's table when he was the Secretary of the Norfolk Naturalists Trust and when they were clearing out, they let him have it. We needed it because there could be 20 people round the table. The table was used for card games and board games too. A favourite was Racing Demons which is like everybody playing patience in a big pile. The person with the longest arms and hardest hands would usually win because they could slap their card down and frighten you.

My brothers had to walk miles over the fields to school in Claxton, even as small children. I think they had it tougher than me because they were older and there were fewer comforts then. Mother normally cooked on a Rayburn but breakfast was cooked on a primus stove as the Rayburn wasn't hot enough.

We had a wood fire in the front room and in winter we did our homework by the light of a Tilley lamp, and we took one when we went to bed at night. We would let the pressure out and go to bed stinking of paraffin. Winter was so cold we had ice on the inside of the windows and sometimes frost on the quilt. I sometimes had my school uniform in bed with me at night and put it on before I got out of bed. We had chilblains but there was a huge upside: we could go out on the water in a boat, have picnics, climb trees, make bows and arrows out of hazel sticks and make dens. I can't say the number of times I cut myself

Suzie with the hens

on the bracken making dens. We had a wild, free life: running about, digging holes, looking at stuff and growing things.

We didn't have pets like cats and dogs. Instead we had chickens and we adopted things like the gosling that followed us about. Things arrived, they lived here and became like pets; that is part of country life. When we weren't running around the woods making as much noise as we liked, we made a lot of noise in the house. Mum was a good pianist and could sight-read to a very old age. We played Bach's Double Concerto and things like that, Mum was quite fierce about our practice and would facilitate it by playing the piano for duets. My grandad had a banjo and ocarina, Mum would bang saucepans and everyone was encouraged to pick up something and hit it.

My father wrote a few fairly decent songs. When he was happy he sang waltzes, especially the Viennese waltz. I think Mum helped him write down the songs and we still have the manuscripts. He wrote the Wherry Waltz and one about the procession with the dragon in Norwich called Snap the Dragon. We sang while doing the dishes, singing harmonies and descants. Mum played the organ every Sunday at Surlingham village church for over 40 years until she could no longer play and we sang in the choir. My father would say he believed in reincarnation; I think his sense of the world approached a Gaia theory and in his mind, nature controlled life and death.

Dad was offered amazing jobs but they chose to live a primitive life here and scrape by, carrying on their ideals. Because he was a naturalist and a scientist, he attracted international attention and on one occasion we had the Japanese scientist who discovered plankton under the ice in the Arctic giving us tips on how to keep our feet warm. In the Arctic, you can put a blanket over the table and a single candle underneath and if you put your feet under the blanket, they won't get frostbite. This was good for Wheatfen!

I remember Beki, the niece of King Freddie of Uganda, who was at Durham University with my sister. There was an uprising in Uganda so Beki spent the summer with us instead of going home. I came down one morning, aged about eleven, and saw this tall, very beautiful African princess ironing her hair with a flatiron on the hall table. Then we had mycologists from Kew Gardens. One had a beard seemingly down to his waist, very thick pebble glasses and rode a motorbike. Our lives were full of these extraordinarily eccentric characters and in the deepest, darkest recesses of a muddy Norfolk fen we had a multicultural society in our house, and an open door policy. It was frenetic a lot of the time and my brother-in-law said he felt sorry for me as I was always called, 'Somebody'. When he came for the first time in the 1960s he would hear Mum shout, 'Somebody wash up; somebody clear the table; somebody go and get some wood…' I was the last one left at home!

Russell Sewell was born at Wheatfen in 1900 as one of 13 children. When he was three years old Russell was getting water from the well when the handle came back and banged him on the head, it knocked him out for days. After that he was treated as if he was stupid which he wasn't, and he told me terrible stories of being beaten at school by the strict Methodist teacher. He had a really tough life but lived to the age of 83.

Russell had worked for the Cockles. He was a great handyman and when he saw my mum struggling with living here he would help her out, and she cooked him a meal. He was unhappy living with his sisters and brother in the village and eventually a deal was struck and he effectively lived here with free board and lodging for life, while tending the garden, growing wonderful fruit and vegetables and cutting reeds. He became part of the family and even though we lived off the land, if it was not for Russell, we would not have eaten so well.

Russell was a proper marshman and such a good influence on us. He would say, 'Come along with me, I've got something to show yer'. And off we'd go into the wood. After a mile we'd find a mushroom with a natural smiley face. 'Look at that!' He'd let us carve our names on young marrows and they would grow with our name in big letters. He engaged with us and he played with us in a way that connected us with him through nature.

Grandfather was interested in Mendelism, cross-breeding plants and breeding chickens and he always made copious notes, I think that's how my father became interested in the minutiae of plant genetics. He also got the drawing and detailed observational skills from his mother – they both had a microscopic view of things, like the old miniaturists. Father left school at 14 and worked in a false tooth factory where the silica probably caused his lung problems later in life.

Russell with coypu

He had his 'apprenticeship' with Arthur Patterson the naturalist when he was 17 to 18, and kept a diary of everything like the naming of species and learning the Linnaean system. Then still a teenager, he revived the Yarmouth Naturalist Society and became a Fellow of the Linnaean Society with a complete grasp of the system. He typed up Arthur Patterson's work and when Arthur died, Father took on much of the work and began writing newspaper articles.

Wheatfen cottage 1960

In the 1960s, my brother John was stationed in Singapore and bought a lovely Pentax camera and that was when Father took up photography. There were a lot of things he thought beautiful like parasites on wasps, and we had endless slide shows once we got electricity. Sometimes we didn't really feel like it. Most of his work was writing articles for the papers but he also recorded Nature's Postbag on Radio 3, he was on Look East and he did a natural history spot for the BBC 1 Friday night programme, Weekend, with John Mountford.

From my perspective his experience of life was going out and observing things, making notes, referring to his vast library of books and connecting information; he was a proper researcher. He discovered various microfungi like one on the bog myrtle catkins which was named after him. He was very academic despite leaving school early. He was poetic and wrote in a flowery, conversational and celebratory style that could be ornamental, embellished and Victorian. He could also write scientifically and UEA gave him an honorary doctorate in 1971. He was a communicator with a lovely, articulate tenor voice. He was a good broadcaster and charismatic, and people liked him. As his children we found that difficult to believe!

My father was really down on farmers using dangerous pesticides and phosphates and we now know these things go through to the water table. He certainly didn't like the government-funded decimation of hedgerows. He predicted that washing liquids and detergents would destroy our waterways because the sewerage systems couldn't deal with them. He was right but was threatened with legal action for publicising that point of view.

He was offered a knighthood but turned it down because a Norfolk furrier had been offered one the same year but I also think he just couldn't be bothered with it. He lived to 77 despite bad health; he had tuberculosis and had suffered from quite disabling sickness in his life. He was quite happy on his fen doing what he could.

My mum felt she was betraying his memory by accepting her MBE but she saw it as good publicity for the Ted Ellis Trust. At Buckingham Palace when the Queen spoke to her I saw the Queen's face drop and wondered what Mum had replied. Later as we sat in Hyde Park having tea in a polystyrene cup, I asked about it. It seems the Queen had said, 'I see you got your MBE for services to the environment,' to which Mum said, 'No, I think you'll find it's for services to conservation'. For Mum, services to the environment meant something to do with a water or sewage company, whereas services to conservation was much more important!

Mum had taught on the Isle of Dogs in the 1930s when she was a student at Goldsmiths. She saw the Jarrow marchers with cardboard wrapped around their bare feet. She taught a class of 60 who had no underwear so she went out, bought cotton and taught them to make their own. I think Mum was a real socialist and believed in an equitable society.

Mum and Dad had rented the parish marshes to keep them as a nature reserve and to stop people shooting; and when the Ted Ellis Trust was formed, the open door policy was kept.

The Trust raised enough money to pay for a warden and we are attracting more young people and their families. My daughter helps this process by running a forest school which encourages the parents of young children to bring them to do some forest work on Saturdays. It is going well, and she is continuing the family tradition of education and nature.

Ellis family 1960

Phyllis and family at the Palace

A life's trickle: childhood

(1953 – 1970s)

Kim Dowe
(b. 1953)

POTTER HEIGHAM

Kim grew up in Potter Heigham. He recalls a carefree childhood roaming the marshes, picking fruit with his grandmother and helping his father on the wherry Lord Roberts.

I can trace the family back to just before 1700 and on both sides there were watermen and lightermen. My father was the wherryman for the Lord Roberts working for a man called Blucher Thain who owned four wherries. He went off to war and when he came back the Lord Roberts had been turned into a motor wherry. His job was transporting goods and I can remember him moving stone, reed, gravel, wire mesh and sugar beet. I used to spend a lot of time with him sleeping on board in the cuddy where we had a lovely warm fire and big thick mattresses with blankets. One thing with my father was that when you went into the cuddy you had to take your boots off. That time spent with him was magic.

My father's cousin Sonny Amis was a piling contractor and used to do a lot of quay heading work. Years after my father died I remember Sonny telling me that Father had the job of going to Heigham Sound to recover parts of a crashed Spitfire. He went down on the Lord Roberts on his own with a load of lifting tackle and lifted off five bits of plane and took them back to Potter Heigham Bridge where the RAF collected them. He never told me anything about it.

My grandmother Annie Howell lived one door away from us. She didn't have a lot of money so she worked at the farm next to the church picking up stones and putting them in sacks. She also did fruit picking with my mother, my brother and myself; we would pack sandwiches and leave our bikes near to where there was a massive great bull which had a good snort as we walked past.

It was seasonal work so in the winter I would go sticking with my grandmother and her friend Eileen down at Picamore. We collected branches and bags full of sticks and tied them on the bikes; it was just another way for them to support themselves through the winter. I also remember Grandmother fattening up pigs for Christmas, one was called Pig-Pig. I spent a lot of time with her and my dog Butch and when I was younger I also worked with my grandfather picking up fallen apples and boxing them so they could be made into cider.

When I was one and two years old, I spent time with my great-grandmother who lived in the old school after it closed, and it was her home for many years. I have a picture of me on a trike with knitted shorts and vest with my great-grandfather's pipe in my mouth. During the war she had Italian prisoners of war brought to her every day by two policemen and she used to feed them; they worked in the village and carved wood and ivory gifts for her. I've been told that behind the old school there was a small building in the woods where an old man lived and he used to shoot duck from his front room window.

Sometime after the war my great-grandmother moved next to the Methodist church. There she had an oven in a hole in the wall next to the fireplace where she made bread. I remember eating cold rice pudding that could be cut with a knife – gorgeous. My great-grandfather grew tobacco there and dried the leaves to smoke.

Grandmother Annie Howell

If I had nothing to do on a Saturday I would take myself down to Picamore or Wagon Hill or Candle Dyke. I liked being on my own with my dog Butch and I would go walking the marshes and along the riverbanks, climb trees and go through orange muddy water in the dykes. If I ventured further afield I would go swimming in Hickling Broad. Before they built the new dyke you could go out of Picamore, over a plank, up a bank, through a few reeds and you'd be in Hickling Broad. It used to have a sandy bottom and I would paddle around for hours and then, still soaking, I'd go back to the woods.

I used to go to Wagon Hill and climb into boat sheds looking for swallows nesting inside. There was a watchtower from where people watched herons and I liked to climb it for the 360 degree views. I also liked going down Marsh Road to see the brick bridge which used to span the dyke. I was told that the RAF dropped two parachute mines on the marshes there and that they spent nearly six months trying to dig them out. I used to lie in the clumps of reeds and just dream. I would look up at the sky and listen to the sounds around me and I can always remember the sound of seagulls which were louder in winter when they followed the plough, picking up worms.

There was a man in the village who worked as a farm labourer who I knew since I was a nipper. He had two cart horses which worked with the tumbler, or small plough, but I never saw them work together. I remember one mangel time when Norman had hitched up the tumbler and I went with him to the fields at the back of the church to where they lay in little piles. He set the horse off while he topped and tailed them and threw them into the tumbler, with me sitting on top, loving it all. When the tumbler was full Norman said, 'Here you are boy, you take the reins', and I set off down the field to the farm and tipped the mangels in a heap.

During the long winter freeze of 1968, Butch and I used to go down to Hickling Broad to see what was going on and I remember a helicopter with some sort of weight underneath hitting the ice on the broad to break it up, as the poor birds had nowhere to swim or feed. They threw out corn and the birds were milling about. I saw a big wooden plough being pulled by a horse up and down the roads to clear the snow, and the milkman knocking on all the doors and telling everybody that the milk wagon was up the road and to help ourselves.

I remember Mr Cray, the 'honeycart man', collecting the 'honey' at the end of the night. He used to come down the road, jingle-jangle and he always stopped at mine to call up, 'Are you awake?' And I always said, 'Yes', because I knew I was going to get something, and he would throw me up a few sweets. He was a lovely man.

I was never a fisherman as such but I spent a lot of time at it; I would find a nice quiet spot and just sit there. I used to go to Candle Dyke too but I was more interested in watching the eel catcher putting his catches in a massive box that was just below the surface before hauling them off to wherever they had to go. I used to stay overnight down there in a little hut. My mum and dad knew where I was so they didn't bother and that was when I got into eels.

I started a Saturday job at the Woods boatyard when I was 13 and was given an eel trap to put into the basin there, but I often let them go again. I also took the eel trap down the river towards Repps using an old rowing boat. My friend David Woods caught eels professionally so he used to take the eels and give me a few pennies.

I was at Woods for about five years earning my Saturday money and got the job through my aunt's father who was the foreman there. He had lots of stories to tell including meeting George Formby, who lived at Wroxham and had a boat built at Woods. To start with I cleaned out the dinghies and made sure that they were ready for the next customer. I then progressed to being the car park attendant, cleaning cars and keeping a couple of batteries charged for when people got flat batteries; that was when I made my money, £3.10s a day.

I also helped my father on the wherry. I remember one time when I was about 14 or 15 he asked me to help him take a wherry full of sugar beet down to Cantley. I had handled the tiller many times but when we stopped at Yarmouth he told me he was getting off and he took his bike and said, 'I'll meet you back at Cantley!' He also said to be careful going under the bridges. And that was that!

I'd been to Cantley before so knew what I was up against. I got onto Breydon Water, chugging along, and was then against the tide for a lot of the way. When I got to Cantley I came in right next to the shoebox without having to turn round. The shoebox was a long concrete container that had a big crane with a grab on top which grabbed the

Victor Dowe wherryman

Wherry Lord Roberts and Beaumont's Mill 1950s

beet from the wherries to put in the box. The sides of the shoebox were painted with different scenes by wherry people to make a big mural about 200ft long; it was beautiful. My father took the last wherry load of beet to Cantley around 1962 and after that there was no need for the shoebox, so it all came down. I was sad to see it go. I always thought that something like should have been kept with all those pictures of the ships that used to come in, and people's names on them. That was part of the Broads history just taken away.

My father carried on working for May Gurney and that is how the wherry Lord Roberts spent her last years. She was then taken to Hunter's Yard and sunk in a little dyke nearby. After a while she was raised and there were hopes that she was going to be put back into working order by the Wherry Trust. She was refloated and taken to Royall's yard in Wroxham where she was moored up and that is where she lies to this day. Everything below the water is still there but she's now covered with trees and her superstructure has rotted away. It is sad to see. I had lots of lovely times on her as a kid.

Albion at Bungay

Around 1964 when my father was still working for May Gurney he was asked to sail and maintain the wherry Albion after Nat Bircham retired. I sometimes helped my father do weed cutting to keep the navigation open for the boats. He would get his contracts and spend the whole day out. We used a weed cutter with 7ft blades – I think there's a similar one in the Museum of the Broads – and we would go to Horsey, Deep Dyke and Meadow Dyke and sometimes up to Waxham Cut.

The fair used to come in August and I would help my father moor the three wherries: the committee boat, the beer boat and the spectator boat. He used to work with Billy May putting the fireworks out on the Repps side for the display on Saturday night. As a kid I would lie in bed and hear the fair going on and during the day it was exciting to watch the dodgems and pick up coconuts and balls that were thrown into the river.

A lot of children today miss out on these experiences but I actually lived it, I was there. And the memories will stay with me. I see the waterways, villages and stretches of marsh all changing from when I was a kid. I just wish that people would change their attitude towards the Broads; not just take but give a lot.

The marshman's daughter

(1960 – 1976)

Sue Goodchild
(b. 1960)

REEDHAM

Sue is the daughter of marshman Bill Lacey and had a wonderful childhood running free in the Halvergate marshes.

I was born in my grandma's house in Reedham, exactly where I live now, because my mum wasn't allowed to be on the marshes when she was heavily pregnant. We went back to Berney Arms the next day to my brother who was three years older and my dad, Bill Lacey, who was a marshman. Our nearest and only neighbour was three fields away and we lived three miles from Berney Arms Mill where there was a row of cottages. We were not far from Breydon Water and that is where we went for our Sundays out if we went anywhere.

We didn't have electricity or running water. As I recall, we had two bedrooms and we went through my parents' bedroom to our bedroom. We had a very 'farm-orientated' lounge downstairs, no carpets but very cobbly and the kitchen had just a sink and a cupboard so there was no luxury at all. But it wasn't a hardship; it was just how we lived. I remember there was an old-fashioned bread oven built into the wall and an Aga, and when the new-born lambs were poorly Dad used to bring them home and put them in the Aga. He'd give them a tot of whisky and warm them up before they went back to their mums.

There was no indoor toilet – the toilet was down the garden and had two seats, one little hole and one big hole, for different-sized bums. It was very cold but I remember the toilet had ivy over it and in the autumn it was a beautiful red. We had to go to Brian Banham's for drinking water; he was based just before what is now the Vauxhall Holiday Camp going into Great Yarmouth. We would go on Saturdays with churns in the back of the Land Rover all the way along the Acle Straight and were allowed to use the hosepipe near the bridge; goodness knows where the water came from. Two churns had to last us the week.

We used well water for washing and on Saturday my brother and I would wash in a tin bath, one each end, in front of the fire that used to roar and warm up the bungalow. There was also a copper with a fire underneath for the hot water. I don't know if my parents ever bathed, I'm sure they must have done something but in those days you didn't think so much about it. When there was lambing we were out all day putting our hands in not very pleasant places to help birth a live lamb, and we would just wipe our hands on some straw and eat our lunch. That is what you did. And, if we were thirsty, the water in the dykes was clean enough. We had a generator for electricity but we had to wait for Dad to come home from work before we could have it. As children we just had to pray that he'd be back in time so we could watch Blue Peter.

We went to school in Halvergate and walked from Berney Arms to the A47, as it is now. I think there were 19 gates and a good two to three mile walk to get there. We had to go over and under and round and through, climb gates and go over liggers, and if my brother was being particularly mischievous, he would try and spring me off into the dyke. He didn't succeed! When I think how tiny we were, walking all that way; I can't imagine it happening today.

One bus went into Yarmouth at six in the morning and returned at six at night and it was always full of workers going to the factories in Yarmouth from the villages. We used to catch that bus about seven on its return trip from Yarmouth to Halvergate and then wait at a friend's house until school opened.

My dad worked where we lived on the marshes so he couldn't take us to the main road. His work was hard and he didn't get time off for being a parent. However, if there was really deep snow he would put a tin sledge on the back of a horse and somehow get us to the A47 for school. We didn't have wet weather gear but we had wellie boots and a coat. I don't think we felt the cold like you do now. Even now I say, 'Put some gloves on, Dad'. 'Gloves? Who on earth wears gloves?' He still doesn't feel the cold.

Mum was a teacher but did not work when we were tiny, so that worked fine. After we moved to Halvergate when I was nine, she taught us for a while; it was really hard because we had to call her Mrs Lacey but it was the time when we became 'civilized' with running water and flushing toilets.

For entertainment in the evenings we had TV. We didn't entertain and hardly ever went out for a meal so the fish and chip shop in Yarmouth was always a treat. When we went out we always saw people we knew. We made friends because there was always a routine: the petrol, the market for some fruit and Woollies (Woolworths) for corned beef. We didn't buy meat otherwise because we produced our own, Dad would kill something during the year and we lived off that. We grew most of our own vegetables so were fairly self-sufficient and very green. There's concern these days about waste products, plastic, and what we do with our lives; that never happened just 50 years ago. So my generation has kind of ruined the world.

Occasionally we went to the Norwich cattle market on a Saturday and even now I can smell the Norfolk Dumpling which was the restaurant there and hear the stools scratching across the floor. Sometimes we brought things to sell and sometimes we bought things. It was a really busy hub and we could catch up with everyone. Dad told us a tale about how he once came back from the market pushing the pram with my brother in it and it went into the dyke. Dad saved the new calf first!

Sue and brother

I loved the life. Even now, I love my wellie-boot days and being out in the muck. There wasn't a track to our house, it was pure mud and when we were out in our wellie boots we'd lose them and end up barefoot but it was fun. The tractor was generally the only vehicle to get right up to the house, just, and in summer a Land Rover might manage it. Now it's very plush with a concrete road.

I remember the postman used to come to Berney Arms by train and then come to us and the neighbour across the fields and then back to Berney Arms. The pub there was a busy place with a lot of river people and locals as well as the many marshmen who worked down there; there was no other social life so once in a while Dad would say, 'Oh come on, we'll go', and it was always lovely to see Irene and her husband who ran the pub.

School friends didn't come to the house so once we got home that was it, we were home. When I was seven we moved to a bungalow a bit further into the marsh, and although we were probably only three miles from Halvergate village, we were still on our own. It was just one black bungalow in the middle of the marshes. The one time people came was for our birthday party. My brother's birthday and mine are close together in August and all our friends would come in the middle day. I suppose they thought it was exciting because it was something different, not many people had a party on the marsh. We didn't see any health visitors or the like; they wouldn't have known how to get there and, for sure, they wouldn't have walked all that way. Nanny and Granddad only came at Christmas because it was just such a trek.

We always had dogs and pet ponies everywhere and we had a horse for hacking around on. Once, when we lived at Halvergate, we were on the marshes and the horse kicked my dad. I drove the Land Rover to the village to get help although I wasn't old enough officially, but we could drive as soon as we could touch the pedals. We had a Massey Ferguson that my brother or I used to drive while one of us dropped the feed off the back. Once I ran my brother over and broke his leg when we were feeding but it didn't cause a big drama, it was just dealt with.

I can remember another time when Dad was hay-carting and Peter and I were helping as we always did – we didn't think of it as a chore. We were on top of the hay on the trailer and as we came round the corner to go to the black bungalow, the hay tipped into the dyke along with us!

When the vet came to check the cows, I remember sitting on top of the pound with my pad and writing down the number of each cow. I would earn some pennies for that and felt very important. I know how lucky I was to have that kind of freedom and I would do it all again tomorrow.

There was lots of physical work but there was certainly no obesity in our family. We just had proper food three times a day; we had a cow so we made our own butter and a Jersey cow for scrummy full fat milk. Sheep-dipping days involved a massive amount of work and we knew we had to help as Dad had about 200 sheep. Dad looked after everyone else's cattle and marshes on his level, a level being an area of marsh. He also had some of his own marshes to help boost his income where he kept some cattle, calves, sheep and a couple of horses. I seem to recall some Nissen huts with pigs in them as well.

We didn't join clubs or groups outside of school, we didn't know they existed, but we went to Sunday school at Halvergate which meant we walked but we never missed, and I loved it. My grandparents were staunch Methodists so if we were at Granny's in Reedham, we used to attend three services on Sunday, but on the marshes we just went to Sunday school.

I remember when Sunday school had an anniversary in July we had to learn by heart something called 'The Bit', which was a poem. We were not allowed to read it and I can remember walking for hours round fields learning it. The anniversary was always held in Halvergate in a massive barn in three sessions. Afterwards we were taken out for a treat and went to Gorleston in the morning, Lowestoft beach in the afternoon, and the Pleasure Beach at Yarmouth in the evening. To me that was the world, a day without our parents and all those treats.

We were surrounded by dykes and Fleet Dyke was the big one where my brother and I used to make rafts out of cans and strap bits of wood on top. Then during the summer we would paddle up and down using another bit of wood as a paddle – we didn't have accidents. If we had a cut they just stuck something on us and said, 'Get on with it', and we did.

There was always wildlife around like ducks and geese, and rats and mice too, they were part of life. In the feed sheds I would squeal a bit when I put my hand into animal feed and a mouse ran up my arm. I also remember the grass snakes and owls and the coypu. There were coypu catchers at that time and we would earn so much a tail when we trapped them. I used to be fascinated by their teeth because they were long orange hooks and I collected them!

There has been an increase in people walking and birdwatching on the marshes since the Weavers Way was established and people learned where they could walk. However, there is also less freedom. As children we could walk anywhere and no farmer was ever offended. Dad taught us to walk next to the dyke so we could escape if a bull or a cow with calves ever went for us. It never fazed us because we were brought up with it and we knew that we could jump over the dyke if we needed to, but we never did.

I can remember the telephone had a shared line. You had to pick it up and listen for somebody else on the line and if there was no-one, you'd press the button and talk. One time we got a call just as we were ready to go out for the day. Somebody had drowned at Berney Arms and Dad had to go to Wickhampton in the Land Rover. I went too, being nosey and needing to know what was going on. We picked up some divers, the police and an Alsatian dog in the back of our Land Rover and drove them to Berney Arms where they dived for the body. Although it was sad, for me as a young girl it was exciting to have all those people in the Land Rover.

I left Acle School at 14 and went to work in a cafeteria in Yarmouth. I loved it because it was busy and I was talking to people all the time. Then my dad said I should get a proper job. I think with the hardship he'd gone through, he wanted better for me. He used to get paid once a year and that had to last, so there was very little money. At 16 I joined the civil service which was dull but I enjoyed being in the town and I liked the life.

Berney Arms 2018

Today I work at a boatyard that overlooks where I was born so I've come full circle. I look out on the marshes now as an adult and see the marsh harriers and every day it takes my breath away. Today we were taking pictures of the moon because there was an amazing sky with a line of cloud and the moon just under it. As a child it was just home and we didn't think anything of it and the Berney Arms Mill was just one of our playhouses. It was an absolutely idyllic childhood. It might be some people's worst nightmare to have no indoor toilet, no water or electricity, a hot water bottle to go to bed with, little entertainment, and cooking everything from scratch, but our life was full with just us four.

Childhood around How Hill

(1954 – 1970)

Stephen Aldred
(b. 1954)

HOW HILL AND SUTTON

Stephen was born at How Hill and has wonderful memories of roaming through the fields and woods and not returning home until he was hungry.

I was born in 1954 at my grandparents' house, Crome's Farm in How Hill. In those days young mothers would go to their mother's home to have their first child. It wasn't an easy birth so my father had to phone Jimmy Walsh who was the doctor at Stalham. Not every house had a phone then so Father had to bike a mile over to Mill House to use their phone. By the time Father got back, Jimmy Walsh was wandering up the path to the house with his bag in his hand, whistling away, and according to Mother he saved my life.

My father was a farm labourer and worked at Mill and Bray Farms, Sutton. He was also a relief milkman and looked after the game shoots on arable land and a duck shoot down in the marshes at Hickling, between Eastfield and Stubb. My mother worked as a typist at Laurence and Scott in Norwich until she married and had the family, then, like a lot of women, she worked on the land picking strawberries, potatoes, apples, pears, holly or whatever was in season.

My first memory of the farm was after my sister was born when I was two, and we moved from our little thatched cottage in Sutton to the Mill Cottages down Mill Road. Father got hold of a little Allis Chalmers tractor and trailer and piled up all our possessions and drove it about a mile to the cottages. Mother walked behind with my sister in the pram and I walked beside her. We got about halfway and I got tired so Father lifted me up and I sat on his lap for the rest of the journey.

I can remember the tractors coming up and down the road and Father working on the farm and when I was a bit older I used to go and help him down on the marshes. I'd check on the cows and count them when they were there in the summer and I helped feed them at weekends. We lived in tied farm cottages until Father became a thatcher in the 1970s and he bought his own house in Sutton.

I have lovely memories of How Hill, it was idyllic. Mother and Father couldn't afford holidays away but every summer we went to my grandparents at Crome's Farm for three or four weeks. Crome's Farm is about a mile from the river and has about 90 acres; it was owned by the Boardman family when my grandparents were there but after my grandfather died they took the land back and they are now farming it.

We had a lovely time roaming about the fields and through the woods, going out in the morning and not coming back till we were hungry. We built dens with bales in the fields and played cowboys in the woods. At harvest time if Grandfather or my uncle, who also worked on the farm, went out on the trailer we would cadge a lift to the fields and watch them load up the bags of corn or bales of straw.

I remember going down to the little marshman's cottage at How Hill because one of our friends was the daughter of the gamekeeper, and we would go down to the staithe and that's where I first saw reed being cut. Bob Smithson and Eric Edwards would cut the reed and stack it all on the staithe.

I first started fishing at How Hill when Grandfather made me a cane rod and float and we'd go down to the river, and strangely enough I actually caught fish. I generally caught eels by accident but later on we went eel babbing and I remember being in a pleasure boat with Father and a few of his mates. They had a crate of beer and had a whale of a time although several eels didn't actually get into the boat; they sort of flew over and landed in the reed bed. Some were 3 or 4ft long and quite thick. There were lots of eels in the broad then.

When I got to secondary school and had my own bike I started fishing, sailing and canoeing, and I'd fish down at Sutton Staithe or the Pleasure Boat Dyke at Hickling, or even at the millpond by Stubb Mill on the Hickling Marshes. My best friend had a two-seater canvas canoe and we used to go on adventures over Hickling and round the backwaters. In those days the water was so clear you could see the weeds and the bottom, and in the backwaters you could see big fish like tench and pike just lying and sunning themselves in the water. We would go as far as Horsey Mere via Meadow Dyke and across Heigham Sounds to Potter Bridge. We even found a way to go as far as Somerton Staithe; so a lot of adventures.

Many of my school friends had fathers who worked on farms. There must have been at least ten men working on Mill and Bray Farms which had about 400 to 500 acres. These days that would be a part-time job for one man.

Father left the farm when he was made redundant in 1970. When the owner died, his son-in-law took over and realised there were too many men to make a go of it. They got rid of the dairy herd so Father wasn't needed. I was 16 at the time and that was the year I started at agricultural college.

Toad Hole, marshman's cottage, How Hill

Eric Edwards, marshman

It's the little things that get destroyed

(1960s – 2019)

Daphne Howlett
(b. 1943)

ROCKLAND ST MARY

Daphne has lived in Rockland St Mary since 1968 and has a keen interest in village life and the conservation issues of the area.

We chose Rockland as we had a boat and wanted a mooring within easy reach so we could go out for weekends on Rockland Broad and the River Yare. My husband Derek loved both river and sea fishing and we found the southern area quieter and easy to get around but with always something to see even if it was just a flock of geese flying over. We used to sit out regularly after our evening meal and enjoy the peace and quiet, observe the birds, and grumble about the insects biting.

Rockland St Mary is a peculiar village in some respects as it is linear, about three miles in length, and we have three distinct areas: the top end of the village, the centre, and the community down in New Inn Hill and Lower Road. As we are so close to Norwich we are a bit of a dormitory village in some ways. There is no actual village hub and I don't think there ever will be, it's not like a village with a village green where everybody lived around it and worked together.

As the village has grown over the years there has been a lot of new development but when we first came there were lots of gardens, smallholdings and orchards which supplied fresh produce to the market in Norwich – a lorry came round and collected it from around the village. They have all gone, the last one being Applebee orchard on the Bramerton border. Most people never retired, they just continued working until they passed on and if there was no-one to take over, the smallholding was sold.

At the end of the 1970s and the beginning of the 1980s the village started to change so now there are very few original residents left, but I remember they were typical country folk who were very independent and kept themselves to themselves. I remember a lot of rivalry between the villages, particularly between Claxton and Rockland; they were very separate communities and people didn't enter one another's villages.

The characters that lived in the village mainly got their living from the broad, rivers and marshes. One such was Archie Taylor who lived in a cottage on the marsh with his wife Peggy and their three children. He was a reed cutter and could be seen on the reed beds around Rockland in the wintertime. One of the smallholders, known as Fudgie, had a market garden where the village playing field is now and I remember picking strawberries there when we first came. He was a reed cutter too, and his son could always be seen with him at reed cutting time, knocking the reed into bundles and bringing them to the landing stage.

There are a number of marshmen's cottages scattered around but you have to look carefully these days as a lot have been upgraded and turned into riverside properties. In old photographs they look like wooden buildings but we know they were lived in as some show linen on the washing lines. Most may have disappeared between the

Marshman's cottage Rockland 1993

wars as my 82-year-old neighbour, who was born here, doesn't remember them. One was razed to the ground in the last year and a large building is being put up.

When we first came, the marsh at Rockland was a cowboy's paradise. The parish council got to grips with it and the shooting rights were let to the Rockland Wildfowlers Association, established in the mid-1970s to regulate shooting during the season.

The pub was still a very old-fashioned one with a tiny entrance porch. There was a wooden hatch that you knocked on and the landlady, Ivy Breech, would ask what you wanted. Then you either went outside or went into the large drinking room which was always smoky and smelled of ale. It was a typical country pub of that era. Most people knew each other but sometimes there would be people from the boats. At that time the boat business was really taking off and sometimes people came down from Brundall or Loddon and moored on Rockland Staithe right at the end of the dyke when it wasn't the big open staithe it is now.

When we first came you could walk around Rockland Broad but you couldn't actually see it because of the bank. It was wonderful though; the bank was covered with hawthorn and brambles and the marsh was just grazed occasionally in the summer and was filled with orchids and lovely wildflowers. The insect life was fantastic and included 14 species of butterfly breeding out there. During the 1990s the marsh was cleared, the banks were rebuilt and the footpath became part of the Wherryman's Way. When we have high tides now you can see water running down the side of the bank and coming out through little mole holes, eroding the banks. When the plants and bushes were there this erosion never happened as the roots were a deterrent to the moles.

The loss of insect life such as butterflies, dragonflies, damselflies and moths was enormous because of the destruction of the bushes. It is so disheartening to go out and see nothing. The swifts used to duck and dive and swish past gathering flying insects as I walked the dog first thing in the morning. It was wonderful.

The Yare is very busy at certain times of the year with holiday and private boats so the dyke coming down to Rockland Staithe has been maintained and was dredged again quite recently. We almost always have a cruiser of some sort in the dyke moored at our end. Village folk have access to it as well as the staithe is owned by the Rockland Poors Trust.

My husband is a very fine naturalist who walks around the staithe and dykes and his records go back many years. His particular interest is in molluscs as it is the little things, like the molluscs, that get destroyed. The Rockland dyke used to be partially dredged every now and then until around 2010, when English Nature wanted it to be

Rockland Marsh

properly dredged and even the water soldier plants were stripped out – it is only slowly coming back. Water soldier are brownish water plants that live in the dykes and the Norfolk hawker dragonfly breeds on them, so it was a long time before we saw them again.

It's a shame that the marsh has been completely altered. It has been overgrazed and now looks like a bowling green rather than a lovely wild area with wild flowers and orchids.

There are salt water meters along the river, one at Wheatfen and one on the corner of Short Dyke and the Yare which record the salinity of the water. They are showing that salinity levels are higher than they should be, more often than before. It means that things that need fresh water such as swan mussels, slugs and snails are being lost from the broad as they can't survive in brackish water.

The muds of Rockland Broad and the surrounding dykes have a deposit of heavy metals. Chemical works quite legally put chemicals into the water until European Union regulations made them clean up their act. Eel catching was decimated as was the eel catcher's livelihood because eels retain heavy metals. I know a local person who used to go pike fishing and keep them in the freezer until the health officer took one away to check for heavy metals and then ordered the rest to be destroyed as they were riddled with mercury. However, there are still people catching and eating the fish!

Living off grid in the marsh

(2005 – 2019)

Julie Williams
(b. 1953)

HALVERGATE

Julie and her husband Philip live off grid on Halvergate Marshes. She describes the use of renewable energy, its challenges and seasonal changes on the marsh.

In 2005 I saw Manor Farmhouse advertised for sale but we didn't find it until a few weeks later, when we were walking across the marsh and saw it. We finally moved in October and I woke up the first morning and wondered what we had done. It was cold and damp and there was a howling wind whipping through the house – we had moved from a modern centrally-heated house! But Philip promised to make it right and over the years he has done a great job of managing the build and making sure that this is a fantastic house to live in.

The kitchen was very damp. The units were fitted with battens holding the cupboards away from the wall but even that didn't stop the damp from penetrating – recipe books in the cupboards would be damp and smelly within days. We only had two gas rings for cooking and for the first Christmas we borrowed a friend's kitchen to cook the dinner, before transporting it back here.

We coped with those conditions for two years whilst we started to get the house straight. We were lucky as we found a young plumber who sorted out the heating and recommended a builder to do an extension. One of the advantages of not building until we had been here for over a year was that we could see the position of the sun at various times of the year, and we had a window put in the kitchen specifically to see the sun setting in winter. It was important for us to capture as much light as possible.

The lack of power took some adjusting to. When we first moved in, the generator was over-engineered and the batteries were not particularly powerful. It meant, for example, that every time I turned on the hairdryer the generator used an hour's worth of oil! So drying hair didn't make you popular.

It was great when Philip installed the new batteries and then the wind turbine. To get it to work at a premium we had sockets wired so they only came on when the generator was running. That was okay but it meant that things like the washing machine could only run if the generator was on, so if the wind blew for two weeks we couldn't use the machine. It wasn't very practical and Philip changed it.

Even now I only use major appliances when there has been lots of wind and sun and the batteries are fully charged. Over the years we've learned that if the battery is at say 60% in the morning but the sun is shining and the wind is blowing, then it will be fully charged by the end of the day, the washing can be done and we can live quite normally. It is noticeable when Philip is away and the computers are not being used how much less energy we use! Of course we have the problem of what to do if we lose power; we can't call the electricity board but fortunately this has only happened twice.

There is half a mile of track to get to the house which nobody maintained. The farmers are used to it and are normally in tractors and happy to go over potholes. However, we wanted access

Mutton's Mill 2016

that didn't do too much damage to the car. So we maintain the track ourselves which requires quite a lot of physical effort – we have stone delivered and then we load it onto a wheelbarrow and push it up the track to off-load. The last couple of times we have had help from a friend with a dumper truck, but even so, after eight hours you know that you have done a day's work.

We have only been cut off once in 14 years because of weather. The snow tends to miss us, perhaps because of our closeness to the coast. In 2018 the 'Beast from the East' hit this area quite severely, due in large part to fallen snow being blown across the track. I went out one day not realising how deep it was, drove to the end of the road and got completely stuck. We tried again the next day but this time Philip got stuck and we had to dig him out, then a local farmer very kindly came down with his tractor and cleared the snow for us.

One time I went for a walk across the marsh with my grandson and just as we were coming back from Mutton's Mill a blizzard came across and there was a total whiteout. It looked absolutely amazing with nothing but little fence posts sticking up. As it was only half a mile we managed to get home safely and he thought it was great fun.

We have had several incidents of wind damage to the house, both times when Philip was away. The first time was one November when we had severe gales and some roof slates came off along with the end of the barge board. I climbed onto the flat roof and with the help of my son-in-law we nailed it back in place; the builder was quite horrified when we told him. The second time there was a roaring gale I could see the shed roof being ripped off, so again I climbed a ladder and nailed it back on, all the while being hit in the face. The house doesn't really suffer in the wind at all now so it shows how well built it is.

Living here you notice the seasonal changes on the marsh. The cows come off at the end of the year and for three or four months there are no livestock and farmers coming by. Then the cows come back about the end of March depending on the weather and it's always nice to see them. The pink-footed geese arrive in late September or early October in their hundreds and it is fascinating to sit and listen to their calls. People say that there were even more here in the 1970s. The geese leave us around the end of February depending on the weather.

The wildfowlers start to come at the end of September and stay until the end of January. They come past with their dogs and rifles and are so well camouflaged that it can be difficult to see them; sometimes you only see their dogs' eyes as the headlights hit them. They are very friendly and often chat; one used to be my son's rugby coach and just after we moved in, he came round to show us how to pluck and dress pheasants. It was useful as they quite often drop geese off for us and I am now quite accomplished at it.

We have people walk across the marsh although not as many since the Berney Arms pub closed around 2015. They would walk to the Berney Arms and either come back or carry on to Great Yarmouth. We have had people lost on the marsh and I remember one evening when we had police cars outside the gate and a helicopter with searchlights. A family had set off and become hopelessly lost when it got dark but the police managed to track them down. Since then white markers have been put on every gate across the marsh so people can see them and follow them back.

We have seasonal birds arriving and house martins used to come back each spring and nest in the eaves. However, about ten years ago we had an almighty downpour and all the house martins gathered at the front of the house getting soaked. Two days later they were gone and they have never nested here since. Swallows nest down the road in the barns and we are thinking of putting up some boxes for them. Over the years we have had eleven barn owl chicks raised in the box we put up and one year we had four chicks which was a really good brood. We are not allowed to photograph the nest but there is a window that overlooks the tree so we can sit and watch them.

We have Chinese water deer and this year we had one who gave birth in the field opposite, a tiny little thing. We also see hares in the garden and one year there were three or four leverets in the garden each evening waiting for their mother to come back and feed them. We try to encourage as much wildlife as possible and we feed the birds all year round and have goldfinches, pheasants and partridge, along with weasels and water vole. There used to be foxes around but not so many now as the RSPB shoots them; they don't want them going after the birds.

One of the reasons we liked the house so much was because of the south-facing aspect looking straight over 12,000 acres of marsh. Nowhere else have we seen such a view.

CHAPTER 2

Water

BOATYARDS

BOATBUILDING

WATERWAYS

BOATS & WHERRIES

REEDHAM FERRY

Wroxham

Wherry Maud

Ships great and small

(1870s – 1970s)

Thelma Waller
(b. 1951)

REEDHAM

Thelma has generations of boat builders in the family including the founder of Hall's boatyard and the builder of wherries Maud and Hathor.

My grandfather was William Henry Hall and he was born in Reedham in 1877. He was the great-grandson of James Hall, a man who moved to Reedham from Norwich in the early part of the 19th century and started a boatyard to build wherries.

One wherry that is dear to my heart is the wherry Maud which was named after my grandmother. The Maud was built in 1899 and my grandfather designed her and worked on her and the rebuilt Maud is still sailing the Broads today. He also helped to build Hathor, a pleasure wherry commissioned by the Colman girls, the Colman family being the mustard people in Norwich. It was used as one of their pleasure boats for sailing on the Broads and was very different from the trading wherries he was used to working on. Like Maud, it is still sailing.

When they married my grandparents moved first to Thorpe and eventually to Oulton Broad. When I was a little girl I used to take Grandfather's hand but not the one with the missing finger. He would make fishing rods to sell and sometimes he had to bend bits of wood using a homemade steam tube that he filled with water and heated on the fire, so the steam would bend the wood. Sometimes the water boiled over and my grandmother would tear him off a strip for making a mess.

When my mum was small the family was quite poor, there were seven children, and in the 1920s and 30s there was not a lot of employment so my granddad earned some extra money making model boats in addition to normal boatbuilding. A man came down from the Science Museum in London looking for model boats and Grandfather built three – a wherry, a beach yawl and a keel. And they all ended up in the museum. When I was eight, I was taken to see them and was delighted to find a postcard of the wherry in the shop.

My father, Herbert Walter Waller, was born in 1917 and trained as a carpenter and joiner at Richards' shipyard in Yarmouth and then Lowestoft; they were building luxury yachts, cargo vessels and ferries. His job was to fit out the boats and build furniture, he was a perfectionist and very skilled. Sadly there is nobody now in the family involved in boatbuilding but I feel very proud of both my father and grandfather because they were working in a trade that is anchored to this area and its history. Although Hall's yard and Richards' are long gone, their ships and wherries were very useful to what went on in this area. I am very proud of my craftsmen.

Hall's of Reedham boatyard (1908)

A boatbuilding family

(1908 – 1960s)

Rex Woods
(b. 1942)

WROXHAM

Rex's father and grandfather

Rex was born into the Woods boatbuilding family but decided to be a marine engineer instead.

My grandfather was Ernest Woods; he originated in Yarmouth but moved to Cantley where he had a small boatyard, and in 1908 he designed and built the Yare and Bure One design which is sometimes known as a 'white boat', or YBOD. Then in 1926 the Cantley sugar factory expanded and he accepted compensation and transferred the yard to Horning where, apart from the war years, my father also worked for him.

There were several Woods brothers. The eldest was Walter Woods and my father happened to be the youngest but they were the only ones involved in boatbuilding. My uncle 'Old Man Walter', as he was referred to, started the Norfolk Broads Yachting Company at Potter Heigham in the late 1920s or early 30s. His son Herbert, who was born in the 1890s and had been apprenticed as a boat builder, took over the company because of his father's ill-health and started to build the Light Class cruisers at Potter Heigham.

I suppose from the time I was born until the age of 22 my life was involved with boats and not just on the Woods side of the family. My mother was a Gilden and her father, Harry Gilden, was a boat builder and a number of his sons and sons-in-law

The last YBOD built at Horning

were too. However, I didn't have the desire to follow the family tradition and fancied the mechanical side of things. So when I had the opportunity I began an apprenticeship as a marine engineer at John Loynes & Sons at Wroxham in 1958.

I worked with Sid Loynes, John's son, who was an extremely active 70-year old who dealt with all the rigging and equipment. If there were problems on the hire boats I was delegated to take Sid and any replacements out in the field so to speak. If

'My family members involved in boatbuilding probably had a better standard of living as tradesmen compared to the average farm labourer but it still was not very good by today's standards. When my grandfather first had the boatyard at Cantley they lived in an old houseboat known within the family as Rudder Grange. I suppose it was there for convenience more than anything but I also think it had to do with finances. It wasn't until they moved the yard to Horning that they built their own little bungalow based on the American homestead with a veranda at the front. I remember as a child going down there and sitting out in the evening sun, provided the mosquitoes weren't biting too much.'

it was a spar like a gaff or boom it was lashed to the roof rack of the ancient Jowett Bradford van, but if it was a torn sail or a damaged shroud we would drive to Sid's house in Wroxham and he would open the garage to reveal a gleaming 1948 Austin 16 limo. Sid hated riding in the van so when the opportunity arose we would cruise in the big Austin to Yarmouth, Beccles or Loddon. Tea breaks and lunch breaks were strictly adhered to when in the field and usually conducted in the roadside or riverside hostelries that were abundant in those halcyon days.

Back then a boatyard engineer didn't just work on engines, we also fabricated bits and pieces to go on the boat and we were involved on the plumbing and electrical side as well. The phrase 'health and safety' hadn't been invented; it was more a case of self-preservation than anything and you just had to be more work-aware. I think we had the same idea as the Americans; you looked out for yourself. You did hear occasional grisly tales though.

I was still working at Wroxham during the 1962/1963 freeze and one of the things I remember most was when the thaw set in. Broads Tours ran the river buses at the back of our yard and they needed to get their boats out to take them to a boatshed down river for an overhaul. They had to cut a channel through ice that was 18 inches thick in some places and they piled it up on the existing ice – it was mid-April before it all disappeared!

I stayed until I completed my apprenticeship, and when I was asked whether I would stay on I replied that you never stayed at the company where you had served your apprenticeship, otherwise you would always be regarded as the boy. They took this as a sign that I wasn't really interested and when the opportunity arose they got rid of me. So I was made redundant before the word was invented. I then got a job at Ross Foods in Wroxham repairing forklift trucks which, strangely enough, had similarities with boats as Coventry Climax built both trucks and marine engines with similar masts and transmissions. I preferred the factory environment which was a lot warmer than being on a cold boatyard.

As a small child, I suppose I thought my grandfather to be a very abrupt and gruff man, but I think most of the Woods family were. He never suffered fools gladly and he was very economical with his words. In fact, he probably didn't have much to say, unless he decided he was going to say it.

Hunter's Yard history: early days

(1932 – 1994)

Tom Grapes
(b. 1929)

LUDHAM

Tom grew up in Ludham and trained as a boat builder at Hunter's Yard. His first job was helping to build the boat the Wood Anemone in March 1947.

My great-grandfather ran the Wherryman pub which was the last pub at St Benet's Abbey. It was maintained especially for the wherrymen as in those days there were a lot of wherries and there would very often be two or three laying there at a time.

After demob from the Royal Marines I came back to Ludham and needed a job so I went down to Hunter's boatyard and saw Stanley Hunter, the younger of the two sons there. He said he would give me a job but only if I also joined the local volunteer fire service which he ran. So I finished up with two jobs on the same day!

The yard had 12 boats from the original fleet from before the war with the first two- and four-berth ones built in 1932. Hunter's then built about two boats a year until the war when the yard was closed and the family went to Potter Heigham to do essential government work, making motor torpedo boats amongst other things. They returned to the yard after the war and in 1945 they were allowed to relaunch their yachts, although the boats had to be blacked out for the next two years. Instead of having white canvas on the side, they had dark green to keep the lights from being seen at night.

From the start Stanley gave me jobs doing more or less whatever came along. We had to be able to turn our hand to anything because, apart from the Hunter family, there were only two of us working there. Percy Hunter was the governor, Cyril his elder son was the boat builder and Stanley did most of the painting and varnishing. I didn't do an apprenticeship; I learned on the job and did the jobs to the best of my ability. My first job was helping to build the Wood Anemone in March 1947, holding the nails while Cyril turned them all inside.

There was no aspect of the work that I preferred as you weren't doing the same thing day in day out. One day you'd be rubbing down and varnishing, another day you'd be scraping the hulls and bringing them back up to scratch. To make a really good job of a boat that had been freshly scraped, you had to put on at least five coats of varnish. It would dry overnight and you would come in next morning, rub it down and put on another coat. Once it was all re-stained and varnished it would look like a new boat again.

The boats were mahogany with oak ribs and insides, some was Brazilian mahogany and some was ordinary mahogany. Mr Hunter would go to Taylor's at Wroxham to pick out trees and they would be cut to whatever thickness of plank he wanted and delivered to the boatyard. We then laid out the wood with little splines of wood in between to let the air go through. It used to take two years before we could use it.

Percy Hunter learned his trade by starting as the manager for Norfolk Broads Yachting Company at Wroxham before going to Potter Heigham and managing George Applegate's. He then decided to have a yard of his own. He was very friendly with a farmer at Ludham who sold him the land where the yard is now, and Hunter's Yard was established. Every boat had its own dinghy so when the first boat, the Lustre, was built they needed a dinghy for it. Percy, or 'old man Hunter' as we called him, set to and built one in a fortnight! They built a number of boats and when there were too many for the one shed, they built another.

In those days there wasn't much in the way of health and safety, and often when there was a high tide, water would come right through the sheds. It used to be ankle deep and you had to be very careful using electric drills. Since the floors were made up we rarely get water through now.

By the end of the war, people started coming back to the Broads for pleasure trips including some of the old customers and I got to know people from all over the country. The majority of the cabin boats were let for a week and the customers would sail themselves, we had to take their word about how competent they were. Anyone we were dubious about I would take out for an hour or so until they were capable of going off on their own. In the main people were very careful but we did notice that the ones who had done a lot of sailing were the ones who knocked the boats about and did most damage! We used to have a group of bank managers come down and hire nearly all the boats and they would sail from one public house to the next; they were known as the Bitter Boys as they drank pints of bitter.

Sailors can go more or less anywhere from Hunter's Yard. In a week they could sail down to Yarmouth and hang on until the tide started to come in and then take the tide across Breydon Water and up the River Waveney to Oulton Broad, or they could sail along the River Yare to Reedham and right through to Norwich. Bookings were always pretty good despite the weather and I have known a time when I had to brush snow off the boats.

The interiors of the boats were varnished mahogany and they had gimbal oil lamps which meant that when the boat heeled the lamps stayed upright. There were only a few facilities on board like Blake's toilets and the odd wash basin in the four-berth boats. The toilet required you to pump the water in from the river and then pump everything out with a separate pump back into the water. You wouldn't get away with that today! When I first started, cooking was done on primus stoves but after a few years they were changed to gas burners and the four-berths got an oven as well.

The sails were made of Egyptian cotton until 1962 when the first boat to have a Terylene sail was Hustler 2. As the other cotton sails wore out they were replaced as well, as Terylene was stronger and could be stowed wet – cotton sails tended to sweat and become mildewed.

Work changed through the seasons. We had to look after the boats during the summer and at the end of the season the boats were all scrubbed out, dismantled and pulled into the shed. We always liked to get them in by the third week of October. When I first started we used an old wherry winch to crank the boats in and out of the water. Fortunately Stanley Hunter was friendly with a manager at Laurence and Scott's, the electric motor people, and he made us an electric motor to fit onto the winch. We then got a gear box out of an old Austin 7 and fitted it to the motor and winch, and from then on we pulled the boats out with an electric winch. It made an enormous difference because having to crank them out was no easy job. The boats were back in the water just after the first week of March and they were usually let by the third week and were always out for Easter.

In the 1960s Stanley took over the yard but when it got too much for him they decided to sell up and the Norfolk County Council (NCC) took it over. They kept the three of us on: me, Roger and Graham. They wanted us to carry on just as before except a lady arrived to run the office and do the paperwork and lettings. It was sad for us when the Hunters left but workwise we just carried on as normal.

When NCC took over we had a warden who was in charge of school sailing courses throughout the county with sailing bases at Filby Broad and Kings Lynn but Hunter's Yard became the main base. Once pupils knew how to sail they used to come along to the yard with their instructors and take the cabin boats out for a week at a time.

In the 1980s NCC decided to sell the yard but also applied for Heritage Lottery Funding. People came down to look around and go through the books to check that we were a going concern, then once the lottery money was agreed the Norfolk Heritage Fleet Trust took over. The trustees got together to run the yard but they left the working side of it to us and again it was not very much different to what we'd been doing all the way along.

They wanted to keep everything as it had been in the 1930s. There was still just the three of us and the secretary. Roger was the first to retire and when he left, two young fellas took his place and when I packed up somebody else came along and learnt the skills as they went along. Graham was the last of the three to retire; he was the boat builder and foreman of the yard and when he left my son Ian took over the role.

Tom and Ian, 1950s

Hunter's Yard 2018

Hunter's Yard today

(1981 – 2018)

Ian Grapes
(b. 1961)

LUDHAM

Ian trained as an engineer for a year before completing a three-year apprenticeship as a builder of wooden boats. He is now the foreman at Hunter's Yard.

In 1981 a position came up here at Hunter's Yard and I put in for it. Norfolk County Council had taken over Hunter's Yard by then and I can remember going for my interview at How Hill which they already owned. We used to have family boat holidays there and it's where I learnt to sail. Father was allowed to take out a boat that wasn't on hire and we'd go down to Hickling; he would push me out in the middle and say, 'Learn', and you know, we had great fun.

I'd grown up sailing Hunter's boats and knew them well, and because they had one of the best fleets on the Broads I knew it was where I wanted to be. I didn't have to ask too many questions about the boats and I had wooden boatbuilding experience so I got the job.

There were about 18 boats when I started and we've been adding to the fleet as the years go by. People offer us boats and we have built boats. When I first started I got the job of doing the varnishing. I got all the bits and bobs to do, varnishing spars, cabin tops, nothing too exciting but as time went by I started doing more.

We always started work at 8am and we never knew what was going to turn up. We knew which boats were going out but we could be called away at any time. People used to hire the boats for a week and come back every year so we got to know them. Now that all seems to have altered as people want short breaks and they book online. Years ago they would phone and you looked at the chart and pencilled them in. You got to know who they were and what they wanted. Now, I think we have lost that personal touch.

It can get very cold working here during the winter and we've had floods come into the shed up to three or four inches. During the October 1987 gale, I remember we had all the boats outside ready to come in and if you look at one post now it's got a lean on it. The shed moved a little bit in that direction, so we need a gale the other way to put it back. The boats were alright though. We did have one boat out sailing at the time and I think they were glad to get it back. In Hunter's time this shed had a soil floor but we raised it up six inches and it is now brick. Soil floors were good for boats because they held more moisture and that kept the boats tight but it is not so good if you're working on them.

Our biggest boat is 28ft. The boats are particularly well designed for sailing on the Broads and will come out of a tack the same speed they went in. Hunter always built his boats very light so they would sail and other boats are often surprised when one of our boats sails past. Other hire yards have put in engines and bridges… but the more weight you put on, the more weight you have to get moving. There are fewer yachts around these days and fewer places that hire them. It seems fewer people want to sail, that's the trouble. We are trying to encourage more people to come, particularly the younger generation through the schools. But I always think the world is a much smaller place now they can go further afield.

Very little has changed on the boats and we do try and keep them as they were in the thirties although we are now going over to electric lighting and have put an electric engine in one of the boats. We had oil lamps before but it was getting very hard to get spares and also some customers burned soot which is very hard to get off. Some customers ask for the oil lamps so we have to try and put one in for them. They like the heat that comes off them, and just going back in time I suppose. The boats are all self-contained and use calor gas. They used to have primus stoves which I can't imagine; I have tried them and there tends to be a lot of flames!

Through the winter months we do boat maintenance. I do most of the sail and awning repairs and all the rigging, ropes and blocks. Since my father retired, I've also taken on the sign writing. As a rule Jeckells in Wroxham makes our new sails and I put the order in at the end of the season for March delivery. They have been making the sails for 70 years so they have all the sizes; on average hire boat sails last about seven years.

We have five people working here, three of them trainees. For many years we had the same people working at the yard and suddenly we got to a point where everybody was retiring and nobody else was coming on. But things look pretty good now with the younger ones, two of whom are very keen sailors. We are hoping they will take over in time.

Being the foreman I have to ensure we have the materials to do the work. A lot of the wood we use comes from this country and we like to get the oak fairly locally if we can. I always want freshly sawn oak as we use steam to bend it and the juices inside the wood help it bend. Mahogany is a different problem, we have to import that and some of the logs are getting very expensive. Not long back the rep said the cheapest log was £10,000 and probably could not be used for seven years because it still had to dry and be stored in a shed. That's a lot of money tied up. The log would be about 30ft long and 3ft in diameter.

Hunter's Yard, 2018

We tend to use a lot of the old tools and equipment but I would say that the glues and materials we put in the seams have altered for the better. In the past we just put normal linseed oil putty between the seams but now we use a construction adhesive which glues both planks together but still lets them move. The putty used to harden letting moisture in until the wood swelled up again and the seams would rot also. But, with the newer products, we don't see that any more. I know we're a Trust and we're trying to keep things the same, but you do have to move on to make life simpler. In the end, our job is to make the boats last as long as we can.

We have all sorts of groups coming. We do ask for sailing experience and many groups will bring their own skipper but we also have volunteers who can knock them into shape. However, we have had boats smashed up. We get most damage with groups sailing together; they want to set off together and often one boat will hit another. On Saturdays when the boats return we go over them and retouch any scratches; that's one of the jobs we always do

Mahogany drying

and it is what Hunter's has always done. The next customer always takes the boat out scratch free.

We did have a group of Italians who were sailing through the new Breydon Bridge and hooked the main sheet on the bridge. The tide dragged them through and they actually sank. We got the call to go down to Breydon to rescue them and what I always remember is that when the boat came up, it was full of little crabs and we had to clean them all out! Fortunately there were no holes. These things happen but that group doesn't come any more!

Today we still have school groups coming and part of the Lottery Fund is to encourage them and they also get a reduced rate. We have volunteers who go out with them or they bring their own skippers and each year they slowly get better. A school group will go out quite disorganised but by the time they come back they have all got their little jobs and have had a great time, and want to come back. I'm especially pleased if they have looked after the boat!

I remember when I had not been here long, the BBC turned up to film Coot Club and The Big Six. They needed a yard that could be turned back to the 1930s so this was ideal and the yard was renamed 'Rodley's of Wroxham'. They hired a boat for 12 weeks with a cotton sail made especially for it and it was my job to look after them and the boat, so they could film where they wanted. We have also had Ben Fogle here and Griff Rhys Jones. I have met Prince Charles and Camilla on a stand at the Norfolk Show and talked to them about the yard. One of our trustees is very keen and goes round the country giving talks about the Hunter's fleet.

I also knew Stanley and Cyril Hunter when they were quite elderly although they were always known as 'the boys'. They were very glad that the boatyard was saved from being split up and Cyril worked here for a time in an advisory capacity when the Council first took over. So it's been quite interesting over the years. The Hunters picked this place because there is such a choice of directions to suit the wind and tide such as Thurne Mouth, Yarmouth, Wroxham, Hickling and Horsey.

I like seeing people enjoy themselves and we are always happy to have visitors because there are not many places in the country where you can look at boats like this.

It's not a job where you always do the same thing. My summer job is totally different to my winter job. I'm dealing with people in the summer and they've gone for the winter. I do like the summers but usually by the end you are glad that winter has come and you can recharge the batteries for the next year.

The atmosphere at Hunter's Yard has not really changed over the years and my job is to keep it as it was because that is why people come. We need it and at the moment, things are going from strength to strength. I used to take people out a lot but now I tend to let the younger ones do it. I'm often asked if I go sailing on my days off but to be honest, I tend to want a day away from boats!

The story of Bee's Boats

(1960s – 2018)

Trevor Beales
(b. 1946)

BRUNDALL

Trevor did an apprenticeship as a carpenter and joiner in the building trade. His father ran the former Red Lion pub in Norwich but left to establish a boatyard in Brundall where Trevor joined him.

We built a speedboat from plans in one of the rooms at the top of the pub, and we got it out through my parents' bedroom, over the toilet roof and into the back yard. Then we built a 12ft cruiser in the back yard. My parents had bought a piece of land down at Brundall, where Brundall Bay Marina is now, and we had the boats there just as a hobby. We then started letting the cruiser and after a few years we bought another to let out and we ran them as a little extra business, until the council stopped us.

When my father left the pub we bought a house in Brundall and looked for a piece of land to develop as a boatyard, and we bought the last site on the Riverside Estate. At its peak there were 13 different boatyards letting boats in Brundall and now there's one. They were all small to medium-sized yards and I suppose the biggest one was running about 15 or 16 boats. A lot of them did morph into something a little bit bigger going up to 20 to 25 boats but we stayed round the middle.

After my apprenticeship I moved around some building firms but eventually finished up with my father at the boatyard. Our land was just marsh. I think we paid around £3,000 for it which was a lot of money in those days. We had a dredger in to dredge out all the soil and peat and put it on the land to raise it up. Then we put in the quay heading but it was a while before we built a shed because we just couldn't afford it. A friend of my father used to go around clearing plastic waste from plastic bottle factories and he would dump it with us to form a kind of bed which we topped with rubble and concrete for the shed to go on. We still say that it was the best thing we could have used but I don't suppose it would be allowed today.

We started running the boats from that very small shed and as we couldn't get the boats in, we just pulled them onto the land and did them up outside. This continued until we had enough money to put up a bigger shed which we built out of asbestos with planning permission – there were fewer building regs then! And we started building boats for the fleet.

Lady Bee, 1965

Very few people lived down there. The council was very strict about it as the road was just a track and prone to flooding. My father and several others formed a committee and from that sprang the Brundall Riverside Estate Association which now maintains the road. I became involved and was Chairman for 15 years and nowadays it is quite a nice little road.

In those days Broom's was not the massive firm it is today so to keep their chaps busy during the summer, they would build wooden hulls, and they built one for us. Father and I fitted it out and did all the engineering work. That was the first boat of any size that we worked on. I could fit a boat out because I had the skills from the building trade but I didn't have the skills to build a hull so I would never class myself as a boat builder. However, we did not need the skills as eventually we were buying fibreglass hulls.

We had self-employed people giving us a hand with the boats and engineering and several people around the Riverside Estate made their living going between the yards. We never actually employed anybody until my father had a stroke and could no longer work. My wife worked in the office and my mother-in-law looked after the cleaning. In the early days people were only too glad to earn a few pounds on a Saturday cleaning out the insides of boats. Later on that did become a problem although we were quite lucky and had some cleaners who stayed with us for years and became friends.

Although a small yard, we still had enough room to moor up all our boats and get them out of the water but we had to help people manoeuvre the boats out of the yard. We would also take them on a trial run up the river and show them how to moor up if they were inexperienced.

We had some good seasons when we could push the business along quite nicely. People were interested in hiring a boat and it was a reasonably priced holiday. The 1960s, 70s and into the 80s were good despite one or two hiccups but, on the whole, it was a reasonable business. We expected to operate between 25 and 30 weeks every year and people could not hire a boat for love or money during the summer holidays. We never earned a fortune but we managed to keep our families going.

We had one very bad year that resulted from an Esther Rantzen programme. Some people had suffocated themselves on a boat out at Stracey Arms. It was during the winter and they had the heaters on with all the windows taped up and they had asphyxiated. That programme tore boat hirers to bits. The thing that came out of it was a code of practice for ventilation on boats. We did it ourselves in conjunction with naval architects and ventilation people and eventually we got the boat safety scheme which is still used.

We did once have a fire on a glass fibre boat; it had a petrol engine which was really quite lethal and the boat was completely gutted. There were lads on it and they were having some problems getting it to run and we think they played about with the carburettor to make it go faster. We went out and set it all up again and left them to it. We have a sneaky suspicion, although we could never prove it, that they had another little go at it. The carburettor developed a leak and petrol got into the bilge and when they started the engine a spark from the starter motor ignited it all. It happened at Horning and luckily no-one was hurt but the boat was burnt to the water line.

We had one or two sinkings which we took in our stride. One boat went out on a Saturday only for them to ring up on the Sunday morning to ask us to pick them up as the boat had sunk. It was at Reedham, and when we got down there all we could see was the top of the roof about 3ft under the water. They had run aground and the stern gear was on some sunken pilings. Once we got it up there was very little water coming in but they said that water had started coming over the floorboards so they had gone onto their friend's boat for the night. If they had rung earlier we could have saved the boat!

Rising expectations finished off the small yards. A big yard can give a bigger service but not the personal touch. When our customers came down I was there to have a chat with them and help. It became necessary to have a 24-hour callout service and as a small yard we struggled to do that sort of thing but we did. I think boatyards made the mistake of putting too many extras on the boats and it ceased to be a holiday one step up from camping. It became a 'glam' thing. We started to put central heating in, colour televisions and then they wanted WiFi. Some of the boats being produced now are very luxurious but a small yard can't raise that sort of money to build them.

Pamelena Bee, early 1970s

The yard was called Bee's Boats. That came about from my mother's name, Beatrice, but she was always known as Bee when we had the pub so we just carried on the name.

To start with we named the boats after family members, like Pamelena Bee and Christina Bee; then we had a boat called Blonde Bee which was really named after my mother again as she had been a blonde. When I packed up the hire fleet 20 years ago I had to change the name so I dreamt up the name Harnser, which is Norfolk for a heron, and I've carried on running the yard just as moorings. There are half a dozen people who live on their boats. I maintain it all the best I can and I don't have to spend every day there. It keeps me occupied.

Ludham Bridge Boatyard: a family business

(1970s – 2016)

Robert Paul
(b. 1954)

LUDHAM BRIDGE

Robert's family owned a boatyard, café and chandlery in Ludham for many years. Robert is also president of the Museum of the Broads at Stalham.

When I left school, I had a year at City College and then decided to go to Southampton College of Technology to embark on a course in boatyard management. My father had retired from the restaurant business and bought the premises at Ludham Bridge in 1966 and some years later he bought the boatyard opposite. I was halfway through my course but I decided to give it up and came back to help run the boatyard.

When we first took over, the business consisted of a small village store and two petrol pumps on the road. We thought the lifestyle was fantastic and we used to sit in deckchairs wearing our sunglasses feeling quite cool, waiting for customers to come and fill up with petrol.

Two lovely ladies ran the shop in the truly old style with scales on the counter and everything weighed out. It had a lovely atmosphere and visitors came in year after year and loved it because it never really changed. Whilst the shop never made us rich, it covered itself and we were all very happy living and working there. Many personalities came in to talk to us like Cliff Richard on his boating holidays, and around 1998 we had an edition of Eastenders filmed in the shop which caused great excitement in the village; it was great fun.

After we bought the boatyard, we opened a chandlery and converted the rose garden at the back of the house into a boat park. We also built a showroom and it all went very well. We had a lot of business and it grew substantially, helped by the public moorings at Ludham Bridge. One thing we did which I don't think anybody else was doing in those days was a 'swap shop'. People would bring in their second hand boat items for us to sell or they would swap them for something else we had in stock. It was pretty simple but people loved it and it worked.

In the 1990s we decided to try a café at Ludham Bridge and my mother, who had some experience of running restaurants, used to make lots of homemade cakes, sandwiches, soup and so on. It was small-scale but people really appreciated the personal touch, she would always be there and we had lovely staff. It was aimed mostly at boat owners and it went very well for several years. We did try to keep it open in the winter for walkers but it wasn't viable. I am pleased to say that there is still a restaurant on that site doing quite well.

Ludham Bridge ca.1980

Ludham Bridge 2005

We had three hire cruisers, one diesel and two petrol, called Bright 'n Easy, Nice 'n Easy and Free 'n Easy. They were good boats and we had quite a few regular customers. We kept the boats for a number of years until it became evident that they were uneconomical to maintain and we had to decide whether to invest a lot of money in new boats or give them up. We decided to concentrate on day launch hire of rowing boats and sailing boats coupled with quite specialised boat repairs. We also offered wooden boat repairs and wooden boatbuilding, and that went very well.

Most yards were members of either Hoseason's or Blake's agencies and we got to know each other at meetings and the annual dinner. We were all very friendly and if one of our boats broke down on the southern broads or a long way away, the nearest boatyard would happily assist in the repair and, likewise, if someone broke down near us we were only too happy to help. We had quite a well-known tow boat called 'Big Tow' and we regularly pulled people off the mud on Barton Broad.

In the 1960s safety on boats was sadly lacking, a lot of the boats still had petrol engines and old gas cookers on board resulting in a lethal combination of petrol fumes and gas, alongside sources of ignition like fridges and starter motors. Even fire extinguishers sometimes were not checked so unfortunately there were a lot of accidents. In the early 2000s I became a boat safety examiner. A lot of people were critical of the scheme and thought it put unwarranted regulations onto boat owners. I agreed that some of the regulations did seem pointless but overall they were very worthwhile. Of course you can never guarantee 100% safety as you never know what people are going to do, but it did improve safety considerably.

We sold the boatyard in 2007 and concentrated on the chandlery and I continued selling boats and doing engineering work and outboard repairs. We then sold the rest in 2016, by which time we had leased out all the parts – shop, café and the showroom which became an art gallery. I have four children, two of them work with boats but none were interested in keeping the business going. I think this has happened to a lot of family businesses in the Broads; the children have perhaps seen that it is hard work and long hours for not a huge return. Their ambitions may be greater these days.

My interest in traditional boats began when I owned the boatyard and it was clear that there ought to be a museum for the Broads. The Broads Society already had a working group and when I became chairman in the early 1990s, I felt able to push the idea and wrote several articles for the Harnser. This area has so much culture, tradition and a fantastic boatbuilding history.

Objects started coming in and, as we had no premises, they were stored at my boatyard until Len Funnell showed us an unused shed at the Herbert Woods boatyard in Potter Heigham, and suggested that we start something there. We went ahead with the idea and then wanted to establish a modern museum. Our application for Heritage Lottery funding was unsuccessful as the site was considered to be in a flood risk area, so we reluctantly had to rethink and we moved to our current site at Stalham in 1999.

Changing times at Cox's boatyard

(1990s – 2019)

Eric Bishop
(b. 1969)

BARTON TURF

The Broads were always a part of Eric's life. He did an apprenticeship in boatbuilding in Brundall and later joined R Moore & Sons in Wroxham and became involved with Cox's Boatyard in Barton Turf.

I got involved at Cox's Boatyard when one of the directors at Moore's asked if I'd be interested in maintaining some moorings for him there. It was a turning point for me and for Cox's as the boatyard was about to become insolvent. David Adler, who is now the chairman, got together other local business people to form a consortium in 1995 and they renewed the lease for 19 years. They wanted to get it up and running in the way they remembered it as children.

Cox's Boatyard goes back to the late 18th century when the Cox family began building and repairing wherries on the public trading staithe at Barton Turf. They had a small shed at that time but they mainly worked on the staithe itself. Their last wherry, Eithne, is no longer around. They were called Cox Brothers initially and the boatyard was passed down several generations. When the family no longer wanted to run the boatyard they began leasing it out and now it is with the consortium.

My job at Cox's was to manage the business, turn it around and increase the mooring, so we started by trying to make some profit to plough back into the business to keep it growing. It began with just me and two brothers who lived in the village and today it has become a thriving business. We started with 50 boats in the marina and now have 187 boats afloat and nearly 100 on the bank including the little rowing boats and tenders.

The position of the boatyard is very important. It is next to Barton Broad, the second biggest broad, and it's where Lord Nelson learned to sail. It is connected by the River Ant which in turn links with the northern broads. During the war they used to land planes on Barton and there is at least one wreck out there.

Cox's Boatyard 1970

When we started much of the marina was silted up so we had to dredge the whole site. It was a difficult time as we were dredging in the winter and moving a lot of mud in the freezing cold. Morale did go down a bit. But we knew, come the summer, the sun would shine and we would try and forget about it. Gradually the banks got new quay headings to make them usable and we virtually doubled the number of boats in the marina.

Cox's Boatyard 2019

After that we started a big development where we got planning permission to replace some of the old sheds with modern workshops, starting with one small shed with a soil floor and not many windows. We also dug into a little basin and designed and built a closed loop system which harvested rainwater off the workshop roof for washing boats when they were out of the water – the water was then filtered and re-used. The Broads Authority helped with funding. We then purchased a radio-controlled boat mover to help move the boats around and in 2013-14 we replaced our main workshop.

We took on a lot of apprentices as we were keen to teach youngsters and keep the skills going forward and many have won awards. We've had one who won Apprentice of the Year for his module two years running, so they are doing very well.

The customer base is enormous and we have people bringing their boats from the Thames as a cheaper way to have their boats maintained. About 50% of the boat owners are from East Anglia and apart from London we have people from Kent, the Midlands and some from Somerset. We do a lot of work for the Broads Authority maintaining their boats and also for the Environment Agency, Norfolk Wildlife Trust and Natural England. We also have breakdown service contracts with them and we'll go and help others as well if they are in real trouble.

Barton Broad was mud-pumped over five years starting in 2000. The mud was pumped into big lagoons on one side which drained and the mud was then ploughed into the field. The pleasure island in the middle of the broad was reinstated as it had deteriorated through birds destroying its banks. All the dredgers had to come out of our yard because it was the only place where they could gain access to the river and broad so it brought in some income for us.

Since it was dredged, the water has been cleaner and deeper including the water at the marina, and sunlight could get down to the bottom. The water is also clearer because of the number of water fleas hatching out and eating the bacteria which in turn allows even more sunlight into the river. The cycle is getting quicker and easier resulting in more fish and more wildlife coming through. In the spring I regularly see kingfishers out of my office window, we see marsh harriers and hen harriers flying and quite a few deer walking around the marina; on several occasions we have seen otters.

We were approached by Natural England to design some floating rafts for nesting birds. We designed them out of glass fibre in such a way that they were predator-proof both from land and water. Some birds nest on a gravel base so we put gravel inside the rafts to imitate a sandy beach and the birds can nest in there and know their eggs are safe. There are quite a few rafts around: three on the Trinity Broads, some on Barton and Ranworth Broads, some in North Norfolk, several in Cambridgeshire and we've even got two in Somerset. Our customers are Natural England, the Broads Authority and Wildlife Trusts dotted around the country.

The plan for the future is to carry on developing the site. We will be knocking down the last of the old workshops which still have soil floors to put up holiday homes with extra space beneath them to store and maintain boats, because our core business is boat rebuilding and boat repair. We'd like to create more moorings but it is going to be difficult because we are running out of land.

There is a great shortage of moorings on the northern broads and it's difficult to build more as there are tight planning regulations and few people are investing in big marinas. The size of boats is getting bigger as well. We find that people start off with a small boat and then work their way up to bigger more modern boats. But there are still many people who like the traditional wooden boats and are willing to keep them going and we put in a lot of man-hours varnishing and painting them.

There are not so many boatyards around which are developing like us. Although boatyards do not need many people, finding craftsmen is hard because the skills needed to maintain a boat are difficult – it's why we have trained up so many apprentices. We find that small boatyards are winding down and selling their land for either moorings or holiday homes so the number of yards around the Broads is decreasing. It is only the slightly bigger yards that are still operating, helped by people who want the yards to keep going as traditional yards. It is a great shame because there is an enormous amount of boating on the Broads and it is a trade we would like to keep going.

Innovation in boatbuilding

(1978 – 2018)

Alan Goodchild
(b. 1957)

BURGH CASTLE

After completing his apprenticeship Alan began his own boatbuilding business. He has been instrumental in developing specialised vessels and equipment for niche markets.

I grew up in Great Yarmouth and Caister-on-Sea and was interested in boats because my father was a chartered skipper. I had my apprenticeship with Maycraft at Potter Heigham under Billy May building clinker fishing boats, and left with his blessing at 19 with the ambition of starting my own business – which happened in 1978.

I initially built wooden fishing boats but quickly moved to more modern methods when fibreglass came in. Our fishing boats were 90% timber with the deck and wheelhouse constructed in English oak as well as imported timber. Forty years ago timber was more readily available, not as expensive and we were not aware of the destruction of forests and the need for sustainability and renewable resources. Timber was chopped down at phenomenal rates and nobody thought about it so now hardwood is very expensive and probably impossible to obtain from some places.

Our first fibreglass fishing boat was put into service in Yarmouth, a bold step as there was a bit of opposition from the fishermen at the time but fortunately for us, the first boat was bought by the most successful fisherman. I bought the hulls from specialist moulding companies and we fitted them out and that process taught me the skills of how to laminate – the emerging market meant there was a lot of learning for everyone on how to build in fibreglass. It is low maintenance, lighter and doesn't leak and there are not the inherent problems of wooden boats drying out and splitting over the winter period. It's a shame because I loved building wooden boats; I loved the smell and the feel.

Fishing boats at the time were supported by grants from the sea fishing industry and a fisherman could gain a grant for a new boat built to a certain standard by a reputable builder. They paid 50% and the government paid the rest. However, as successive governments reduced their support for the fishing industry the grants stopped after I'd built two or three boats, so the writing was on the wall. New boats were built for efficiency and not to increase the overall number and this together with the introduction of fishing quotas was reason to look for other opportunities.

Convincing what was the Yarmouth Port Authority to buy a new fibreglass pilot boat was our breakthrough and I focused on the market for pilot and survey boats. This was hard to break into because of the strong competition from established commercial builders so our only chance was being competitive and local. I was only 22 at the time and I battled hard to get the first one into service. I still remember it. It cost £66,000 and it is still in service.

My first boat was built in a converted piggery at Scratby. There were pot floors with things like flower pots upturned and concreted over to keep the pigs warm. I had to smash them out to make a suitable floor for boatbuilding. We outgrew the site after two years as it limited the size of

Alan, early 1980s

the boats I could build – the bigger boats had to be built outside under a tarpaulin sheet over scaffolding. It was not an ideal workshop but that was how everyone else was doing it in those days.

The search for more suitable premises led us to buying a yard which originally traded as Bure Marine in Great Yarmouth opposite the yacht station. Whilst it wasn't directly on the river it lent itself to lifting boats in and out with a mobile crane and we built a lot of boats there. However, it became evident the market was for bigger boats and we had outgrown the facility so I was very lucky that Beck and Martin's yard came up for sale at Burgh Castle. It had a timber-built shed with tinned cladding and soil floors, and a slipway that was good for nothing. It was a massive investment to buy the site and to get planning permission for a new shed. This transition period wasn't easy. We were trying to build and finish the Caister lifeboat whilst it was afloat in the river and the yard took nearly a year for builders to complete rather than the scheduled six months. We were trying to get other things completed and finding the extra money. It was a nightmare looking back, but it is what you do.

Breydon Marine boatyard was next door and ran a very large operation for coasters. It was a difficult decision to buy it when it went into administration but we were congested, being a large shed on a very small plot. What allowed us to get a bank loan was our building the first travel hoist in Norfolk for lifting boats out of the water. Travel hoists were common on the South Coast but not in Norfolk. It became very popular and it didn't take long for people to find us. Winter storage was very popular and the hoist helped to keep everything clean and secure in good conditions.

Buying Breydon Marine was fantastic. We were able to demolish the blister hangar which had occupied a massive amount of land and we dug out the derelict slipway in the middle. We had the marina at the end which overcame our lack of moorings and boats afloat space, and we tripled our presence on the river front.

At this point we were emerging in the pilot boat market, gathering momentum and name. We supplied as far as the Shetland Islands, the Channel Islands, Ireland and even France. It is a competitive and specialised market and I think it would be a hard one to break into now as port authorities and buyers will only buy proven vessels and not from drawings or a good sales talk. They did when I first started and I was able to convince them through looking at the fishing boats I had built.

As we built pilot boats for ports like Aberdeen we became familiar with that market, its clients and customers and it became obvious there was a market for small survey vessels. They wanted to survey their own ports to see where dredging was required so we made multi-work boats – vessels dedicated to the maintenance of the port. These were followed by survey vessels and then wind farm boats.

Multi-work boats tend to be heavier and based on fishing boats while survey boats tend to be catamarans due to the equipment. We developed a lot of products for this niche market. I've always focused on these markets because the more specialised and robust you make your product to

Wherry Maud being hoisted on land for maintenance

address a certain problem, the less the competition. It's a bit more challenging but I like that.

The wind farm off Yarmouth on Scroby Sands was the first off-shore wind farm with 30 trial turbines. We built a small survey vessel to survey the sandbank for its suitability for piling and building the wind farm and it became obvious the crew would need to travel to and fro so we began focusing on support craft. Initially a 12m or 14m catamaran was sufficient but as the market emerged it required 17m, then 20m and now we're building 28m wind farm boats.

The survey vessel market diminished once the surveys were completed and other wind farms moved further offshore where bigger vessels could do the surveys. However, as the small survey vessel market dried up, support craft were needed and we adapted the designs and built specialist vessels for that market. We also provided maintenance and a 24-hour call-out as these commercial boats are usually contracted to third parties so there is a penalty for not having the boats in service.

We are now building the UK's first hybrid pilot boat and I believe it is also the world's first. We've sold it to the Port of London Authority who invested in it as part of their green strategy – there's a lot of pressure for greener ships going into city centres like London, Liverpool and Southampton. There are technologies to make ships hybrid but the challenge for our new pilot boat is to balance speed and weight. We need to design the boat to be as light as possible with a low drag coefficient and able to accommodate the hybrid equipment without compromising overall strength. The hybrid equipment weighs an additional three tonnes for a 13.6m pilot boat but we are achieving 15 knots with hybrid propulsion whereas, according to our calculations, a traditional pilot boat design achieves 8 knots. The interest is amazing.

I think we import too many spare parts and materials and it reflects on successive governments not focusing on manufacturing and I'm concerned by the loss of two generations of skilled tradesmen who can teach the skills. We train our own apprentices so we have people who understand our methods and standards. We embrace new technologies and write software to increase efficiency. We design in 3D CAD (Computer Aided Design), invest in CNC (Computer Numerical Control) machines to cut the materials, and we train young workers to run the machines along with a young design team.

Thinking about memorable projects, the most rewarding contract was building the Caister lifeboat – the first self-righting one. It was a 38ft beach-launched boat and it has saved the most lives on record for that station. It could go over sandbanks and was only pensioned off because of its speed to attend to vessels.

Our most unusual project was probably the dredger we designed to dredge the marina that can walk on the river bed. A traditional dredger has spud legs, basically tubes or piles going up and down and spiking down to the sea bed. We wanted the new one to spud down when it was working to anchor it, and also be able to lower easily to transit under bridges. So, if we were going to the expense of making hinged spuds, then a pin would allow them to move 30 degrees from upright in either direction. Effectively they could spud to the bottom and then walk! It also eliminated the need for a propulsion system because the boat could be walked into position instead. It was a specialist piece of kit and it sold to dedicated marina operators as it could go under pontoons and boats without moving them.

I watched the Fastnet yacht race in the late 1970s where several people sadly lost their lives. Many of those rescued by helicopter were dead on arrival having survived in the water for 11 hours and it sparked a massive inquiry whose outcome was twofold. The body produces a chemical when in a state of panic due to the survival instinct. However, it stops production when the person thinks they are rescued. The body almost shuts down. As a result, the RNLI changed their training methods so now people are never told they are safe until they are physically out of the water and they really are safe. Instead they say, 'We've got you but you're not safe yet'.

The other change was to do with being rescued by helicopter because lifting someone out head first induces cardiac arrest and many die of a heart attack. As a man-overboard system is compulsory for pilot boats, I designed one which would lift the body out horizontally. The platform can be immersed under water to 0.5m so the casualty is floated on top of it and lifted out level. We gave our first one to the Hampshire police when we built their patrol vessel. It was trialled extensively and we're now on version 10. It's on every pilot boat we build and there are inquiries from all over the world.

Prospects look bright for the future and it helps us retain our work force, most of whom have been with us many years. It helps us recruit people as they can see we have a good order book which shows stability. I think, of all the things people need at the moment, it is to feel there is a bit of stability in the world.

Float my boat

(1954 – 2004)

Ivor Broughton
(b. 1939)

WROXHAM AND OULTON BROAD

Ivor wanted to be a boat builder as a schoolboy and completed a five-year apprenticeship with R Moore & Sons in 1954. In 1990 he began teaching at the Boatbuilding College (IBTC), Oulton Broad.

My first job involved helping the men lift planks to put round the boats and just generally watching and learning. They would quiz me on the names of different parts of a boat and I learned to have a good sense of humour! We built several 28ft mahogany Rebel One design half-deckers, many of which still sail at Horning Sailing Club, and some small launches for the Admiralty which were still on the order books from the war.

We worked in big corrugated iron sheds also left over from the war and the only heating came from one tortoise stove in the corner; it was my job to keep it going although it didn't really have much effect as the sheds were about 70ft by 50ft. One shed had sleepers on the floor and when there was a high tide they would squelch and move about although the water didn't actually come through; it was eventually concreted before I finished my apprenticeship. The sheds where the boats were stored for winter had large double doors onto the river and as the water came up the slipway, a cold draught blew through the gap at the bottom, and when the sun came round, we got condensation which made it difficult for the guys to varnish the boats.

Before Easter, the boats were put back in the water. They were pulled out to the slipway with the winch wire and it was my job to work it with another person. The boats were fitted out for the holiday season and I helped put down floorboards and bunk boards along with the cushions and mattresses which had been aired on sunny days. Once the interiors were finished, we had to get the gangplanks, boat hooks, life belts and so on out of storage. The boats were then driven down the river to the other premises in Wroxham where a gang of women would hang the curtains, put in cooking equipment and add the finishing touches. The boats were then brought back ready for hire.

Inevitably there were more repairs when boats returned and each Saturday they all had to be cleaned. Any dinghies would be paddled up to the boathouse and if fishermen had hired them, there would be lots of insects, maggots and mud in the bottom. I also rowed the painter around the yard so he could retouch any marks on the varnish. I did these jobs for a couple of years and then I was allowed to do repair work.

Building a wooden boat

A Peter Duck ketch

This gave us the chance to do four or five hours of overtime, a substantial sum of money for us, and it also provided another bonus. The customers' groceries came from Roys in Wroxham and arrived in boxes with little tickets stating there was a shilling refund. We would wait until the boxes were put in the dustbin and then discreetly put them somewhere safe. On Monday mornings I could make a little fortune, five shillings being a fortune, and I could fill my motorbike with petrol that lasted the week. I also put the dustbins out once a week and if I was lucky there might be a soda syphon which meant more petrol money and a few extra miles.

As I worked through my apprenticeship I began to consider my future. The money was not very good but I was happy. Then the Enterprise dinghy came along in 1957. It was a smaller boat designed by Jack Holt with fewer sails and more affordable. With the backing of the Daily Express, Ralph Moore wanted to bring the Enterprise to the general public so he built the dinghy in his spare time away from the office and I used to help him. We planked it up and recorded everything as he wanted to know how much work and expense was involved. He bought the first mast but eventually, when production was in full swing, we used to do a dozen masts at a time. Eventually the dinghies were mass-produced which perturbed me.

I moved onto Scorpions, Wayfarers and some Ospreys, some of which were Jack Holt designs, but all were eventually mass-produced so I decided to leave with my signed apprenticeship papers and the princely sum of £5 and went to work at Porter & Haylett's. They were building up a new hire fleet and I worked on four cruisers there, good experience as I learned an entirely different method of working.

While there, three friends asked if I would be interested in helping them build a boat and I drew up the plans based on magazines about boat design that I had borrowed when at Moore's. I asked the foreman about an unfinished mast up in the roof of the shed as I wanted to buy it for the boat. I told him I'd done the plans and he asked to see the boat when it was completed. As good as his word, he went down to Hickling Broad one night and after that he gave me the job of lofting out boats, some designed by Jack Giles whose work I admired.

The Peter Duck was the boat we made most while I was at the yard and I worked on about 30 altogether. It was a little 28ft double-mast ketch, originally built for Arthur Ransome. One of his books was called Peter Duck and told of his adventures sailing the boat.

We built some seagoing yachts including one for Humphrey Barton, a great transatlantic sailor and a director of Laurent Giles – he was one of the first men to sail the Atlantic. Jack Giles came down to Wroxham for a trial sail of a boat he had designed, it was a rough day and there was only the owner, me and Jack Giles. We sailed off Lowestoft in different directions, winking the mast up, turning the rigging and all the rest of it. Jack then decided to test the genoa which is the large sail used when reaching to get as much speed as you can. It was blowing a force 7 at the time and he asked me to take the tiller! By the time they got the sail up,

Jack and the owner were in water up to their knees on the forward deck and I wondered what I'd do if one of them went over the side. It was good news when they decided to take the genoa down.

I moved on to work with Jason Borthwick at the Deepdale boatyard, Brancaster Staithe, for a few years. The real draw was the house that went with the job as I was getting married and we had a nice little brick and flint cottage overlooking the salt marshes. They had a small class of Jolly boats at the time, a fast 18ft boat decked all around with just a cockpit in the middle. The last one I built was done especially for Jason to enter the Jolly boat championships. The boat was supposed to weigh 250lb but no-one had ever achieved it, so I began whittling away everything I could and even used lighter plywood for the decks, but we still couldn't get it down. I think I got it to about 260lb without making the boat dangerous. Anyway it must have done alright in the championship because he came home without it.

After four years I moved back to the Broads. I had tried to keep away from mass-production but fibreglass boats were becoming the big thing and all the yards in the Broads area were advertising well-paid jobs. So I started working at Moonraker on the Ocean 30 from Aquafibre. They asked if I could read a drawing and I attended a meeting at which they discussed building a Moonraker boat from drawings by the boat designer, Robert Tucker. I got the job to loft it out and was given a shed down by the river and locked in to keep it a secret. I lofted it out, made the frames, set them up on a big jig and then we skinned the boat with plywood. It was basically a powerboat design. After many coats of paint to create a perfect finish, the fibreglassers moved in to make the mould and then the hull. We then made the pattern for the superstructure and that was the beginning of a very long line of Moonrakers.

Herbert Woods at Potter Heigham was advertising for boat builders to build 70ft trawler yachts. It appealed to me as it would be a new experience. I got the job and rejoined some of my old mates from working on wooden boats. The yacht was built using iroko (a teak substitute) for planking onto oak frames. We had a nice new steam box and with a plank that size we had about six or seven men running up the shed with it to wrap round the boat before it got cold. We used 2ft G clamps and extra-long screws left over from when Woods was building Admiralty craft.

One gang of us worked on the hull and another on the wheelhouse and cabin. As the boat couldn't go under Acle Bridge to reach Yarmouth, the superstructure was made separately and was designed to slip onto the hull later. It was put on a trailer and the hull was towed down to Yarmouth on its own. Several men went with the superstructure to get rid of overhanging tree branches along the way – apparently, that is what Woods did during the war with the MTB (motor torpedo boats) for the Admiralty.

Eventually Woods stopped building trawlers and concentrated on its large hire fleet but it wasn't the type of work I wanted to go back to so I found a job with Charles Ward who was setting up a boatyard in Fakenham to build seagoing yachts. It was a lovely West Coast design, with a wooden frame covered in fibreglass and with foam in between. I carried on working there until I was made redundant.

I went self-employed for a while until I saw an advertisement for a boatbuilding training instructor at IBTC. John Elliott had set up the college in 1975 as he felt there was a need for the boatyards to have a school where people could learn the business. I started in 1990 and found it very strange at the beginning showing people what to do rather than doing it myself. Some students really wanted to learn the job but there were some whose parents had sent them there because they thought it would be a good idea. There were also people like solicitors and accountants who wanted a change of career as they were tired of the rat race. Interestingly, the foreign students seemed to do better than the British with many getting good jobs all over the world.

I gave lectures on fibreglassing and lofting. Some students had a problem getting their heads round lofting out, which didn't surprise me as I've always said that if you haven't got the feel for a boat, you can't do it. A boat is all about sweet curves and if you don't get a sweet curve it will look terrible.

I feel lucky to have had a career which I thoroughly enjoyed. I worked with lots of good people and I only ever had one day off and that was when the boatyard flooded one winter and we were sent home. I've designed and built two boats for myself, and I've enjoyed going for a sail at weekends.

After I retired I decided to volunteer at the Broads Museum at Stalham and in 2018 I was involved in renovating Henry Blogg's hoveller – a crab boat with a foredeck so they can spend a few days at sea. We got it from Stiffkey and brought it to IBTC. The back half was in a bad state so we built a new front using pine and oak planks, the same as in the original – there was no money to renovate it all. It now overlooks the cliffs at Cromer and is Cromer's memorial to Henry Blogg who saved so many lives and was the most decorated lifeboatman in the country.

The Norfolk boat builder

(1944 – 2012)

Mike Fuller
(b. 1930)

NORFOLK BROADS

Mike began as 'a boy' at Herbert Woods yard in Potter Heigham at age 14 and worked many years as a boat builder. In 2000 he became a volunteer at the Museum of the Broads.

My first job was in the stores for three months learning about screws; it was invaluable because even now I can pick up a screw and tell you its length. Then they moved 'us boys' into the machine shop to learn how to work the machines and then the carpenter's shop where we built our own toolboxes. By the end of my first year I had started doing odd jobs on airborne lifeboats with two boat builders. This was 1945 and Woods had a contract to make 50 with 25 going to South Africa. When us boys had finished our part, we built the boxes to put them in to send to South Africa.

Two months after the war ended they started bringing in all the boats that had been anchored out on the Broads during the war to keep German sea planes out. Most had sunk and because they were heavy in the back they had lain with their noses out of the water so that wood was rotten. Some of us got to strip out all the rotten pieces, quite an experience, then they put one boy with each boat builder and we went round repairing them and getting them ready for the new season. The boats had motors and just enough electricity to start the engines. They still had hurricane lamps, paraffin stoves and sails until 1947 when they started changing all that.

On Saturdays we all did different jobs and I worked with the electrician for a year, moving batteries about. Then the next year, on Saturday, we did something else.

The first summer after the war finished I was put on what they called Herbert Woods Norfolk dinghies, a special class of 14ft dinghies, and I learned to make clinker boats. Then I got the chance to do three months on the Yare and Bures, a one design boat that Herbert Woods built after the war, so I learned from different people.

In 1946 six Summer Breezes were built. By then Herbert Woods had bought Southgate's at Horning so we were able to use two stocks and us boys helped – it was always a boy's job to plane the bottoms. They finished the first for the start of the 1947 season but when they moored it at Horning, lightning struck the mast and blew a hole through the bottom of the boat and it sank. We had just a fortnight to get number two ready. They didn't worry about youngsters working all times of the day but we did get good bonuses and I sometimes got more bonus than I did for my working wage. And we had some good times; I'll always remember them.

Woods got short of work and got rid of a few men. One chap who had been a fisherman before the war went back to fishing and gave me a lot of his old tools. He was a lovely chap but I used to get wrong with him sometimes and he even slung me into the wet dock one day. The work continued like this, being a boy and learning the trade, until the autumn of 1946 when the foreman said, 'I've got a job for you, Boy Mike', as he used to call me. I was given a section of a shop

Loading the beam at Yarmouth 1984

up in the corner and was told everything in the yard was to be looked at, patched, varnished, new masts made, whatever was needed. I was to get it all out again by the next Easter. I loved it!

Then he said, 'I'm giving you a boy.' 'I'm sixteen and a half', I said, 'what do you mean, giving me a boy?' I got started and the boy came with me. We were working till 6.30, but funnily enough at 5.30 every night I would miss him, then one day the foreman asked, 'Ha' you seen your boy?' 'He's gone home?' 'No,' he said, 'he h'e'n't clocked off yet.' We found him sitting in one of our dinghies in the dock, fishing! He didn't last too long. Anyway, I think I did about 90 dinghies on the yard; it really taught me boatbuilding.

I remember all the good times, especially summertime… There were no divers and sometimes people got a rope round the propeller, so a few of us would be asked to jump in and cut the rope. I suppose that made another ten shillings of pocket money between us.

Every summer there was a regatta at Potter Heigham and Herbert Woods would tell the boys to take a dinghy and do some sailing. We used to have swimming contests like having two boats side by side with a gap between. Then we would dive off one boat and swim across to the other, drink a quarter pint of milk and swim back again. The first time I didn't know how I got back – your tummy's full of milk, you're in the water, still drinking! Another game was when a round pole was put across two boats and you'd sit on it with a pillow and try and knock the other boy off. We'd also jump off Potter Heigham Bridge. There would be about 20 of us; I never won anything but I enjoyed it.

That was my life until August 1947 and I'd done three years. I got a notice to say I would be called up when I was 18 and I served as an airframe fitter in the navy for seven good years. I left in 1955 but didn't do any boatbuilding for 13 years until Billy May, who built crab boats in Cromer, asked if I'd like to go back to it. I put up his new shed and I built five crab boats for him.

The fishermen up there wanted the very best as they could get a grant from the government. They were not allowed to say what they wanted but the boat had to be up to standard. We didn't have plans; we just set up for a 22ft or a 19ft length, cut the keel and away we'd go. The fishermen would come down to see us every now and again; they'd walk in the door and just stand there… and I'd wonder what they going to say. Then it was, 'Blast, thass nice, m'boy.' And that's all I wanted to hear.

Richard Davies, who was skipper for the Cromer lifeboat, came down one day and asked me to build him the biggest crab boat we had ever done. Well, that came out at 23ft 3in. He was also the first one to put in a diesel engine at Cromer. He used that boat for a year and was ever so pleased with it; then he said he had another little job for me. He had damaged the boat by dragging it up the beach with too much weight in it – six tons of cockles and mussels. 'Well', I said, 'you've caused me some trouble, h'e'n't you?' When I finished he gave me a bottle of whisky.

After seven years I told Billy I wanted a change and I went back to Woods who were building their last three wooden boats ever. I stayed three years and did many of the troubleshooting jobs. A memorable incident involved a boat sinking in Yarmouth Harbour. They had a hole by the waterline and every time a wave washed over, it filled the boat and there was only two inches above the water. I stripped out where I thought the hole was and stuffed it with an old pair of socks. I then made a proper patch and screwed it on with my usual putty and grease. Next I made a big patch using fibreglass and held my hand in the water until it set. That was the sort of job I did. I built boats and sometimes I put boats right and made sure they didn't sink; you don't want to see them sinking.

I then joined Powell's at Wroxham. They had some concrete boats and I was asked if I could put them right and was given a shed of my own for the winter. I did ten and they came out nice and I launched them with just a bloke to help. They were 28ft long with four berths and there are still a few on the Broads but you wouldn't know unless you were told. They were built with layers of concrete and mesh steel which ended up about two inches thick with three layers of steel inside.

There was a bad winter where I couldn't get to Wroxham to work so I started with a chap at Womack near Ludham who had a little boatyard. He was an engineer so he made sure the engines were right and I looked after the ten boats. This went on alright for two years until he suddenly said he didn't have a lot of money. His father and another bloke put some money in and I was told I could run the yard for the next year as he was going to work in France, then it was sold.

I worked for myself for the next 12 years until I retired in 1995. I enjoyed my life. Never look back and never wish for anything, I always say. Well, everybody wishes for more money sometimes but I didn't worry about it. Anyway, by the time I retired in 1995 I'd done 51 years and two days at work.

About 1982 I had begun doing little bits to Wherry Albion. I was paid for some and on Saturday mornings I would go as a volunteer as I'd realised what it was all about. I had seen her on the Broads and thought nothing of it but now I'd started to take an interest in wherries. In 1984 she needed a new main beam, 14ft long, so we went down to Yarmouth Harbour where May Gurney gave us one of the old pilings – the barnacles were still on it! We scraped them off and I made patterns of the old one out of ply. A friend took out handfuls of rot all round where the old beam was. Albion was nearly 80 years old then – when wherries got to that stage years ago, they just built a new one and shoved the old ones into the side and used them as banks.

By the 1990s, I'd helped repair and replace all the main bits. Then, at a Wherry Trust meeting, I told them I was retiring and I'd like to work on Albion as a volunteer for five years. I had a friend who was a retired policeman who wanted to help and we did the five years together replacing more planks and whatever. I finished when I was 70 and after a while the Wherry Trust made me a Vice President. I go to meetings and they ask me about things now and again.

In 2000 I decided to volunteer at the Museum of the Broads in Stalham. The President showed me around what they called the wherry room and asked if I could build the back end of a wherry to put on the wall. Two of us finished it in four months. I made it out of ply and ordinary timber to look like oak and they were pleased as punch with it, and I've been there ever since doing little pieces. I've had a good life and I still work a little bit.

Sailing through work

(1957 – 1980s)

Roy Forder
(b. 1942)

BRUNDALL

Born in Reedham at Ship Cottages next to the river and the swing bridge, Roy left school wanting to work on boats. At age 16 he began an apprenticeship with Bell Boats, Brundall.

In 1957 our local River Inspector told me about a vacancy for a boatbuilding apprentice at Bell Boats in Brundall. He put my name forward and I went to the interview with my father. I worked on cruisers which varied from 27ft to 52ft in length and also looked after private boats. With a small yard you didn't do just boatbuilding, it was also a general job and I worked on their caravans and bungalows as well.

We sold a Shark 8 to a guy in Littlehampton and he sent his son, an oil tanker captain, to collect it. The foreman drove to Yarmouth to watch him go out to sea and all he could see was the mast once the boat left the harbour. The captain went back to Littlehampton without stopping to refuel because of a huge storm and was in hospital for three days from being thrown around. The boat was fine though. He said he'd take it anywhere.

We built a 32ft Aquafibre hull for an army captain based in Germany. The army intended to equip the boat with gear to catch drug smugglers but unfortunately the captain died halfway through the build and the boat was put up for sale. A Mr Bertie Buxton looked at it and asked why it was not furnished with crockery, linen and utensils and we said it was for the owner to decide on their own requirements. He went on to form his own company, Buxton Marine, which bought boats from Aquafibre and then equipped them for sale.

One day while working on the boatyard, a couple of minesweepers came down and my friend said, 'Stand beside this flag for me and just watch.' I could see the crew cleaning the deck. Suddenly he moved and our house flag came down. Everyone on deck shot round to the back end and dropped their flag in salute to us; it was the traditional thing to do but quite amusing.

Another time we were checking one of our hire yachts at the edge of the river when a steam train went by and the reed bed caught fire. We carried on because we knew we couldn't do anything and it was harmless. A police boat pulled up. 'Come on, boys, give us a hand to put this fire out. Come on, do as you're told!' We followed them and one of them charged straight into the field. Next thing he was shouting for help; it was a bog and he came out smelling… quite lovely. Fortunately there was a houseboat close by and the lady had some spare

Shark 8 at Bure Quay

clothes. Through this we formed a good friendship with the police and they would pop in every time we went down that way, always at the right time for a cup of tea.

The actor Jack Douglas from the Carry On films had a Moonraker built in our yard and he came with a group of friends to see it launched. They had lunch in the café at the front of the quay and he burst out laughing at the duck footprints in the concrete where we couldn't keep them off. Our clerk came from Potter Heigham where Cliff Richard moored his boat, Pamanda. He persuaded Cliff to store Pamanda at our yard and I put in a new bilge pump for him.

Working on Crossbow

(1974 – 1980)

In 1965 I went to work for Tim Whelpton at his boatyard in Upton where they had a small hire fleet of wooden boats. I was involved in building one wooden boat as soon as I started but then they went into fibreglass and I began fitting out the hulls.

In 1974 we got involved with Crossbow which Tim Colman used for his world speed sailing record in 1972 when she achieved 30 knots. It was built by Reg White in Brightlingsea but Tim wanted a new hull and we did the work and he upped the record to 35 knots. Later on we worked on Crossbow 2, a fast machine designed by Rod Macalpine-Downie. The hull was built elsewhere but we finished it off. The speed attempts took place in Portland Harbour in Weymouth where Crossbow 2 eventually reached a speed of 36 knots in 1980, a record that stood for six years. These were big 60-65ft boats but the record was beaten by a sailboard! A Crossbow 3 was started but never finished as, unfortunately, the designer died.

Paul Reynolds
b. 1937

Engineering: a vocation, not just a job

(1960s – 2003)

John Cooke
(b. 1943)

RANWORTH, REEDHAM

John completed an apprenticeship in marine engineering at age 21 and worked for various marine companies around the Broads and on Reedham Ferry.

During my apprenticeship in Lowestoft I did a variety of work, building and fabricating machinery. We were the main agents for Gardner Marine Diesels and when the Scottish fishing fleet came down every year we were extremely busy. We could be sent out to a boat at Yarmouth and probably not come off it until midnight. It gave me a grounding in marine engineering. To help me read the specifications and drawings for the machinery we were building I took a night course on technical drawing. I managed it very well despite my dyslexia and it proved an asset for both me and the company.

After a variety of other engineering jobs I was told that Moonraker Marine in Brundall was hiring and I was offered the position of plant engineer, which suited me down to the ground. They were building a range of luxury sea-going power yachts at the time and I was responsible for looking after the fabric of the many buildings and all the lifting equipment and compressors. They had a fully automated GRP (glass reinforced plastic) shop which was powered by machines called 'drosstones', an early way to spray on fibreglass.

The company was owned by Colin Chapman of Lotus cars who also had boatbuilding enterprises on the Hethel site in the old hangars. I was seconded there as project development engineer to set up the woodworking sawmill and upgrade the power supply whilst still being responsible for the operation at Brundall. When you build a boat and start fitting it out, you work off a mezzanine floor which is like a quarry quay heading. My job was to maintain it. There were some problems with the hangar floor not taking the point loadings required at one end – it was an interesting time.

I also ran the operation at Ranworth pulling boats up the slipway and into the yard or putting the boats back in after they had over-wintered. During this time I worked with the Cator family and Charles Cator was my immediate contact. He was a gentleman farmer and loved getting amongst all the muck. I had a very nice letter from him on my retirement saying that he looked back on our days of rummaging about in goodness knows what, with great affection.

Another job was working for South River Marine at St Olaves where they specialised in the restoration of classic and vintage boats. A lot of the boat owners wanted original-type engines in their boats, the type of engine I had worked on during my apprenticeship, so I knew them inside out. We would take out the engine and Mike Barnes, one of the directors, researched for an original type engine, and I basically rebuilt it as best possible with whatever spares I could access.

One such was a stepped-hull hydroplane called a bat boat which was built for experimental work on the shape of hulls on seaplanes – they were using hull design to try and get the hydroplanes out of the water faster. The one that I was involved with had a Spanish SPAD fighter engine in it, so how the new engine was researched and sourced,

I haven't a clue. It was an absolute monster, a 12 litre V8, and you needed a shoehorn to get it into the hull.

My involvement with Reedham Ferry was one of those things that just happened. I was phoned up one day by a gentleman saying that the ferry had come back from a refit the previous week, suffered a complete failure on the hydraulics and they couldn't get anybody out to deal with it. I went immediately and found that one of the steel lines had corroded and burst so I spliced a temporary repair into it and got it running again. I said that really all the lines should be in stainless steel and was asked to fit them. That was the start of my association with Reedham Ferry and it continued for the rest of my working life. After the Bowbelle ran the Marchioness down on the Thames in 1989 we had to do various tests on the ferry to check buoyancy and loading capacity. The biggest problem was fear of capsize but the ferry came out with flying colours; it did have a good safety record.

The construction of the ferry is quite advanced being steel framed with oak planking and very heavily built. It has a ballast tank at each end that can be flooded to adjust the ferry's height according to the tide as Reedham is very tidal. It is powered by two diesel engines which run the hydraulics but it can run on either engine; it doesn't need both. I replaced the engines with modern diesel engines and as a by-product we discovered that the smoother engines extended the life of the chains which winched the ferry across the river.

As my business became more established, I started getting work in the Newmarket and Cambridge area on the River Cam. I got a call from a professional photographer to the racing fraternity who had a petrol engine Seamaster and wanted to dieselise it as it was almost impossible to buy petrol on the Cam anymore, and petrol engines are notoriously thirsty. I liaised with Peachment Marine at Brundall and was given the job. Over a number of weeks the old engine was taken out and a new one put in and re-engineered. The owner was delighted. The boat had a lot more torque and was easier to handle and he wrote an article in one of the yachting magazines which brought me another identical job.

A bat boat

Rebuilt diesel engine

The conversion to diesel is expensive, basically the value of the boat again, so a lot of people just sold their petrol engine boats and bought a diesel one. It was interesting work and I still have contact with a lot of my customers; they have almost become personal friends which is not good in business as you tend to be too kind to them!

Nature in the raw

(2009 – 2019)

Geoff Doggett
(b. 1945)

RIVER WAVENEY

Following retirement Geoff canoed the length of the River Waveney and later helped form the River Waveney Trust (RWT) in 2012 and then the Waveney Heritage Group in 2017.

When I retired at 64 I needed to do something and I wanted to do a volunteer-based activity in the community. In 2009, Stewart Orr, a great sailing friend of mine, had just finished building a beautiful 16ft wooden canoe in Ipswich. I had helped him but then he didn't know what to do with it so I suggested a trip down the Waveney from its source to the sea.

The Waveney has always been a good canoeing river and we just wanted to be 14-year-old boys again for five days. We started at Redgrave, Lopham Fen, which is close to the source and paddled our way down, camping overnight. It was a phenomenal trip which allowed us to see the river from the swan's-eye view which is even better than walking along it because canoes are virtually silent. You creep up on things, you get surprised by things and you leave no footprint.

We did the trip in May, a good nesting time for swans and spring was bursting out everywhere. Near Flixton we went round a corner and an angry cob started to flap his wings behind the canoe and attacking the back where I was sitting. We pulled into the side and sure enough, half a mile further on, we saw the hen sitting on her nest; he was just doing his stuff and as soon as we passed, he gave up.

Rivers join communities and people which I find fascinating. On the Waveney we have four wonderful market towns: Diss, Harleston, Bungay and Beccles. They are almost equidistant and each has its own culture and community but it's the river that unites them. The Saxons, Romans and possibly people before that were using the river for transport, there was nothing else. The river has an impact on those who live near it, its flow has a soothing effect and it is also something on which our communities have been built.

The Waveney is a classic lowland, slow-moving and lazy river, dropping only 50-60ft from its source to Yarmouth, 60 miles away. It has little gradient but it has been interfered with dramatically, first by the mill owners in the 18th century and more recently by the Environment Agency (EA) which is trying to protect us from flooding. We are fortunate to still have two dairy herds in the upper Waveney so the marshes are still used for productive purposes rather than being more like tidal marshes.

After the canoe trip, the Waveney became very important to me and I wondered if I could start an organisation with like-minded people and in 2012 the RWT was set up as a charity. A hundred people turned up to the first meeting. The Rivers Trust movement in England, of which RWT is a part, is all about trying to maintain good water quality, the ecology of the river and its water bodies. We got to 200-300 members very quickly so we split the membership into five separate groups along the river, each with their own stretch based on the four market towns. It meant the work done was local to the members and volunteers. We built relationships with the EA, the Broads Authority and Norfolk County Council all of whom began to get involved in issues faced by the Waveney and its catchment areas.

The River Waveney

The catchment for the Waveney is from Pulham Market to Mendlesham in Suffolk and from the west of Diss down to Yarmouth, so it's a big geographical area. I began to explore this and realised just how important the tributaries were. A little tributary like Starston Beck, our local one in Harleston, is only four miles long but it has its own ecosystem. If it was polluted it would endanger the main river but if it's healthy, fish will get out of the main stream to breed because they like the quiet life in the tributaries.

We also began looking at the marshes in depth to try and understand them. The Waveney marshes are interesting because they have two distinct types of ecology. Above Ellingham, which is three or four miles upstream from Beccles, is the 'tidal gate'. All the water below is tidal, so Ellingham through Beccles to Oulton Broad and Breydon has two tides a day and different fish and invertebrates live in the more saline water. The other side of the tidal gate, upstream, is called the fluvial or freshwater stretch and the EA controls the water and sluices there.

Long before the EA there were constant battles between farmers and millers because farmers didn't like the water being held back by the mills and the millers needed the power from the river to drive the mill. Funnily enough it was often the farmer's grain that was being milled!

Upstream we have lovely grazing marshes which used to support a very big dairy industry. Our groups got very involved with the local farmers and found that the grazing marshes have very few ecological challenges; they have lots of little dykes which act to provide an incredibly well-behaved flood plain. The tidal marshes below Ellingham include the massive Carlton Marsh and Peto's Marsh near Lowestoft and have some of the most magnificent marsh landscape anywhere in the East of England, and possibly the country. Further downstream is the magnificent estuary of Breydon which is a class act in terms of estuaries in East Anglia, with its wildlife and walks on both banks, and then the river ends in Yarmouth at the seaside. I hope the future will include as much access as possible to the grazing marshes upstream where much land is now owned by the RSPB, Norfolk Wildlife Trust and the National Trust.

One of the pieces of unfinished business when I retired from the RWT as a Trustee was the heritage and history of the river, its catchment and communities. So, in 2017 a group of us in Harleston formed the Waveney Heritage group based at the former Brockdish School, to do projects and establish an archive about the river; we are about to start a big project on river crossings.

Memories of a river man

(1987 – 2011)

Tony Risebrow
(b. 1961)

HORNING

Tony was a Chief Mate on container ships and sailed the world. He then worked as a River Inspector for 24 years, mostly for the Broads Authority.

I finished my career on container ships in 1986 and on my last trip I took along the Yellow Pages and typed about 180 letters to different employers, one of which was the Great Yarmouth Port and Haven Commissioners. They wrote back offering me the job of River Inspector. Fortunately they didn't tell me what the salary was as it was half my salary at sea!

I started as a relief River Inspector in April 1987 and spent my first day at Ludham. I can remember coming out of the boatshed and thinking, 'This is absolutely beautiful!' The first six to eight weeks were spent being trained and then I went out with a senior River Inspector to make sure that I was a safe pair of hands. The Port and Haven Commissioners were sensible; they employed ex-seafarers because they knew one end of a boat from the other as well as all the technical stuff, so they just had to give us their information and point us in the right direction, and off we went.

Nobody in their right mind would leave a River Inspector job when I started. We were given a nice 30ft launch and could decide where we went each day, and we were encouraged to go into the pubs at lunchtime so we were known. We were part of the community and information just flowed in to us. It wasn't just about enforcing speed limits; it was about knowing all there was to know. Our role was to manage our area and as long as the office wasn't getting too many complaints and we could be contacted over the radio, they were happy; it was a very different era.

I had been working for the Port and Haven Commissioners for a couple of years when the Broads Authority (BA) took over in 1989. As the same people were still in charge, the transition was very smooth and nothing really changed for several years until the BA decided to look at our terms and conditions. The chief executive was unhappy with our little add-ons. We had a low basic salary and he quite rightly said that he would rather put up the salary and do away with the extras. Everyone viewed it positively but there was a perception that the BA didn't understand us which persisted for many years. They kept the work patterns the same and they eventually introduced a new, less intimidating uniform, more like a ranger's.

It was decided to divide the area into two teams, North and South. I had been looking after Norwich but with the changes I was moved to Wroxham which had a far more 'touristy' feel about it and was much busier than Norwich – Norwich was very much about large stretches of water, fewer hire boats, and more local people using the river. Friday and Saturday nights were interesting at Wroxham as boats coming out of the boatyards were all looking for somewhere to moor and Horning was the place to go. It didn't have that many moorings so I would go out in the evening to help people as they could get quite panicky.

I started using volunteers in 1998 and my first one was a local person who wanted to come out on the boat. I used volunteers extensively from then on although they didn't become an official thing until about 2003. All they really wanted to do was drive a boat and you could tell if they would be any good within a couple of minutes. By the time they reversed out of the boatshed, you knew if you could teach them; it's all about spatial awareness with boats. Initially their role was to support the staff but later they went out on their own in launches clearly labelled 'Auxiliary Navigation Rangers'. I always tried to look after them buying cake and making them tea and coffee.

During the winter months we went wherever we were needed but it was mainly clearing trees from the river banks. We were given a work boat in November and told what needed to be done and that would really be it until the following Easter. We would log on and off each day so they knew where we were and what we were doing, and as we were cutting down trees, they could see what had been done and, in the early days, we were allowed to collect firewood and bring it home.

We had a lot of rigs moving around the system which we escorted during the winter months. The enormous Flood Alleviation Project around the Broads involved lots of barges moving about and dredgers moving from one site to another. We would escort them all as some dredgers effectively filled the river.

In the 1990s we also escorted the Blackheath taking oil up to Cantley. Towards the end of my time I was one of the mud pilots so I would go on board the Blackheath and help the primary pilot. He had been on coasters so he was the one who actually told the captain. They used to say 'master's orders and pilot's advice', because the master is always in charge but the pilot tells him where to steer. We would take the coasters up and down the river with a launch in front, to make sure everyone got out the way. Over the years we had problems with ice and once we had the Blackheath iced in at Cantley sugar factory. We couldn't allow it to leave even though it was able to smash through as it would have sunk every boat on the way down, with the ice slicing through the hull of any moored boat.

Broads Authority patrol boat 2006

I remember going out after the hurricane of October 1987 at the end of my first season. I was told to go to Wroxham and on the way I saw a yacht which had been blown down a dyke and thrown over pilings! Even more extraordinary, an island in Bridge Broad, upstream from Wroxham, had blown across the broad and had attached itself to one of the banks! We ran an echo sounder across the former area of the island and it was the same depth as the rest of the Broad. One of the worst-affected areas was at Dunburgh on the River Waveney – there were so many trees down you could walk across the river and I think May Gurney was there for three months clearing them.

There is a natural rhythm to the river and I used to work with it; it tended to start about 10 or 11 in the morning and finish about 6 or 7 in the evening. However, on Fridays and Saturdays I would start and finish later especially when I worked around Horning. It probably doesn't work in the same way now as resources have to be focussed where they are most needed and rangers are far more multi-skilled than we were.

We spent time talking to people and that is hard to measure, it was just different. We would spend time gossiping over a cup of tea and information might come out which we found useful. I miss that, I miss helping people, I miss towing people off when they were stuck. Things like that really make somebody's holiday. We would let a young lad come on board and drive the boat, or help holidaymakers find a mooring as it was getting dark and they all thought it was wonderful.

Technology has helped rangers enormously. Nowadays they have smart phones and cameras. We used film and had an arrangement with a guy at Wroxham to develop the pictures really quickly if we needed them in a hurry. I can remember getting my first mobile phone; it was wonderful. We used to have boards up at the mouth of the rivers and the police had SOS boards. If they were looking for someone that would go on the boards, and we used to say that we could find someone between 45 and 90 minutes, wherever they were on the Broads. In those days all the services, the police, emergency services and River Inspectors worked closely together, there was a comradeship and we all felt part of the same team.

More regulations have been introduced, and they were needed. Stability requirements are preventing accidents and there are fewer incidents of drowning. One of the biggest beneficial changes I have seen over the years is the improvement in safety and especially the wearing of life jackets. Self-inflating life jackets allow people to wear buoyancy aids all the time. When I first started, all we had were Board of Trade jackets which were used on deep-sea ships; they were full of fixed foam and enormous so it was a job to get out of the narrow cabin door. Self-inflating jackets made such a difference and we wore them all the time as a fine example to others.

My favourite areas to work were Wroxham and Horning because I was helping people, and that is where the job satisfaction comes from. I also was interested in protecting the wildlife by trying to stop fishermen disturbing it in winter. Horsey Mere is voluntarily closed in winter, but that did not stop fishermen from trying to get up there for the female pike, full of eggs. There were some real fanatics, some of whom travelled from other parts of the country. I worked with the National Trust on the Horsey Estate to try and get these fishermen out. They would go to enormous lengths: launching before sunrise, covering their registration numbers, even wearing balaclavas; they didn't worry about the voluntary ban at all.

My last winter on the launch was 2010-2011. I remember going down for an early morning escort from Runham on the Lower Bure, and because we were running quite quickly the water was coming over the bow and freezing on both the foredeck and the windscreen. I can remember thinking, 'I'm getting too old for this'.

The Broads is one of the best-kept secrets; it is like a great big village where everybody knows everyone else. It has such a lovely feel and those of us who have lived here a long time have such a connection. Unfortunately we are losing it, as everything is changing and becoming more focused on technology, rather than people.

Bridge Master and River Inspector

(1982 – 2006)

Gerry Jarvis
(b. 1941)

NORWICH

Gerry grew up in Norwich and joined the Royal Navy in 1965 as a Writer handling clerical and financial business. He left in 1982 to become the Bridge Master at Carrow Bridge.

Becoming Bridge Master of Carrow Bridge seemed a strange step but it was a good move. The bridge was on the A47 before the bypass was built so it was a very busy road and it meant I had to stop the flow of traffic whenever the bridge was lifted to let ships through – quite interesting! We had control of the traffic lights at the junction of the old Riverside Road and Carrow Road, flashing lights on either side of the bridge meant the barriers were due to come down, and we could open and close the bridge quite quickly. Opening it on match days was especially difficult as the bridge was very near the football stadium but we had some support from the police who would help hold the crowd back.

I worked very closely with the River Inspectors and I thought that was something I would like to do but it was a case of waiting for a beat inspector to leave. So when I saw a vacancy I applied and became a relief inspector. There were eight permanent beat inspectors for the eight launches based around the Broads – four on the northern rivers and four on the southern – and four relief inspectors who rotated around the different launches to cover rest days, holidays and sickness and the like. The inspectors covered the 120 miles of navigable water which make up the Broads including the tidal River Wensum as far as Carrow Bridge in Norwich.

When I became a permanent River Inspector I had my own beat and a boat based at Thorpe. My duties were to patrol the area, enforce the many regulations, check licences and also help the fire brigade, ambulance service and police as needed. I remember an incident when an inspector on the Upper Thurne was asked to collect a lady who lived upstream of Potter Bridge, and he transported her downriver in her wheelchair on the top of the engine cover, so the ambulance crew could take her to hospital.

Speed causes lots of problems on the Broads because the wash from a boat can cause damage to moored boats and also damages the riverbanks. As you travel along the rivers you can see erosion largely caused by the wash from boats.

One time I was carrying out radar speed checks at Brundall when a colleague downstream radioed to say that a boat had gone past exceeding the speed limit. I speed checked them as they came by and informed the six crew members of the problems they were likely to cause. Later I learned that they were all newly qualified solicitors on their celebratory outing and they wrote to my boss calling me Lombrosian. I eventually found out that this comes from an Italian count called Lombroso who thought that criminals inherit their criminality, so you could just look at a person and know he's a criminal. They felt that I'd done this to them! Lombrosian was a title which stuck with me my whole career.

Police launch

Later on I was quite famous… or infamous is probably the word. Under the Merchant Shipping Act the Union Flag can only be flown on boats which are specifically authorised, so when I was on the River Waveney and saw a hire cruiser moored up with a big – and I do mean big – Union Flag hanging over the side, I pulled over. I let them know that they were actually contravening the Merchant Shipping Act and that the penalty, if convicted, was four figures, and off I went. The following day I was in the London papers and the EDP for saying the little girl couldn't wave her little flag!

Being a River Inspector was such a varied job with no two days alike. So many things could make your day good or bad: the weather, the tide, the boat traffic… When you were assisting the police and fire brigade to recover bodies from the river it could be very depressing. One incident which has always stayed with me involved a young boy of about six on the Waveney. His parents made him wear his life jacket all the time he was on board apart from when they were inside. They were having their tea when some swans went up to the boat and the boy ran out to the back of the boat, went straight over, and the tide took him away.

The water can be dangerous but lots of people don't wear life jackets and adults are the worst. Whatever we were doing as River Inspectors, we always wore life jackets. Even on the banks while we were cutting down reed in the winter or building staging or whatever, we always wore them. I think I have personally fallen into all the rivers in the Norfolk Broads.

The job also involved some conservation work. In the days when wherries sailed the rivers they cut down trees as wherries needed to let their sail right out over the land when they were close to the bank. Since then trees have grown up at will, so some of us did this work in the winter. We also built habitat piles for animals and generally tried to help conserve a bit of nature as well as make everything safe and open for navigation.

I did quite a lot of work with schools and Scout groups so children could learn how to behave around boats and get the chance to go on the water and appreciate the environment. We also helped on Fun in the Broads days which were often held at Salhouse Broad, and we would have things like a rope and knot display teaching children how rope is made and how to tie knots. Those days were enjoyable and were well supported.

Mariner and River Inspector

(1982 – 1989)

Mark Lockwood
(b. 1950)

NORWICH

Mark joined the army and served as a seagoing soldier on landing craft all around the world for 12 years before becoming a River Inspector on the Broads in 1982.

At my River Inspector interview, I was asked how often I had been aground and when I replied, 'Hundreds of times', the interviewer's face sort of dropped until the harbour master whispered in his ear that when you're on a landing craft and you beach or ramp down, you are technically aground. When I received my start date and was given a warrant to prove my authority as a River Inspector, I thought it was a joke, because it was dated the 1st April 1982, April Fool's Day!

I had 16 weeks training going round the various beats with different inspectors learning about the areas they covered and getting their views on how the job was carried out. Everyone had different ideas but one of the inspectors on the southern rivers said something I still remember: 'Not everybody knows everything but everybody knows something so between us all we know the lot!' We had two-way radios on board and he said I shouldn't be afraid to ask questions.

There are about 200 navigable miles of river but I found there was a lot more because each inspector showed me the nooks and crannies of his beat; all the little dykes and inlets and I learned that the rivers today are not what they were hundreds of years ago. I'm not talking about the making of the Broads and peat diggings, but about the actual rivers that used to flow around here and have changed their course. Some were dug out and are actually canals, but not very long ones. For instance, the River Bure coming downstream out of Horning, past the River Ant and St Benet's Abbey is actually a canal – the river used to take a sharp right and go down almost to South Walsham Broad. I learned this when the inspector on that beat said, 'We'll go on the old course of the Bure', and we disappeared into the reeds. We went through the reeds very slowly and all of a sudden we popped out. It was amazing.

After the 16 weeks I became an inspector on relief duty. Our uniform looked like a naval petty officer's but without the badges. Initially it was a black jacket, black trousers, white shirt, black tie and a peaked white hat. The black jacket was replaced shortly after I joined by a navy pullover which was a lot more comfortable and the blue waterproof parka was replaced by a jacket that the police used but said 'River Inspector' – we didn't want any confusion!

In the morning I would book in over the radio and then head out; a note was left by the previous inspector to say if anything needed checking. If there was nothing I picked my own route, and would go downstream one day and upstream the next. I had a packed lunch and facilities on board to make hot drinks, and that was it.

Our job was to enforce the bylaws made by the Port and Haven Commissioners which related to the speed and condition of vessels and vandalism to property along the rivers. One problem was people coming out of clubs and pubs in Norwich late at night, going down to the yacht station and casting off the boats. We had quite costly and large signs at Thorpe which said, 'Free Mooring 24 hours', and one vandal used to take the sign off, turn it upside down and bolt it back on!

We saw differences throughout the year. In the holiday season we had people who had never been in a boat before so we would give them a lot of leeway because they would biff and bang things, and plough into things. They were only there for a week and then they were gone. We used to pull people off mud banks and tow them when they had broken down, or radio the boatyards.

After four years I became a regular beat inspector and took over from the guy who ran the beat from Beauchamp Arms down to Breydon Water, including the River Chet down to Loddon which was virtually reeds, reeds, reeds all the way down. I enjoyed working on my own and the peace and quiet – when I was on my own, that is. When there were holidaymakers wanting to know things and getting into trouble, that's when it became hectic!

I often had people tell me that there was a bloke on the bank in a sleeping bag. Well, it was always a seal as seals used to come up between Breydon Water and Reedham to calve. Going upstream towards Geldeston one day I saw a turtle. The Broads Authority (BA) had just started up an information centre so I went back to tell them and it turned out to be a green snapper, probably a pet which had been discarded when it got too big. It just sat there, brazenly bathing in the sun. Apparently they hibernate in the mud over winter time and were regulars on the rivers.

I left in 1989 as the BA was starting up. It was a time of change for life on the Broads. The BA had already set up information centres and was carrying out projects like damming off Cockshoot Broad near Horning. We got a new guy who was employed as an engineer to inspect hire boats and private craft, raise standards, reduce pollution and stop them leaking oil everywhere and breaking down. The BA wanted cleaner water so boats had to clean up their act; it took time because some hire craft were in a terrible state.

Under the BA the job of River Inspector changed considerably and they are now called rangers. They lost the uniform and patrol boats and use work boats instead, and they spend a lot of their time ashore rather than on the water, whereas we were on the river all the time. I wouldn't wish to be a River Inspector on the Broads now because we did get threatened a bit when some people took exception to being told what they were doing wrong. But in the main it was a very enjoyable job, watching bird life, watching wildlife, looking at turtles … It was quite an enjoyable experience.

A life on the waves: barges and coasters

(1960s – 2008)

Robin Bowling
(b. 1943)

GREAT YARMOUTH

Robin was interested in the sea from childhood and worked on cargo-carrying coastal barges for 30 years. He later became a River Inspector for the Broads Authority.

In the 1960s I wanted to learn how to handle a barge so I applied to London Rochester Trading Company for a job as crew. As it was the policy of barging companies for the master to train the crew, I was taken on as mate on the Northdown under a very experienced skipper who taught me a great deal.

The skipper had bought the 200-tonne coasting barge as a wreck and converted her into a little motor ship. She had what at that time was called a Yarmouth Dover Load Line, meaning she could transport a full load anywhere between the ports of Yarmouth and Dover and the near continent.

It was economically advantageous to carry as much cargo as possible as we were paid by the share, so we would stow as much as we could and it also made the ship more stable at sea. Most barges work on a share system: the owner takes 50% and of the rest, the master has two-thirds and the mate one-third unless he has little experience and the master has to do more work. After two years or so I became a master by learning on the job.

We'd go to Yarmouth, Lowestoft and Norwich. The cargo for Great Yarmouth was mainly bags of cattle food but we also carried fertiliser to Bunn's in Yarmouth. We were booked in advance but if we were held up by the weather we couldn't call ahead as we didn't have radios. A journey from London to Yarmouth was a 16-hour passage unless the weather was bad and we had to do it in stages.

Lowestoft was tricky to enter if the wind was in the south but the tide there only goes up and down. Yarmouth was harder because the tide flows out for a long time. There's a very restrictive bar at the entrance which wasn't a problem for our barge unless there was a big swell and the wind was anywhere in the east – I still have great respect for Yarmouth pier heads! Yarmouth is a 'harbour of refuge' which means you can go in through stress of weather without having to pay dues. I believe it's the only one between Harwich and the Humber and, although Yarmouth is quite a busy port, you can always find a berth.

I moved on to work for Sully's, barge owners, and stayed for 18 years starting as a relief mate on the Peter Robin. During this time I learned many skills including general navigation, chart work, and how to navigate in fog as we still didn't have radar. You always relied on seamarks and landmarks so when approaching Yarmouth we would see the power station, a tall concrete building with a large chimney which was visible from a long way out to sea. Later when Peter Robin was fitted with VHF I took my restricted radio licence with the GPO.

The loads we carried on the Peter Robin came from London or the continent and it was just me and the mate on board. Canadian wheat was exported to Tilbury and we would transport 200-tonne loads to Read's Mill in King Street in Norwich. We'd get alongside the mill and the wheat would be grabbed out with a crane and grab. Later on, in the Subro vessels, we brought soya from the continent up to Riverside and unloaded it into lorries using the grab roughly opposite to where the swimming pool is today.

It was the Master's job to 'order the bridge' when going from Yarmouth to Norwich and I would try to do this two hours before high water in Yarmouth as I would have the full flood to get to Norwich, a six-hour journey. The bridge was the railway bridge at Reedham which was controlled by flags at the time. Two red flags meant that the bridge wouldn't open. One red flag meant it would open and they would slide out a board with the opening time.

Occasionally, if the Bridge Master wasn't keeping a good eye out I would be approaching the bridge and it would just say 'The bridge will open', and then they slid out a board saying that the bridge would open in ten minutes. It's quite difficult to stop a barge with a flood tide under you! The Reedham Ferry was always pretty good. When he saw us coming up the river he would pull to one side and drop his chains to the bottom. I never had a problem there.

The New Cut behind Thorpe Island was cut to accommodate the railway and avoid having two extra swing bridges but we had to navigate it with care as there wasn't much water. One of the hazards going through it was passenger boats and if a boat came past us hard, he would draw the water away, and we would sit on the bottom for a minute or two. No-one had priority; it was just care and courtesy, although sometimes the River Inspector would ask us to hurry along because the Bridge Master at Carrow Bridge wanted to get the bridge shut for the evening traffic.

I left Sully's and worked on coastal tankers before being made redundant. When I first started, you could make a living in a 130-tonne barge. By the time I finished I had a 2,000-tonne ship nominally for a crew of 20, yet we were running her with five and still finding it difficult to make a living. Whilst working at a factory in Rackheath, a job as a River Inspector with the Broads Authority came up and in 1997 I started working with them on Breydon Water and retired in 2008.

Throughout my time with the Broads Authority I was the pilot up to Cantley taking up heavy machinery including one of the biggest loads in length and size ever seen. It was a long pontoon-lighter, more or less the width of the river, with a tug on the bow and stern. Radio Norfolk announced that Reedham Bridge was the best place to see it going through, which was just what we didn't want. You don't need 200 people flashing their cameras when you're manoeuvring such a heavy load and entering a bridge with only a foot clearance either side. Luckily there was no damage!

Subro Valour

Large load going through Reedham Swing Bridge

Keeping the waterways clear

(1970s – 2012)

Victor Gosling
(b. 1944)

GREAT YARMOUTH

Victor worked on trawlers for a few years and later worked for many years on a dredger helping to keep the waterways open for cargo boats.

I was about 17 when I went on the trawlers at Lowestoft beginning as a deck hand on the steam boat, Silverfish. When I started I worked eight or nine hours a day but as soon as I got my ticket that went up to 14 hours working both day and night. We had two hours trawling then up to four hours gutting the fish, all the while chucking the lumber or fish guts over the side. We used to dock at Boston or wherever had the best prices, unload the fish and go back to Lowestoft. On the day off we would pass by the dock to see how much money the catch had made because the crew got a percentage. We needed to check they weren't robbing us! There was another day off when they iced the boat up and away we would go again. It was the hardest job I've ever done.

I got a job at May Gurney's at the dockyard where they were doing a lot of piling work on the groynes at Yarmouth Harbour for the roll-on/roll-off and also at the lifeboat pen near Breydon Bridge around Stonecutters Quay. Then after an operation I was allowed back on the dockyard as a fireman and that's when I met Billy Fox.

Billy! Well, there ain't another chap like him, he was a really nice old boy and would do anything for you. His father was the agent who ran all the wherries carting sugar beet, and Billy's job was to get them there. He would often sleep on board. If it was a loaded wherry it could rise up and start twisting all ways so Billy would lie there with one foot out of bed, with his sock off. When the water touched his foot, he knew it was time to pump the water out; this was before my time in about 1958 to the 1960s. Billy knew the wherry Maud over many years. He always said that the Bell, Dora and Maud were the best wherries for carrying sugar beet.

I worked as mate with Billy and we dredged the river from Reedham Ferry up to Norwich to keep it clear. It had to be 10ft 6in at low water all along the river because at Colman's, there used to be a big, cast iron sewer pipe which coasters couldn't get over if their draught was any more. We used to put the dredgings on the shore wherever we could or else it was wherried away.

While I worked with Billy, eight or nine ships were coming up to Norwich all year round. There were several occasions when we had to pull coasters off the horseshoe bends at Surlingham when they had come round the corner and run into the bank. We would take the dredger down beside the coaster and if the load was coal we would put it in the old wherries so the coaster could float itself off and we would tow the wherries up to Norwich. That's how it used to be. We were actually servicing a lot of the industry and businesses in Norwich.

One time we were dredging at Riverside Road where the pipes from King Street go out to the river. We would blow our boiler to clear out all the muck from the bottom and I used to stick a pipe through to help clear it. Then the boiler was

Dredging

turned on and steam would come up out of the water; people walking past would wonder what it was. We did this twice a day and then we refilled the boiler. One particular day I had done the same thing but after I pulled out the pipe, a pigeon came out without any feathers, completely bald!

I remember we used to take odd bits of steam coal home. It was called Newstead Hard and it had to have a good draught to burn, but it lasted for ages. It was unloaded by hand down at Trowse and put into the wherry. We laid in at Surlingham Broad one day outside the pub and the publican asked if he could have a little bit of coal. We got up the next morning and all the coal had gone. Every time we went past after that we got a free pint.

Early one morning we were sitting round the boiler keeping warm and having a cup of tea like we always did and as we sat there, the pressure gauge went up to 50. When we looked again it was up to 55, but we didn't know it had gone round twice. It turned out that one of the chaps had taken the safety valve off the boiler the previous weekend for repair and the valve had been screwed down again far too tightly. Old Sam came over and hit the throttle with a big stick and it made the engine go really fast – we had to open the boiler doors and it took a good hour for the steam to escape. If that boiler had blown up, half of Ranworth would have gone with us.

Looking back I remember that everyone was helpful. If there was a problem or you had to stop a night with your wherry or boat alongside a property, you could knock on the door and they would let you moor there. The most satisfying and enjoyable times of my working life were spent on the dredger. You could turn round and do your toast on the boiler and sometimes we would put a little bit of wire netting round a kipper. That was ever so nice.

Sailing is what I do

(1960s – 2018)

Jamie Campbell
(b. 1950)

BROADS

Jamie first sailed on Wroxham Broad as a six-year-old. He has raced competitively all his life including at international level, and also has a great interest in maritime heritage.

I went on a racing course at Filby Broad, the Norfolk schools' sailing centre, and that's when the whole thing started for me. Sailing was part of the school curriculum and I was eventually captain of sailing at Gresham's School as was my son later. That enabled me to race competitively and I've continued all my life, including 25 years of racing internationally. You have to travel to get better, do open meetings and experience different conditions, and that's what I did. I sailed initially in Enterprises around the Broads and then went into 505 dinghies which are the most beautiful dinghies in the world.

In 1949, when the country was effectively bankrupt and against a background of rationing and short supplies, Jack Holt, to whom dinghy sailing owes a huge debt of gratitude, produced the Hornet and the GP14, both very successful plywood dinghies – plywood had been used for aircraft manufacture and they were still producing it. The prime fleet was the International 14 which cost £350 in the mid-1950s. Quite a lot of money but they were works of art. In 1958 my father bought his first Enterprise and paid £100. It came with a trailer and two sets of cotton sails – racing and cruising.

Dinghy sailing exploded because fuel was rationed till 1956. From building 35 International 14s a year, Jack Holt began producing 28 Enterprises a week and suddenly people could have a boat and I can remember Horning weeks having to race three or four fleets of Enterprises. It was really good fun because we were all teenagers together, having an absolute ball. My father would give me a fiver at the beginning of the school holidays and I'd go off in the cruiser with the dinghies at the stern. Actually I had to win races otherwise I got awfully short of beer by the end of the holidays.

We spent the summer holidays going from one regatta to the next. It was new and it was vibrant, and with all the pirate radio stations in the background, everybody felt it had never been done before. It was nearly all due to Jack Holt who just happened to be in the right place at the right time and became the most successful small boat designer in history.

The problem with dinghy racing now is that it has all got much more expensive, which is why it's a declining sport. Better equipment gives better performance so children want the expensive kit. The Jack Holt growth was a baby boomer activity. I'm one, and when we fall off there will be a gap behind us. I always say the Broads are a great place for old men and children and I somewhat regret filling the former category now. There are many more options for young people today but if you are going to race seriously you have to need to win; it has to be the most important thing in the world.

Up to the Second World War we had a remarkable dinghy sailing team based on International 14s that mainly sailed at Oulton Broad under the aegis of the Royal Norfolk and Suffolk Yacht Club. The club is one of the oldest established clubs in the UK, running since 1859. By 1936, the Prince of Wales Cup was the principal event for

505 World Championship 1978

International 14s in the country and that year, the Royal Norfolk and Suffolk put out a team to race against the Canadians that consisted of 19 winners of the Prince of Wales Cup!

As I've got older I have become more interested in maritime heritage and East Anglia is particularly rich in that. From Victorian times, yachting on the Broads was 'money no object' and that drove development with the first Victorian Skimming Dish being built in Brundall. It was a boat designed to go over the water and not through it and it was a year before the Thames caught up, so we were well ahead of the game here.

Banjo restored

(1985 – 2019)

Philip Webster
(b. 1939)

BUCKENHAM

Philip trained as an engineer in the RAF. In the 1980s, he bought and then restored Banjo, a wooden steamboat built in 1897.

I trained on Spitfire engines in the RAF and then worked mainly on repairs and modifications. My work was very technical and so after leaving the RAF, I tried a variety of jobs, hundreds of them. I had jobs with garages and anything that came along.

My ideal job was working at Clays in Bungay in engineering development, it suited me down to the ground and I loved it. I was there for eleven years and then the firm was taken over and I was made redundant. I then got a job in a boatyard in Loddon being jack of all trades which also suited me. It was my first connection with boats and water.

Whilst there I met a chap whose father ran Broadway Cruises and was retiring. He knew I liked old boats and said, 'Dad's got one he wants to get rid of, why don't you buy it?' So I had a look and found Banjo and liked the look of it. It was 22ft long and very streamlined. I didn't really know what it was but it was cheap so I bought it, and then started writing letters. I had a reply from a chap at the Steamboat Association who said he knew exactly what Banjo was – an 1897 wooden steamboat registered in the Lloyds Register of Boats. I decided it would be fun to restore it to being steam.

Originally I was unaware of Banjo's connection with the Colman family but found out by writing more letters. I heard from Timothy Colman and Lady Mayhew that Banjo used to belong to Russell Colman and they sent photos including a lovely one taken in 1902 of Russell with his brother Alan and sisters on Wroxham Broad.

Colman's boatyard was on Oulton Broad and the family's boats were stored there during the winter; 'Banjo' is written on the first door on the left. The Colmans sailed both socially and for sport and Banjo would tow the fleet through Lake Lothing up to the Royal Norfolk and Suffolk where they sailed. It also acted as a rescue boat and I have a letter from a chap who was rescued by Banjo from a dinghy off Lowestoft on a choppy day.

Russell Colman left Banjo to a friend who had no use for it so he sold it to a boatyard on Lake Lothing where they fitted petrol engines, and had it as a harbour service launch for several years. Then Broadway Cruises had it for many years as

Russell Colman in Banjo 1902

Banjo's first outing in 1995

their harbour service launch pulling cruisers off the mud in Breydon. By then it had a big Scamell two-litre engine which had been converted to run on paraffin, which just after the war was much cheaper than petrol.

When I got Banjo in the mid-1980s, it was an empty hull with no engine or boiler and its only machinery was a prop shaft. A friend from Acle gave me a propeller and I'm sure that it's the original as it fitted perfectly, it's the correct pitch, it goes very well and we are still using it.

I kept Banjo at home and it was several years before I did something positive with it. I knew a lot about petrol and diesel engines but had never touched steam. Father hated steam having grown up on a farm with it and when they transferred to petrol engines it was a great liberation for him. But steam engines became my retirement project.

We got it steaming on the water for the first time in 1995 after several years of development. I started off with a gas-fired flash boiler, then converted to paraffin and then scrapped all that and went to coal. We use six horsepower and at a squeeze I can take eight people.

I have a crew of two or three who are good pals. One likes to helm, the reason being that he is the only one who can concentrate long enough to steer a straight course. I like to be busy all the time so I'm engineer and stoker and John is in the galley. We have a very well-appointed galley nowadays and a salon at the stern where we can have guests.

The first man on board lights the fire and checks the water in the boiler and it takes about 30-45 minutes to get up to steam. We usually run at about 150 pounds per square inch and we can comfortably average five miles an hour wherever we go. We have only 300 rpm on the engine, very sedate, and we slip through the water with hardly a ripple.

Our longest journey is up to Stalham which means going through Breydon, and it takes us eight or nine hours using 50 kilos of coal. With the price of petrol and diesel these days it is actually cheaper to run a steamboat. As well as decent coal our latest thing is scrap pallets, which we chop up and burn. It goes well on wood but wood does soot up the tubes a bit more quickly. These days what I try to do is set off on coal and then after lunch get home on wood and I save about a third of a bag of coal.

Banjo 2009

Maintenance costs more than the fuel. Boiler tests, insurance, river toll and compliance certificates have all got to be paid annually. I need a pressure vessel inspection every 14 months by law and it passed the last inspection with flying colours. I wouldn't want to operate a steamboat unless it was perfectly sound; the amount of power in a boiler is phenomenal and if anything went wrong the only way is over the side!

We try to clean the boiler tubes once a month as they get sooted up and it knocks down performance, and afterwards we have a short trip and a pub lunch – we are getting quite organised these days. I keep her on the Yare at the Buckenham Sailing Club where I have been a member for the last 50 years. At the minute, unfortunately, we are very short of sailors there as all us youngsters have grown up and we have run out of new youngsters.

There are a lot of steamboats around. The steamboat list has over 1,000 and there is a handful the same age as Banjo, although most are replicas. The Museum of the Broads has a steamboat which they use regularly to take people for rides. Recently another one turned up during a money-raising event for Waveney Stardust where we give disabled people rides. It went puffing past and I thought it looked familiar so we chased after it and it turned out to be the steamboat Ermintrude, which I had been on 30 years before. Another steamboat called Bess has arrived recently in the bay where I am.

A lot of steamboats are kept in garages and come out once a year to go to rallies. However, we are on the water every Friday; it's good for her as the engine can soon seize up. Banjo was originally an open boat but I have put up sides with rigid windows and a canopy so we can use it all year round including New Year's Day!

I am over 80 now and I have thought a lot about what to do with Banjo. I would absolutely want it to go to someone who would keep it in the water but I shall certainly keep using it until I can't! Banjo gives everybody a lot of pleasure, it is still an unusual sight and wherever we stop I have to go over the history, but that is more of a pleasure than a problem.

Sailing into education

(1956 – 1970)

Leslie Gee
(b. 1930)

LUDHAM

Leslie first visited the Broads with his school in 1945. As a teacher he helped form and then run the Norfolk Schools Sailing Association (NSSA) based at Hunter's Yard.

In 1956 I moved to Norfolk at age 26 to start teaching. The following year the Chief Education Officer agreed to teachers setting up a sailing course at Martham for children and teachers during the summer holidays and in 1958 the Norfolk Schools Sailing Association (NSSA) was formed. I was appointed to the development committee and subsequently to the committee to run the place.

The sailing courses were based in Martham Primary School with safari camp beds in classrooms and outside toilets which had to be emptied. Then in 1962 the Norfolk Broads Yacht Club, where I was a member, allowed us to organise a teachers' course at the club. It had to be run during the Easter holidays and was restricted to four days midweek as they raced at the weekend. Then, through the good offices of Major Power, an ex-Commodore of the Yacht Club and a landowner round Filby, we managed to negotiate with Great Yarmouth Water Board for the use of Filby Broad and it is still used today, although it's no longer teacher-led.

Things expanded and we decided that teachers who wanted to be instructors should have instituted instructor qualifications. We were not alone; school sailing associations across the country were coalescing to form a National Schools Sailing Association and creating instructor qualifications. We were possibly the first to introduce qualifications for young people, necessary when we moved to Hunter's Yard with its bigger boats and we needed senior pupils to take charge of them.

There were no health and safety regulations at the time. Everyone had to be able to swim and that was thought enough. The first time we used buoyancy aids was at Filby and they developed into the BSS 3595 life jacket, a two-stage life jacket which was developed in conjunction with the British Canoe Union.

We started running intermediate courses around 1962 or 63 using Wayfarers and little 11ft Norfolk dinghies called Bitterns. We needed our boats to be portable so they could be trailered to schools for maintenance. In 1965 I was given an office in Wensum Lodge and took over what had been the coopers' workshops and we had people coming in to maintain boats there but most were allocated to schools to be maintained. Eventually NSSA became too much for the school PE staff to organise, so in 1965 the job of Sailing Instructor Fleet Warden was advertised and I applied and got the job.

A permanent base was needed to accommodate the boats and about 140 sites were submitted to Norfolk County Planning but were turned down. Eventually I suggested Hunter's Yard which was up for sale. Although this was initially rejected, Norfolk County Council wanted to establish an outdoor education centre in the Broads and they agreed that if there was enough money left over, Hunter's Yard was an option. How Hill was sold at auction to Norfolk Education Committee for £37,000 with 350 acres, and in 1967 we got Hunter's Yard which cost about the same.

There were a couple of interesting boats at How Hill. Bobs was built in 1900 or 1901 as an apprentice's master piece by Ernest Woods, who later designed the Yare and Bure One Design and built many other significant yachts on the Broads. Bobs was a Decimal 3, 13ft long, beautifully built of Austrian oak with thirteen planks on each side trimmed with teak and she sailed wonderfully. She was a wedding present from Mr Colman to his daughter who was marrying Mr Boardman and it ended up at How Hill. Bobs was moved to Hunter's Yard and I used her on several sailing courses before she went to the Museum of the Broads for a while. Shrimp was another boat at How Hill, she was a Norfolk Punt Number One and Christopher Boardman learned to sail in her; he later raced in the 1936 Olympics. Shrimp was given to Bob Smithson, a marshman, who used it as a punt as it was a little boat which could do all the dykes at How Hill.

In 1968 I was told that I had three years to make Hunter's Yard pay. The boatyard was to be run commercially much as it had been previously but during the holidays, our schools would have priority booking at a reduced rate. I worked with Cyril Hunter, Percy's son, and he loved being involved. He did most of the boat repairs and I helped where I could, being a woodworker, and we did the turn round of the boats between us. I had a wonderful secretary and I took over Hunter's Yard with Cyril's help; I couldn't have done it without him. We had Roger Nudd and Tom Grapes and that was it.

At this stage NSSA was mainly teachers with some youth leaders and we depended on volunteers for instructing. The instructor courses were run at Easter, and at the start of the summer holidays we had beginner courses for about 70 youngsters and 30 staff, mainly on the northern rivers, Hickling, Horsey Mere and up and down the River Thurne.

Wood Rose

The intermediate course sailed much the same area but was based at Acle School. We also had an advanced course in Bittern dinghies based at Fleggburgh School.

Fleggburgh School had a wonderful cook and the courses really relied on the catering and caretaking staff. The children's rooms were inspected every day and a prize was presented to the winning dormitory. Everyone enjoyed it. The courses were residential and after breakfast there was a statement of who was going in which boat, where we were going, what to expect from the weather... We would be at the boats around nine and we sailed until five, in all weathers.

I left Norfolk in 1970 and didn't return until 1997 after I'd retired and, of course, I had to go back to Hunter's Yard. I couldn't keep away! I joined the Friends of Hunter's Yard and was elected to the committee and a couple of years later I became Chairman. I used to do their two-hour sails but when I was over 80 I thought it wasn't a good idea to keep going, particularly as the Wherry Trust just up the road from Hunter's Yard, had put an age limit on their skippers, so I thought I'd better put an age limit on this one.

The Royall family story

(1909 – 2019)

Nigel Royall
(b. 1964)

HOVETON

Nigel's family connections with boats go back to the 1770s and include a bit of smuggling. He recalls stories of Uncle Billy and tells of his own work on the wherry Solace.

My grandfather, Ernest Robert William Royall, known as Ernie Bob Billy, was born in 1909. He went to Carrow School which was supported by the Colman family and when he left, his first job was in Colman's sawmill making boxes. Later his father got him an apprenticeship at Jack Powles in Wroxham building their little sailing hire yachts.

When he finished his apprenticeship, he began boatbuilding at Jenner's in Thorpe then around 1948 he wanted a boatyard of his own. My grandmother rented out some houses which had been left by her father so these were sold and Grandfather took on a small shed for £5 a year that had been the rowing club at the back of the Ferry Boat pub in King Street, Norwich, and he built a boatyard there. The family all came from King Street so they knew everyone.

In 1949 they built their first wooden hire cruiser, Royal Times, in the back of the lean-to of the pub. I expect he built one a year as that was the normal way and also did any repairs there. The boatyard was handy to the station and in those days most people didn't have a car so my grandparents would shove the boats across the river to the yacht station, and people arriving by train would be ushered on and sent off down the river for the week.

Wood was still on ration but they had a permit to go to Taylor's in Wroxham to buy oak and mahogany to build boats about 30ft long, quite small by today's standards. Grandfather seemed to get on alright in King Street, there were only a few hire firms around at the time and he was there until 1960 running the hire fleet, and a little longer doing repairs.

After a time my grandfather acquired a ramshackle old building from cousins in Brimbelow Road in Hoveton. They were also related to William Royall – known to all the family as Uncle Billy. The building was pulled down and a new boatshed built. The last boat built in Norwich was the hull of the Royal Tudor in 1960. It was launched with just an engine and a sort of rudder so they could steer her all the way from Norwich, across Breydon, to Hoveton for fitting out.

After that they built two more wooden boats and then in 1964 they moved properly to Riverside Road in Hoveton which gave them more space. My father bought one or two extra bits of land over the years just to expand a little more and the company changed from E Royall to Royall and Son Ltd. The pennant on the hire boats had been green with a yellow circle; we think old Ernie had just looked across at the football club from King

Chris and Alice Royall at Ferry Boat pub ca. 1960

Chris Royall at Hoveton 1962

Street, saw the colours and thought he would put a ball into the flag. However, when they became a limited company the pennant changed to red with a yellow crown.

Before I left school, I helped out at the Riverside Road site on Saturday mornings and then, aged 16, I was off to the Oulton Broad centre for a year for some training before returning to work full time.

There were a lot of hire boats so it was very busy and we used to do them at the weekend and then work on the private boats during the week. We also did a lot of work on Broom's wooden boats; Grandfather had worked there for a while before the war and built several of their big Admirals. In January 2017 we sold the hire side of the business to Barnes Brinkcraft which was next door.

The Solace is one of the very few remaining big pleasure wherries; she was built in 1903 by Halls of Reedham and is 67ft overall. She was built on speculation so she could have been finished as either a trading or a pleasure wherry. Commander Rogers from Ingham Hall bought her and wanted her finished as a pleasure wherry and she has had only three owners since she was launched.

I do all the maintenance on Solace, apart from the engineering, if I look at an engine it just conks out. As she is old now, there is a fair amount of work apart from general varnishing; the decks have all been redone and last winter I did the cabin sides and put in a long section of planking. Quite a few planks have been replaced over the years along with a few frames.

Solace is used as a family boat and is moored on Wroxham Broad during the summer and comes back to Hoveton late September and into her winter shed for repairs. Every third or fourth year we have her out of the water to check the hull and do any planking. Nowadays we go to Goodchild's at Burgh Castle and they lift her out. The hard bit is getting materials and a lot of people are using stuff like European oak and the like because they cannot get anything else, but it isn't half as good and won't last half as long. A few years ago we got two massive oak trees which were sawn up and now have plenty of great long grade A1 boards.

When I was about 15, I was on the river and saw an old wherry sunk at the back of Old Woman's Pulk near Salhouse Broad. The tides were very low that year and she stood out of the water. I found out through talking to an old wherry man called Jimmy Gorbould, that she was the Cornucopia. After that I used to visit wherrymen and I picked up a lot about wherries and my family, and it linked in with everything my grandmother had told me when I was a child.

The wherries were doing alright until the railways took away some of the trade. Roads didn't really affect them until after the First World War when lorries used by the Army in France were brought back in 1918, and flogged off cheaply. That was the beginning of the end. Wherries hung on for a while and then Colman's did away with their wherries and that was really the end of them. Uncle Billy and Spray traded until November 1927 and one or two sailing wherries worked up until the start of World War Two.

Uncle Billy with Prince on the King St Ferry 1933

I used to visit my grandparents, Ernie and Gladys, on a Saturday morning and there were odd times they would chat about family history. My grandmother was very good and knew a lot about my great grandad but Grandfather wouldn't say much. Robert Malster's book on wherries and waterways had come out and it mentioned the Royalls doing a bit of smuggling. Grandfather was out one day soon after and was asked about it and he didn't like that one little bit and clammed up on anything to do with wherries!

We know that Christopher the Older was on the keels in the 1770s and that he was the one who was the smuggler. Then we had Christopher Senior, then Edmund who was born in 1818 and was Uncle Billy's father. Unfortunately Edmund was crushed at Yarmouth between the quay and a wherry and was killed. I know most about Uncle Billy because his granddaughter lived with him and I used to see her when she was an old lady, and oh the stories she told about him; he was famous with the older generation of the family.

Uncle Billy's wife was Mary Ann Bullen and she owned Number 5 Rayner's Yard on King Street. Apparently she was fairly well off so what she was doing with Uncle Billy I don't know, because he only ever washed twice in his life and one of those was when he was dead. The first time he washed was when Mary Ann made him. 'I'll catch me cold,' he said. He did and was laid up so he didn't bother again.

There were two types of trading wherries: north river where wherries went between places like Aylsham and Yarmouth, and Norwich river wherries. They didn't really cross over that much. My family were involved mainly with the latter, trading between Norwich and Yarmouth although Uncle Billy also traded up to places like Bungay.

Uncle Billy's boat was a classic wherry called Spray. She was built about 1860 and lasted until 1936. She was all oak, had a little cuddy with two bunks and could carry 40 tons. She had sprung a leak while loading granite off a ship and sunk in Yarmouth harbour in 1901 and Uncle Billy bought her the day Queen Victoria died. According to Spray's toll book she carried coal, stone, tiles, grain, cement, barbed wire, paraffin, timber, flour, groceries, matches, sugar beet and ice.

When broads froze over, which didn't happen as often as they would have you think, the old wherrymen used huge hockey sticks with iron bands on the bottom to smash up the ice. Then using an ice didle, which was a long pole with a hoop and net on the end, they used to didle the ice into the wherry. It was rough old stuff with weed and other matter and they took it to the ice houses at Lowestoft or Yarmouth for the fishing fleet. However, when ice cut in the lakes in Norway was brought in, their business decreased as ships could carry a lot more.

Eventually ice was manufactured by the Lowestoft Ice Company and crushed ice was sold to the fishing fleet. Uncle Billy then began carrying three-ton blocks of ice which were crystal clear with no bubbles, having been agitated for a week. He would go to Lowestoft in the morning, use Spray's mast to load the ice and would get back home the following evening. It was mostly summer freight so the ice was protected from the sun by the hatch covers and brought up to the ice house at the back of Dragon Hall on King Street. From there it went to the local morgues, the fishmongers and so on. Uncle Billy would carry the ice on his own, quanting or drifting on the tide as needed. A lot of the wherries used to moor up at night at the pubs but Uncle Billy liked to load up during the day and if the wind and tides served, he would start home and just keep going.

Uncle Billy also loaded and carried timber on his own for firms like Cushion's, Colman's, Jewson's, Ranson's and Porter's. The timber would come from the Baltic and Russia and was brought up by wherry before they used lighters. He was a hard worker Uncle Billy. His sons had a go at working with him but it was too hard for them. Sometimes he sailed the wherry Leveret for William England and his son Chris went along with him. His wife used to say, 'Owd Towzer nigh on kilt the boy Ernie'. This translated as 'Old Billy nearly killed Chris by over-working him' – Towzer was Billy's nickname and Chris was known as Ernie!

Uncle Billy always carried a set of creepers on board his wherry Spray. Creepers are like a grapnel anchor and were used to drag the river for bodies. They were paid half a crown and in earlier times it didn't seem to matter where they found them, they would still get their money. But eventually it was ruled that the bodies had to be within the Norwich City limits. At one time there used to be several morgues in King Street and one by Foundry Bridge under the Compleat Angler pub which was cold as it was near the river. There was also a morgue where Zaks restaurant is now at Petch's corner, opposite Cow Tower.

His last freight was ice for the East Anglian Ice Company in November 1927 and then he laid Spray alongside his two old cottages and ran his ferry boat from the Ferry Boat Inn in Norwich. He was a bit of an old devil because he used to load her with so many people they had to stand stock still.

Uncle Billy seems to have had an arrangement with the Dutch boats moving coal to Norwich and I think the crews must have been selling him sacks of coal. He would scuttle them across the river in the old ferryboat to either his little cottages at the Ferry Inn or his house opposite at Rayner's Yard. I believe that there was a room in there that was full of contraband he sold on. He'd call it 'trucking and trading'.

One night he made a deal with a Rotterdam collier and tipped the coal into Spray's hold to be moved once things quietened down but someone told the police that he was up to no good. When it got really late Mary Ann told her granddaughter to 'get Billy off that wherry' because he used to spend the day sitting in Spray even if she wasn't going anywhere. But he wasn't there. She asked a few blokes about him and was told someone had rounded on him and he was in the police station.

So Mary Ann sent the granddaughter to get some of the relatives who lived nearby, and they got hold of the manager of General Steam who went to the police station. 'Come on, you can't hold Billy in here all night, he's old'. Uncle Billy was sitting in the cell with his dog Prince saying, 'Don't touch me, don't touch me, the old dog'll have you', because Prince was a feisty little thing. In the end the police let him go for the night but said that they would be round in the morning for the coal and they would deal with him then.

Next morning they couldn't find the coal, it had gone, so they couldn't arrest him. Apparently Billy had gone straight to old Spray and chucked it all overboard. He knew there was a concrete platform under the water where Spray was moored so all the coal was piled up there, then a few weeks later when things had calmed down Billy didled it out, bagged it up and sold it on!

My life with Wherry Maud

(1979 – 2018)

Linda Pargeter
(b. 1951)

RANWORTH, UPTON

Linda was introduced to the Norfolk Broads by her millwright husband, Vincent, and they decided to raise and restore the wherry Maud.

My first introduction to boating was learning to row on Rollesby Broad. Subsequently we had our own 12ft 6in clinker dinghy that we trailered up to Norfolk. Then a friend who was an antiquarian librarian in London decided to arrange trips on traditional sailing craft, the first was on the wherry Albion and the next on a Thames sailing barge. This gave Vincent, who had the necessary woodworking and metalworking skills, the idea of restoring a wherry himself. It seemed a shame that Albion which was carvel-built with smooth sides and butt-jointed planks was the only restored trading wherry when the typical Norfolk wherry was clinker-built with overlapping planks on the hull.

In 1979 we started looking for a clinker-built wherry hull that could be restored and we were directed towards Ranworth Broad where there were several wherry wrecks. Maud was actually visible at low tide and the hull seemed to be intact – she looked like she would float if we could pump her out. She was built for the timber trade on the River Yare and Yare wherries tended to be larger than the others. She is approximately 60ft long, plus the length of the rudder which is another 8ft.

She was owned by the Norfolk Naturalists Trust who gave us permission to move her. She was pumped out and floated. After being sunk in mud for 15 or 16 years the smell was terrible! Then Paul Reynolds came with his boat from Upton boatyard and with Tim Whelpton, they towed the Maud round to Upton Dyke where we prepared her for being lifted onto the bank.

We had two of the largest mobile cranes that we could find and I believe they said that she was on the limit of their lift: something in the region of 14 or 15 tons. They placed her gently on the bank and Paul and the Eastwood Whelpton staff supported her on the bank and left her for us to roof over and get ready for restoration.

We had to make sure that the support arrangement was exactly right so that she would maintain her graceful shape, which was quite difficult on marshy ground, and we spent much of the next year adjusting props. We also built a temporary roof using some second-hand lorry tarpaulins so that the inside of the hull provided a workshop area.

One of my jobs was to scrape the dried mud and old tar off the outside planking. It was uncomfortable lying underneath the boat, especially as tar dust landing on the skin tended to burn rather badly. We tried various arrangements to cover up and protect my face. Anyway, section by section, it was done.

Maud pumped out at Ranworth 1981

The planking hadn't looked too bad when we first lifted Maud but as it dried out, gaps opened up. The worst planks had to be replaced whilst the better ones were repaired. But first the framing had to be replaced. Researching and then obtaining the timber for the framing was quite difficult. We needed seasoned 4-inch oak with a natural curve as we cut the frames following the grain of the timber. Timber yards don't often stock such timber these days so we had to find the curved oak and season it ourselves. Most came from a very large timber yard in Hull where we bought several trees and had it sawn to the required thickness.

For the first five years we worked on the framing, just the two of us. We would take one piece of timber home on the trailer together with its pattern and Vincent would cut it out, then a couple of weekends later we would take the frame back to Upton and endeavour to fit it. Fitting frames in the hold area was not too complex, but fitting them in the curved areas at the bow and stern was much more so. After five years it was almost complete and we started to think about how to replace the long sections of oak planking. Quite a challenge as everything had to be done on site. We needed a boat builder to work with us for six weeks every summer and luckily found Colin Buttifant who was just starting his own business, having trained with Broom's.

All Maud's planks are curved to a greater or lesser extent and had to be steamed to shape. The thicker planks were soaked in Upton Dyke for a few days first. Then, rather than construct a steam chest which would have taken up space we didn't have, Vincent decided to use tubes of tarpaulin material on trestles instead. We had small steam boilers either end to feed in the steam and cook the planks for three to four hours. It was a very hot day when we started this, and we were swathed in thick sweaters and gloves as handling hot planking was quite hazardous! The planks were then clamped in position with large G-clamps so they would assume roughly the shape needed. Once they had cooled and dried they were taken off for final shaping. We did this for five or six weeks every year until the planking was completed.

Maud's bow after restoration

Maud was re-launched in 1995 when the hull was ready and was towed round to Colin's yard at Womack: the Swallowtail boatyard. The local press and television were there. At the yard one of Colin's men made up hatches for the boat and Vincent framed and boarded the foredeck and also built the cabin which is very snug with cupboards and a wood-burning stove.

Maud was now pretty well complete apart from her mast: a story in itself. We had got together with the other wherry owners to import six baulks of timber from Central America to make up masts and the baulk for our mast was taken down to the International Boatbuilding Training Centre where they shaped it according to Vincent's plans. I believe a total of 18 apprentices were involved. One of them came on board Maud for a trip a few years ago and was able to write a story for our website about how the mast was constructed and he provided photographs of the whole process.

Maud was taken round to Eastwood Whelpton boatyard at Upton again and Paul Reynolds and the Eastwood Whelpton crane lifted the mast on board. It fitted beautifully. The completed wherry was then towed round to Womack where we had negotiated a mooring with the Norfolk Wherry Trust, in the same shed as the wherry Albion.

Maud's restoration took 18 years in the end rather than our five-year plan. It was largely financed by us; however, we had grants from the Broads Authority in the first ten years for which we were very grateful as it enabled us to buy timber in advance.

Maud was finally readied for her re-commissioning party on Wroxham Broad and, of course, it was a bit of a cliff-hanger. At midnight, two days before the party, we finally finished rigging her and the next day she was sailed round to Wroxham Broad. Sailing a 12ft 6in lug sail dinghy was the limit of our sailing experience but we managed to find experienced wherry skippers to do the job for us. In the morning we had Mike Sparkes of the Norfolk Wherry Trust and in the afternoon we had Peter Bower of Wherry Yacht Charter. The press, everyone involved in Maud's restoration and people with family links to Maud were all invited to the celebrations.

Maud was built in 1899 for Walter Christmas Bunn to haul Jewson's timber from their yard in Yarmouth up to Norwich. Maud was one of the later wherries to be built and Bunn owned her until 1908. She then carried general cargo such as coal and coke as well as timber for Henry Newhouse until about 1918. In her latter days up to 1945, she transported sugar beet. Then, as she went down in the world, she carried mud dredgings. Her final owners were Hobrough's, who were bought out by May Gurney, and she was sunk in Ranworth Broad in the mid-1960s when May Gurney no longer wanted wooden wherries – they already had iron wherries which were easier to maintain.

Maud was designed to carry about 42 tons of timber under sail. It was a comparatively light cargo especially as it was mostly softwood imported from the Baltics. They would take the hatches off, load the timber in the hold and then stack it up on the side decks until it was level with the sides of the hold. Then they laid timber across the hold to form a raft. A slot was left down the centre to allow the mast to be lowered to go under bridges, and the wherrymen manoeuvred with a quant, walking up and down on top of the timber stack. I imagine the wherryman on the tiller had to stand up on the afterdeck rather than down in the steering well. Traditionally trading wherries were operated by a wherryman and a mate but I think two wherrymen couldn't have operated under these circumstances; unfortunately, there is not much documentation about how it was done.

It was a hard job especially before the wherries had engines and Maud didn't have one until 1918. Operating without an engine meant you had to know your tides and use them to your advantage and wait for a wind that was good for the direction you were travelling in. So if they were stuck and had to get a cargo to Yarmouth, the wherrymen had to quant all the way. Then at Yarmouth where the tides are strong, they had to get to the port.

The wherry skippers tended to be small and wiry so how they did it all, I don't know. In winter the decks were covered in frost and a descendent of one of the old wherrymen told us that they used to take cinders from the stove and sprinkle them on the decks to make them less slippery – it's amazing what they did.

After Maud was re-commissioned we decided that it would be prudent to ask wherry skippers, largely from the Norfolk Wherry Trust, to come out with us and take responsibility while we watched and learned and Vincent felt confident enough to skipper Maud himself. Then as we both approached retirement age, we needed to secure a future for Maud and with a couple of others we formed the Wherry Maud Trust.

Maud at Reedham Ferry 2019

On a wooden boat there is always work to be done and every three years Maud has a thorough survey and out-of-the-water maintenance. She has been back in the water now for over 22 years so it is inevitable that some of the wood not replaced in the 1990's was replaced in 2014, when about 70ft of new planking was put in. This was relatively minor as next time we'll be doing some major re-planking of those remaining from 1899.

We are hoping that the various Wherry Trusts can involve young people so they are keen to carry on the traditions and ensure that the wherries sail into the foreseeable future. Most of our wherry skippers these days are either retired or nearing retirement so we do need more young people to train as wherry skippers and as boat builders. We need youngsters enthused so our wherry history and the whole context in which the wherries operated is not forgotten. Wherries are part of the history of the Broads.

The Wherry Yacht Charter story

(1950 – 2018)

Peter Bower
(b. 1943)

WROXHAM

Peter grew up in Wroxham with a love of railways, sailing and wherries. He helped set up Wherry Yacht Charter (WYC) first as a business and then as a trust to preserve and sail five wherries.

I have lived in Wroxham since 1950. My father had a sailing yacht with a little lugsail dinghy and he just let me go out in it and I learned to sail by having a go. I first worked at Wroxham railway station for five years and left when Dr Beeching's railway closures were taking place. I then retrained as a teacher and taught at Cromer High for 18 years but by 1986 I was heavily involved with wherries and couldn't do both so I continued part time for another two years before leaving. Cromer High was one of the first to send youngsters to How Hill, Norfolk County Council's outdoor education centre, and from 1969 to 83 I took a group there every Christmas for a week's course. In later years I took them there by wherry.

I was into old things but apart from seeing wherries Albion and Solace from time to time, it was very rare to see other wherries and I began to think that they were disappearing in the same way as the railways. So in the early 1970s I scoured the Broads to see if there were any left and saw several being used as houseboats. Then in 1974 I saw an advert for the wherry Sundog but she was in a very poor state, her back was broken and she was leaking badly. However, her owner who was living on the wherry yacht Olive said he was thinking of selling her later in the year. Olive was basically complete with mast and sail, or looked as if she was, so I went back and did a deal, and ten days later I brought her back to Barton House in Wroxham.

I had never sailed a wherry before but she had an engine so we brought her home under power and then sort of learned to sail her by trial and an awful lot of error. I could write a book on how not to sail a wherry and what can go wrong.

That December I took kids up to How Hill on Wherry Olive for the first time. In the morning the wind was quite calm and we sailed up to Barton Broad and back but when the wind got up a bit in the afternoon the kids wanted to go for another sail, so we decided to go in the other direction towards Ludham Bridge. I was very green then and I misjudged it. We were roaring up with the wind behind us towards the bridge and I yelled at the kids to get the sail down. As they did, the old canvas sail ripped from top to bottom. They stopped and I had to scream at them to carry on. I got them ashore with a load of lines and we pulled up about 10ft short of the bridge; quite frightening and the first of many terrifying episodes on wherries.

It didn't put them off but it almost put me off when I found out the cost of a new sail, and then a couple of years later the cost of a new mast, and I realised I couldn't afford to maintain Olive unless she generated income. So I started doing charter work at weekends which grew into weeks during the school holidays and by the late 1970s I was doing more and more.

Things changed in the early 1980s when I was approached by a certain Barney Matthews who owned the wherry yacht, the Lady Edith, as she was called then. Barney was a local man and when he retired in 1983, he decided not to sell her but to do her up. We teamed up the same year to do charter work and got on like a house on fire except when we were having fearful arguments, but as Barney would say, 'Ahh purely academic, purely academic'. In 1984 rumour had it that Martham Boatbuilding and Development Company had the pleasure wherry Hathor for sale and Barney and I decided we better have it, so in December 1985, Hathor ended up at the bottom of the garden. We then had three wherries, the Olive, the Lady Edith who we renamed Norada when she was 75 years old, and Hathor.

Hathor is unique among the wherries on the Broads. She was built for the Colman family when two sisters Ethel and Helen decided in 1904 to have a wherry built in memory of their younger brother. Alan Colman suffered from tuberculosis and in 1897 the family embarked for Egypt where they hoped the dry clean air would prolong his life. His dying wish was to see something of the Nile and they embarked on one of the dahabeahs which happened to be called Hathor which means Goddess of Love and Joy. But when Hathor was moored at Luxor he sadly died aged 30. It had a profound effect on the family and when the two sisters were thinking of having a wherry, they decided to call it Hathor.

The hull was constructed by Halls of Reedham, then Edward Boardman who was their brother-in-law and a prominent Norwich architect, was commissioned to design the interior with Egyptian hieroglyphs. He sent one of his employees, Graham Cotman, who I believe was related to the artist John Sell Cotman, to the British Museum to sketch subjects in the Egyptology section. Consequently, Hathor's interior decor is unique with light sycamore panelling inlaid with teak which is a darker wood. It is full of symbols and

A detail of Hathor's interior

lotus leaves and flowers. It really is something quite special and when people come aboard there's a real wow factor.

Barney and I decided to form WYC but it was a 'business' very much in inverted commas because businesses usually make money! After we got Hathor we worked very closely with the Broads Authority who gave us a terrific amount of support both financially and in terms of activities. Then in 2002 WYC became a trust with the sole aim of preserving the wherries for future generations to enjoy.

The ownership of the wherries was transferred to the charitable trust and then, quite amazingly, we got the wherry yacht, White Moth. When the boatyard at Horning was sold, most of their boats went to Martham on the other side of Potter Heigham Bridge, a low bridge, so White Moth wasn't suitable. One of our trustees, Andrew Scull, kindly bought her for the use of the Trust in 2011 with the eventual aim that she would become part of the Trust.

She arrived at a low point because as each wherry came up for its survey in the 2000s, we didn't have any money. Hathor was the last wherry to sail but was laid up in September 2009 and for a couple of years we had no wherries in commission. The Trust had been formed and

Wherry Hathor

we had a Heritage Lottery grant but we had to rebuild our base before we could do any work on the wherries. So when White Moth arrived still in sailing condition, we were able to start generating income. Even more surprisingly, by the same process with Andrew Scull, we got the pleasure wherry Ardea as well.

The Ardea was built in 1927 for Howard Hollingsworth who owned the store Bourne and Hollingsworth, and she was the last wherry to be built of any sort. He was a very rich Lowestoft man and it is said he commissioned the Ardea to relieve the depression in the boatbuilding industry. The huge wherry was constructed for his private use; it was 65 ft long, much longer than any other wherry and was built of teak, the most durable and expensive wood. When she was commissioned Mr Hollingsworth had a dinner for all those who had worked on her and at the side of each plate was a golden sovereign, a considerable amount of money then.

Mr Hollingsworth had her for about ten years and then she passed through several owners until in 1959 she was taken to France and moored on the Seine near the Eiffel Tower where, it is said, she was used by one owner as a place for ladies of the night to rest. Later in the early 1970s, she was bought by a Parisian, Philippe Rouff, in a totally derelict condition having been impounded by Customs. He initially lived on her, and then commissioned her for charter work. For years she travelled all over France and the waterways of Europe and is probably the most widely-travelled wherry in existence.

In 2005 she was sold to Phillip Davies who had previously bought White Moth and had also established the Norfolk Broads Yachting Company boatyard at Horning. He brought Ardea back to this country and spent an enormous sum restoring her to a high standard for his own use. He enjoyed only a few years as he sadly died too early. His widow used the Ardea for a year or two before getting in touch with Andrew Scull and we then had five wherries at the bottom of the garden.

I have skippered wherries since 1974 but I'm now winding down a bit. In the early days I had various people help me sail and when I did charter weekends in the early days with the Broads Authority, the staff and volunteers would crew. The situation now is that the Trust has formed a friends' organisation so if people want to crew they join and then train as crew or skippers. We're always looking for new recruits.

When we put the wherry programme together it was important that we also had an educational programme. We decided that the best place would be How Hill which is now a residential educational centre. We have sailed Hathor and some of the other wherries up to How Hill for a few days at a time for the youngsters there, but then I thought that the best use of Hathor was to have her on show at How Hill and allow people to look round her. So starting in 2018 Hathor has been moored at How Hill from the beginning of May to the end of September. At least twice a week school parties staying at How Hill come aboard and we also do some day cruises there which I still skipper.

I think we have established that the Olive, Norada and White Moth are the most suitable for day and weekend cruises. They all have small electric engines and counter sterns where people can sit. I would like to see Hathor becoming part of the Broadland scene at How Hill; it's such a special place where people go to experience the Broads. The Ardea is a little more difficult as she is restored to such a high standard so we would really like to develop her for luxury day cruises; we did a couple last year with all meals provided and they seemed to go down very well. I think that dividing up the usage of our wherries is the way to move into the future.

Ardea in Norwich 2018

Wherry yacht Olive

Sparkes on wherries

(1840s – 2019)

Mike Sparkes
(b. 1951)

TROWSE

Mike's interest in wherries was inspired by his family's historical connections. He is a skipper with the Norfolk Wherry Trust (NWT) and has researched the history of Wherry Albion.

In the 1980s my mother told me that the family had worked on the wherries; it really interested me as it helped explain the connection I felt for the water. After talking with both my grandmother and mother, I learned that my great-grandfather Stephen Field was a wherry skipper who worked out of Norwich on the old tar wherries. He would sail to the tar works at Yarmouth to collect liquid tar which was pumped into two large tanks especially built into the hold of the wherry. Back in Norwich it was pumped into two huge tanks near the Adam and Eve public house, the tar was fairly warm so it could be pumped in and out.

George Gibbs, son of a boatbuilder at Coldham Hall, once told a tale about my great-grandparents on the wherry John Henry: 'Stephen Field would sail up to Coldham Hall, where he would stop for his usual drink. However on this particular day Field went back onboard and decided to have a sleep. Mrs Field realised that they needed to keep the wherry moving to catch the tide, so she got George and his friend to raise the sail and she set off for Yarmouth steering the wherry. When asked how she would manage at Reedham railway bridge, Mrs Field replied, 'He'll be awake long before then'. She picked up the bucket with the lanyard and said, 'He'll certainly be well awake by then'. Jane Field often sailed the wherry with her husband, except for certain extreme weather conditions; she was a tiny lady.'

My four times great-grandfather Stephen Field Senior was a master boat builder. He started at Carrow Abbey boatyard on the River Wensum in the early 1840s and in 1865 he built Alexandra, the first steam wherry to be propelled by a screw (propeller), previously used only in paddle steamers. He worked for Britchers, later Field and Britcher, at the yard near Girlings Lane which looked straight up Thorpe Reach and Norwich. Stephen Field Senior also built large yachts for prominent people including the Cigarette in 1886, which went across to the Kiel Canal, between Germany and Denmark. Also his boatyard was used as a temporary morgue during

Stephen and Jane Field on the John Henry, by Harry Clow

the great train crash of 1874 when two steam trains crashed on the road crossing close by.

The wherry Albion was built in 1898 for the Walkers who were the maltsters of Bungay. At that time all wherries were built using a clinker contraction method but because they sustained damage to the planks when going through the brick locks to Bungay, the Walkers asked William Brighton, a famous boat builder, to build an iron wherry to save on maintenance. Brighton refused and built a wooden carvel wherry instead which was much easier to maintain. It also had less shear (shear is the curve of the hull) to make it easier to quant. She was built in Suffolk on the north side of Lake Lothing in an old ice house to carry 35 tons.

Albion's first skipper was Jimmy Lacey and his mate was his nephew Jack Powley. They had worked together on an older wherry, also called Albion. Their first cargo on the new Albion was carrying 44½ tons of cattle cake from Lowestoft to Bungay. She continued working for the maltsters until the 1920s when she was sold to the General Steam Company based in Yarmouth where they renamed her the Plane, and she sailed under that name until her restoration in 1949. Like many wherries during the war, she was stripped of her sailing gear and used as a general lighter – lighters were towed in numbers to Yarmouth behind steam tugs to move goods at speed during the war.

In June 1942 Plane was moored to the side of the wherry Eudora in Norwich, and during the night an incendiary bomb went through Eudora's hatches during one of the Baedeker air raids. Sadly Eudora burned and sank on the spot. Wherry Plane was saved only by being cut adrift. She then went to Colman's.

Once she was acquired by the NWT, her sailing gear was restored, she was again named the Albion and she started carrying cargo once more. But sadly over the next few years it became harder to find goods for her to carry, so the Trust decided to put her up for chartering during the summer and in the winter months she would take sugar beet to Cantley.

Albion sank in 1966. Nat Bircham had moored her near Berney Arms for the night but the weather changed and it came on to a strong blow. Sadly in the morning they found Albion sunk with just the mast sticking out of the water. They had to remove the mast and the sugar beet with a crane, then Albion was pumped out and raised. The wherry I'll Try also sank just a quarter of a mile upriver that night.

Albion first sank in 1929 when they were building the Haven Bridge in Yarmouth and had built a temporary bridge close by to take the traffic. Wherries would sail down to Breydon Water and on entering Yarmouth they would drop their sail and mast, then a mud weight was fixed to a very long chain and dropped overboard. The wherry would slowly turn on the mud weight to face the last of the ebbing tide and would go backwards with the tide down through Haven Bridge – by turning the wherry to face the tide and going slower than the tide, the skippers were able to keep their steerage. This time, however, Albion hit one of the pilings for the new bridge whilst passing under the temporary bridge. After this incident wherries were no longer allowed to drudge or dredge through Yarmouth (the name given for going down backwards with a mud weight) as Yarmouth Port decided that all wherries should be towed through the bridge. She also sank during the 1950s in Langley dyke. It's thought she sat her bottom on a spike at low water.

The NWT was formed in 1949 with the aim of preserving at least one wherry. It was the brainchild of Roy Clark who had skippered a landing craft to the beaches on D-Day. The sight of dykes filled with yellow water lilies alongside the battlefields reminded him of his Norfolk childhood when wherries plied the main rivers

Wherry Plane (Albion) at Colman's

and he decided to restore one. In February 1949 Roy organised a public meeting, chaired by Lady Mayhew of the Colman family, and NWT was born, funded by donations from the public.

The wherry Plane was found moored at Colman's works stripped of her sailing gear as she was last used as a lighter. My father worked at Colman's and remembers her lying close to Carrow Bridge, near to the flour mill he was running. He said that she was used to move sacks up and down the river to other parts of the factory. The NWT acquired the Plane which had originally been named the Albion, and she was towed to Yarmouth for restoration.

I joined the NWT in 1985 after I found my family had worked on the wherries and I sailed as mate with an excellent skipper, Sid Chettleburgh. In those days Albion was moved only by quant poles and sail so sometimes we would put all the charterers on the shore to tow her along. I was mate until 1991 when I was given the chance to skipper Albion when Sid had to go to hospital and I was asked to bring her back from Barton Broad to our base at Ludham. I didn't have a mate but was told not to worry as the young scout leaders on board had sailed on her before. We set off at 6am and managed to quant out backwards and suddenly we could hear all the waterfowl coming onto the broad through the mist. The mist cleared and we raised sail; the youngsters were so good that we tacked against the tide and wind all the way from Ant mouth to Thurne mouth and we did it in two hours.

I became the archivist for the NWT in 1986 just a year after joining, and I still do it. I began researching and collecting information on wherries and researching my own family tree of watermen. I joined the main committee and was given the box with the archive – today three of us run the archive and a website.

Our volunteers enable things to keep going so well. Our sailing season is May to September and September to May is used for restoration. The internet has helped attract a lot of public interest and we hold open days around the Broads which is a great way for the public to see a wherry. It is strange that there are more wherries now on the Broads than there were after the war.

In the 1960s and 70s the river banks were kept tidy, scrub was trimmed back and farmers cleaned out the ditches. Sadly today the River Tas is so overgrown you can't see the river mouth where it joins the Yare. Every autumn the leaves go into the water and it's like the arteries in your body: if they clog up only trouble will follow. Letting these small streams clog up will cause a major problem for the main rivers in years to come. Water quality has improved and this has brought back the water lilies but the sides of the Yare have become choked with them making the river narrower, and they get in your prop if you're too close to the bank.

They reckon salt spring tides in the Broads were not such a problem in the late 1700s when they were protected by the sandbar across Yarmouth harbour. Old newspapers have articles about keels from the north bringing coal down and hitting the

Albion at Womack, Ludham 2019

sandbar. Wherries could sail over it but big ships from Scandinavia couldn't, so wherries would sail out to offload their cargoes. In the 1880s they wanted the bigger vessels to come into Yarmouth so they started to dredge the harbour mouth and this allowed the salt tides to push further up the rivers, particularly the Yare and the Waveney. On the northern broads it reaches Potter Bridge, which does hold a lot of the salt tide back.

The large build-up of reeds on the river banks also makes the rivers narrow, and with certain wind conditions it takes longer for the salt to flow back out again. The problem then gets worse when the next tide comes in on top of the last tide still flowing out. It is the build-up of reed that is holding up the water, sadly this will only get worse with rising sea levels.

On a more positive note, over the last two years I have noticed more people in canoes and on paddle boards which can only be good for the waterways. Electric boats are being used more these days which is good for cutting down noise levels and helping with pollution. However, their engines may not be powerful enough when going through Yarmouth if they get the tides wrong. I learned early in my skippering years on Albion that you really need to know what you're doing when going through Yarmouth because of the strong tides!

The Cambria

The Thames barge, Cambria, was built in 1906 and was the last sailing barge to trade. In the 1940s and 50s she used to sail regularly to Norwich.

To mark 25 years of the Broads Authority, she was chartered to come to Norwich in 2014. She sailed from London to Yarmouth where a pilot boat was to tow her the rest of the way. However, on the day, that particular pilot was on leave and no other pilot would take on the job. Luckily the wind was south-east so the skipper decided to sail in, right up to Town Hall Quay in Yarmouth. The masts and spars were then laid flat (the main mast was 100ft) so she could get under the new viaduct on the Southern Bypass. The tug took almost a week to tow her from Yarmouth to the 'bus stop' at Whitlingham Park, a jetty built for passenger boats. She was tied there overnight and then towed the rest of the way at 2am when the railway bridge could be opened. The bridge had to be raised by hand using a winch and a 16-man rail crew from Colchester because the turning motor wouldn't work. Eventually, Cambria tied up at the Riverside berth and was re-rigged and ready for visitors the next day. Numerous people visited her – it was a big point of interest for Norwich.

Robin Bowling
b. 1943

Wherry memories

(1960s – 2019)

Kim Dowe
(b. 1953)

THE BROADS

As a child Kim helped his father on the wherries Lord Roberts and Albion and much later he became involved with wherries again as a skipper.

I finished working offshore after many years in 1992 and then had the opportunity to skipper the wherry yacht White Moth for 19 years and also the wherry Albion. White Moth was a lovely vessel and the number of people I met was unbelievable. I used to take a group out to Horsey on the Albion, moor up for the night and have a barbecue and big tubs of strawberries. I had already been on the Albion with my father in the 1960s and spent many years sailing on her, and in the 1980s I helped my father-in-law, Mike Fuller, and his friend restore her. For quite a while now I have been sailing with the wherry Maud, a trust has been formed and I like my involvement with it.

One of my claims to fame when I was sailing Albion was having the Duke of Edinburgh on board. We had lots of things in common: we both liked boats and I had worked on the Bacton Gas site which he opened in the 1960s. We got on well, he was a nice man.

In 1996 Norwich Cathedral celebrated its 900-year anniversary and the Wherry Trust was asked if the Albion would take the Caen stone to Norwich. The stone had been brought from France by boat and then by tug to Yarmouth Bridge where we were waiting to receive it. The stonemason had cut three balls into it to indicate that it had been through customs.

The weather was horrible so the Broads Authority strapped one of their boats alongside to take us through Breydon Bridge. We did manage to sail part of the way and later on we had a family cruiser alongside us which helped us up to Norwich. The Mayor of Norwich and the Bishop of Norwich came on board at Coldham Hall.

As we came into Norwich we were met by the Sea Scouts with a big rowboat and six or seven kids on the oars and they towed us as far as Foundry Bridge. There we were met by more Sea Scouts who towed us up to Pull's Ferry.

Albion on the River Bure

Before we got to the railway station people had started to gather; there were hundreds on the bridge and up to Pull's Ferry, all cheering and clapping, and ahead of us wherries were pulled up to welcome the Albion. I had a lump in my throat as I usually do when it comes to things like that. We came to May Gurney's big lighter and crane and were told where to lift off the Caen stone. We decided how we would do it while the Bishop was doing his ceremonial bits and bobs – there was a lot going on! We managed to get it off and it was pulled away, and that was it. A really memorable day.

Life and times at Reedham Ferry

(1949 – 2019)

David Archer
(b. 1934)

REEDHAM

David's father took over Reedham Ferry Inn and ferry after the war and David has been there ever since, taking over the business in 1969.

Father used to come up to Norfolk from London before the war to do a bit of boating. He knew the Broads to a degree so when he saw an advert for Reedham Ferry Inn and the ferry he went with a friend to have look at it and later put in an offer. When my mother and I arrived by steam train, the inn looked fairly dilapidated but had a charm about it and because I was interested in fishing, I thought it was going to be heaven for me.

We took over in 1949 when I was 14. The Buckenham and Surlingham ferries had disappeared just before the war so Reedham Ferry was the only one in Norfolk at the time. The inn was just a beer and cider house so Father applied to the Blofield and Flegg Courthouse for a spirit licence. He always told the tale that when the Clerk to the Court asked, 'Why do you want a spirit licence Mr Archer?' he replied, 'Well somebody came in after falling in the river and all I could offer him was a pint of beer!' So we got a spirit licence.

The Inn was a very small building originally, just the bar room, a private room, a garden where the conservatory is now and the cellar which now has the pumps. There were steps down to the cellar where the barrels sat on a stillion and we would open the tap and pour a pint. We'd walk back up and they'd say, 'Can I have a packet of crisps?' and we had to go all the way back down again.

There was no electricity, it was either paraffin lamps or Tilley lights, but then we got a little generator which did a few lights until finally we got mains electricity. There was no water either, so we used to go to Reedham for it and eventually had a well bored out the back. They drilled for several weeks before they hit water at around 100ft. It wasn't the best water as it had a high iron content but nevertheless, it saved us trotting up and down the road. I put in mains water many years ago.

There was no sewerage originally, just 'a bucket and chuck it' so we put in a small sewerage system out the back. In the end it couldn't cope with the increased number of people and now we have a big holding tank and a couple of pumps to pump it up to the road and the main sewer.

The ferry was a chain ferry which had to be hand-wound across the river. It was very hard work so at first we used a sculling boat to take foot passengers and bicycles over the river as in those days there were few cars about. The sculling boat could carry half a dozen passengers and was easier than winding the ferry over by hand. The ferry didn't have ramps to begin with. Instead there were wooden shocks or various-sized blocks made

Early photo of Buckenham Ferry

Tug towing lighters at Reedham Ferry 1950s

David Archer on old ferry 1960s

out of elm, which allowed for the rise and fall of the tide. So as the tide rose the blocks were in the water, and when it fell they had to be taken out.

When the sugar beet harvest started and Cantley was in full swing we could manage the small trucks being used when they were empty, a lot were ex-Army Bedfords, but they were too heavy when loaded. There would be four or five queued up in the late afternoon. We eventually started to get a few cars and taxis but still a lot of bicycles so we put ramps on the ferry and also a little Lister diesel engine so we could chug across.

We had times if the current was very strong when we couldn't operate and one such time was the first Easter we were here. The gear was fairly worn and Father and I were on the ferry when it broke. I managed to grab hold of the chain and we swung round on the quay head and the ferry sat there all Easter. Eventually when the wind calmed down, we used the sculling boat to put a new link in and we were back in business. It's always been a chain ferry, we did look at cables but what with the stretch on them and the river traffic it was a no-no. In those days there were coasters, tugs and lighters coming up to Norwich from Yarmouth and we had to keep an eye open for them.

Coasters would fill up lighters and then a tugboat, including one called the Gemsteam, would tow about three lighters all the way up to the power station in Norwich. The river is 18ft here and in the early days there was just one chain on the ferry which we would lower into the mud to let them pass – the new ferry runs on two chains.

In the early 1950s we would have a few private boats coming and then the hire boats started up as people got more into holidays and this began to generate income. There was a time when they had to get here by three in the afternoon or not get a mooring. Because the ferry could only take one or two small cars, there'd be a queue round the corner, particularly at busy times. I remember one year when the Show was on at Raveningham, we started first thing in the morning and carried on until late at night. As people began holidaying abroad though, business on the Broads started to ease off.

We used to get a few horses and carts coming across too. A lovely old boy used to come from the other side of Loddon on his way to Acle Sale. He had a little dairy and made his own butter. He used to give me the odd pat of butter and you could actually see an imprint of his hand on it and whether that was washed, or not… Acle Sale day was always quite a thing; they sold livestock, including cattle and pigs, and it was always a busy time for us.

We used to keep chickens, ducks and some pigs out the back and I'd walk the sow up to Reedham to get it serviced, I can't imagine walking a pig up the road now. I remember the wherries coming through up to the late 1950s and carrying sugar beet to Cantley. They would come down from the Raveningham Estate to the Cockatrice on the other side of the river here and upload the beet straight off the trailers, forking it in by hand.

In the 1953 flood, the bank opposite broke and the river flooded the marshes. I managed to get a rowing boat through the bank and I rowed all the way across to Haddiscoe on the flood water. We were lucky the pub wasn't flooded, it was touch and go.

The new ferry was launched in August 1983 down at Newson's Yard at Oulton Broad. Fred Newson was a lovely man and we used to kick a few ideas around and eventually we drew a plan for a new one. We gradually added to it and I suppose it took two-and-a-half years to actually materialise. The old ferry was driven by V-belts, which are like large-scale fan belts, and because they had been so successful we went for them again, but that was a bit of a disaster. The old ferry was timber-framed whereas this one is steel and it struggled getting over the river against the tide. So she went back to the yard to be converted to hydraulic power.

She had a refit in 2016 and was out of the water for six weeks. She was towed down to Oulton Broad and then through the locks and onto the yard. She's 35 years old so she needs a lot of attention now. It is similar in design to the first one but about 10ft longer – we can't go too long otherwise the tide would catch her and make it difficult to get her in. She's slotted-built so when the tide hits her it just goes under. However, there are times when you get a wind and tide together and then it can be difficult to get her in, although the engines are powerful enough. With the old ferry, we had to use a block and tackle and pull her in by hand!

Reedham Ferry 1950s

Refit 2016

Today there are three employees for the ferry during the week and others covering the weekend. Various checks are carried out on the ferry at 6am to get it going by 6.30 for people going to work, and business is pretty steady all day now, especially in the summer. Nowadays people mainly use the ferry service as a shortcut and some even buy multi-car tickets but there are still plenty of people coming across with bicycles – we had 30 during the course of the day recently.

After the Marchioness disaster on the Thames in 1989 when a passenger vessel struck a dredger and 51 people drowned, the Maritime and

Coastguard Agency (MCA) came into being and ferry operators had to come up with plans for the capabilities of their ferries. So now we get an MCA inspection on the ferry twice a year and ferry operators meet annually to discuss various rules and regulations. We've been meeting for years now and it's like a club with Reedham ferry being possibly the smallest ferry and the only one on the East coast. Fortunately we've had no major issues regarding health and safety.

We've got about 50 acres of land here including marshes and when we first came there was an opportunity to run the drainage mill. The old boy that was doing it was retiring so I took that job on and I still do it. I have to check the water levels are right, clear out the weed, and just check everything is running smoothly. I have a vehicle to get to it now, but at one time I just used the liggers and I had them in a straight line across to the mill and would run one way and walk the other. There's been the odd time when the fog came down and I went astray; I knew where I was, but I didn't know how I got there. It's crazy with fog when it gets you like that.

We get a lot of walkers as well as cyclists as after the 1953 floods the riverbanks and the paths were much improved. Hopefully the Wherryman's Way will open up from the middle of 2020 so they will be able to go all the way to Yarmouth along the river wall or to Loddon in the opposite direction.

I like to think that over the years we've become more of a destination pub. We use local produce wherever we can, we've got a couple of fishing lakes and fishing on our riverbank and there's scope to expand the moorings in the future although the boating side has declined from the Yare and the Waveney, but there are more private boats around. I took over in 1969 from my father and it still very much a family business with my daughter Harriet following in my footsteps.

Reedham Ferry

(1958 – 2016)

Keith Patterson
(1942–2018)

REEDHAM

Keith was a ferryman all his working life on both the old and new ferries at Reedham.

I started full time at Reedham Ferry at age 15 in October 1958 and worked as the ferryman until 1963, after which I continued part time right through until I retired in 2016. On the old ferry you could get three cars on if they were small enough, but by the time the new ferry came along cars were increasing in size so generally speaking it could only carry two.

The old ferry was much harder work. It had two chains but only one was a drive chain, the other was just a guide, and because the power drive chain was on the upside of the ferry I had to pull it in on a rope to get it square when the tide was coming up the river, otherwise I couldn't drop the ramp for the cars to get on and off. If the wind was strong as well, I had to pull the ferry in on a block and tackle. It all took more time and was much harder work, unlike now with the hydraulic ramps on the new ferry.

The new ferry came into operation in 1985 with a power drive on both chains so if it's not square, it can be nudged in on power instead of being pulled in on a rope. We don't have to wind the ramps up and down either, it's now done by simply pulling a lever.

Our 'till' in the early days was two Mars Bar boxes, one inside the other. We threw the change into the middle while the notes were put in between the sides and the amounts were written in a book, and that was it. We also sold sweets, cigarettes and bottles of pop in the summer to the holidaymakers. And regulars from Reedham, or those living on the other side of the river in Heckingham and Norton Subcourse, would sometimes pop down to buy a packet of cigarettes.

I worked from 8am to 5pm and David Archer, his father and I used to share the shifts between us. Now there are a number of ferrymen because most are quite happy to be part-time, so they all fit into the pattern of the week.

Holidays in the Broads were very popular in the 1960s and 70s and holidaymakers with cars would come especially to use the ferry. When more people had bicycles we often took the bikes and pedestrians over the river using the sculling boat. This was a large wooden boat with a single oar

Reedham Ferry 1970s

Reedham Ferry 2018

at the stern which was manoeuvred in a figure of eight in the water. I was trained by David's father when I started, on a boat tied to the quay head and he used to make me practise doing a figure of eight with this big oar. When he thought I was capable, he let me go.

The wind and tide could cause problems. If the wind was going one way and the tide the other it would balance you up, but if you had a low tide and the wind was howling down with the tide, it was much more difficult to get in and get the ramp down. Summertime was much more pleasant, when we had holidaymakers and boats everywhere and there were people to talk to. I remember some of the names like Old George and Young George who were poultry farmers and used to go to Acle Sale every Thursday, and Weedy Hall and Snowy Gaze who were lorry drivers. I've only bumped into them a few times since I finished, but we always have a chat.

CHAPTER 3

Mills

Thurne Mill

Horsey drainage pump internal layout

The mills are part of the marshes

(1990s)

Michael Knights
(b. 1946)

THE BROADS

Michael studied planning and architecture in 1965, a new field at the time. In 1990 he began as Head of the Historic Buildings Team at Norfolk County Council (NCC), where he stayed for 20 years.

In the early 1990s at NCC I was involved in a major project about drainage mills in the Broads, and travelled around the marshes registering their condition in order to produce an overall strategy for their protection. It was part of the Broads Authority Windpump Protection Programme (WPP) which had been set up in the 1980s. I remember some mills were very difficult to get to because of the dyke system in the Broads but we assembled all the information and it is now lodged with the Norfolk Windmills Trust.

Traditionally, mills tend to take either the name of the man who looked after them, such as High's Mill, or the name of the level they were draining, such as St Benet's Level. Other mills like Stracey Arms might be named after the landowner or by the distance up the rivers from Great Yarmouth, like Five Mile House.

Most mills on the Broads drain the land and the earliest ones did this by simply lifting water from one level to another with a scoop wheel. Later adaptations meant that some had vertical turbines installed which acted like centrifugal pumps. While some drainage mills such as Turf Fen near How Hill had two external scoop wheels and others had one internal scoop, most had just one external wheel placed next to the mill race or leat.

Early mills were usually either simple timber skeleton mills like Boardman's Mill by How Hill or smock mills which were bigger and very common in Holland and on the Fens in west Norfolk. The only example of a smock mill left on the Broads in Norfolk that I know of is Tunstall Dyke Mill, a derelict mill repaired under WPP. Mills probably didn't exist much before the 17th century and the earliest mill in the Broads is Oby Mill, built in 1753. They really flourished in the 18th and 19th centuries with about 280 in the Broads at one time. These are iconic structures and a very important collection of industrial monuments and I can't think of anywhere else in England which has a larger group of such monuments.

Over the years there have been many ideas about the best ways to protect them and make them wind and watertight. In the early 2000s a bid was made to the National Lottery called Land of the Windmills to bring 15 drainage mills on Halvergate marsh and Acle Straight back into sail. It was a very ambitious programme but the Lottery decided that we could do just two sections – the group of mills and pumps alongside the River Yare on the Reedham Marsh, and two old mills on the River Bure: Stracey Arms Mill and Ashtree Farm Mill. The latter was a brick tower mill built in 1912 with lots of cast iron machinery which contrasted with earlier mills which tended to have timber wheels and cogs with fruitwood teeth.

The group by the Yare included Polkey's Mill which is a large brick tower mill with an external scoop wheel; the derelict Reedham Marsh steam engine house; and Cadge's Mill, another traditional brick tower mill with little machinery left. There was also a 1940's green, corrugated iron shed housing two large Gwynne centrifugal pumps powered by Ruston diesel engines. Next to them is an electric pump that now does the job. This is the only surviving group of such buildings on the Broads where you can demonstrate power sources from wind, steam, diesel and electricity all together. Over a few years we brought Polkey's Mill back to full working condition and carried out repairs to the others.

Most drainage mills were built on the soggy, marshy ground of what was once the old estuary flowing from Norwich to the sea. Billy Nudd, a marshman in the Hickling area, told us about one of the techniques used to construct these heavy structures which could have 30 to 40 tons of brickwork. First, a cone of brickwork was put on the marsh and left to settle for a year or so, then another cone was put on top to take it up to around 20ft and left to settle. Each layer may not have run in the same direction but finally, once everything had settled nicely, the cap was put on. Billy heard about this method from his father and grandfather and the technique can be seen at both Buckenham Ferry Mill and at Brograve Level.

Brograve is a derelict mill near the Waxham Cut and you can actually see the horizontal mortar lines meeting at a point. Sometimes timber poles were rammed into the ground to provide some stability but it didn't work as the weight of the brickwork still had to be stabilised.

We met Bertie High, a lovely chap, who was born in the early 1920s in the middle of the marsh where High's Mill still stands and both Bertie's father and then Bertie looked after the old cloth-sailer. This meant it didn't have patent sails with individual shutters but canvas cloth like many of the Dutch mills. The cloth would have been rigged on sail bars like a yacht, depending on the strength of the wind that day. It was also pole-winded which meant that if the wind changed direction, the sails were pulled around to face the wind by turning the cap round with a long tail pole. By the 1990s the mill was in poor condition and leaning quite a bit so we employed a specialist firm to underpin and lift the brick tower to a vertical position. Bertie later moved to Potter Heigham where there is also a High's Mill.

Billy Nudd was born and actually lived in Stubb Mill, Hickling; most mills were sophisticated machines for doing work but some did have overnight accommodation with a little fireplace which allowed the marshman to get out of the weather – mills only do their job when the wind blows. The mill is now owned and maintained by the Norfolk Naturalists Trust and acts as a look-out point.

Draining flooded marshes was a serious problem. There could be a storm on one day with lashing rain and plenty of wind to turn the sails, but water levels could rise after the storm had passed and the winds had dropped, which meant the mill was unable to work. The marshman might then see a wall of water heading his way and be unable to do anything about it. The invention of the steam engine was a wonderful thing as it could be fired up and worked even on a windless day. Diesel pumps arrived in the 1920s and 30s and the internal combustion engine was easier to manage as they didn't have to shovel coal and get the steam up. It meant that the same amount of land could be drained with one engine rather than 10 or 12 mills.

Mills in the Broads tended to have four sails which are connected to the brake wheel via a windshaft to slow and stop them. This worked most of the time but there are stories of the brake wheel getting too hot and causing an explosion in storm conditions, and a lot of mills did burn down. Sails need to face the wind at all times. However, in this county the winds can veer rapidly and if the wind gets behind the cap, the sails could be pulled off. So the first

Brograve Mill 2018

mills had to be constantly stopped and the sails turned to face the wind. To overcome this problem, patent sails were invented in Norfolk by William Cubitt in 1807. They consisted of a range of shutters which were operated by lever mechanisms and ensured that when the wind picked up, the shutters opened and spilled the wind.

The fantail, or fly, is a bladed wheel at the back of the mill at right angles to the sails and its job is to turn the cap – as long as the cap faces the wind the sails will turn. They are connected via the brake wheel to a crown wheel and a central upright shaft. The shaft runs perpendicular to the base of the tower and is attached to the pit wheel via a gearing system which in turn is coupled to the scoop wheel.

Scoop wheels worked alongside a narrow channel and lifted the water rapidly from one level and deposited it via sluices on the other side. When they became defunct, turbines proved to be more

Scoop wheel Polkey's Mill 2005

efficient, acting like a centrifugal force within a chamber, with the water rising to the edge and spilling out in the same manner as when you stir tea with a spoon.

Caps on Norfolk mills are boat-shaped with the heavier timber at the front designed to sweep off the rain. As long as they face the wind they survive very well. However, as soon as the mill stops turning, rain can get in through the back, rot sets in and over a period of years, internal machinery and floors are lost. It can happen quite quickly as these buildings are in the middle of nowhere.

The early mills were a primitive skeleton framework of timber, and sails could be connected very quickly to begin draining the land. There is still some evidence on the Broads of very simple timber structures which could be moved around while landowners waited three or four years for the main mill to be finished; a sort of portable mill. These timber structures were protected from the weather by wood tar, something familiar to anyone working on boats. I have done some research and experimentation and I am an advocate for wood tar as a preservative on soft wood but not on brick or masonry as the tar seals in water and damp. However, where the brickwork is already heavily tarred as at Polkey's Mill, there is little choice other than to replicate the finish.

Restoring old mills creates an interesting dilemma. Once you decide to bring them back to working condition you have to employ people on a permanent basis to operate them, take the brakes off and let the sails go round so they don't become stuck in one position and allow water in. There have been some spectacular collapses in the past so it is important that the sails are turned regularly and the fantails are greased.

If mills are not easily accessible then the problems re-occur. I know of mills that were put back into good order at the beginning of the 1990s and then 20 years later were back on the buildings-at-risk register. It was always because people were not working them – if funding for mill maintenance isn't built in, then you have to question the purpose. However, these are important listed buildings and should be kept in good order for future generations to enjoy.

It was the job of the marshmen to work the mills but it was never their sole task. They usually had a house on the marsh and worked for the farmers. They were out in all weathers keeping everything flowing, the ditches clean and the animals safe, setting the mills to run and keeping them greased. They didn't necessarily sit in the mill whilst it was working; Bertie High told me that each mill had a unique sound, it might be click, click.....click, click. As long as it was a regular beat, he would carry on with his other work.

We were happy to get Polkey's Mill back to working condition, it is by seeing the scoop wheel moving and the sails spinning round that you get some idea of just how powerful and important these machines were. I feel lucky that I spent so much time out in the marshes and met such interesting people. And even though I have plodded around in filthy weather in the middle of nowhere, soaked to the skin, it was well worth it.

Thurne Mill

(2002 – 2019)

Debra Nicholson
(b. 1955)

REPPS

Debra visited the Norfolk Broads on family holidays and now runs both Thurne Mill, built in 1820, and the Wind Energy Museum. It's as much about the place as it is about the machines…

Thurne was my favourite place as a child and when my own family first moved here and my husband was working away and the children were at school, I decided to do an A level in photography and picked Thurne Mill as my project.

I knew the mill had been saved in 1949 but I thought the man who did it would be long gone. I looked in the phone book and found R. D. Morse so I gave him a ring. Bob was so helpful, he got out all the photographs and told me about the mill and what he had done over the years.

Once I passed my exam I phoned to thank him and he cleared his throat and said, 'You'll have to excuse me, I haven't spoken to anybody all week'. I thought that was so sad and I began to phone him every day just to make sure he was alright, and then it got that if I hadn't phoned him by 5.50 pm he would phone me, and he became part of the family.

Bob bought the mill from the Internal Drainage Board for £75 when many were being demolished for their ironwork after the war. So Thurne was lucky. It took Bob just a year to restore it and Albert England was employed to help – Albert was a direct descendent of the millwrights that originally built it, England & Co of Ludham. We have a lovely journal in the museum which explains how Bob took stuff down to the boat and along the river, how long it took, how much petrol he used, the paint and supplies he bought, everything. It cost only £7 6d to paint the tower and that included the paint and Albert England's wages! Nowadays, maintenance costs up to £10,000.

Bob had been interested in windmills from childhood and when he was seven he picked out a colouring book with a windmill on the front. Two years later he made a balsa wood model of the mill which we still have along with the book. It wasn't until he was 81 that he found out that it actually exists: North Mill in Kent. It's where his inspiration came from and from the age of seven he wanted to own a windmill.

He gave his life to wind power and once Thurne Mill was restored he leased it to the Norfolk Windmills Trust and began creating the collection which is now in the Wind Energy Museum in Repps. The museum has a lot of local exhibits including the scoop wheel from Whitlingham Lane

Bob Morse 1951

in Norwich which drained the marsh there, and the Holmes steam engine from Hemsby with its turbine – the only one left in existence. So Bob has done Norfolk a favour in preserving this history.

He was the youngest of three brothers who all enjoyed engineering but Bob never had a job as such. He never married so in a way he kind of adopted me when I took such an interest in the mill. Bob asked if I would take on the collection about five or six years before he died in 2007; quite a tall order as I am not an engineer. I had long talks with my husband and in 2002 we decided to take it all on, so Bob would see we were determined to keep things as they should be and could advise. I just wish I'd listened more.

We opened to the public in 2001 and when the Norfolk Windmills Trust restored the mill in 2002 we had a big party with 250 people – we did things like that throughout which was nice for Bob to be part of.

Thurne Mill is one of the few working windpumps on the Broads and can pump water in its own circle of water for demonstration purposes. People see it from quite a distance and moor up when the sails are going round. Our lovely volunteer, Paul, dresses up as a marshman and gets it going most Sundays. It will be 200 years old in 2020; it's white, it's visible, it's accessible and it is probably the most photographed mill in the Broads.

Maintenance is always an issue and it's constant. Unfortunately in 2013 the mill was attacked by a red algae which I understand came from Europe to Cornwall in 2007 and worked its way north. It was eating away the paint and turning the mill pink so we had to pressure-wash it quickly. In 2018 we painted the tower, cap and insides thanks to our volunteers and that should last five to six years. We also have a millwright who comes every month to make sure everything is okay.

Thurne Mill

The mill ceased working in 1936 when it was overtaken by diesel and electric power so we have a little green shed at the end of the staithe which pumps the marsh, and is nowhere near as attractive. Without our little green sheds scattered all around the Broads the marshes would just fill up.

When I first took it over, it was all about the machinery and I knew I couldn't do it alone, so I started to get volunteers to come and help. They have a sense of ownership and can talk about everything as if it was their own. It made me look at the whole site. We're two and a half acres of marsh, it's quiet, it's peaceful, and I began thinking it was as much about the place as it was about the machines.

We wanted to use the windpump as a backdrop to this lovely place so we created a social enterprise. Now more people come to relax and get involved in activities that help them, than paying customers who come to look at the exhibits. We work with schools, opened a Men's Shed, and have had the Duke of Edinburgh scheme and the Prince's Trust at the mill. Apprentices from the 3sun Group do some work for us and people from The Bread Kitchen support organisation come along and run workshops to teach them woodwork. It is all so varied and it's not all about machinery.

Falling in love with Keswick Mill

(2016 – 2019)

Juju Vail
(b. 1967)

KESWICK

Juju and her family live in Keswick Mill and she relates some of its history and their ideas for the future of this former flour mill.

We saw Keswick Mill online in 2016 and it reminded me of similar properties in Canada where I grew up, being a wooden building over a river. It is on a long thin island populated with huge poplar trees originally planted to make matchsticks. I fell in love with it and we finally moved in in 2018.

The ground floor is a rough, open area where I paint and where my husband does his woodwork and projects, and fixes our bicycles. The bedrooms are on the first floor and there is a large communal living space with windows on all sides – the views are incredible.

The previous owners left us a large folder which tells the history of the mill and its last miller, Mr John Brock, and of the two owners who lived here after it was decommissioned in 1976. The miller's son, John, remembers working here as a teenager and young man, and has told us how the mill looked before it was converted. A later resident, Mrs Pearson, ran needlework courses at the mill, and rented out the second and third floors as student accommodation. The last owners used it as a holiday home from 2001 until we bought it, and they laid out the mostly wild gardens very beautifully.

After the mill stopped in 1976 it fell into disrepair, then in the late 1980s the next owner re-clad the outside, put in lots of skylights on the south side, divided up the space differently, moved the staircase and made it into a liveable building. Nonetheless, it is still relatively easy to walk around and understand how it would have worked with a system very similar to Letheringsett Mill. There is no millstone but there is a large cog room on the ground floor and a lot of what appears to be spinning-type wheels. Our neighbour has a millstone outside his place and it is assumed that it is one of the original five millstones.

Upstairs, as well as chutes for the grain and a hoist, there is a trap to an area which ran over the north-facing bridge. From there the grain would have been transported to the top floor before

The mill interior 2019

Keswick Mill

moving down the various chutes to the millstone, where it was ground and shot out onto the ground floor to be packed.

Records show that there has been a mill here for over a thousand years. It would have burnt down and been reconstructed many times. The current building is half-Georgian with wooden beams dating to the 1760s and half-Victorian with iron beams from around 1860. I understand the mill used to be bigger and in one spot you can see where a wheel turned on an axle. There were two wheels early in the last century but when the mill became residential the area was concreted over and the ground level was raised.

We have the original toilet on the ground floor; it's just a hole over the river with a toilet seat. Apparently we still have the right to use it! There is also a trap door in the ground floor where you can see the river rushing underneath and we've been told that the students used to jump in and ride the water into the millpond. Because mills often burned down there is also a brick column with an iron store for records and money.

When the meadow is mown annually, muntjac and all sorts of creatures run out from cover. We've seen a family of otters, water voles, lots of mice, moles and shrews and our cats are very good at managing the population. There are lots of birds

The mill race

in the millpond and wagtails nest all summer long underneath the arches of the mill where the millwheels would have been, and we just sit outside and watch them.

We also use the river in the summer, swimming and rowing, pulling out weeds as we go to keep the water relatively clear. The miller's son said that when he was a lad he would take a boat up the river to buy groceries but he hated it because he would have to lie flat as he went underneath the train tracks. I can imagine it was scary, especially when a train went over.

It seems the millers earned a large portion of their income by catching eels and the last miller also put a net under the mill in the summer months and caught lots of them. Now there is a mill race where water bypasses the mill and a mill ladder at the sluice so eels can climb up and carry on up the river. I haven't seen any but we have seen fish, including a huge fish with no head out on the water meadow. Otters eat just the head and brains so they are obviously active around here.

When the mill was converted, the local authority took over responsibility for managing the sluice and put in an automatic system to control water level. It opens when the water starts to rise so water can run through to the millpond, and if it gets very wet the fields around will flood. In the last very wet winter there was a lake all the way to the train station.

We hope to buy back the sluice in order to put in a water source heat pump and generate our own electricity. My husband is an electronics engineer and has worked in various kinds of sustainable power management so we already have a big bank of solar panels but he regrets all that water power going to waste.

The mill became a listed building when it changed to being residential so we see it as our responsibility to maintain its historical features for future generations. We would like to have an annual open day perhaps with guided tours and we hope to build our own working models of how the mill would have worked. If we get our pump we would also like to open the mill to environmental groups interested in looking at alternative forms of energy.

And the mill came with the house

(1979 – 2007)

Nick Prior
(b. 1948)

THRIGBY

Nick worked many years as an offshore hydrographic surveyor. Whilst living in Thrigby he discovered the remains of a historic mill in the grounds of his house and decided to restore it.

I had about 40 years working offshore and during this time my wife and I bought a house with a bit of land at Thrigby. In the grounds was what looked like a cut-down tower mill – it was actually a roundhouse and the remains of the trestle of a post mill sitting on four big piers. Post mills were the earliest type of mill and go back to the 1200s but this one dated to the 1700s. The roundhouse was about 25ft in diameter and had been added on afterwards. It was just an outbuilding, riddled with deathwatch beetle and you could see where carts had been kept under the trestle and damaged the piers.

We found a photograph in the Record Office in Norwich and that started it all. It was taken around 1880 just before the mill was pulled down and it's a tiny picture showing the miller, his brother, the miller's wife and their baby. The mill is in full sail with a pair of commons, which were just plain canvas sails, and a pair of double shuttered patents. It was a flour mill used by the local farms and it stood on a little hill where it would have caught every breath of wind coming up the rise – there must have been a mill there for hundreds of years. There were quite a few of these mills about at one point; old maps even show some on Yarmouth seafront. But when I bought it there was only one other in Norfolk, at Garboldisham on the Suffolk border.

John Lawn, the millwright from Caston, had been involved with the mill through the previous owner and knew a little bit about it. He donated the windshaft from Tottenhill post mill, just outside King's Lynn. He had grabbed it as the scrap merchants were demolishing the mill! We reckoned the windshaft weighed about a tonne, the weight of a fully armoured stock car, so we got hold of a car trailer and early one Sunday morning loaded it up behind my old 1600e Cortina. The trailer bent, but we balanced the windshaft behind the car and I drove at 20 mph all the way from Caston to Thrigby. It started to break the back of the car which was rusty anyway, but I made it.

I took the damaged windshaft to Dennis Burrell who was in charge of Burrells Engineering at Yarmouth but made the mistake of saying I wasn't

Thrigby post mill 1880

Sails in place 2003

in a hurry for it, and we forgot all about it. About three or four years later I went to see them and they then started work. They used their early Victorian lathe that had made prop shafts for drifters and ships; its faceplate was a monster and apparently, so the story goes, they had used it to turn the turrets of Churchill tanks during the war.

I made a model of the proposed post mill by working out its rough size from the dimensions of the roundhouse and the old photo. I had help from Richard Seago, John Lawn and the expert Vincent Pargeter, who was with Essex County Council and had experience of post mill restoration. I altered the model to incorporate Vincent's ideas and after he had a good look over it and put me right on a few things, I ordered the timber and got started.

A post mill sits on a trestle which is two big bits of timber in a cross laid on the piers, then diagonal props about 20ft long come up into the main post. The buck is the body of the mill that sits on top of the main post. There are three storeys: the bottom is the sack floor where the flour goes into the sacks; the middle floor with the grindstones is known as the stone floor, and the top bit has the brake wheel and bins where the corn goes in. The post in the middle is known as the main post and is about 20ft long by 2ft square and built out of one piece of timber. Although most trees that size have been cut down, we luckily found one down at South Cove in Suffolk and got it to Beccles, where it was milled into a square and then transported to Thrigby.

A lot of lifting was involved. To get a crane in the early 1980s was pretty straightforward but it would be hard to do the same job on the site today because of the high voltage lines running past. I did most of the practical work, chopping out joints, testing them for fit and getting it ready to put together. Come the day that I wanted some help, I just whistled up friends from the village.

The whole ethos of Thrigby Mill was to have it look as it was towards the end of its life, so there was nothing fancy to it. It was just sawn-finished, using picked-up timber that fitted, a make do, except for where it really counted, namely the trestle and the framing for the buck. I wanted a place that was 19th century with unguarded machinery, flat belts and wooden shutters, no glass.

The mill was never finished. I got it to the point where the sails were on and turning. They were safe with the big brake wheel on and with the tail pole to pull them into the wind. The next stage would have been to put in the grinding machinery and all the stuff to produce flour, but that never did happen.

My aim was to put something back into the landscape, something that had been there – it's a kind of museum piece I suppose of what life was like in the 1800s. Hopefully somebody, somewhere, will pick up the gauntlet and finish it.

Restoring Mutton's Mill

(1975 – 2017)

David High
(b. 1943)

HALVERGATE

David bought Mutton's Mill with his friend Paul Reynolds and set about restoring it, a process which involved some trial and error to begin with and turned into a 40-year labour of love.

Paul Reynolds and I both worked at Eastwood Whelpton at Upton Dyke. We were really keen to restore a mill and we ended up buying Mutton's Mill in 1975 for £3,500. It was known as Mutton's Mill because the last marshman who worked the mill was from the Mutton family and it was traditional for sons to follow fathers into that line of work.

Most mills were in operation up to the war and after that many deteriorated. I think Mutton's Mill must have been kept in quite good condition before she stopped working around 1947, but by the time we bought her she was in a poor way. Most of the cap was missing, the doors were off and cattle were using it as a shelter.

The mill had a pair of stocks in place and not much else. Stocks carry the sail frames and shutters which catch the wind to turn the sails. There is a big driveshaft through the middle of the mill with a paddle in the bottom which lifts the water up into another dyke and on to another mill, before finally emptying into Breydon Water. Mutton's Mill has an internal scoop wheel to lift the water which is quite unusual as most of the others have wheels on the outside.

We installed a new cap and a new stock, and put on some sail frames. We also fitted a fantail on the back so it would always head into the wind. The original fantail had deteriorated and was only facing one way when we took it on although the remaining two and a half stocks still managed to turn the cap in a good wind. We did have a problem with the fantail we put on in the 1980s because the housing moved up and down on the spindle and damaged a couple of the blades, but that's all running well now. Our restoration work has involved quite a bit of trial and error really.

The brake wheel had just about disintegrated but we had a few bits and pieces, and as Paul is good at working these things out, we managed to save it. One day when we were working on the mill we got chatting to the lady who used to look after Berney Mill. She told us that half a stock had been lying there since new sails had been put on Berney a few years before. We managed to get hold of it and we spliced it together with Mutton's stock to form the set we needed.

Mutton's Mill 2017

Brake wheel

There was a bit of subsidence in the tower and a bad crack so we put three big steel bands round it to hold it together. As the mill has an internal scoop wheel it means there is an archway which causes a weak point and these mills were built on only a very rough wooden raft. I suppose at the time they didn't imagine they were going to be standing for another 150 years. Anyway, she is quite steady now. We took a few measurements which showed the mill had not moved much in her lifetime but putting the steel bands round has done a great deal to keep it together.

When we were working on the mill we sometimes spent a week camping down there and I remember once we decided to walk across to the Berney Arms pub. By the time we came out, the mist had come down. It's an eerie place to be when you can't see too far in front of you. We eventually got back to the mill but only after struggling to find a gateway and then following the dykes round each field until we reached the next gateway and the next. We only attempted that once. We do more work on the mill in summertime although now we don't do as much as we used to. In the winter the tracks get very muddy and it's a cold old place out there when there's a north-easter blowing.

The mill is about 32ft to the top of the tower and slightly higher again with the cap on and there's a beautiful view from the fan staging. You can see right out to Berney and Yarmouth and the towers of Filby and Thrigby churches one way and Wickhampton and into the distance across the River Yare the other way. If people come along they don't always like the idea of climbing to the top, but it's worth it just for the view.

It is surprising the number of people who walk past while we are working and just ignore us, but probably they are not interested in mills. The funny thing, though, is when we go down to do some greasing up or whatever, we know we have had visitors because they have opened the gate and not shut it properly. It doesn't matter at all about them going in, but they just don't seem to know how to shut gates!

Around November 2016, the BBC wanted to film some derelict mills because they'd read about the Water, Mills and Marshes grant to restore some mills on the Broads. We are now part of that project and just happened to be at the mill so they filmed us!

The mill can still lift water but it would only go round in a circle now and not into any of the main dykes. Sluice gates were put in after the war, then about 10 to 15 years ago as part of flood alleviation works, the sluice gates were replaced with Dutch sluice gates and now Mutton's Mill is nearly on its own little island.

Today the tower needs tarring and pointing up in places and the cap will want repainting. Also another stock and set of sails would be very handy. When Paul and I bought Mutton's Mill in 1975 we never imagined we would be working on her over 40 years later! There's a High's Mill on the Halvergate Marshes not far from Mutton's, so whether there is a family link back there and that is the reason I've been interested in windpumps, I don't know.

Mutton's Mill

(1975 – 2017)

Paul Reynolds
(b. 1937)

HALVERGATE

Paul has a background in boat building and along with his friend David High, he bought and restored Mutton's Mill. He also worked on Oby Mill, the oldest mill in the Broads.

Around 2000 I worked on Oby Mill but it wasn't my first job on a mill as I had already bought Mutton's Mill in 1975 with David High. I had always thought when I first started boating around the Broads that I ought to save one of these mills – some like Stracey, Horsey and Thurne mills were being saved but a lot were just left derelict.

I was at St Benet's Mill one day after rescuing what was to become my crab boat from a dyke, and I got talking to two millwrights who were working on several mills. They said that Mutton's Mill was coming up for sale so David and I went to have a look at it before it was advertised and we bought it from the farmer. I had several boats at this time, so I sold my crab boat and a half decker and managed to scrape enough together for my share.

Mutton's Mill was built by 1837 and was named after generations of Muttons who were the local marshmen. It was fairly derelict but had all the essential bits and pieces. We took the sails off and repaired enough for just one pair. Then we took the stocks off thinking that one might go back on but it wasn't possible but we did manage to slice a piece off a discarded one from Berney Arms to repair it. Next, it took a few years to gather enough wood to make a new cap frame using old timbers and it was built in my new workshop.

During this time we got several grants to help with the work, first from Mr Raynor, a Windmills Trust man at County Hall and then from Steve Earl also at County Hall. At the rate we worked we didn't need much money all in one go. We would work through our holidays and sometimes if we had a big job like putting the cap frame back on or getting the sails on, we took several days in a row to work on it.

We never really felt that we had taken on too much, although we did get to the stage, probably about ten years ago, where we were finding that we had to go back to do things again as rot had set in or there was storm damage. And when cracks appeared in the tower walls after the sails were up, we had to put bands around the mill to hold it together. We discovered that the mill was built on a timber raft and that the wood underneath the foundations was rotten and there wasn't much holding the two halves of the mill together!

The mill is part of the Water, Mills and Marshes project so we hope it will be finished. I am over 80 now and would like to see it finished as I am not able to do as much heavy work as I used to.

I got to know the owner of Oby Mill at the boatyard in Upton when he was working on his launch. He needed it to get to the mill from Upton as access wasn't good by land. I helped him make the mill safe to start with and we took off the cap frame and removed the stocks. We left just the windshaft up and fitted a temporary cap. After I finished the owner wanted me to do some more restoration work but he eventually had to sell the property.

Oby Mill

The present owners approached a retired millwright from Essex, Vince Pargeter, who was keen to see Oby Mill restored. Unfortunately he died and no-one else has been able to take on the work. The mill was built in 1753 and is Grade 2 listed; English Heritage, the Environment Agency and the Broads Authority are all involved, so what's going to happen now I don't know.

There is quite a lot of public interest in the mills or at least the ones that are easier to get to. There is a footpath running past Oby and also one which runs near Mutton's Mill but people walking down to Berney Arms usually turn off a couple of hundred yards before Mutton's so we tend to only get the odd visitor who has lost their way.

Hardley Mill

(2000 – 2019)

Mike Stephenson
(b. 1938)

HARDLEY

Mike retired from a career in the Civil Service in 1998 and became very involved in the restoration of Hardley Mill.

In 2000, my neighbour thought that I was looking bored so he took me to see Peter Grix at Hardley Mill. Peter was an architect from Norwich who had always wanted to restore windmills. When he retired he looked at several, including Brograve and St Benet's Level, but was unable to lease them. Eventually, he turned to Hardley Mill. Rather oddly, all three had internal appold turbines, a pure coincidence I think.

Many mills have a scoop wheel which turns on a horizontal axis, scooping water up. The appold turbine was developed in the mid-19th century and was exhibited at the Great Exhibition. It spins on a vertical axis at 100 rpm or faster, and has a circular turning rotor which turns and throws the water out sideways by centrifugal force. It's more efficient, as a lift wheel can only lift a third at most of the diameter of the wheel, so if you wanted a 5ft lift you would need a 16ft wheel. An appold turbine can easily lift 5ft and we have ours running at up to 120 rpm, lifting six tonnes a minute.

Hardley Mill was commissioned by Thomas William Brograve Proctor-Beauchamp who owned all the land and he contracted Dan England, a Ludham based publican and millwright, to build it in 1874. In one of the censuses Dan England said that as a millwright he had three employees. We think that the entire cap was built in a shed in Ludham and was then taken apart, loaded onto a wherry and reassembled on site.

Proctor-Beauchamp wanted the mill built to improve the marshes. Digging ditches to drain a marsh required a large capital investment so the pattern of the ditches tends to stay the same. If you look at the map of 1842 and the present one, the ditches are all in the same pattern.

Around 1900 a steam pump was installed where the electric pump now stands and in 1926 the mill was restored, however, in 1949 the cap was back-winded. When the great surge of 1953 burst the bank down towards Hardley and most of the marshes were under water, it was decided to get the old millpump working again. A small tractor was rafted in and set up outside the doorway and a hole knocked through the wall. A new low-level countershaft was installed with an inverted turbine wheel and a smaller pit wheel. I think these were all salvaged items as metal teeth were driving wooden ones which millwright Vincent Pargeter said were typical for flour mills, but wrong for pumps. It didn't work.

A second, bigger tractor was rafted in and another hole made in the south wall of the tower. The two tractors worked well in tandem until it was found that once started the bigger tractor could be stopped – it seems the depth of water in the turbine weighed about four tons so it was not surprising that the small tractor struggled to get the water in the well to spin at the necessary speed of over 110 rpm. A local man would row across from Langley Street every morning to refuel and fettle the tractors and then row back to switch off in the evening – his dinghy was moored to a pear tree in an orchard!

It was at about this time that electricity reached Hardley when a line was brought across the

Hardley Mill in May 1989

Cap lifted 2009

marshes and a big electric pump was put in. Our mill with its ruined cap was no longer used, the wall by the doorway was patched up and corrugated iron was nailed across the doorway. I've been told that teenagers in the area got inside the mill and went up to the first floor but decided it was unsafe. It does make me wonder just what it was like if three teenagers in the mid-1950s decided something was unsafe!

The Langley estate sold the mill to the Internal Drainage Board in 1944 and they leased it to Norfolk County Council who then leased it to Peter. In order to get a European Union LEADER Plus grant, a Trust was formed and the lease was transferred to the Trust.

The mill was in a shocking state. Only two of the main four ribs were left in the cap, half the brake wheel was in the cap and the rest lay broken on the floor, while the wind shaft which carries the brake wheel had disappeared. Peter collected a group of friends to help him and they bought a Nissen hut that had started life as an 8th Army Air Force hospital to use as a workshop, the cap was taken off and a crane was hired to lift out the innards.

Peter spent a great deal of his time restoring the mill. He would work by himself on Tuesdays, I would help him on Wednesdays and sometimes my neighbour would help. He then did some more work on Thursdays before driving home to Hounslow on Thursday evenings. The Friends of the Mill was established in 2005 to help and roughly 20-30 people were involved. I enjoyed woodwork and knew how to use a chainsaw and I discovered early on that I could tie knots in ropes or, being pedantic, 'bends', so I took over all the tying and joining of ropes.

After we put the floors in I suggested we get the turbine turning and Peter agreed. The old turbine couldn't be repaired so Peter produced a drawing which we passed to a pattern maker. The old one was taken out using a 300 weight chain hoist which used to belong to the Coal Board and we dismantled what was left of the turbine mounting – the original turbine wheel had disappeared and a different one had been put in upside down!

Finally, a crane lifted the cap on and the stocks and clamps were fitted. Towards the end of the afternoon Vincent Pargeter sat on the clamp and moved himself to the end pushing the big galvanised U-bolt. He reached down and put the plate over the ends and it just hung until he produced a nut from his pocket, and fitted it. He then produced a second nut for the other end and a spanner to tighten them. I hadn't realised he was pushing so much stuff in front of him and it was all done with no safety harness. We were gob-smacked. We then had to turn the sails so the same could be fitted to the other sails. Peter never saw the mill working as by that time he was wheelchair-bound at home, but I did send him a video clip and he was almost speechless with joy. He has left us a tremendous legacy and inspired us all.

Once LEADER Plus decided that we were doing things seriously they were very helpful and advised us to get a visitor centre and a mooring. They were right because 90% of visitors use our mooring and once the sails were turning we started getting more visitors including people walking the Wherryman's Way, as they could see the sails from below Reedham, ten miles away. These days we have everything screened with heavy-gauge wire and I tell people that this is as close they will ever get to a turning brake wheel.

Once the restoration was finished I realised that we needed an ongoing maintenance campaign. We fund all the work ourselves and currently the lower brickwork needs repointing. The mill is a timber structure, exposed to the weather and 40ft high, so we need to keep it in good order despite the lack of millwrights around.

We are always in need of volunteers and we need young people who are comfortable working at heights. We also need people who are prepared to tackle the 40ft climb to the top to take parties round. We charge adults £3 a head to go round the mill, children are free and we charge if boats are moored overnight. We have volunteers who run the visitor centre and serve very nice cakes I'm told.

Hardley Mill today

Centrifugal pump installed 1950, Herringfleet Mill

The millwright's story

(1944 – 1998)

Peter Gowing
(b. 1928)

NORFOLK

At age 16 Peter began work at F Flowerdew & Son in Norwich and trained as an agricultural engineer before becoming a millwright. He worked all over Norfolk and many parts of East Anglia.

I'd spent my school holidays working on a farm and always thought I'd like to be an agricultural engineer. Flowerdew's were agricultural and general engineers and I joined them in 1944 during the war. They explained that they could not take me on as a signed apprentice because their workshops in Temple Road had received a direct hit and they had lost most of their machine shop equipment. They had some premises at Gowings' farm, no relation, on Hellesdon Hall Road where they had a blacksmith and a carpenter shops so they moved there, but they explained that if anything else happened, they would not be able to set up again.

My first day on the job was at Stammer's Flour Mills, East Dereham and I found it a bit overwhelming. We went in the car with Mr Flowerdew to fix their big Crossley twin-cylinder gas engine at their gas producing plant. When the engine was started they would put one cylinder onto town gas and the other was used to draw the fire up on the gas producing plant. Once their own gas got going, they switched over and used it instead. It was one man's job to keep the fires going and it was the only gas producing plant we knew of in Norfolk. The clutch was slipping so we had to adjust it so it could drive the machine and the mill. I'll always remember that first day.

I worked from 8am till 6pm and my position was similar to being the teaboy, so all the dirty tasks of cleaning bits of machinery were mine and if we were out on the marshes to fix a pumping station, I was the one who carried the bag of tools on my back. In the early days we did a lot of work on farms fixing binders and old grass cutters and I was privileged to see the start of combines coming into fields and to work on the early ones.

I didn't have to do National Service as I was on work of 'national importance'. My work with Mr Flowerdew included farming, land drainage pumps on the marshes and the mills and, as such, we came under the Ministry of Agriculture, Fisheries and Food.

In the early days when it got dark we used Tilley lights and hurricane lamps but later when mills got big diesel engines to drive their machinery there was a dynamo for lights. However, if the engine had broken down we often ended up working with just a candle stuck on a piece of wood!

Over the years my job evolved and I mostly worked on mills as they moved from steam to diesel. The flour mill at Stalham still had a steam engine when I first went there, but on Reedham Marsh, the mill and its steam engine had stopped so we looked after the new plant and the two diesel engines which pumped water from the marsh at 100 tonnes a minute. In heavy weather those pumps ran 48 hours at a time to keep the marshes from flooding. So if a pump broke down we would get an urgent call and had to get there quickly.

The railway line from Acle to Yarmouth passed along the marsh near Reedham and if the pumps broke down and the marshes flooded, it could also inundate the railway line. In winter we couldn't get to the pumping stations by vehicle so we had to walk and carry everything on our backs. At Reedham we had special passes from the railway so we could walk up the railway line till we were opposite the pumping station and then we just cut across.

When electric pumps started to come in, we had to learn to deal with them. All the work in my early days involved hand tools so there were no electric grinders, saws or files – if we had a piece of 3-inch solid round steel to cut through, we did it by hand with a hacksaw. Some of my tools would be museum pieces now, like the ones we used for corking up pipes and boilers. How some people today would manage makes you wonder!

We did quite a bit of work at Mundesley which had the only remaining overshot water wheel in Norfolk with the water coming over the top of the wheel. Unfortunately it burnt down but you can still see the wheel although it's in a state of disrepair and the buckets have gone. We also put the diesel engine in at Letheringsett when the cogs got too bad.

In the early days if you set foot in a mill or a barn you had to deal with everything, it didn't matter if it was plumbing, woodwork or electrics, the miller or farmer would expect us to do it all. When people began manufacturing cubes and pellets for animal feed and required a steam boiler, we put in the boiler and steam piping as well as the electrical controls. That was just accepted in those days and as a millwright that is what you did.

Many farms had a number of little engines to drive machinery but these in turn we replaced with electric motors as electricity came in. I am still interested in those little old barn engines and, in fact, I've got six of them and I belong to the Norfolk Internal Combustion Engine Society. I go to the rallies and I think how we threw the old engines on the rubbish heap when they were no longer wanted – I wish I had some of them now because they're worth quite a bit of money! Mills also had little engines for driving odd bits and pieces, and farms had little Lister engines to drive the well pumps so the farmer could have a tank up in the roof rather than draw buckets of water from the well.

There was a big well pump at Kirby Bedon in a 90ft well that was used for cooling milk – cold water from the well would run through a grid to cool it. We always laughed and said that come the bank holiday, as sure as eggs, we'd get a phone call to fix the pump. Mr Flowerdew always went down the well and we stayed at the top to pull the bits up and down. It's nice if you go down a well and look up because you can see all the stars in the sky. If you go down in summer it feels a little bit cool and in the winter it feels warm because the temperature doesn't change. The Maltings at Whitbreads in East Dereham also had pumps in the wells to soak the barley and get it growing. So again if those pumps broke down we had to go straight away.

Both mills and farms used wheels with wooden cogs and one of our jobs was to re-cog the wheel when they wore out and we preferred to use either hornbeam or beech. Around 2000, I was contacted by Michael Grix at Burgh Mill, Aylsham, to re-cog his water wheel because the BBC wanted to use the mill with the wheels going round for an episode in the Campion series. We re-cogged it together and my photograph was in the local newspapers. I got the vast sum of £8 an hour from the BBC for doing it, which is more than I ever earned in my life! That was quite an enjoyable job.

I kept with Flowerdew & Son until they eventually packed up the business. I had worked with the son, Mr Albert Flowerdew, who was a

Flooded marshes at Reedham

gentleman through and through. He was a big church man who carried his principles into his work and we were told if we used bad language we could look for another job. When he retired he asked if I would like to take over the business but I decided against it. He said it was a wise decision because when he went on holiday he had to take a bag of tools with him in case he was called back. I went instead to Allen & Page who were milling animal feed, and worked as engineer and production manager for 25 years. When I retired I was offered a job in Horsford one day a week to keep the machinery going in the mill and that finished up full-time, and I carried on until I was 70.

Most of the mills I worked in are no longer there; some were pulled down but a lot have been converted into dwelling places with the water running through underneath. I enjoyed my career very much. Obviously conditions were not as good years ago as they are now, it was a different way of living and working and you accepted things as a matter of course.

A passion for mills and machines

(1960s – 2019)

Richard Seago
(b. 1958)

SOUTH WALSHAM

Richard has been interested in mills since his youth and began restoring his first mill at age 17. He has worked on numerous mills as a millwright and has built his own mill at South Walsham.

My father was brought up in Caister-on-Sea and from his early teenage years his main passion was ornithology. He spent a lot of time around the Breydon Water area and I would often go out on the marshes with him, but rather than looking at the birds, I was far more interested in the old drainage mills although most were in a poor state. When I was about eight my father bought me a book called The English Windmill by Rex Wailes and I was particularly keen on the chapters on Ashtree Farm drainage mill and the Saxtead Green post mill.

In the 1960s I saw a picture in the Eastern Daily Press of a post mill at Syleham in north Suffolk, and I plagued Dad to go and see it although it had stopped working and was getting decrepit. The 1987 hurricane smashed it to bits but it was this mill that really fired my interest in post mills in particular.

I became a cartographical draughtsman and did a course in building construction which has proved pretty useful and I tried to get a traditional craft apprenticeship in wheelwrighting or blacksmithing but in the 1970s, no-one was taking youngsters on. I got a job fitting Alfa Laval milking machines which I did until I was 25, and then I became a self-employed dairy engineer which I combined with picking up small repair jobs on windmills.

When I was 17, I acquired the remains of a hollow post mill, called Palmer's Mill. It stood in a reed bed at Acle and was relatively small at 15ft high but had drained two or three acres of meadow. I was given the mill on the understanding that I took it away and fortunately I managed to find a site behind the boatyard at Upton Dyke.

Two good friends, Paul Reynolds and David High, helped me dismantle and transport it to the Upton boatyard and it took me four or five years to restore. That involved repairs to the substructure, pumping gear and mill body and I made new winding tails, a new windshaft and new sails. As well as providing a site, Tim Whelpton, the owner of the boatyard, was always helpful in providing assistance and some of the timber for the sails.

Syleham Post Mill

Palmer's Mill, Acle

While the work on the mill was still underway and I was 19 or 20, I acquired Howard's drainage mill on Halvergate Fleet from the Fairhaven Estate. It was a traditional Broads tower mill with a boat-shaped cap and scoopwheel. It had worked until 1947 but was gradually decaying. The estate was pleased to be rid of it and I repaired it gradually over a period of 20 years, putting in new doors, floors, windows and lintels. I took the cap off and rebuilt it and put in new winding gear.

Gradually my dairy work declined and as interest in mills was growing, I was able to pick up an increasing amount of millwrighting work. My first professional job was on the Herringfleet smock mill for Suffolk County Council, building a new hoodway and carrying out various repairs to the scoop wheel.

In the early years, I had to supplement mill work with other joinery and roofing work and I even produced rocking horses. As there were no apprenticeships I was largely self-taught but I got to know some of the established millwrights especially John Lawn from Caston Mill who was for some time in partnership with Phillip Lennard from Essex. I spent time with them and with Vincent Pargeter during the 1980s and quite a lot rubbed off. I also knew Bob Morse from Repps whom I first met at the age of 10. Bob was ahead of his time when he bought Thurne Mill around 1949 with the aim of restoring it, as mills were still being demolished at the time rather than repaired. He was a great influence.

Palmer's Mill, Upton

I bought the smithy and cottage at Pilson Green, South Walsham, in 1981 to provide a base in the Broads, and I now work on mills all year round. I like to use traditional methods but I use power tools to make things somewhat easier. I do all the timber work and the vast majority of iron work myself including the pattern work, apart from very complicated patterns like a wind shaft, when I'll get a pattern maker to do it.

South Walsham Mill 2017

Working on mills is very labour intensive and the materials can be expensive and difficult to obtain especially oak and other woods, so most of the work these days is reliant on grant aid of some form or another. I am currently working on Stracey Arms Mill which is a Lottery funded project. If the listing of the building is high enough, Historic England will sometimes part fund and Norfolk Windmills Trust has funded numerous mill projects in the past.

I have probably worked on a couple of dozen mills in the Broads. The most important ones have been the St Benet's level mill near Thurne, and salvaging the remains of Clayrack Mill (a hollow post mill) from the marshes at Ranworth where it hadn't worked for a hundred years, and rebuilding it at How Hill as a working mill.

The repair of Ashtree Farm drainage mill was also a Lottery funded project. It's in a place called

Nowhere near Yarmouth and was the last drainage mill to operate in Norfolk until it finished in the great gale of 1953. I did a total overhaul and brought it back to working order. St Olaves Mill is a skeleton mill which I rebuilt and then repaired twice! The first time was when the cap was tipped off in strong winds.

I have always been interested in the styles of different millwrights and the more local mills I have worked on, the more I have learned about their different construction methods and engineering preferences. No two mills are identical.

As Norfolk post mills had all but disappeared – apart from one at Garboldisham on the Norfolk/Suffolk border that is relatively complete and a more recent reconstruction at Thrigby – I decided I would like to build a new post mill incorporating local features and original components from collapsed mills. So in the late 1980s I developed the idea of a post mill at South Walsham with buildings and a dwelling. I started collecting timber, and following the 1987 hurricane I got hold of a number of oak trees that went into some of the framing in the mill. The project has been self-funded and I suppose that is why it has taken so long.

The mill is 44ft to the ridge which is average for a post mill in this area and is based on mill designs in the county around 1830 to 1840. The footings were dug out in 1995, the piers and round house went up in 1996 and I've been working on it ever since. I had someone do the brickwork and some people from the village have helped with the assembly. There has been quite a lot of interest locally and it's rather been adopted as the village mill which is pleasing. It will stand out even more once the sails are on.

Over the years I have collected various steam engines and vintage tractors and more recently I have become interested in traditional farm wagons and have rescued a few – sometimes from the bonfire. The idea is to develop a museum alongside the mill. We have open days in July and last year we had over 200 people in three hours.

I think that we will retain the majority of the mills in the Broads but we may fail to keep their authenticity. It is difficult to obtain the materials to maintain them and the traditional skills are now very scarce; there are perhaps 10 or 12 millwrights in the country. Millwrights have to be adaptable because it's not just timber work or just engineering but a combination of all kinds of skills. Mills have always been a passion of mine and I think it is a passion for most people who work on mills in this country; it is not something you go into just as a job.

CHAPTER 4

Marsh

- MARSHMEN
- AGRICULTURE
- ANIMAL HEALTH & KNACKERING
- REED CUTTING & THATCHING
- CANTLEY SUGAR BEET
- OTHER MARSH ACTIVITIES

Horsey Mill and marshes

Laughter brings life to the marshes

(1930s – 1990s)

Bill Lacey
(1927–2021)

HALVERGATE

Born in Reedham, Bill was a well-known marshman on the Halvergate Marshes for many years.

I was born in Reedham but before I went to school we lived on a wherry for a couple of years; it was moored at Cantley and was quite cosy. Then Father took a job with the East Norfolk Rivers Catchment Board and we moved to Haddiscoe and I went to school in Lowestoft. I took the train, which didn't take long as we lived alongside the station. At the outbreak of war my sister and I were evacuated to Barnham Broom and Mother used to come over from Haddiscoe on a Saturday. I left school when I was 14 and began looking after cattle, starting at 6am to do the milking with another cowman, and then we did the milk round.

I carried on like this until just before I married. I had been working on the marshes in Cantley for a time but when I was offered a job by another marshman at Berney Arms, I grabbed it. There were 400 acres to look after and I worked alone and was really in charge of myself. The main things I did were the dykes and drains in the wintertime and tending the cattle in the summer. I would get up in the morning and decide where I needed to be first. If it was the dykes, I would do the middle one first, then all the little dykes afterwards, and I had to walk a fair distance as it wasn't possible to drive or ride a bike.

I lived on the marshes. There were four houses for marshmen all addressed as Berney Arms – they were on the old road as you came from Halvergate towards Lock Gate Mill, before the A47 was put in. The four marshmen were Freddie Mutton at Manor House, Carter on Sutton's level, another Carter further down and then me – there was also another marshman on the other side of the Fleet. My house was nice and it's still there today. We had no electricity so we used candles and oil lamps but we did get a generator eventually and we used a Rayburn for heating. We drank rainwater right up until my daughter was born when the nurse said that we had to have fresh drinking water.

We shopped in Yarmouth once a week and began bringing two milk churns which we filled with water and carted back from Yarmouth station. We eventually managed to scrounge enough to get a motorcar but before that, my father-in-law used to meet us on the Acle New Road and we would walk the mile and a half across the marshes with the churns. We used the water sparingly and would still wash using the rainwater.

Our post was delivered by the marshman at Berney Arms, Mr Hewitt. After he had seen to his cattle, he would walk across and put the letters through the door, even in winter. The children started school when we were in the marsh house

The milk round

at Berney Arms and Peter used to walk the mile and a half to the New Road, where the bus would pick him up. He did this twice and then he was late home; something happened with the bus driver and he dropped the poor little fella off in the wrong place. Peter walked over the first marsh, then along the railway line and was heading for home when I came across him. He was very young, only five, and hadn't been to school above a week, but he got home in the end. Times were quite hard with the children holiday-wise but we used to go down to Breydon Water at low tide where there was a sandbank, so it was like a beach.

We were loaned a horse for the winter months. It spent the winter with me and in the summer it went back to run on the sea front at Yarmouth, taking customers up and down; not a bad life for a horse. Snow and ice were the worst for us. One time when we lived in the marsh house, we couldn't get out but I managed to get Bunns from Yarmouth to bring a lorry from the A47 right across to the house – it was so hard but they brought food and everything for us.

The work day would start about 8am, and if I was clearing the dyke I would take a scythe, a meg and a short cutter with me – a meg is a long pole with a scythe on the end and a short cutter is another type of scythe, only bent. We got used to carrying them. The scythe would be sharpened every hour and a half using a rubbing stone which I carried around with me. I never wore gloves or had any accidents, and I've still got all my fingers! These were our three main implements, nothing mechanical, until later when they brought in some drain cutters that were put behind the tractor and we drove it along like a little plough. I used them for a time until we were no longer allowed to do the drains as they wanted the water levels to be higher.

When I was clearing the dykes and drains and looking after the cattle I would walk a fair distance each day. If I walked to Halvergate from the house that was three miles there and back, and I would tend the cattle once a day, sometimes twice, so that could be twelve miles. Eventually, after two or three years we managed to save enough to buy a jeep. I got a left-hand drive jeep from an auction near Norwich which ran on petrol and it made a tremendous difference. I wouldn't see anyone during the day; I would take a snack and my wife would have a hot meal waiting when I came home.

After Berney Arms I moved on to work for Sutton's Executors, on the condition that they sold us a piece of land to build a bungalow at Halvergate. I was still working with cattle as Sutton's had Irish cattle coming over weekly via Birkenhead. We used to refer to them as 'marsh cattle' but they were no different to the ordinary ones.

Sutton's had their own grazing marshes and the cattle went out on the marshes at the end of April until about October. There were some sheep about too and I had some of my own. The only time I thought that it was a bit too much and didn't want to go out, was when it was snowing. We had some hard winters especially around 1962 and 63 and we couldn't work for a long time as the marshes were frozen, so that was hard. We didn't have any special clothing to keep us warm and dry, just the normal.

I remember one Christmas when we were at Berney Arms, everywhere was frozen and I went to feed the sheep and they had gone. They had walked down towards Halvergate but the dog went down and rounded them up. I think they had got almost to the Manor House.

We were paid once a year for clearing the drains and dykes, it was like piece work and we got so much a chain. I can't tell you exactly how much we were paid but it was peanuts. The measurements were all passed down and when a marshman left, he gave you the measurements so you knew roughly what was what.

Over time as more mechanisation came in, working hours on the marshes got less so it became important to find other ways to make a living and I began looking after other people's sheep, tending to them like I did with the cattle. Initially I didn't do any shearing but later on when we moved to Halvergate I hired some marshes and got my own sheep, and then I did some shearing, learning mostly by trial and error. The wool went off to Stamford, so that was a reasonable bit of extra income.

I also had my own cattle, the number varying depending on what I had reared during the winter, how many small calves I had, and whether I sold them in the spring or waited until they got fat. I also picked up work like checking and mending fences and doing maintenance for local land-owners.

Other marshmen also had extra jobs. Yoiton Hewitt looked after the Breydon Pump as well as the one near Ashtree Farm. I looked after a pump at Stracey for a time, just making sure that the water levels were right – if it was getting too high I'd pump the excess into the river.

As I got to the end of my working life the biggest change I'd seen was caused by the RSPB who wanted the water level to be high. This meant the dykes were no longer cleared as they thought that was better for nature, I suppose. In the early 1970s the Ministry brought in diggers and the marshmen no longer cleared the middle dykes, so they took our work away. It was the beginning of the end for the marshmen as we didn't have as much work to do. There used to be nine or ten marshmen between Reedham and Yarmouth and as they retired, nobody replaced them, and by the time I retired there was only one still working.

When I first went on the marshes there were plenty of coypu but it was thought that they were destroying the river banks. They did make a mess, but not that much. The government paid a shilling a tail so we would take our guns when we were clearing out the dykes and drains. I suppose they thought it helped conservation but I don't agree. I think that grazing was the important bit, the cattle helped with the grazing and we cut all the thistles so the marshes looked clean, but they don't today. The marshes seem empty now, hardly any cattle. It's all horses.

Bill shearing sheep

Four generations of marshmen

(1940s – 2017)

Brian Mace
(b. 1951)

HADDISCOE

Brian grew up on Haddiscoe Island and also worked there as a marshman, following in his father's footsteps. He describes the life and its isolation.

My family has lived on the marshes for generations. My grandfather, Reginald Mace, was a marshman on the Reedham level and he had a large family of four boys and four girls. Times were very hard then and they had to live off the land. During the war he would shoot starlings and one day he got 76 in one shot. He would take them to Pettitt's in Reedham and got about a penny a piece for them. During the war, an American bomber crashed at Reedham and he helped to carry some of the crew to Reedham on a gate used as a stretcher.

My father became a marshman working on the opposite side of the River Yare to my grandfather. He went over for a week's work mowing thistles and stayed all his life, and was awarded the BEM for helping to prove that copper deficiency in the grass affected the cattle. He also had a hard life and lived off the land shooting ducks, rabbits and hares, but we had a good life.

My mother, Violet, was the stationmistress at Berney Arms and also looked after the Post Office, she was the driving force behind Father and shared the hard times. Her grandfather was a marshman, her uncle was a marshman and her father was a ganger on the railway looking after the section of the track from Great Yarmouth to Reedham. When we lived on Haddiscoe Island she used to make butter and take it by boat to Reedham to sell. We didn't have a telephone so we had to go to Reedham to use the phone box if any of the animals were ill; then later on Grandfather got a phone on his side of the river so we could go there.

I was born at Berney Arms and lived there until I was five. Then we moved to Upper Seven Mile House on Haddiscoe Island where I had to go to school by boat. To begin with my father and grandfather Albert rowed me up the river to Reedham, then later on we got a little motor launch and when I was 14, I drove myself to school. I was an only child and all on my own on Haddiscoe but some of the boys from Reedham would walk down the river wall and give a shout when they were opposite the house, and we would set off down the river for the boat and have a few hours together.

I wasn't keen on school. In the big winter of 1963 the river froze so I had a bloomin' good excuse for not going! I went shooting nearly every day of the week I think. I had a 410 gun at the time and I would go after ducks and pheasants and whatever was about and they ended up on the table.

Violet Mace lighting the lamp at Berney Arms station

Haddiscoe 2019

We had a run of snares on the river wall to catch coypu and we also used to shoot them. I had a little Scottie terrier that absolutely hated them and she would swim in the dyke when one was in the water and wait until it came up and grab it at the back of a neck and kill it. We got a lot of coypu like that. This was before the coypu campaign started and the owner of the marshes used to pay us sixpence a tail to kill coypu because they did so much damage to the banks, and when cattle put their leg in a coypu hole, it would break. When the coypu campaign started, they more or less took the credit for our work. I once shot one during the hard winter of 1963 but the tail had frozen off so I was most annoyed to miss out on my sixpence!

When I left school, I did various jobs before deciding to go self-employed and I began reed cutting for several years; it was hard work and I earned every penny but it was a good time. The reed from the Island was some of the best in Norfolk and it went all over England, there was even an order for some to go to Disneyland in America.

We used an Allen Scythe when I started cutting reed before going for a Mayfield cutter which was a bit bigger and quicker but by the end, we were using an Olympia rice harvester that actually cut the reed and bound it. The main disadvantage with the Olympia was you had to cut all the strings, clean it all out and then retie it all again. It was very hard on the hands.

We had one patch of reed that was 500 yards from the river wall and we used to carry the reed off the rond, over the top of the river wall and stack it at the base. We tried many ways to do it faster. We started by putting ten bunches into one big bunch, hoisting them on our backs and walking. Then I made a sledge out of some old gates and we pulled that across the rond with a tractor and long rope. But the rope would stretch and the tractor could be half way across the marsh before the sledge moved, then it came in a hurry if it came at all. It was different when my father and grandfather did reed cutting, they used a hand scythe, tied it up and carried it off, but it took a lot longer.

In the past most people had to walk around the marshes but a few had a horse. My uncle used a horse to go round the cattle and for shopping they had a horse and cart. Eventually he got a bullnose Morris motor car to get about. Life was very hard on the marshes then. I can remember Father had to walk two miles to get the cattle off the lorry, then walk them to where they came over to Haddiscoe and then down to the marsh.

I packed up reed cutting and began looking after cattle on the marshes after the Pettengill family moved out and I took over their level. When they hire out the marshes, they hire the marshman with the marsh so I was taken on automatically and I've been doing it ever since. These days I start as early as I can, about 6am, and go round the cattle using a four-wheel drive: a lot easier! Some people use a quad but I prefer a four-wheel drive. I check the cattle to make sure they are all in good health and nothing is wrong, no colds or pneumonia and no foul in the foot. If there is a problem I phone the owners and it is up to them to get the vet in and sort things out or take the cattle home.

The cattle calve on the marshes and sometimes we have to help them. If a cow is in trouble I automatically call the vet and if a caesarean is needed then it's done down here and we'll cart water and everything down so all is clean and fresh. I work with the cattle for 30 weeks a year and in the winter I mend the gates and posts and supervise the dykes being cleaned out; they use a digger nowadays where we used to do it all by hand. There are also sheep on the marshes and I have a farmer who owns marshes and has anything from 300 to 500 sheep as the marshes are dry enough for them.

I think the marshes are going downhill all the time as there are not so many cattle to graze them. There used to be only dairy cattle down here but now we've got suckler herds and smaller numbers. They don't seem to put the money back into the marshes as they used to; there is less thistle-spraying and thistle-cutting now.

My grandfather, my father and I were marshmen and my son is still on the marshes but working for the mink control project. They are getting on top of the mink quicker than they did with the coypu. Mink just kill for the sake of killing and will kill rabbits and chickens and not eat them, they'll get into fish ponds and kill the fish and they are spreading into places like Bradwell as well.

Haddiscoe Island

(2001 – 2006)

Roy Baker
(b.1935)

HADDISCOE

Roy studied zoology and has been a naturalist from a young age. With two friends he undertook a five-year study at Haddiscoe in 2001 ahead of flood alleviation works. He describes the New Cut and his encounters with a well-respected marshman.

In 1832 it was decided to cut the 'New Cut', as it is called, from Reedham Ferry to St Olaves. This was to stop the ships from Lowestoft having to go all the way down the Waveney to Breydon Water and up again, and it became the 'New Cut' in six months, creating Haddiscoe Island. There were a number of winding creeks on the marsh and the local owners started to build dykes and slowly it moved from salt marsh to grassland. On a map the dykes are straight lines and they are the boundaries on the island from the 18th century. It is thought that the Dutch built the walls as there are no bushes or hedges and grazing cattle and sheep are kept in by the dykes.

Derek Howlett and I first met Bob Mace on Haddiscoe Island in October 2001. I knew what the east coast was like so we were wrapped up but Bob was there in a woollen shirt open to the waist. He was so immune to it. He was a remarkable character and had a hard life. He grew up on the marshes and he described how each year they would have to work on some of the dykes. They could do about 200 yards in a day pulling out weeds and cutting the banks. If they had to get rid of mud, they would just wade in, fill up buckets and throw it out. Bob said:

'Dyke clearance is phased normally over five years but often it's on a needs-only basis. In earlier times the dykes were maintained by marshmen using traditional Norfolk hand tools: meags, didles, cutters and cromes. Winter work was to draw dykes – this involved cleaning 13 miles of dykes and 18 miles of drains to keep them clear of weeds. It was all knee and wrist work.'

Summer work was looking after the cattle and sheep. A couple of marshmen and a shepherd live off the island but Brian (Bob's son) is the only marshman living on the system now.

As it is a salt marsh there are two sluices to keep the water suitable for the cattle and sheep to drink. The water coming down from the Waveney is fresh water and sea water comes in from Breydon Water. The fresh water will float on top of the salt water, so at the height of the tide the sea water is coming in and the fresh water is still going out, one is flooding and one is ebbing. The sluices

New Cut looking towards the River Yare. The river bank drops down to the main soke dyke on right.

Six Mile House Mill, Haddiscoe, 2021

at the top are opened and fresh water is then pumped around the dyke system and keeps the level of salt water very low so that cattle and sheep can drink it. This management has been going on from time immemorial.

Bob recalled that after the floods of 1953 he lived in the Six Mile House Mill:

'We nailed sacks round the walls to keep out the draughts and there was an old grate in which we burned scrap wood to keep warm. We only went home to get fresh grub. Two of us worked four-hour shifts using a tractor and an admiralty pump to clear the water, for seven weeks!'

In 2013 there was another huge surge which overtopped the river walls and the whole of Haddiscoe was under salt water. It overtopped again in 2014. The actual rivers are much higher than the land – if you go to the Mace's cottage you can look up and see the New Cut and the boats passing by higher than the cottage!

Derek Howlett, Keith Clark and I got involved with the island in 2001 when the Broadland Environmental Services started to rebuild flood defence walls in the Broads. On Haddiscoe, the first defence is the rond before you come to the wall and the fold behind the wall. There is always a soke dyke after the fold so any water that overtops or seeps through the wall can collect in the dyke.

We were asked if we could survey the dykes on the island and also on the other side of the River Yare before they started work. Well… you're talking about 12 miles around the river wall and 100 miles of dykes! It took five years to do because often we couldn't walk into the fields because there were bulls and we were not brave enough!

We produced a report and it is all about how the landscape developed but remains largely unchanged, and how conservation and land management for farming can live together.

Best job ever out on the marshes

(2011– 2019)

Paul Remblance
(b.1964)

HADDISCOE

Paul began working with cattle on the Haddiscoe marshes in 2011 and says that marshmen never seem to retire.

When I was about nine years old I started going down to Norton marshes with my dad to shoot duck from the first of September. We shot mallard and geese which would have been greylags or Canadas and we always ate them. We were a family of eight and that used to feed us all. We would go shooting about once a fortnight. My dad was on the marshes all his life but only for the shooting. After leaving school I did lots of jobs in Lowestoft, Beccles and Southwold before coming to work on the marshes with Gerry Meadows, the Beccles marshman.

I didn't have any training but I knew a little bit and learned a lot as I went on. The cattle get New Forest eye disease, foul of foot and other things going wrong with them and we are responsible for checking them and reporting what we see to the farmers and normally the farmers come down and give us a hand. We catch the cattle, put them in a crush, put a halter round them, pull it nice and tight and get some cream in their eyes or inject inside the eye or the foot for foul foot.

I look after cattle for whoever hires the marshes and this year I've worked for about seven people. At the moment we are looking after more than 500 cattle, some beef and some dairy cows. The farmers get them to market but we get them into the pen ready for pick-up.

Cattle give birth on the marshes and sometimes we jack the calves out. I've had about five born on the marshes this week and the farmers came and took them home; the cows sometimes stay on the marshes but this year there was less grass so they go to where there is more and the cows can make plenty of milk.

The wildlife is really nice. We see a lot of hares, ducks, geese and all sorts of different things coming in. I've had 12 hares running around one day and hurtle right past me. I've seen a little leveret born and I've seen Chinese water deer born – they are breeding like anything now. They are not like coypu yet but they are getting that way and they can put us off when we're getting cattle in. We might get the cattle through the gate then a deer runs out and they'll turn back again! I've been on the marshes early in the morning and seen a marsh harrier fly off with a snake, wiggling about in the sky. There are quite a few marsh harriers now.

During the day we only see other marshmen or we may see the odd jogger coming through the tracks. It's nice to be out there early in the mornings and in the evenings. That's lovely. I'd like to see the marshes keep going the way they are but with the changes, you never know. They could become flooded in time; I think they would let them flood. But marshmen don't seem to retire, they just keep going.

Cows for company

(1970s – 2017)

Tony Clarke
(b. 1945)

HADDISCOE

Tony has lived on the marshes since childhood and used to go out shooting with his father. Later he became a marshman on Haddiscoe.

When I was a child my father was allocated some coypu cages and became a coypu trapper and we used to help skin them and send the skins to Wisbech. We'd get ten bob, sometimes thirty or whatever we could get. Sometimes we'd boil up the meat in an old copper outside – it was really good grub, like rabbit really. I remember one particular coypu which was dead but the belly was moving, I think the dog had got to it. So we cut it open and took out three babies which were born with all their fur and their eyes open, they had everything. We took them home and kept them as pets in a run for a few months until they escaped.

We used to do a fair bit of shooting and swimming and general messing about, and then they dug a nice soke dyke and we swam there. I shall never forget one boy who couldn't swim but would come down and watch. One day he said, 'Let me have a go'. I said, 'Alright, go on boy, dive in'. So he dived in but he never came up. We hunted about and found him stuck in the mud. We had to pull him out and get him going, he nearly drowned. We got him sorted out and away he went again. We also used to swim across the River Yare and try to beat the Reedham Ferry; we normally did because the ferry would drift down the river on the tide while we managed to swim straight across. They were really good times.

I got a job as a cowman at Norton Hall about 1966 and worked there for seven or eight years and later I put in for a marshman's job on Haddiscoe and was lucky enough to get it, but on condition I got a phone. I did, and I gave him the bill. And I've been here some 40-odd years and had some good times.

Basically, a marshman spends most of his time looking after cattle on the marshes. We don't have to feed them because they live on the grass but we move them about from one marsh to another, so while a bit of grass is being fed off, another one is growing back. Cows like the reed that grows on the side of the dyke and will go for that first; there is some goodness in it that they like. We have copper deficiency on the island which means most autumns the farmers supply us with mineral buckets containing calcium, iron and copper. We used to give the cows an injection of 5ml of copper but it's put in the mineral licks now.

If the cattle are ill, I ring the farmer and he deals with it or he will ask me to get a vet out to them. We do get wooden tongue and foul foot along with a bit of mastitis, also New Forest eye which is an infection in the eye.

At the end of March we have a marsh letting at the Bell Hotel in St Olaves where Gaze, the Auctioneers from Diss, let 1,000 acres of grazing in parcels ranging from 5-30 acres. They are all dyked off as we don't have any fences. The farmers come to the marsh letting and the highest bidder pays anything from £50 to £100 an acre and they hire us as well for 30 weeks from the beginning of April to the end of October. Sometimes it runs over a bit when the weather is nice and they let the cattle stay down on the marsh a little longer.

Tony on the marsh

I have my patch of 600 acres to look after and sometimes I have had almost 1,100 head of cattle. When they hire us we set our fees. It isn't really enough but we're happy and we keep jogging along, and making a living.

I had one particular old farmer who gave nothing away but he once gave me an aniseed ball and once he turned around and gave me 50p. 'Here you are, Clarke, here's 50p', he said, 'you've done a good job getting them cattle in there'. I went home and said to the wife, 'The old man ha' give me 50p tonight'. I went through all my pockets but I couldn't find it so I thought I would have a look round the next morning, but I couldn't see it anywhere – I say to this day that the old man had it on a bit of string!

We control the water level with an electric pump and I look after it for the Drainage Board. I only run it in the winter as I want the water in the dykes for the cattle in the summer. It is a good old pump and can pump out 30 tonne a minute – that is moving some water. In case of flood we have the pump going and going. I used to clear the mill dyke years ago. I used a long-handled knife to cut out the reed and then used cromes to clear the dyke so the water could get to the pump alright. We laid the waste on the side of the dyke but the cattle didn't eat it as it was just little bits. In the winter we cleared the foot drains to help the water run off the marsh. We had a tractor come and it pulled a gadget a bit like a plough which would throw out a little muck from the foot drains. We used to get a quid or two for doing that. But they stopped all that, just as they have stopped about everything now.

In 1976 we had a drought and we couldn't get water up and out of the river. The water in the dykes turned brackish and wrong and the cattle which drank it got saltwater poisoning and died. Saltwater poker we called it. We had well points sunk about the marshes, going down 60ft to get to water and I went round with a little pump hooking it onto the standing pipe and filling up the bowsers. Then with a tractor and bowser I went round the marshes filling the water tanks. I did it twice a day, seven days a week; I nearly lived down there for a while.

The cattle belong to a lot of different people so the dairy cattle have freeze brands, which are numbers frozen on their bums, and big ear tags, either yellow or orange, with a herd number. Every farmer has his own herd number so if we get a mix-up then we have the ear tags to help sort them out. We know the number in a herd and how many are on each marsh so if one is missing we'll have a hunt round. It might be in the dyke or with someone else's cattle because they can walk through the dykes and they can swim. One year I had a cow in a cut in the river and we had to get the fire engine out. They put straps on it and we pulled it out like that.

As for the future of the marshes, I'm 72 now and I don't know how many more years I can keep going or who is going to take over when I do pack up but I'd like to think the marshmen will still be here. The work probably hasn't changed in a hundred years; cattle have been on the island all that time and people have looked after them. But I don't know whether it will continue another hundred years, the number of animals has decreased so much.

I can remember when I was first started on the island I had a lot of black-and-white Friesians. This year I have just one dairy herd, whereas, 20 years ago I had seven or eight different dairy herds to look after. I understand there are now about eight herds of Friesian milking cows left in Norfolk! I did have a few sheep once but not now, I don't know why. Horses have never been allowed on the island and I'm not sure if there is some law against it. However, the marsh letting catalogue says, 'No horses'. They do have them down on Haddiscoe Dam and Acle Straight though.

It's obviously been a very varied job in terms of what I do and also in the amount of time I spend on the island. It is very seasonal and you never know the amount of work you are going to have. But once the cattle have all gone home I can spend a bit of time with my Labradors and we go out shooting. I certainly would recommend the job of marshman and I would especially recommend it to my grandson, but the wages are going be the thing. Nowadays people want double what I earn, they can't live on what I can, so I don't think he'll take it on – but I would recommend it. If heaven's as good as them marshes then that'll do me. Bury me down there!

Farmer, marshman – always animals

(1961 – 2018)

Paul Harvey (b. 1946)

ALDEBY

Paul was born on a marsh farm and with his twin brother he was involved with the work from an early age. He now works on the marshes as a marshman mostly looking after horses.

I lived at Waterheath Farm in Aldeby in a cottage with my parents and my twin brother, Peter. As a boy of seven or eight I used to help my dad who was a horseman, and sometimes I helped with the ploughing. If they were drilling I would harrow in behind them and sometimes I flattened the clods in front of them. I didn't hold the plough, I mostly walked with Dad beside it. I used to do a lot of harrowing, flat rolling and ridge rolling (or rib rolling) of the corn and barley. Flat rolling is when the corn is up and you squash down stones and crack the clods so when the cutter cuts the corn, there's nothing to blunt the knives.

Our school used to keep pigs and I looked after them, mucking them out, feeding them and cleaning rather than doing lessons, I didn't like school at all. We kept pigs and cows at home too and I used to look after the stock before I went to school and when I came back. I enjoyed working and I've been interested in animals and livestock ever since. We used to kick a football about and sometimes we met up with the gang but I didn't have a lot of leisure time. I never really worried about that because most of my time was taken up with the animals.

I left school at 15 in 1961 and my brother Peter and I went straight into the farm business. In 1978 we were made redundant and I worked for the NRA (National Rivers Authority) as a lorry driver. My brother went self-employed and did relief milking. At the same time, my brother and I kept sheep and cattle down at Whitehouse Farm which we started renting. I left the NRA when I was 61 and took on my brother's job as a marshman after he died and I've been doing it ever since.

We kept sheep as they were the best thing going at the time and because the marsh grass was a bit rough where we were. Sheep were the best way to make better and firmer grass and tidy the marshes. We gradually went into cattle and purchased suckler cows, either Hereford or Hereford-cross Friesians. We also had pedigree Simmental bulls and beef bulls which were mostly sold on as store cattle. We would take them to the Norwich cattle market and try to sell well on the day.

Foot-and-mouth disease caused problems with moving the cattle. We had to get a licence from vets through the Ministry and take the cattle to the abattoirs ourselves. We didn't have too much bother though, we just disinfected the straw, our boots and all the vehicles that went on and off the premises. It only lasted one winter through to the spring and then the restrictions were lifted.

I don't look after many cattle now. Instead I've had 60 horses in from Hillside Sanctuary these last few years. They are no more trouble than cattle and if there is a problem you just ring up and they come

Ponies on the marsh

down and deal with it. However, horses do pull the grass a little shorter and you do end up with tufts, and they don't feed the grass as well as cattle. I have cattle and horses in separate parts of the marshes and I go twice a day to check their health.

Four or five years ago there were very few horses on marsh grass, but now there is more demand and the owners are getting more money for the rent. The horses go back to Hillside at the end of the season as the marshes become too wet. Then the following April, the owners return to bid for the annual marsh lettings at the Bell, St Olaves. I try not to get too attached to the horses because you know they will go, but you do have your favourites. You'll get the one that stands at the gate waiting for you and if you give it an apple it will be there waiting for you every time, so I don't encourage it, and I don't do it.

I've enjoyed my life, well most of it. I was self-taught and I learned mostly after I left school. I wouldn't want my son to be a herdsman though; he's earning more than he ever would in agriculture. I don't know what will happen in the future. I just hope there will always be cattle and we don't all go vegetarian!

The sugar beet story: farming

(1944 – 1974)

Robert Fransham (1930–2012)

FREETHORPE

Robert Fransham worked for 30 years on a mixed farm in Freethorpe. He describes working with sugar beet and cattle and how machinery increasingly took over much of the arable work.

I left school at age 14. There were seven of us children so Mother had a full time job. My father was a farm worker, the same as I was going to be, and my three older brothers also worked on the farm for a time and then went into various jobs at Yarmouth and Norwich. I started work on my birthday in 1944 on the same farm as my father, doing the sort of general jobs done by boys, and my first job was taking a horse to the blacksmith.

It was a good time to be working on the land as it was the last year of the war when the Americans were doing their daylight raids and we were out in the fields weeding. They took off from Seething and all the aerodromes round and they just formed up until they got hundreds of them up there, and off they went. And in the afternoon we'd see them come back again. They didn't come back in formation like when they went out, and you'd see them shoot flares sometimes when they had injured on board. It made you forget you were at work – you didn't think about the number who had been killed, that didn't come into it really.

There was haymaking in the spring, then hedge trimming, and at harvest all you did as a boy was drive the horses to the stacks of beet and just keep things going for the horses. I also had to stay with them at lunchtime when they had their feed. Boys didn't get involved with sugar beet; we just did straw carting and looked after the animals and that sort of thing. Normally, apart from harvest time, we went home at lunchtime as we lived five minutes away by bike – lunch was an hour and a quarter.

We picked up the job as we went along. There were perhaps two or three boys together and I can always remember our foreman saying, 'One boy is as good as a man, two boys is as good as half a boy, three boys is no good at all'. And that was right… you know what it's like! When we were 18 we started hoeing sugar beet and became more involved with the harvest and everything else.

They used to drill beet pretty thick at one time so we had to chop them out and single them, and take any weeds out as well – most areas were fairly clean but there were rather too many beet, we thought. As time went on they began to drill single cell beet seed or monogerm and the drill could single-plant about 10in apart. This made for easier work but they didn't pay quite as much for that. They began spraying for weeds as well so we didn't get the rubbish and that also made the job easier, and not quite so well paid.

One of my first jobs during harvest was riding on the binder. That was quite nice but dirty – you'd get plenty of dust. Binding was when we tied up the sheaves and people would put them together in shocks so they dried out before they were carted. Then the combines came in and I worked

Shocks of grain stalks

on those. The first combines used to bag the corn on top which wasn't very good. It was dusty work and whichever way you went round a field, there was one side where you got covered with dust and at the end of the day you were in a bit of a state. Another job then was going round collecting the sacks for the trailer to take to the barn. It was very labour intensive until it got so that it all went straight into the trailer – much better.

It was the same thing again with the beet harvest. When I first started beet was all dug by hand using a digger. In September the ground was so hard that it used to play our hands up and we finished up with bandaged wrists. But, as the season went on it got easier to dig, the wrists got better and we got over it. The digger was a wooden handle with a v-shaped piece on the bottom and we just had to ram it in the ground beside the beet, lever and pull it up, hopefully without breaking too much off the bottom. Then we went round chopping the tops off – we'd hold them in one hand and cut the tops off with the other and throw them in heaps. Again, very labour intensive. That improved when they brought in the squeezer, a machine that moved two rows of beet together, pulling them out of the ground, and left them in a row. That took a lot of the hard work out of it. Then the harvesters came in and all we had to do then was dig the corners so they could turn round!

When I first started there were about 15 men, 12 horses and one tractor and that's all they had for years. The farmer liked his horses so we kept them for several years after other people were nearly all tractors. His idea was to employ more people as they were needed with the horses. That worked a treat but the wages weren't the highest. We had a job but we didn't earn as much as some other people. It was about £6 a week in the 1960s and that slowly went up a few shilling a year. By the time I left it was up to about £9.60 – that don't sound a lot now! It was better when we had piecework like hoeing or pulling sugar beet because we could earn twice as much then.

As a rule there was a gang of ten of us for the hoeing and we all worked more or less together doing the same amount of work – that worked alright. However, when we took up the sugar beet we were more individual and did our own acre, working at our own speed. Sometimes two of us worked together and we worked quickly doing what we could. It really played up the wrists and later on I suffered from carpal tunnel. Hoeing was better – that just made our backs ache!

We also worked on wheat, barley and oats and there was one field of clover a year for the horses. For about two years after the war we grew flax or linseed, as they call it now. It was grown for the fibre, not the seed, and we used to pull it up by the root. They took the whole plant miles away, but where it went, I don't know.

When I first started we did a 45-hour week with a Saturday morning. That slowly came down to a five-day week. We had one foreman who looked after two farms so he would give the chaps their orders at Halvergate and then bike to Freethorpe to give us our orders, so we always started an hour later and at harvest time we would work until dark. They had a price for the harvest which was the equivalent of three weeks work, so the quicker we got it done the better and we tried to finish in a fortnight by working to 8.30pm – a good long day.

Transporting sugar beet

The owner had a lot of cattle and once the sugar beet was finished there wasn't a lot to do apart from feed them. In October the cattle went into the bullock sheds and were fed on sugar beet tops to start with, then wet pulp from the sugar factory and finally dry pulp in the latter part of the year. We would also do some regular straw carting to keep the litter dry and that kept us busy most of the winter until about March/April, when they were sold off as fat cattle.

The cattle were imported from Ireland and it was a boy's job to drove them from Reedham Station either to the farms to be fattened up or, during the summer, down onto the marshes. We used to go from Reedham, through Wickhampton to Berney Arms. I don't know how we kept going all day – we were running about for hours at a time. But very often they were late coming in so we would take them from Reedham to Freethorpe, put them on the meadow behind the school and sort them out in the morning – they were all marked so we were able to sort them into their right group. They were shipped from Ireland to Birkenhead and the poor things were often a bit thirsty by the time they arrived. There could be 200 cattle sometimes and we had to hold them in the yard while we unloaded the rest, and there could be several trucks… That was quite good fun at times.

I finished up on the farm feeding the bullocks as my winter job, seven days a week. That wasn't too bad, apart from 1963 when we had a bad winter and every morning the pipes were frozen. The only way to thaw them out was to dig up warm muck and put it round the end of the tank. It was hard work to keep the bullocks watered but we kept going. Food wasn't so bad although it wasn't always easy getting it in, but we always had a supply of dry pulp in the barn so there was always something. That lasted from Christmas to March, a long winter. You'd see birds like woodcock round the buildings trying to find food – you never saw them as a rule, but it was a terrible winter.

I left the farm after it was sold and another farmer bought it – he was a good farmer and he put money in if he thought he'd get profit out. We got 10% more money if we were qualified. I thought I was qualified but he said I wasn't so I decided to leave. As it happened my two neighbours were both foremen at Cantley and they said there was a job going, and that was it. I started at Cantley Sugar in October 1974 after 30 years on the farm.

A Neatishead farm boy

(1953 – 1956)

John Horner
(b. 1938)

NEATISHEAD

John left school at 15 and went into farm labouring until he started his national service three years later. He recalls life on the farm over 65 years ago.

I left school in 1953 and went to work at a farm just up the road in Neatishead. One of my winter jobs was to turn seed corn sacks inside out because old corn would hang on to the insides. I'd scrape them off with a piece of wood to be sure that only new corn seed was in the sacks for the next year. Hamilton was the foreman, he was a very big bloke and the two of us did all the arable work and looked after the bullocks and ducks.

After a while I heard that they wanted someone at Irstead Hall so I left to do the ploughing and cultivating there. There was a chap called Bell who we all called Ding Dong and another guy, Teddy, who had been there since doomsday. They still had an old horse, called Prince, and Teddy would sometimes do some light work with him. I was asked to plough a field that went down to a point near where the boardwalk is now and we used to do just one furrow there with a drag plough. It had to be deep to loosen the soil for the sugar beet but I had never learned how to do that point properly. So, I ploughed as best I could and then Ding Dong told Teddy to take some harrows or rollers with Prince and roll the field. When Teddy came back that night he said, 'What the hell you done in the corner of that field?' 'What do you mean?' I said. 'God, you left some furrows there, Prince fell in them and couldn't get out!'

Irstead Hall had a dairy herd with about 70 cows and Rolly, the cowman, would start at 5am to do the milking and then go home for breakfast. I would be working in the fields with the tractor ploughing or cultivating and when he cycled past with his old army greatcoat hanging over his handlebars he would probably be one of the few people I saw all day.

We grew kale for the cows and in the winter we cut them at the root with a hook. Because the leaves are dish-shaped they would be full of ice and would deteriorate quite quickly when cut, so I would just start the tractor and let it run across the field and I'd pile the leaves onto the trailer.

When it came to sugar beet, I used to plough, harrow and disc the field to get a good tilth on it. We would sow rows of beet about 15 inches apart and each seed would put up four or five shoots. When they were about an inch and a half out of the ground we had to chop them out by hand with a hoe and leave one plant every eight or nine inches. We also had a thing called a horse hoe that would go between the rows to cut out any weeds. I was on £2 10s a week then, but me and Teddy would do the sugar beet on a contract basis for about £7 10s per acre. We would get there about 7am and work on separate rows but I could never keep up with him; he'd been doing it all his life and I was only a 16-year-old. One of the fields was on a slight hill and he would gain on me and get to the end of his row, lean on his hoe for a little rest and wait for me to come down the hill. As I reached him he would head off again so I had to chase him all the way back.

We would take bottles of tea wrapped in socks to keep them warm as we didn't have flasks; our sandwiches were in Oxo tins. Teddy used to make me laugh. He often brought pork chops for lunch and as he was always there before me, he would be well into his chop before I sat down. He would open up his Oxo tin, reach into his pocket and get out his penknife, carve off a few bits and put them on a round of bread and then eat, eat, eat; a swig of cold tea and off we went again. I thought, 'One of these days, I'm going to catch you up Teddy', but I never did.

We lifted the beet by hand in all weathers including ice and snow pulling two this side, two that, and placing them on the ground with the roots facing each other. Teddy would go down one side of the row and I would go down the other, cutting off the tops with a hook and loading them onto a trailer to cart down to Irstead Shoals. We would let the tops die back a bit before taking them up to the farmyard to feed to the pigs, bullocks and cows – we didn't use them when they were fresh as it upset the animals' stomachs.

We would load the sugar beet onto a wherry at Irstead Shoals, 40 tons at a time, and Teddy and I did the loading. Luckily most of it was downhill or at least on the level. The wherry would chug off to Cantley Sugar Factory, a three-day round trip, and by the time he came back, we would have another 40 tons ready to chuck on. My brother used to work for another farm up the road and when I was about 13 he would say, 'Come and give us a hand', and he would back the lorry into the field where the sugar beet was always piled up next to the gate. He would drop the sides of the lorry, take the extension bits off the top, and we would throw the beet on until it was as full as we could get it, then the sides went back up and we would continue to chuck the beet up for another 8ft.

On the other side of Irstead Shoals an old guy used to stack up all his reeds for thatching opposite to where we piled the sugar beet. There was a dyke there where they cut a tremendous amount of reed and it made me laugh to see their boat piled up high and the cutters sitting in the back rowing or pushing the boat, not able to see where they were going. Reeds were big business then but I understand that they are not allowed to stack them at the Shoals any more. Recently a chap told me that the reed had to be gone in one day now, he was waiting with some reed for a lorry to pick it up and take it to Bedford.

I had a lovely job in the springtime. There were meadows down by Irstead Shoals where you could see the sails of yachts on the river across the marshes and How Hill in the background. My job in spring was to drain the meadows so the cows and bullocks had more grazing. Where a house is now, there used to be a tin shack with a double-fly-wheel stationary engine attached to an eight-inch pipe to pump the dykes out. It was a bit of a swine to start and a bit temperamental so Ding Dong would tell me to stop down there and make certain the engine kept running, and the water-cooling tank was topped up. You can't have it better: birds singing, engine running and water flowing past you. I would be there all day long. I've told the owners of the house about pumping water off the marshes some 65 years ago and it seems the pipe work is still there but the engine has gone unfortunately.

There are water carriers for the cows still kicking about in the meadows. They were wheeled tanks with a single iron wheel at the front and two at the back. I remember one was in a bit of a state and Ding Dong asked me to paint it. I said that I would need to get inside and was told to stand it on one end to do it. I set to work cleaning off the rust and then I used a no-rust paint and the fumes knocked me out! Luckily, Ding Dong looked out of the kitchen window, 'What's the matter with you?' I'm still here anyway.

When I was 18 I had to do my national service and didn't go back to farm labouring afterwards, but I have been very fortunate to return to my beloved village of Neatishead to retire.

A marshland farmer with Scottish roots

(1920s – 2019)

Peter Cargill
(b. 1955)

NORTON SUBCOURSE

Peter is a third generation farmer in the marshes; he relates how it all began there and how things have changed over the past 100 years.

My grandfather came from Stonehaven in Scotland in 1922, and took up the tenancy here at Norton Hall which is part of the Raveningham Estate. The farm was found for him by his brother Charles who had come down to Norfolk and Suffolk during the First World War to purchase horses for the army. The reason for their move from Scotland to this area was that it was marginally less tough and they brought a way of doing things that allowed them to thrive where others had not perhaps. My grandfather had been a tenant on a small farm and I believe this farm was taken free of rent for the first three years, as it was in a bit of a mess and he was given the opportunity to turn it round.

Grandfather's first winter was in the Cockatrice pub on the side of the River Yare whilst he filled the farmhouse with the seed potatoes he had brought with him to plant in the spring. His wife came down in 1923 and the seed potatoes were discouraged from being in the house. He retired in the late 1940s but lived at Norton Hall until 1966 when he moved into Norwich. My father was born and raised at Norton Hall but when he first married, they lived in the house at High House Farm, also on the Raveningham Estate.

Initially Norton Hall Farm was a traditional farm of about 280 acres on the edge of the marshes. It had poor quality land: marshland to the north, sand and gravel to the south. Grandfather had brought his Ayrshire cattle and they fed out on the marshes but he milked them here. So around the yard there were all sorts of little cubbyholes with five cows in this one and ten cows in that one. He built up the farm and with his brother, he acquired interest in other farms either by way of tenancy or purchase, over a period of 30-40 years. He also took on the tenancies of Carr Farm at Raveningham which is only half a mile down the road and High House Farm, which took the holding up to 688 acres or so.

At that time there were other Scottish farming families moving down to Norfolk and I understand that a number of the Alstons were earlier and the Pattersons were a bit later. They brought a different way of doing things that enabled them to find a way to make a profit: different rotations, more potatoes… I think they also brought with them a willingness to co-operate and share; something that was perhaps not so prevalent in this part of the world at the time.

Brothers, cousins and other families would collectively do things together, and out of that, any number of co-operative organisations eventually appeared, including the Loddon Farmers more recently. Grandfather, his brother and others got involved with breeding cattle and the original AI Centre, prior to being at Beccles, was at the farm at Benacre. The young vet they took on to look after their organisation subsequently became the chief vet at the Milk Marketing Board.

Towards Raveningham 2019

Father was born in 1926 but didn't start work at the farm until 1943/4. The first farm in his own name was when he took over the tenancy at Carr Farm from my grandfather in 1948, and in 1952 he took on the tenancy of Oaks Farm at Bixley, on the Crown Point Estate owned by Timothy Colman. So between the two he farmed about 700 acres in his own right. After the war his older brother George took on a tenancy on the Kirby Cane Estate, Loddon Hall, as well as the High House tenancy which my grandfather had from the Raveningham Estate.

Dairy was a feature on all of these farms and Friesians became a principal interest. Indeed my father was quite successful showing in the late 1950s and early 60s. I always find it interesting that during my grandfather's time the cows were there to scavenge the bits and bobs that were left over from the arable crops: strawberries, raspberries, broad beans, runner beans. But in my dad's time, the emphasis changed and cows became the main business with the rest of the farm there to serve them.

Grandfather had some of the marshland as arable cropping during the war as anything that could be turned into arable was used. Then the 1953 flood did a lot of salt damage on the marsh and it took a while to get it back to grazing. Norton has a mixture of clay marsh and fairly deep peat marsh and there are also fringe marshes, particularly up the River Chet. At one time the family farmed about 750-800 acres of marsh but I now only have about 450.

I am third generation and I spent my childhood at Oaks Farm in Bixley until I was 21. It was predominantly arable with quite light land towards the river and a bit stronger up towards the Loddon Road. It had a chunk of marshland that my dad brought back into production in the 1950s just after they took it on. It had quite deep peat and we grew potatoes there. As a lad I would go around with my father on the marshes and the family thing to do during the summer was to have a picnic lunch on a Sunday and go round the marshes looking at the cattle.

As well as the home marshes at Norton we had young stock on the Haddiscoe Island marshes and a suckler herd on the Nova Scotia marshes at Caister which was still in grass at the time. In the early days at both places, us kids used to get paid a penny a gate to open the gates. If we did the full tour it was, with lunch, a sort of four-hour job with 30 or 40 gates!

As a teenager in 1973, I did a year at Shuttleworth in Bedfordshire on what was referred to as the Farms Course; most were like myself from family farms. I didn't get a certificate but I learned more about life and was a keen participant in all things apart from the educational side; that came a bit later. Prior to Shuttleworth, my education on the farm had been dealing with muck. I would dig it, push it, pump it – all the things that one ends up doing as a lad on a farm. Tractor driving came later.

I went back to the farm and was effectively apprenticed to our farm manager who looked after the cattle business for the whole family. He was a chap called John Francis and I owe him a considerable amount. We worked with the suckler herd at Caister, Uncle George's dairy herd at Loddon Hall, one of my dad's herds at Bixley, the herd at Carr Farm and Grandpa's two herds here at Norton Hall and Heckingham Hall – about 750 cows in six herds. Around this time my father made some changes. My grandfather had died and Crown Point offered Father the opportunity to surrender the tenancy at Oaks Farm and we left in 1975 – the Norwich Southern Bypass was going to cut through the farm whichever way it went.

I suppose one of the big changes on the marshes was in the 1970s. It led to alterations to the drainage and a drop in the water levels, and brought a lot of the marsh into arable production. We ploughed the marshes at Caister through the 1970s. The suckler herd went and a big chunk of the marshes was turned into arable, some of it very good land. The number of drainage pumps increased and the bores amalgamated, and some marshes had the new Archimedes screw pump put in to further increase water management efficiency.

After my Uncle George died, the Loddon Hall tenancy was surrendered and the herd sold. So we then had one herd here at Norton and one at Heckingham. At that stage we were milking about 350 cows, quite a big reduction, but they produced more milk. With the milk quotas and various other things there was a bit of a boom but when prices no longer covered our overheads, we took the pain for a while and then sold the herd.

From about 1989/90, we have managed the marshes for suckler cow grazing. It was originally my first wife's enterprise and it works well; it is absolutely traditional with low input grazing. We run the sucklers through to weaning then the great-nephew of my grandfather's best friend takes all the calves to fatten up. Norton now has a total of about 900 acres of which about 450 acres is permanent pasture and managed under a variety of environmental schemes – either the old HLS system or the new Countryside Stewardship begun in 2018.

In the arable areas around 20% of the land is taken up with a variety of margins and corners and we leave overwinter stubble to provide a food source. We no longer plough any of the marshes at Norton, only at Caister where the main business is potatoes. The soil there is very fertile, it's that wonderful combination of land that will hold moisture but also drains. I like to joke that its subsoil is better than the topsoil at Norton.

When my grandfather first started farming in Norfolk he grew everything, diversified into anything and employed a lot of people. In 1974 when I first started on this farm there were 24 of us, now there are two! The world has changed and we now have to specialize. We have gone from Grandfather growing everything including bulbs, daffodils and tulips to my father growing mint and mustard for Colman's for a while at Oaks Farm. Nothing stays the same. It is circumstance, technology and world politics that dictate change and you either bend or you break, so hopefully we are bending as much as we need.

There's a great tendency to look at marshes and think of them as all being the same but there are differences in the freeboard and also in land type. So when we turned the Norton marshes into arable we had issues with the clay fraction becoming like slurry. Then we ran into problems with sterile brown soil. So when the original set-aside scheme came in, it seemed an ideal opportunity to revert to grass.

We are involved with Natural England and most of them want to make the various schemes work, although people on the phone don't always understand what I'm asking them. The schemes are well thought through but not necessarily well

Redshank

joined up. My current officer understands my view that the object is to get a result and not to tick a box and she reminds me that one of my crops nowadays is birds – which is fine! So if I am going to grow birds, I'm going to do it as well as I can. The implication is that this may become even more important in the future.

My personal view is that there will be periods when the world population's demand for food will outstrip our ability to produce and that will put non-productive land under considerable pressure. This is a very good place to grow food and it's also a very good place to give the environment the room it needs to do its thing. Both have their place but finding that balance is… I don't know.

Two of the indicator species that get picked up on are the brown hare and the grey partridge, both of which we have always had as it suits them. We have seen increased numbers of breeding waders and the lapwing and redshank are being studied on my patch by a UEA and RSPB project to investigate numbers. The British Trust for Ornithology also did some trial work around understanding the survival of small birds and various other birds throughout the winter hunger gap, doing replicated trials of feeding or not feeding over the winter. I then got involved with the project the RSPB asked the UEA to do around predation. This one looked at what impacts on the success of nesting birds, particularly redshank, lapwing and snipe.

Unusually I am a commuting farmer and now live in Norwich with someone else living at Norton Hall. It means my two young children are not immersed in the farm as I was as a child. So I think in terms of Norton Hall, because I'm a tenant, I honestly don't know if either of them will take over from me. They are very young still so I would like to leave doors open for them, so they can choose whether to step through or not.

Farming the marshes

(1932 – 2018)

Richard Basey-Fisher
(b. 1938)

LANGLEY

Richard comes from a long line of farmers. He recalls marsh drainage and catastrophic flooding and his father introducing a bucket plant to milk 'the Gascoyne way'.

My father started farming at Low Farm, Ashby and kept pigs and cattle. About 1932 he took over Lower Farm, where I was born, and began a small dairy herd. He then built up a mixed farm growing sugar beet and cereals as well as a few pigs. His father was born at Hill Farm and was one of four brothers who all went into farming. I don't know how many generations of farmers are in the family but in Ashby St Mary's churchyard there are some interesting tombstones from the late 1800s of my great-great-grandfather and great-great-grandmother; one is feeding the turkeys and one is feeding the geese – both used to be walked from Ashby to London for Christmas. Most of my family has always lived in this small area; my oldest sister still farms at Aldeby, my second sister farms at Burgh St Peter with her husband, and my youngest sister farms at Hempnall.

As a child I can remember getting the cows up with the dogs and keeping a few ducks for the eggs. Then after the war, at age seven or eight, I really started my own thing and my few ducks became 50 with the eggs sold to the local packing station at Loddon. I only went to school to play sport and when I took on Manor Farm at Langley in the spring of 1964, I was on two sticks because I'd torn ligaments in my ankle in a scrum. I didn't go to City College or Easton Agricultural College because my father was unwell so I went back to work on the farm when I was 15.

Father had taken on Hall Farm, Carleton St Peter, in 1946 and I was very involved there, mostly with the cows. I remember carting sugar beet tops and cutting kale by hand for them, and loading it on the trailers ready for the weekend when it was thrown out onto the meadows. We fed it to them both night and day. In winter we hated the job especially when it was cold and wet.

I was never great at ploughing but Father was fortunate as he always had a good ploughman so I helped with the dairy herd. We started off hand-milking with a bucket then Father had a bucket plant put in so we would milk the Gascoyne way; many people may have seen the slogan 'I milk the Gascoyne way'. Father also had a milk round which took quite a bit of our time and I remember doing the round with ten-gallon churns and a two-gallon can, and ladling out the milk with half-pint, pint or two-pint measures. It was unpasteurised but when the Milk Marketing Board was set up we started bottling.

In the late 1940s we changed over to the herring-bone parlour. At one time we ran two herds because TB testing came in and they found some reactors in the herd at Lower Farm, so my father started a completely new herd at Hall Farm using its old bucket parlour along with a pipeline and airline, and we carried buckets in and out of the dairy. We ran the two herds for two years building up the Hall Farm herd and using different trailers to feed the cattle. The old herd was then sold and Father expanded the new herd and parlour and we eventually got up to over 200 cows. They were all Holsteins.

We bought Manor Farm, Langley in 1964 when I married and we came to live here and that brought our acreage up to 500 acres. The previous owner at Manor Farm had got rid of his cows after the marshes flooded and the grass was killed off and he converted the cow sheds and stables for chickens in 1962. I got to 2,000 hens and kept going for 15 years until it was no longer viable, I then invested in cows again. Over time we went up to 980 acres including 300 acres of marshland and we bought more marshes in the late 1980s when prices were very reasonable.

The marshland revolution started about 1965 when various farmers through this valley began cropping their marshes. The previous owner here began ploughing after the flooding with Ministry of Agriculture encouragement and with the various grants available at the time.

We actually under-drained our marshes until plastic piping went in. I remember seeing the machine putting in the trenches with a laser controlling everything to get the correct pitch. Once the marshland began draining we grew sugar beet, wheat and maize and we had a bit of shrinkage that went on for a few years. The marshland was difficult to farm at first because there was so much weed in the peat and soil, then Bethanol came in and we could band spray. I suppose this cropping went on for about 10–15 years. We still crop some of our marshes but because we have had so much shrinkage of the peat, the alluvial part is now exposed to clay, and the clay is either wet or very dry which makes it difficult to get seed to germinate. Some marshes round here have been put back to grass as a result.

The arable side of our farm has changed considerably especially in the size of the machinery. We are still growing a good range of crops such as sugar beet, vining peas, maize for the beef cattle, wheat and malting barley. This is very good land for malting barley and it's now our main upland crop.

Every farm serving this valley had cows but gradually they have all disappeared. I can remember when the road from Carleton St Peter through to Langley and Hardley, and perhaps Chedgrave, had 14 different dairy herds. That dwindled until I was the only one left between Loddon and Norwich on this side of the A146. My dairy herd went in 2015 as a consequence of BSE, unpredictable milk prices and the rise of supermarkets controlling the buyers. We had never milked on the marshes and it became more and more difficult to get the cows to the grass because of the traffic; we had all this grass in the valley but to use it the cows had to walk up to three quarters of a mile each way, every day. Enough was enough and the dairy cows went.

Electrical pumps were put in before my time and gradually the levels of the marshes were lowered. I was Chairman of the Lower Yare Second Internal Drainage Board for several years and that involved running three pumps on the marshes: Claxton and Langley, Monks and Hardley. They pumped the Hardley marsh level over something like 2,800 to 3,000 acres.

In about 2000 the Government decided to do away with all the little drainage boards and we merged to become the Lower Yare and Lothingland Drainage Board covering the area between Rockland boat dyke, the back of Great Yarmouth, Haddiscoe, Diss and the Waveney Valley. It's a big area. There is farmer involvement but the District Councils have a big say especially for the land at the back of Yarmouth. South Norfolk has a big say too because we take a lot of water from building sites. It seems to be working successfully but it doesn't have quite the hands-on effect we had when we were a small board.

We are still responsible for cleaning out our own mill ditches and dykes which service the pumps as

Flooding at Langley 2007

well as some of the subsidiary dykes, to keep the water flowing. There are three pumps on this level and one is on our farm but I don't run it. I know the Monks pump shifts about 30 tonnes of water a minute, the Hardley pump shifts 40 tonnes and the Claxton pump about 30 tonnes a minute. There would be complete flooding without the pumps due to the lowering of the marsh, rising sea levels and the Yare being higher than it used to be.

In the great flood of 1953 both Claxton and Hardley were completely flooded but this section at Langley was spared. Since then, when the others have not been flooded at all, we've been flooded! One of my earliest memories was filling sandbags in the 1953 floods at Rockland. Gangs of us schoolboys went from Langley to help fill the breaches. Once when Langley Dyke burst on the day Norwich City were playing Sheffield United in the great FA Cup run (1958–59), I couldn't go because we woke up to find the marshes completely flooded.

We have been flooded three times since, twice fairly seriously when the riverbank broke. When Langley Dyke broke in the mid-1960s, I remember we were drilling oats on the marsh. We realised the water was coming and took sandbags over to stop it but thank goodness we withdrew; the water was coming over too quickly. The bank went and the river pushed out onto the marsh. It took several weeks to mend the breach and four years to get rid of the salt and get the marshes straight again; we couldn't get any financial help or insurance.

The flood had a big effect on the wildlife and the fish in the dykes were just floating about. We couldn't put the cattle on the marshes as they were too salty and there was no grass for two years. Gradually we re-seeded and got them going again. It was one of the worst points in my farming career to see those marshes flooded like that, all you could see were the tops of gateposts sticking out of the water. No properties were flooded

Monks Pump, Langley 2007

because they were just high enough. About four or five years ago they completely re-topped the Yare and did a very good job, it made us feel a lot safer here. They took a 20-30ft width of marsh and put it on top of the river banks and since then we haven't had any problems.

We now let some of our marshes to fellow local graziers mainly for suckler cows, and we still use a lot of the marshes ourselves. We have built up to 400 beef cattle which we fatten up for sale. A lot of our Holstein Friesians supply meat to McDonalds so anybody buying a burger should know they have good beef! Some of our pedigree dairy herd went to Beeston Castle in Cheshire, so our cows were highly desirable, and their milk now goes into Colston Bassett Stilton cheese. We kept all our young stock when the dairy herd went and this beef goes to continental-style slaughterhouses like the one near Eye in Suffolk and on to local butchers' shops in the main.

These marshes are part of the picturesque Yare Valley and are a haven for birds. We get a lot of migratory swans in early spring, up to 120 at times; they are not always to my liking because they do so much damage and always seem to pick out the new reed seed grass, which is young and tender. Ducks, plovers, oyster-catchers, wigeon are all here and I have seen kingfisher, heron and marsh harriers.

My son came into partnership with me in the late 1970s when he was 24 and my wife took over some work so we are all partners in the farm. My son has a son who is today trying to keep the rooks off the winter barley, and he will be going to Easton for a two-year course. My daughter has two little boys but they are not so interested in the farm although they are very keen on chickens and have been hatching them along with pheasant eggs.

The doings of the Dewings

(1954 – 2015)

Richard Dewing
(b. 1931)

SOUTH WALSHAM

Richard always wanted his own farm but limited opportunities in the 1960s and 70s meant that he became a tenant farmer with Norfolk County Council (NCC) and found it hard to progress.

I finished university when I was 20 and in 1954, after national service I came out of the army and looked for a job. The first one was with the Agricultural Research Council obtaining identical twin calves for research but I knew in my heart that I wanted to farm on my own account as I had been brought up on a farm. I decided in the mid-50s to take a job as an assistant farm manager to the Duke of Grafton, at the Euston estate in Thetford although, in reality, I was the stockman for the herd of Herefords.

My wage was £9 a week which was more than agricultural workers were paid and I had free accommodation and milk. Whilst there, I was on the NCC waiting list for a holding as I didn't have the money to buy a farm. Then, in 1958, a small 50-acre farm came up at Bressingham. It was half of a 100-acre farm really and was mainly arable with some livestock. I kept a few cattle and bought a tractor and plough with a £1,500 loan from the bank, a lot in those days.

I employed casual workers in the autumn or winter to harvest the sugar beet by hand as harvesting by machine was very much in its infancy. They would work six days a week on the sugar beet and my brother also helped with the harvest. The casual workers were people who were happy to do a bit of work now and again and be paid by results. They didn't have a union but I had to pay what they wanted and they were happy with that; I had a good relationship with them. One chap never turned up on Mondays because he drank so much over the weekend but when he came he was okay.

At Bressingham I did everything else myself apart from the sugar beet and contracting out the combine harvesting for the cereals. It was hard labour but it was the only way to do it and I never had a day off. I kept about 15 beef cattle, fattened them up and sent them to the Norwich market and I kept a cow for the house which I milked by hand. I was teaching biology three days a week at Swaffham as well which I enjoyed doing.

Eventually in 1973 we were offered a slightly larger farm here in South Walsham where I kept hens and sold eggs. I did earn more when I moved here; it just wasn't possible to make enough money on a farm the size I had in Bressingham, especially with five children. I was offered this farm in South Walsham on condition that I stopped teaching, which I did, but when we moved I found that every person with a smallholding had another job and I've always regretted having to give it up. But I wanted the farm and my wife wasn't terribly happy at Bressingham because it was very isolating. When we came here, she was able to set up her own bed and breakfast business in the house, so that helped.

We had always said that we wouldn't stay on the smallholding because the idea was to step up, but

I couldn't get any further. There were hardly any farms to let at the time. However, on one occasion a 120-acre farm came up for let in Suffolk. They wanted the person to be a family man and a supporter of the church. Well, I was church warden at Bressingham and I was also a reader in the church here but I didn't get it. I discovered that the bloke who did get it was the son of a large farmer and single, whether he had something to do with the church, I don't know. It was a lesson that in life, it's not what you know but who you know, and I knew I would never get another farm.

When I came here the sugar beet was all mechanised. It's difficult to do things on a small scale and easier to get somebody in to do the work so I had contractors in to plough, put on the fertiliser and spray. As I had some marshland that couldn't be ploughed I kept a few more cattle to use the grass.

At one point I did try dairy but I didn't want to sell milk to the Milk Marketing Board. I had five Jersey cows and I bottled the milk and sold it here, but the day I sold my first pint they brought in milk quotas, and I couldn't get a quota. Despite the Ministry giving me advice I couldn't get a quota unless I joined the NFU, which I didn't want to do. Members were supposed to say how much milk they sold if they had a quota but they didn't always declare when they sold more. For the first five years they did okay but in the sixth year, for some reason they went wildly over and my profits went to the ministry. I stopped doing the milk then but I'd proved it was possible to sell milk without a quota.

By the end I wasn't doing much; everything had changed and I gave up the cattle around 1990 but still had about 200 hens. The council controls people around here; they had always promised me more land but were never able to supply it. However, if you did get more land you had to sign an agreement to retire at 65, whereas, on my agreement I could carry on forever.
As a result, they gave me a reasonable golden handshake to give up the farm in 1997 when they wanted the land.

I had wanted to buy the house when my neighbour bought his in 1980 but they wouldn't sell to me. In the end they did, and although the golden handshake didn't pay for the house it helped towards it and we've been here ever since. My wife still runs the bed and breakfast to a limited extent and people who have been coming for 20 years still come. It's a very worthwhile thing to do and we have made some good friends over that time. So, it's all worked out very well.

Cows, hens and holiday-makers

(1970 – 2018)

David Burroughs
(b. 1952)

ALDEBY

David grew up on the family farm at Aldeby and attended Easton Agricultural College. He had a special interest in pigs but ended up expanding the dairy side. It is still very much a family business.

Oaklands was a mixed farm with cows, pigs, chickens, and turkeys for the Christmas trade, and we grew a variety of arable crops. I can just remember the last horse being used to roll some barley, and when he died the tractors came in.

I left school in 1969 aged 17, helped with the summer harvest and then went straight to Easton College. Easton was very different from what it is today as we were hands-on in all its enterprises. They had pigs, chickens, cows and we had to do stock duty at weekends; we hand-hoed sugar beet and moved irrigation pipes individually for the potatoes, so we were virtually a workforce while still doing our studies. We got one weekend off in two when I went home to help Father out and give him a few days off.

My father bought the farm from his father and moved here in 1942, so it's always been a family concern and a mixed farm of about 400 acres. We had roughly 50 milking cows and 40 sows with all the pigs going for bacon. Like most farms in this part of the Waveney Valley we had areas of marsh and upland, so stock was kept on the upland in the winter and on the marshes in the summer where we milked them in what was called a 'milking bail'. This was a six-stall-abreast parlour on skids. We milked mornings and nights and moved the cows onto clean pasture after a day's milking. It was arduous but in those days it seemed quite modern.

We used to collect the milk in churns and put it in one big container but our biggest problem was keeping the milk cool enough. We transported the churns from the marshes in an old three-ton trailer, tying them on as best we could, and brought them back to the home farm to be further cooled. Later on we bought a refrigerated tank and we could tip the five or six churns into that.

Arable crops were a very important part of the farm; we grew barley, not much wheat but a fair bit of sugar beet. We also grew kale and stubble turnips for the cows when they came home from the marsh in the autumn. The beauty of sugar beet was that nothing was wasted, the root went to the sugar beet factory and the tops went to the milking cows which stayed out day and night.

When I left Easton College I went home because I loved pigs, that was my main interest, but we had just entered the Common Market and the pig industry was very volatile so my father was reluctant to expand that side of the business. We had been contract-farming Wheatacre Hall for several years and knew the land so when the owner died in 1982 we took the opportunity to buy the farm.

We had always bought marshland as Father was very progressive and never stood still; he'd buy 50 acres here and 70 acres there. So when this farm came on the market it was a big step for us and doubled our acreage. The cost of buying marshland was certainly an attraction. In the early days Father

Discussion on ploughing up the marshes 1960s

bought some marshes at Worlingham for £10 an acre and then they went to the dizzy heights of £50 an acre; it gave us scope to do things.

We saw others growing exceedingly good crops on their marshes and we thought perhaps we could do the same and we began ploughing up the marshes as well. It was very difficult the first year because of the thickness of the old grass and it was a job to turn in. But we got it ploughed and drilled with wheat, and we just couldn't believe the yields we were getting in those days.

There were grants for drainage work so we put in a big drainage scheme to keep a low water level for the arable side but we had to put dams in for the grazing cattle. That was a big event for us and quite costly. We put in tile drains one chain apart with stone on top and it worked very well, but in later years we used plastic piping because that was thought to be the thing, but it didn't work so well.

At that time I was milking 60 to 70 cows back at Oaklands but I couldn't expand there. However Wheatacre Hall bordered the marshes and that opened up a great area for me to expand the cows and graze the marshes. So the cows moved there in 1991. We put in a brand-new greenfield site and went up to 150 cows and a one-man unit, and we've milked with that for over 20 years.

In 2017 we put in a new rotary parlour which is capable of milking up to 800 cows. The herd is up to 400 now and we could quite easily go up to 600; we never stand still. We have decided to do this as a family as we wanted to expand the cows and our strength and depth in business; I'm getting nearer to retirement so this is going to be the next generation's baby.

I've always used British Friesian. I love the breed, it's really a native cow that loves grazing and they just suit my system. They are dual-purpose as they also produce very good bull calves and their lifespan is one or two lactations more than some of the modern cows. They're well-suited for the marshes and they don't mind walking – some of my cows have to walk a mile after milking.

Our marsh grazing now is nearly all cows. The rest of the level has been put down to grass for forage and silage, and a proportion of the upland is used for growing about 100 acres of forage maize that blends well with the grass for a balanced ration in the winter. We also decided that we would put in a chicken unit when we moved the dairy cows from Oaklands to Wheatacre. As the fields at Oaklands were small with hedges, they were not well-suited for modern agriculture and big machinery so free range chickens looked a profitable enterprise at the time.

When the ESA came on the scene in 1987 they wanted to stop the cultivation of the marshes and return it to grass. The biggest problem was that we were not allowed to put enough cows on per acre and the worst thing you can do with grass is under-stock it; it just goes back to reeds and native grasses and spoils the whole job. I feel that joining it was a disaster as it never suited us. So we actually came out of the scheme early and we've gone for producing new leys and good quality grass, because that is the only way I can get enough milk from grazing cows.

When we first ploughed the marshes in the 1960s, there was a lovely peat layer under the grass flag

Ploughing up the marshes

Combining on the marshes

before you got to the clay. It was very fertile and when we ploughed we wanted to mix the peat with the clay. The idea was good but it never came off, because the peat oxidised and actually disappeared before we got the benefit of mixing it with the clay. So in the latter years of growing wheat we just had a bed of clay; it got harder and harder to get a seed bed because the peat had gone, the yields decreased and the soil structure was poor.

In the early 1940s and 50s, Wheatacre marshes were well-known for grazing horses; there was something in the soil they liked, perhaps the selenium or the salt. A lot of horses were reared for the First World War on farms in this area and when we first ploughed up the marshes we picked up a wheelbarrow of horseshoes. The horses were loaded onto trailers and taken to Aldeby station to go off to war. We now have charitable organisations coming into the market for marsh lettings and because they have readily available funds and a lot of animals, they are pushing the rents up to new highs. So for the typical farmer, the marshes are becoming less attractive and there will be a point where they cost too much and we have to look at alternatives.

When we bought Wheatacre Hall we were cropping the marshes but as we expanded the cows, more acres have been taken up with forage and our arable side has decreased to about 600 acres. There came a point in the last few years when we decided that we couldn't afford to buy machinery to farm 600 acres, and as our concentration is on milking cows, we made the decision to contract it out.

I think the most exciting times we have experienced were when we were ploughing up the marshes and everyone was looking for high yields. There wasn't the pressure on chemicals like there is today and we were making serious money. The first wheats we grew meant we suddenly went from two to three tons and we thought it was absolutely marvellous; there was a buzz from being able to expand. I'd like to see the next generation get as much excitement and thrill out of it as I did. I think the low point now is the pressure on prices; there's just not enough margin now. Our costs keep going up and we have no control over the prices we get and it is hard work these days. I think as we go into the future if we don't diversify, arable farming as we know it will be a struggle.

We have diversified: we have holiday homes, my son has taken over the dairy role, my daughter sells eggs and milk which we want to expand for the premium market, my niece looks after the young stock with her father and my sister handles the chicken enterprise. So it's a complete family working farm. We employ a head herdsman and a second man for the cows and the rest is casual labour. We had a family meeting before we spent the money on the new dairy and it was agreed we all wanted to farm, we wanted to do it well, and we wanted to milk cows. Good luck to them.

As a farmer you never retire. I'd like to have the odd day or two off, but I know if I have a day off, I'll be down to the cows to see how they are. Yeah, I'll never finish really.

Changing times in farming

(1920s – 2019)

Henry Alston
(b. 1970)

BILLOCKBY

The Alstons started arriving from Scotland almost 120 years ago and have been farming in the Broads ever since, experiencing the ups and downs of the dairy industry and varying government schemes.

It started with my predecessors coming down from Scotland to Norfolk and parts of Suffolk from 1900 onward. The biggest moves were from about 1925 to the Second World War during the agricultural depression in East Anglia. What commonly happened was that various members of the family and extended family settled in Norfolk and either bought land or became tenants, and there are some great stories about them having the land for free as long as they built a cowshed for 70 cows as part of the mixed farming system they wished to adopt. So one family member would come and get established, then others would visit on holiday and look for the right opportunity and the person here would help them. That's basically how various members of the family got started.

My great-uncle, Alan Alston, was the first of my immediate family to come in 1927 to Green Farm, East Tuddenham. My grandfather, one of the many James Alstons, came in 1930/31 to Park Farm, Wymondham and my great-uncle Willy, whose farm I am fortunate enough to have, he came in 1937/38. The family was attracted to Norfolk because of the world of difference and opportunity between having just livestock on the side of a hill in a valley in Ayrshire, compared to Norfolk. There are an awful lot of Alstons and other Scottish families still farming here today.

Many of my family and the other Scottish families came from the Ayrshire area around the same time and they all brought their cattle on the train. It was quite common to milk them before they left Scotland and milk them in Norfolk when they arrived. Most started with Ayrshire cattle and gradually went over to British Friesian, then those who kept on in dairy ended up with the Holsteins. The Ayrshires did well in Norfolk because of the better forage and climate, and the flat marsh grazing was a plus factor too, a great help after windswept hillsides.

I remember many happy days as a child on Heigham Holmes riding around on the tailgate of my father's vehicle, and then chasing cattle along the marsh tracks to the pound in the middle of the island. It was ideal for a boy who was interested in agriculture to have that freedom and involvement. In 1937/38 my great-uncle bought the majority share on Heigham Holmes and then between my uncle and my father we ended up owning the whole thing, until we sold it as a family to the National Trust in 1987 to buy other more productive farmland. We are still the tenants of Heigham Holmes but now it is just summer grazing under conservation parameters.

We used to milk cattle on Heigham Holmes. The farmyard is in the middle of the island and in its heyday there were two cowsheds and 140 cows could be milked in the stalls. In those days we took the cows to the grass and not the grass to the

Cattle at Marsh boundary

cow. This went on until the early 1960s when my father put a stop to it. It was fraught with issues to do with the ferry over to the island and milk tankers; also we had herdsmen travelling from Billockby to Heigham Holmes on mopeds, falling and injuring themselves. So the next phase was to use Heigham Holmes to make a lot of hay to feed the cows in the winter and the cows were milked at Billockby all year round.

Sadly, my father passed away when I was 12 and so two uncles, Alan Alston and Gavin Paterson who was also my godfather, took over the business until my brother and I were able to take an active role along with my mother. Prior to that I went to agricultural college and had three very happy years at Cirencester. I'd done some travelling before college and came back and started to get involved because my uncles, as trustees, were looking for me to do that. I was just rising 23 when I started to get involved in the management.

We farmed about 1,500 acres and we have managed to build the business up quite substantially over the years, especially the arable side, by purchasing good-quality land and contract farming for other people, which means farming land on a profit-share basis. We also have about 600 acres of our own grassland.

We have 300 acres of drained marshes, mostly drained in the late 1970s and early 80s, and we have continued draining bits and pieces where possible over the years. Mostly the marshes are alluvial clay with patches of peat ideally suited to wheat and rape. We have grown sugar beet and on occasion we have grown peas as well. Elsewhere, we grow 550 acres of potatoes for McCains which doesn't involve marshland as the land is too heavy and too low-lying.

Farming has changed hugely. We have gone from the 1980s which was purely production-led to the introduction of ESA schemes in the late 1980s which encouraged grazing and a softer management for the conservation of the grass marshes. Then in 1992 we had the introduction of set-aside on arable land which meant that marshland was the obvious target to use as set-aside, as it was less useful for arable.

Now we have all the Waste and Resources Action Plan schemes where we can't fertilise within so many metres of a watercourse. It has limited what we can do because all the marshes are surrounded by ditches and watercourses. To some extent it has made the marshes less attractive for farmers. Conservation bodies have had a huge impact because they are extremely well funded by donors and they want to come in and buy blocks of marshes together to try and prove their way is right, which is a balancing act.

The Milk Marketing Board (MMB) was formed in 1933 and was a saviour for a lot of farmers because it gave a stable, average price in the UK. Then, in 1983 we had the introduction of milk quotas despite the UK having never been self-sufficient in milk and dairy produce, not even in 1983 when there were butter mountains and milk lakes in Europe. We were basically given a quota to produce 90% less milk. Then it was decided that free trade was the way and the MMB was disbanded in 1994. I'd started farming by 93/94 and I could only see the dissolution of the archaic MMB as positive for milk prices. The milk price rose from 22p to roughly 26p in the next two to three years and we all thought it was wonderful. Needless to say it crashed and milk has been treated as a mere commodity ever since.

We persisted in milk production and tried to expand through it and become bigger and more efficient, and we got up to 450 cows with year-round calving on an intensive system, and selling to a large co-operative milk buyer. We invested in a new parlour in 2009/10 when world predictions said there would be a steady 2% growth in demand for dairy produce annually. This was followed by the unforeseen Russian embargo on dairy produce in 2014 and a slowing Chinese demand, and we saw prices drop from 33p a litre to 19p. I made the decision that we were haemorrhaging money at a huge rate and there was no light on the horizon so we should stop. We sold our cows in batches as they calved, to maximise the value of fresh-calved production animals, and we kept the calves and young stock as a separate venture to graze on permanent pasture.

We still have a heifer-rearing enterprise on grass and we run what I can only describe as a 'bed and breakfast' for a herd of cows from the Isle of Man. However, the difference was that I sold my last milk in October 2016 at 19p, and 12 months later I sold the Isle of Man milk for 31p a litre. Quite a volatile market in 12 months!

We will continue to have livestock because of our area of permanent grassland, and we are continuing the heifer-rearing enterprise, serving them with sexed semen so we should get a heifer calf every time – it doesn't always work but the number of bull calves has greatly reduced. I would like to think we might go back to milk production in a smaller, simpler way in the future, as I still have a mothballed unit and a good milking parlour and one herdsman left. However, it all depends on market forces.

Following the cow's tale

(1984 – 2018)

John Stafford
(b. 1944)

HEIGHAM HOLMES

John was the herd manager at Billockby Farms and still works part-time with cattle on the island of Heigham Holmes.

When I was seven we moved to the edge of a village between Wisbech and March where there was a small farm just down the road. They had four milking cows and I loved being on the farm and that's how my interest started. After I left school I did a three-year apprenticeship locally and I remember my second day leading the horses for the potato harvest and pulling out the potatoes with what they called a spinner. A gang of women would put them into baskets, and a man went along picking up the baskets and throwing them to another man in a horse and cart. Of course, there were quite a few horses about then.

I then went to Easton College for 12 months and in 1964 I began working with first beef and then dairy cattle until the milk quotas were introduced. In 1984 I answered an advertisement for a job at Billockby Farms which had about 1200 acres, 200 milking cows and a big new herringbone milking parlour and I also got a tied house just 500 yards away.

There were two of us working 12 days with a weekend off and going in at 4.45am. The most important thing was to get the cows milked so the milk was ready and cooled when the tanker arrived. We'd be done by 7.30am and then everything had to be cleaned up. We were rearing our own calves so they had to be fed before we had our breakfast. After that, we did the straw and feed for other young stock until lunchtime. We had two hours for lunch, went back at two, checked everything was alright and turned out the cows ready for milking again at three. I left the milking side in 2006 following a stroke but the milking carried on to 2018 when they stopped the dairy herd as it was costing more to produce the milk than they were getting paid for it.

I also had responsibility for the grazing. Most of our young stock and calves were grazed on Heigham Holmes or 'the island' as we used to call it. It was owned by the Alston family until 1987 when they sold it to the National Trust (NT). It is an island of about 500 acres and the only way across is by a floating bridge. When I first went, the ferry was a floating bridge hinged on the rudder bar from a drifter which was concreted into the ground. It was built in the 1930s and it sank a few times in 1986. A new one was installed in 1987 with the same design and hinged from the same point. Then in 2012 the NT installed a new bridge with hydraulics and electrically-driven pumps but now it takes four times as long to get across! We can get two or three vehicles on the ferry at a time, and the cattle are taken across on a tractor and trailer.

Any cows dried off for autumn calving go over to the island so we can reduce the herd grazing at Billockby as it only has 120 acres. The cattle drink from the ditches and as calves we train them to stay within a ditch system as there are no fences. That means in summer we definitely had to watch the salt levels in the ditches. At Heigham there is a big seam of gravel that runs along the coast and when there are very high tides, the salt water tends

Early photograph of Martham Ferry

Martham Ferry open, 2018

to be pushed through into the nearest broads and waterways, and that increases the salt levels here. The marshes are lower than the river and although all the salt water is pumped off, the salt can sit at the bottom of the ditches below the fresh water. Then in summer, the clear water evaporates and leaves salty water.

I take regular samples and someone from the Drainage Board tests them. If the level reaches 10 it would be poisonous to cows. However, the highest we have reached is eight. So I let in water from the river as it's usually lower than eight to build up the water level. Then the mixed water is pumped out and the salt levels lower. If it ever got to ten, we would have to carry fresh water over in water tankers; I hear that's been done a few times on the Acle marshes.

There is a system of dykes and gates for each marsh so you can only go from one marsh to another through a gateway and you have to know where they are. Over the last few years the marshes on the island have ceased to be primarily for grazing and are now a wildlife habitat with some grazing tagged on, and water levels have been allowed to rise. This means that the foot drains that were put in years ago to drain the marshes are now full of water, creating mini rivers across the marshes. New, so called, foot drains have been put in recently which are about 4ft wide so you can't walk through them – you really do have to know where you're going on these marshes now!

It is common for cattle to fall into the dykes. When it happens, we loop a rope round their head and pull them out on their side with a tractor. I've only ever lost two in about 30 years. When I check cattle on the marshes, I check to see if they are all still on top and I check their state. One health problem peculiar to these marshes is keeping a look-out for animals bitten by adders.

We are not allowed to graze on Heigham Holmes in winter. When ESA came in, we had to be off by 1st December but now with HLS we are supposed to be off by 1st November – we can get permission to graze a bit later if there is still good grass.

There are 37 different marshes on the island ranging in size from 2–35 acres. Since the introduction of HLS, our biggest problem is that we are not allowed to cut anything to conserve it. All the grass has to be grazed despite growing at different speeds at different times of the year, and we are not allowed to undergraze either. The whole island is grass, although the two big marshes in the middle grew wheat when I first came in 1984.

Billockby doesn't have enough cattle to graze all its grass so between 80 and 90 suckler cows and calves come on from a local farmer to help keep it down. This does have its problems though as the cattle are split into three herds and at certain times of the year we have a bull running with each

Heigham Holmes 2018

group, and they have to be kept apart. And you can't have a bull on either side of a ditch because it just doesn't work – they wind each other up. It's not easy to keep the bulls apart, everything fed and keep the grass neither under- or overgrazed! I do it all on my own, but once you have a reasonable plan, it seems to work.

NT wants us to reduce the stocking rate early in the year so the cows don't tread on birds' nests. However, the reduced number will happily graze all the palatable grass and leave the rest. Later, when we are allowed to increase the stocking rate, the cattle won't eat that grass because it's even more unpalatable as it has matured. When that grass seeds, we get more of the same. It just doesn't work on some marshes and things are just getting worse and worse.

With regards to conservation, there's a big balancing act going on and really each marsh wants managing separately to achieve the aims of both parties. The trouble is the one-size-fits-all policy. The marshes here contain tall fescue grass which needs to be eaten off early but we are not allowed to go in early so there's a load of rough old grass that nothing will graze on; it just doesn't work. Also, if you want food for geese and waders, you need short grass!

I've carried on working on the marshes, partly because I was asked to do it and partly because of the wildlife that I'm finding more and more interesting. We get quite a few Eurasian cranes and various ducks and geese dropping in. I can remember one day when there were four different types of swans here: mutes, Bewicks, hoopers and two black swans from Wroxham Broad. That's not a sight you see very often. There are muntjacs, Chinese water deer and a growing herd of red deer, 37 at my last count. I saw a kingfisher recently, only the second one I've seen on the island in 35 years.

The Norfolk animal health officer

(1954 – 1996)

Eddie Macdonald
(b. 1941)

GREAT YARMOUTH

Eddie was interested in the countryside from childhood. He started by working on a farm and later went into animal health. He describes the work and its challenges.

In 1954, at the age of 13, I started working on the neighbouring farm during weekends and holidays. It was an old-fashioned farm where we used a binder, stacked up the corn and used a threshing drum to thresh it during the winter. It was very hard work. A lot of the sugar beet was done by hand too but it was good money. I left school in 1957 and just continued working on the farm. It was a mixed farm with arable, pigs and fat cattle. I was involved in working with the livestock which helped me a great deal in later life. During this time I went to evening classes and day release to get extra O-Level exams and agricultural qualifications.

In 1964 I changed careers completely and worked in Great Yarmouth for five years. I still wanted to work in agriculture and by chance picked up a copy of the Farmers Weekly and saw an advert from the Ministry of Agriculture's Animal Health Division, looking to recruit technical assistants. I had the right qualifications and started in the Norwich office in November 1969, and carried on working for the Ministry in various jobs until the Norwich office was downgraded in 1995 and I took early retirement.

The Animal Health Division was set up mainly to deal with notifiable diseases such as foot and mouth, sheep scab, fowl pest and salmonella pullorum in poultry. It was also involved with various eradication schemes like TB and brucellosis which were a priority at the time. When I first started much of the work was blood testing poultry flocks for salmonella pullorum and I would take a sample from every bird and do an instant test to identify positive cases. Working conditions were not pleasant, there was the constant smell of ammonia and often lots of dust so I would wear a dust mask most of the time. I was expected to test at least 1,000 birds a day and the work tended to be a bit boring, especially in large flocks of 10,000 plus. But if you worked with two or three others and good farm staff, you had a bit of banter which helped.

The TB eradication programme was underway for some time when I started and it is still ongoing. Brucellosis testing was starting and there was a lot of work around milk sampling and helping the veterinary officers with blood tests for the cattle. In the 1970s it was a voluntary scheme and we had to persuade cattle farmers to join so we could take samples at milking times. If the cattle passed it became an accredited herd which had to be kept

On the cutter aged 18

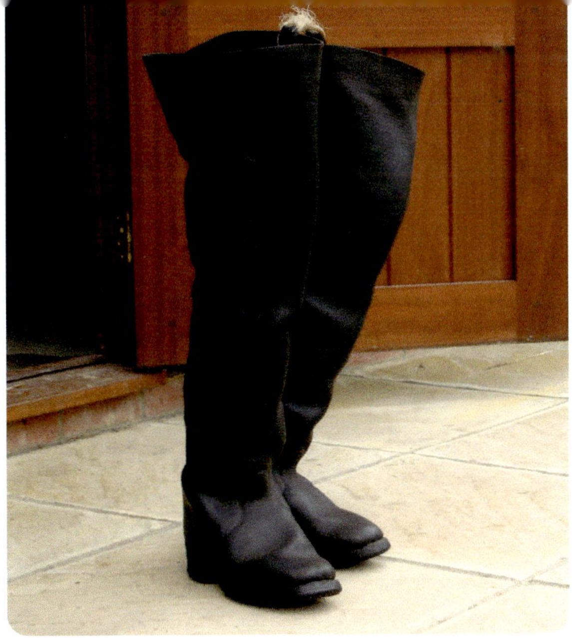

Thigh-length boots

separate from herds of non-accredited cattle and herds with brucellosis-positive animals. So part of my job was to inspect the boundaries to make sure they were double-fenced or had a wide dyke.

I did a lot of this, especially on the Halvergate and Acle marshes. I remember I had large six-inch Ordnance Survey maps which I colour-coded for the various categories of cattle: solid green for accredited cattle, striped green for non-accredited; another colour for steers only as they were not considered a risk, and a fourth colour for areas of marsh which were arable. I built up quite a library of these old maps.

In 1973 I was involved with the first case of swine vesicular disease in Norfolk, just north of Norwich, and experienced my first mass slaughter of livestock. It was certainly not the last. In 1975 I went for a promotion and worked with a lot of the ports and dealt with meat imports and animal products, checking that certifications were correct to prevent the introduction of diseases. In the 1970s we had a lot of livestock exports through Great Yarmouth port and my job was mainly to check on animal welfare.

The thing I remember most about the marshes is they are completely flat with very few landmarks apart from the odd drainage mill, and I had to remember where the crossing points were for the dykes. I also had to rely on the liggers which these days would need an instant health and safety assessment to check whether they would take your weight or not. I just marked them on my maps.

One of the things I liked about the job was meeting and working with all kinds of interesting people. Marshmen were real characters. They often had some of their own livestock but were generally contracted out to some of the bigger farmers to take charge of their cattle grazing out on the marshes. I knew Bill Lacey for many years, almost from the time I first joined the Ministry. He looked after the Halvergate marshes mainly and was a very knowledgeable and pleasant chap to work with. If you wanted to know anything about the marshes or the people who had cattle, he was the man to see, and I often called in for a bit of information and a piece of Betty's cake.

Another marshman I got on very well with was Stan Hewitt who had a house at Berney Arms and because he kept a few cattle I'd visit from time to time. To get there I drove across the Haddiscoe marshes to the top end and met Stan or his wife with their boat. I would transfer all the testing gear and equipment into the boat, set off across the river to the Berney Arms, do my work and then go back again. I am not a swimmer so, as with the liggers, this was a bit dodgy for me. When I drove up to the gate of another family on Haddiscoe, I would be met by a gaggle of geese running up. This was fine as they were in front of me, but when I left, they would be behind pecking my legs – I'd end up walking out the gate backwards!

Another character I saw regularly was Percy 'Jim' Hewitt who had a lonely job operating a dragline and dredging the dykes all year round. Sometimes he could be seen alongside the Acle New Road and at other times he was a dot in the distance way out on a marsh. He was also a good source of information and despite the nature of his work he was a very sociable person, and a great friend of my father-in-law. Most of the marshmen were nice people to work with and were ready to assist. Their knowledge was the thing and they dealt with almost everything on the marshes; their passing is a great shame because the knowledge is being lost.

There would be times when it was not so pleasant working on the marshes. There was no shelter and I just had to get on with it the best I could. We were issued with plenty of protective clothing. My favourites were the thigh wellington boots with a waterproof coat on top – I didn't often get wet.

Part of the job was sheep dipping, mostly done on farms with proper sheep-dipping facilities but some was done on the marshes. I remember one place used a tin bath as a temporary dip because they had just a few sheep. At the time the dips were organophosphates, but on one visit we were using a dip which added detergent to the main ingredient to help get it into the fleece. They were a couple of characters, a farmer and his son, and I was helping them work out the correct proportions. I remember the son saying, 'Steady on. We don't want to use all that detergent up because Father uses that in his bath!'

I carried on working like this until in the late 1980s and early 90s I began some work with the Veterinary Investigation Centre which involved cases of salt poisoning in cattle on the marshes down towards Yarmouth. This occurred if salt water from Breydon Water got into the freshwater dykes and was more prevalent in dry weather or when there was a high tide. My job was to visit the marshes and take salinity meter readings and warn the farmers if fresh water was needed for the cattle.

Norfolk horn sheep at Catfield

I don't think we had any more fatal cases.

In the same period we had the salmonella scare which often meant working unsocial hours at one of the local hatcheries, and collecting dead chicks for testing. Then in 1992, the roll-on/roll-off ferry services at Yarmouth ceased and our port work dried up and I retired early. I feel my work was worthwhile, particularly the animal welfare, disease prevention and eradication aspects of the job, and I enjoyed the marshes and the sense of isolation. It was the silence. I would be out in the middle of the marshes on a lovely summer's day by myself and all I could hear was the birds singing.

The knackerman

(1969 – 2004)

Edgar Hoddy
(1955–2020)

ASHBY ST MARY

Edgar worked in the family business of farming and knackering when he left school in 1969 and went all over East Anglia and the Broads collecting fallen stock from the farms.

Sometimes the beast had been dead for quite a while and was, as we said in the trade, 'ripe'. It could be very foul-smelling at times but it was something we got used to. The meat we collected in the 1970s was sold as pet food; it was cooked and sold on Norwich Market and then all the waste was bought by a company which rendered the bones down for fertiliser and the offal for animal food. It was a dirty but profitable job and nothing was wasted. Then BSE happened. It peaked in 1993 and almost decimated the business. My brother still does the job but all he does now is collect the carcasses to take to a central place where they are all incinerated or rendered.

I was once called to the Halvergate marshes to pick up a donkey. We called at a house in the middle of the marshes where an elderly couple's pet donkey had expired. The gentleman was in his 80s and drank in the local pub, and he had asked some of the lads to dig a hole to bury his donkey for the price of a beer. After a boozy session they dug a hole which they thought was adequate but by the time they finished, rigor mortis had set in and it wouldn't bend, and the feet were left sticking out of the ground! Donkeys are considered unlucky for the knacker and we hated picking them up. We couldn't do anything with them, they weren't skinned and the flesh wasn't used. I think it had something to do with most donkeys having the cross of Jesus on their backs.

Some of the worst things we had to deal with were horses. We attended every meeting at the old racecourse in case there was an accident and there were several horses with broken legs that we had to put down. The vets would call us in to do it as they said we were the professionals at the job. It was a bit heart-rending because people were very attached to their animals but it was necessary and a release for the animal which was suffering; we were doing a service to the animal and the owners.

We had a very interesting life going from farm to farm, meeting lots of different characters, all shapes and sizes. I can't say there was one of them I didn't like, we were doing a service and they appreciated what we did. The social part of the job basically kept it going. One farmer who used to call me Porridge and whose sons I knew well, would ring up and say, 'When Porridge has finished his breakfast tell him to get down here', and it was to pick up whatever poorly stock he'd got on the farm. I'd turn up and he'd say, 'You better come up to my office, boy'. And we would go into the old blacksmith's forge on his farm and I'd have a cup of tea with him, and oftentimes have a yarn and just catch up on things.

We were warmly accepted at some farms we went to but at others we thought, 'He'll either be alright with me or not!' Nine times out of ten they were fine because we were just doing a job. They're not happy about losing a beast but they know they've got to get us in to clear it up. In the early days, in

Ashby St Mary

my father's time, we actually paid for fallen stock, now they are charged a lot of money to take fallen stock away; that's how things have changed. I wouldn't say farmers looked forward to seeing us as they got nowhere near the value of the animal, but at least they got something from us.

A lot of the farming people in the area were related. There were three or four farms where they all had the same surname but they have all gone now; the whole family moved on or got older and decided to cash in and retire. One family with five farms finished and they all left, that's the way with a lot of places in Norfolk now. My family also farmed a 100-acre farm as a family unit for the best part of 30 years but the dreaded BSE disease made the job less profitable so it could no longer sustain the family.

We've seen a lot of changes in farming infrastructure. It used to be mostly small family units with sons and daughters involved but now they have all merged into 1–2,000-acre farms where the small farmer can't compete. I used to visit lots of farms where I knew the grandfather, the father and the son and they were all working the farm together. Even my small farm has been put out to share farming now, and it's farmed by some big conglomerate which has a lot more machinery and acreage than we ever had.

When I first started, the marshes were full of cattle and every village had at least one dairy herd. In my village alone there were three good-sized milking herds. They all went when the price of milk fell through the floor and the farms decided they just couldn't afford them anymore. Where the marshes used to be full of cattle they are now sparsely grazed and have become more of a wildlife habitat than grazing marsh. There were once thousands of cattle on the Halvergate marshes, now I think there are more geese.

A veterinary life

(1973 – 2013)

Roger Clarke
(b. 1940)

ACLE

Roger was always interested in animals and followed the local vet on his rounds during school holidays. He qualified as a veterinary surgeon and describes his work in the Broads.

In 1973/74 we found a house in Acle with a big garden in which we designed and built the Anchorage Veterinary Hospital and it opened the following year. By 1976 I employed my first assistant, a very stout fellow and a Methodist preacher who never approved of me swearing. Everybody used to tell me what marvellous sermons he gave on Sundays in the village chapel.

I've no idea why we were so successful but we did have the only registered veterinary hospital in Norfolk and I think we gave a good service. We saw everyone, and night work and call-outs were just part of life. I was always prepared to turn out at midnight on a Sunday and put a calf bed back in the cow. You just accepted you were in a caring profession and you got on with it. You knew what you were letting yourself in for before you started and in many ways it led to a very agreeable way of life. People were grateful although they always grumbled you were far too expensive!

We are ten miles from the sea and between Acle and the sea there is nothing but marshes so traditional dairy farming was very big. In Oby, Filby and Caister-on-Sea there were lots of dairy farms because of the cheap grazing. Similarly, Reedham and Wickhampton had lots of dairy. Of course, dairy farming was grist to the mill for a veterinary surgeon because fertility was everything and my earlier experience in Glasgow meant I was very competent at pregnancy diagnosis – this sort of stuff hadn't been heard of much before in Norfolk. But then they began ploughing up the marshes.

I owe an enormous debt to a chap called Andrew Lees who was the original conservationist of the Norfolk Broads. He convinced the Ministry of Agriculture that the Norfolk Broads, which runs to about 150 square miles, were the last great marsh wetlands in Europe. The result led to the creation of the Broads Authority and to farmers being paid not to plough up their marshes. So we had a great resurgence as it became profitable for farmers to keep calves again. However, it faded once more when there was less money in milk. Getting labour also became more difficult for farmers and a generation of farmers' sons were less interested in the seven-day-a-week commitment that was dairy, but mostly I think it was because it was less profitable. When I left the Acle practice there was only one sizeable dairy farm left whereas, at one stage, we looked after 3,000 dairy cows.

Pigs disappeared the day I joined the Veterinary Pig Society! Wall's Ice Cream had a company called Wall's Supermeats that made pork sausages, not a very fine product, but they had a multiplier farm at Limpenhoe. I remember the Piétrain crosses that came from Belgium and how technical it all was. Fattening pigs never made any work for us but, on the other hand, any parish you went to had people who worked on the land and had large gardens, and most kept a few calves or pigs in the back yard. They would ring up and say, 'Can you come on Sunday?' My response was, 'Of course we can do Sunday', because I knew it was the only day they were at home.

We had quite a big horse round. We were very lucky to do work for Ray Cook at Oby who

Roger 2005

single-handedly saved the Suffolk horse. They were down to about 40 births in the stud book around 1970 but Ray hung on and really saved the breed, and had one or two quite big studs. We were lucky also to have Brian Banham who had Shires and a big Shire stud, which was very interesting work. We didn't have any racehorses just a few eventers and lots of kids' ponies; at that time gymkhanas were very big business and made good work for us. We also had a splendid American who bred American quarter horses which again was quite interesting and gave us something different to do. We did three caesarean sections on mares which you wouldn't dream of doing in general practice these days, but we were all there was and if we didn't do it, the mare would die. So it was all a challenge.

A fairly unusual thing about being at Acle was the stock of old farms out on the marshes. That certainly could make things difficult. From Acle to Great Yarmouth is roughly nine miles and Acle New Road is a most horrifically dangerous road. It was built in 1831 and is straight with one bend, and has a single railway line on its south side which runs from Norwich to Yarmouth via Acle.

We had farms that were off the Acle New Road on the right-hand side going to Yarmouth and when it was busy, it was a nightmare. We would be waving out of the window, flashing lights and still people would overtake!

We then had to find the right gateway which, even when you had done it a hundred times, could be amazingly difficult. Having survived that, we had to cross the railway line which was always a problem but particularly when it was foggy; you had to park away from the gates, clamber up the embankment, open the first gate, prop it open, walk across the line, open the second gate then hop back in the car and hope, if it was foggy, you could hear a train coming. As soon as you got to the other side you'd hear the train go swooping past and you still had to shut all the gates!

Some places were just horrendous to reach. We used to service the farm at Berney Arms which is beyond the Berney Arms pub; one of the few pubs in Britain to have its own railway station. To get to the farm meant 23 gates to open and two railway lines to cross and then I had to drive up on Breydon Bank to get to the farm. I was ever so grateful if I had veterinary students with me so somebody else could do the gates. There would be 23 lots of cattle trying to get through the opened gates so I had to open the gate and run at it with the car. Also, each gate required its own locksmith. They each had their own technique; some you lifted, some you pushed, some you tied with string; you could lose a finger on those damn gates.

Once on the way back, I lost control on top of Breydon Bank and my car slid down the bank and almost into the soke dyke. I was completely stuck. Someone came along with a tractor and radioed my garage to pick me up from that godforsaken place – no mobile phones then. So… fee for visiting and treating the cow, seven guineas; garage bill to tow my car, £88.

When we went to Clippesby Mill, which is upstream from Acle Bridge, the only way to get to it was by river and in the summer a boatyard at Acle Bridge used to let us borrow a little day launch. One Saturday after watching Norwich City play, my wife said that dear old Mr Bailey from Clippesby Mill had rung to say he had a ewe he was worried about. So I went to the entrance on the Acle Causeway, parked on the main road and then walked about a mile and a half across eight different marshes to Clippesby Mill. I had to take gear with me, and as I set off it began to snow with the wind blowing from the east as normal. By the time I got to his house about 7pm, I was like a snowman. I rattled the door, and nobody came, so I rattled it again and heard about 15 chains and locks being freed up and Mr Bailey stuck his head out and he said, 'Oh it's you. I don't think we'll bother her now, I've taken my boots off!'

They were all Muttons or Mallets on the marshes. Freddie Mutton was a tiny man but a very good marshman and he would always carry the calving jack for you, which was quite heavy. He used to walk at about 15 miles an hour with tiny, tiny steps and by the time we got to the cow, I was just exhausted trying to keep up with him.

I sold the practice when I was well into my 70s and they have dropped the farm work and the hospital status. When I retired I kept on with driving horses which I have had great fun doing for over 20 years. My last driving mare is 30 now and is out on the marshes at Thurne.

Acle Straight 2005

Acle Straight and River Bure 2004

Marsh gates

My varied life: reed cutting

(1951 – 1960s)

Bernard Sheppard
(b.1926)

SUTTON

After farm work at age 14, Bernard became a Bevin Boy for two years and then worked on herring drifters at Yarmouth. At age 25 he became a reed cutter.

We used to go reed cutting from Christmastime to the end of March or until the reed started to colt or grow – if the tops are cut off the colt, you get a shorter reed next time and you spoil the reed beds. We used a scythe and did it all by hand.

We dressed the reed at the bottom to remove the rubbish using a dresser – a bit of wood about an inch wide with three six-inch nails through it – and we would cut a fathom of reed which is 6ft, the same as a fathom of water. A fathom or bunch of reed was five shoves and when we stood five shoves together we would bind them around the bottom. We usually cut a long hundred of reed a day which was 600 shoves or 120 bunches. It was hard work with the scythe!

A lot of the time we were in water so we would double-swathe the reed. We mowed it with the scythe so it lay in the reed and when we had gone far enough, we'd turn round and go back the other way cutting back into it so it stood up at a sort of angle and didn't drop into the water. If we had just mowed it straight down it would probably have got wet.

One day my mate and I were trying to get across a deek or dyke before we started reed cutting. I got across with the water just above my ankles so I told him he was alright to cross there. He went across in the same place and went right in. 'Yar got some bloody high ankles', he said. We were wearing three-quarter boots. Another snag when we were cutting round the Broads was caused by the old coypu rats. They used to live on roots and you'd be walking across the reed bed and drop in where they had burrowed down.

When we first cut reed we would cut and sell it for so much a fathom, but after a while I thought we should sell directly to the thatchers and make a bit more money. Then one year we were cutting round Meadow Deek at Hickling when a boat pulled up and the bloke came across and asked what we did with the reed. He was from Devon and he wanted to buy from us.

They used to come down on a Friday night about 6.30. On Saturday morning my missus gave them some tea and toast and we'd go down to where we'd stacked the reed. They were loaded up about 11am and went straight back to Devon. It was all for thatching and we got about £1 a bundle, a lot of money then.

Bernard 1952

Hickling Broad

I remember when I first started cutting reed we would cut for a bloke at Horsey on the marshes around Horsey Mere. The marshes there had what they called 'needle reed', right thin reed. It had tracks through it which we used to get in and out. It was so tall you had to know the tracks to find your way out as you couldn't see over the top of it. That was beautiful reed but it all went to nothing in the end.

We didn't wear gloves as we couldn't tie the reed with them. When I first started I tied the reed with bond; this is when you use single wale as it is more pliable and you make a bond by twisting it up on your arm. Nowadays they tie with string which is nowhere near as smart.

It was hard work. I never bothered if I put a bit of weight on before reed cutting because I knew I'd lose a stone despite reed cutting giving a good appetite. Wintertime was nice out there. You'd see all the little old birds and I'd think to myself, 'Little ole birds out there, they took all that frost and everything and they survived it'. That's amazing really, ain't it? That was a good life. I enjoyed the marsh work. I have known us to skate across the broad to work; I reckon that ice was about 2ft one year.

A family in reeds and thatching

(1970s – 2019)

Stephen Aldred
(b. 1954)

EAST RUSTON

Stephen would help his father do reed cutting at the weekends and in the 1970s he joined him to learn the art of thatching. He has been involved with it ever since.

Father began reed and sedge cutting by hand at Hickling and Horsey with his mate, George Newman, and they made a good living out of it. Then they used an Allen scythe which they walked behind and made the job much easier as they could cut more reed and they just had to dress it out. They tried to fit in other work as well to help see them through the year and one summer they were working at Somerton doing repairs on council properties when they were asked if they knew of a thatcher – there was lots of thatch on the council holdings and they couldn't find anyone to do the work.

Father knew a bit about thatching because, when he first left school, he lived at Martham and spent some time with the local thatcher, Billy Tungate, so he bluffed his way in and said, 'Yeah, I can do that'. He was told he had the job and he started thatching on his own doing repair jobs and gradually working his way up. He was largely self-taught because there were no official training schemes then. In the late 1970s and early 1980s, a thatching college started at Northampton and a lot of apprentices were sent to learn different types of thatching but it's no longer going.

I went to Norfolk Agricultural School at Easton and when I came home at weekends, I helped Father with the reed and sedge cutting and carrying the reed off the marshes. I didn't do a lot of thatching then because he was still doing small repair jobs. Several years later when he had too much work and I was made redundant, I started to learn the trade properly.

Norfolk reed was traditionally the best but it lost its way in the 1980s and 1990s as it wasn't managed as well as it should have been. The reed beds and ditches became clogged up and more intensive agriculture on the grazing marshes meant more land was ploughed up for arable crops and the reed quality deteriorated. To maintain good quality, reed needs to be cut either every year or every other year. Around this area if it's cut every year, it's called single wale, and if it's cut every other year they call it double wale. It depends entirely on the reed bed whether you can cut every year but some you leave for two years so the old growth protects the new.

Since the late 1990s local reeds have been managed a lot better, the quality has improved and the thatch is probably back to the days when Norfolk reed was good. However, not enough is being produced because of a shortage of reed cutters so thatchers cannot obtain sufficient supplies, especially if they are working on a big property. Today, the majority of reed for large properties is imported from Ukraine, Poland, Hungary and sometimes Holland, depending on the value of the pound. We used reed from China several years ago when the value of the pound fluctuated but it wasn't quite as good as the Eastern European reed. Another source is Turkey where there are large reed beds round the Black Sea.

The big advantage of imported reed is that it's brought in on a container and is delivered straight to site and we can get it unloaded in a few hours. It costs a bit more per bunch but there's less handling. It's important to cover the reed with tarpaulins as it deteriorates if water gets in when it's on the ground. Thatch lasts so long on the roof because only the stub or butt end is exposed to the weather. The benefit of using Norfolk reed is that it is closer and you can pick it up yourself but it takes longer as it's in individual bunches. To load 300 bunches onto a trailer and bring it back would probably take the best part of half a day so getting enough reed for an average-size property could take three to four full days.

Currently the best local reed is at Horning and How Hill although Hickling reed has got better; I can't comment on others because I haven't used them. These sites have been designated for wildlife protection and conservation and they get grants to cut the reed and maintain the area for the wildlife. They could do more but a lot of the reed beds are hard to get to. Up to the Second World War and just after, all reed around the edges of the Broads was cut along with a lot of reed which was difficult to get to. It was cut because there was a big labour force that had been cutting all their lives. As soon as they stopped, the skill was lost, so now only the best areas get cut. It is also a question of whether it's financially viable to cut in the more secluded areas.

Today the reeds are mostly cut with machines like the Allen scythe. As it cuts the reed you can go only so far then you have to stop the machine, take armfuls of reed off and stand it up, dress it, tie it and then turn it into bunches. If the reed is cut with a scythe it has a better edge on the butt but it's very hard work. It's hard enough cutting by machine and it's definitely the way the younger guys prefer to work.

When you are thatching listed buildings it doesn't matter how the reed is cut but it is often stated that Norfolk reed should be used. It's accepted, however, that if you can't get hold of Norfolk reed then you can use whatever is available. Ukrainian and Polish reed is very similar to Norfolk reed and probably as good if not better. It's very heavy reed, very strong in the stem and has very hard butts so it has become an acceptable substitute.

I learned the basics of thatching from Father and then in the early 1980s, I decided to go on my own. My brother, who is also a thatcher, joined me for a couple of years to learn the trade and we went into partnership until 2006 and did a lot of interesting work together, and he's still thatching today.

When you start on an old roof, the first thing you do is strip the thatch off. It's a mucky, dirty job especially in the hot summer when it all sticks to you. Once it's cleared, a fire barrier is usually put on with batons across so you have wooden splines to fix into rather than the rafters. Then starting at the bottom, the eave course is laid on and shaped nicely. The next course shapes the brow of the roof and that is done with the traditional leggett – a square piece of wood with a handle, about an inch thick with horseshoe nails in it. Modern leggetts are aluminium, roughly the same size. Once the brow course is on, the angle of the roof is set and you then work up one course at a time. The thatch is at least 1ft thick depending on the length of the reed – the longer the reed, the thicker the thatch.

The ridge is generally built up with three courses of sedge grass which is more pliable. The first course is the skirt which gives the thickness and the length of the drop for the ridge. The next is a packing course which fills the middle out and ensures there is plenty of thickness to brotch into. The reed roll goes on top and runs the full length of the property and levels out the ridge and also gives something to fix into. Once it's fitted, a saddle course is put over the top and covers the roll to make it watertight and it covers all the brotches holding the sedge on the layers below. Once the sedge is on, you can start the pattern work.

Thatching 1980s

The pattern work is done with hazel rods and hazel brotches and forms roughly the same pattern across the country although it's a bit more ornate in Norfolk. You start at the top of the ridge in the centre and run a hazel rod across to secure the saddle; then you work from top down putting four leggetts on to give the spacing to the bottom of the ridge. The pattern work is put in each space and is normally triple diamond which means, if you look across the pattern work at an angle, you can see three diamonds.

Each rod is held on with a brotch which is like a two-feet-long wooden staple. It's got a point either end and when you bend it over you get a twist in the middle and it's pushed about 12 inches into the roof. You need very strong hands and you've got to make sure every brotch, or spar as we call them, goes slightly at an angle to avoid water getting into the roof.

The ridge is all done by eye and once you get to the bottom you're left with a step up between the sedge and the reed. At that point the finish depends on the thatcher and it is how a thatcher can tell another thatcher's work. Each will leave a mark on the roof with slightly different angles on his pattern, with slightly different drop patterns, or by varying the distance between his drop patterns.

The average cottage takes between six and eight weeks to thatch with two thatchers, and if the reed is put on well, a Norfolk reed thatch should last 50-60 years. Combed straw reed lasts about 30-40, and long straw lasts 10 years. The ridge lasts 15-20 years, mainly because it's exposed to the elements.

Nowadays, my son and I do between 10 and 12 jobs a year. Most are re-ridging and repairs and the occasional small re-thatching job. We have

Making roll for ridge 1983

done a lot of churches in the past and I'll soon be doing a re-ridge for Lessingham Church. When I was in partnership with my brother we worked on churches at Lessingham, Brumstead, Bacton, Edingthorpe, Swafield and Claxton, to name a few. They were all big jobs and took a long time. We also worked on lots of boatsheds around the Broads including about a dozen boatsheds at Hill Common in Hickling where we either re-thatched or repaired.

Boatsheds can be quite difficult because we work over water, especially at the entrance, and I've taken a few tumbles into the water on those. In the past we worked on agricultural barns the farmers wanted to maintain but these days they are becoming redundant as they are not big enough to house modern machinery, so most of the barns we do now have been converted into housing. I've also thatched one or two bus stops which can be a bit fiddly and a few village signs such as Sutton's village sign.

We work right through the year. For me the worst time is the middle of summer as it can be unbearable on the roof with the sun beating on your back, it just takes the energy out of you. The thatch reflects the heat so when the temperature is 30°C, the roof is probably nearer 40-45°C and that is reflected straight back at you. In the winter, when it's cold and wet, at least you can put extra clothes on, and once you've warmed up, it's not too bad.

I have had one or two falls in my time. My worst was in 1992 when I was on my own and had started work on a small barn stripping a hole in the roof. As I started to thatch the gap the sky turned black, and going up the ladder with three or four bunches of reed, an almighty gust blew down the full length of the scaffolding and caught the reed on my shoulder. I tried to let go but wasn't

Cutting and trimming completed ridge 1983

quick enough and the reed pulled me down. I fell backwards about four metres and I thought I was a goner but luckily there was a two-metre-high trellis behind me, and whoever had fixed it to the post had only used small nails, so the trellis actually popped off and I slid down it hurting my shoulders pretty badly and spraining my leg.

I couldn't stop because there was a big hole in the roof and it had started to rain so, with a bad leg and bad shoulder, I put the tarpaulin over it and made it watertight. Then I had to load the truck with the old reed which was in the owner's drive and take it to Scratby and burn it. By that time I was soaked to the skin as well but I didn't need to go to hospital!

Traditionally old thatch is burnt, but it's becoming harder now as farmers are not allowed to take that sort of stuff for environmental reasons. We have tried to find ways of using the old thatch but it's difficult as there is a huge amount of it. We can't shred it because it's quite tough and it's not economically viable. At the moment the only way to get rid of it is to burn it and I can do some on my grounds.

There can be a fire risk in a thatched property if the chimney is not maintained and swept on a regular basis. Old cottages can have holes in the chimney or faulty wiring and recently fires have been caused by the new efficient wood burners that create so much heat. It's not usually a flame that starts the fire, it's the gases that build up around the chimney flue that ignite, and it usually happens after the wood burner has been on all winter. The heat has built up and if there is an easterly wind fanning the heat, the thatch can catch fire. These days we put on a fire membrane, which is like a roofing felt, and it can provide protection for 90 to 120 minutes. If the fire catches on the outside of the thatch the membrane usually gives the fire brigade time to scrape the thatch off and stop it falling into the property, and it also stops water damage.

I have been to a lot of properties where I've been surprised they have not caught alight already. I have seen smoke coming out of the thatch and when I've stripped it from around the chimney, the acid in the soot had eroded the bricks on the inside of the chimney so much that there were holes. In some cases the remaining brick was only a few millimetres thick. Years ago, a farmer asked me to have a look at some thatch because the tenant thought there was steam coming from it but he thought it was smoke. We pulled the thatch off and round the chimney was so charred, the only thing that stopped it from burning was the carbon that had built up on the thatch and stopped the fire spreading. There were holes you could put your arms through, both sides of the chimney!

My son started helping me about ten years ago and I'd hoped he would take over but I don't think it's going to happen. I'll carry on for a while and then I'll have to retire because the body is beginning to say it's had enough. It's a really physical job and a hard but enjoyable life.

A man of the marshes: reed cutting

(1962 – 2018)

Wally Mason
(b. 1947)

ROCKLAND ST MARY

Wally worked on a farm and then a mink farm when he left school while helping his father cut reed at weekends. He prefers the traditional method to the noisy modern machine.

I have always done reed cutting. Even when I had a regular job I did it at weekends so I worked seven days a week. When my dad was still reed cutting I would give him a hand and I've got three sons now who all keep their hand in today. These days people don't use the river to get to the reed like I did, they prefer to drive up to the banks. In my day it was a case of going out on the broad all day, rowing, cutting the reed, bringing it home and putting it on the staithe. That was a completely different thing.

I have always used a hook and scythe. I've tried it with a machine but it was too noisy for my ears so now I am probably the last hand cutter in Britain who can do it. The old wooden scythes have two handles on the side, so when you swathe or swing your blade into the reed, you take down a metre at a time. You walk a bit, swathe – you have to get into the rhythm. Then you lay the scythe down, gather the reed up and clean it, dress it, knock it on a wooden board and tie it together so the bunch of reed is ready to go on a roof.

When you cut by hand all the small pieces come out, whereas the machine takes in everything as it goes and leaves about two or three inches of stubble exactly like a combine on a corn field. Thatchers find when they buy machine-cut reed that they have to do a lot of the cleaning themselves, so they are not really buying a whole bunch but three quarters of a bunch, yet the price of hand-cut and machine-cut reed is about the same. You can't win today because for the last 20 years foreign reed has killed the job completely. It comes from all over and now we are told what the thatcher will pay; you can't bargain with them like you could years ago.

Cutting reed depends on the weather, wind and tide, and how you feel. On a good day we could knock out 50 or 60 bunches and the thatchers would come and even offer to carry it. What they call Norfolk water reed is the best and it will last up to 70 years. However, combed wheat which is about 4ft long is also used for thatching but isn't as good.

Years ago there were lots of hand cutters around the Rockland area and the other broads, perhaps 16 or 18 of them. Bless the old boys, they're all gone now. They used a 20-25ft heavy ligger to cross the dykes and they often had to drag it to the next marsh to chuck across. The old liggers that the old boys used before us are still there and I still go on them. You have to be careful if they are not pegged down because they move if the tide comes up, and if you are carrying a bunch of reed, you'll get wet!

I have also worked on shoots in Rockland and cut out duck paths and hides with the scythe, and the wildfowlers let us have the reeds and muck. I don't shoot myself as it wouldn't be fair to shoot their

Wally on the marshes

Reed bunches

birds but I'm free to walk round their 400 or 500 acres and go fishing when I like; they know I'm about and looking after the place.

Another job was making faggots from thin little branches of trees. On a wet day I used to make a big bunch and tie it three times and make a load to take down to the boatyards. In the past before the liggers came in, they used faggots instead and if you check around on farmed fields you can find blackened sticks still in the drainage – anything underwater like that will keep for years. When boatyards dug out a slipway to take boats in and out of the water they would timber the sides and wait for a low tide. Netting was put in the bottom and the faggots were chucked in, next day they would be like a float forming big square pads. These were then sunk on the sides of the slipway to keep erosion down.

I'll never stop going on the marshes and I still like cutting reeds. I go out on the liggers, I still do duck paths and I just muck in. It's more of a hobby now than a living. As long as it pays for the boats and the diesel in the truck, I'm happy. The best time on the marshes is when spring comes in early April. The birds are getting about more and making nests, the weather is getting better and the nights are pulling out. I can stand on a reed bed and without turning round I can tell if there is someone on the bank. I go by the wildlife on the bank and can sense straightaway.

A life in sugar beet

(1989 – 2007)

Alex Mason
(b.1941)

CANTLEY

Alex always worked in the sugar industry starting in Scotland and finishing in Cantley via a job in Iran and was responsible for modernisation and increased production at Cantley.

Cantley sugar factory opened in 1912. It operated for three to four years before closing in 1916 and reopening in 1920; it has been operating ever since. The whole construction process started in March 1912 and smoke was coming out of the chimney and sugar processed by the end of the year – quite an achievement.

In 1989 the company decided that a change of management was needed and I was asked to take the job. When I arrived it was not operating particularly well and I drew up a plan detailing the changes needed and over the next year or two they were implemented, and during my last ten years, we became a well-oiled, well-running machine.

Although it was hectic working under the sugar beet campaign conditions, it was actually quite routine. I would be in work by 7am, put on my overall and walk through the factory. Unless something caught my eye, I would go straight to the laboratory to look at the throughput results from the previous day together with the overnight logs. Initially when we were trying to change things we would have a daily production meeting at about 9am and talk through the issues of the day and the plans.

When I left in 2007 the throughput was 9,000 tonnes a day, whereas when I started it was 6 to 7,000. Interestingly though, the number of loads had not gone up, the lorries had just got bigger – at one time, farmers delivered the beet on tractors and trailers.

Once the season ends, the factory goes into maintenance but there is always a section processing the sugar, bagging it, screening it and getting it ready for the customers. Cantley produces only industrial sugar for British Sugar and two-thirds of the production is shipped abroad from Felixstowe. There is a perception that industrial sugar is lower grade but of course it's not, because domestic sugar is not analysed for grain size, whereas industrial sugar has to be.

The retail side of British Sugar is Silver Spoon, and when I came to Cantley there was a Silver Spoon production area where we made icing sugar and more specialised sugars like jam sugar but now that has gone to the plant in Bury St Edmunds. The impurities left after the sugar comes out of the beet are mixed with the spent beet, then dried and pelleted, and sold as animal feed mostly to Wales, Yorkshire, the Lake District and Scotland as there is less stock in this area.

The process starts when the sugar beet is brought in and the farmers paid on the sugar content of the beet once it's analysed. Some of the beet is stored on site and transported into the factory in water channels, or flumes as we called them. The first stage is to remove any stones, a simple process because sugar beet floats and stones do not, and the stones pop out through an opening at the bottom of the channel. Rakes take out any green material and the beet is washed by tumbling it around and finished off with high-pressure sprays so it is clean.

Cantley under construction 1912

Cantley 2018

All this is done on the north side of the railway line at Cantley, then a conveyor takes the clean beet across the track to the factory where it is sliced to resemble McDonald's chips. The sugar is then extracted by mixing it with hot water in a diffuser. The water goes in at one end and by the time it reaches the other end it holds all the sugar as well as some impurities. The raw juice is then purified using quicklime and carbon dioxide which precipitate calcium carbonate, which in turn gathers up all the impurities. The calcium carbonate is filtered out leaving the purified sugar juice which is evaporated off to leave crystallised sugar. The first product is white sugar, it's not coloured, and this white sugar goes off to be dried and stored in big sugar silos. There are various grades of sugar but the two main products at Cantley are ordinary granulated sugar and caster sugar.

Sugar beet doesn't like heavy frost and frost also makes it difficult to process which is why farmers store the beet to stop it from getting damaged. There have been years when the beet was damaged and we couldn't get enough good beet coming into the factory.

Over the years we have had some interesting characters working in the factory and one thing that always amused me was that nearly everyone had a nickname – I never found out what mine was but I cannot believe I didn't have one. In the early days most of the workers came from Cantley and local villages and a lot of the seasonal workers were bused in from Great Yarmouth. As the requirements changed and the workforce got smaller and more skilled, they would come from further afield.

Over the years there have been some terrible weather conditions but during my time we kept everything going the whole time. In 1987 the factory was cut off by snow for four days and we had about 70 people stuck in the factory and they had to fly the food in.

Looking back the thing that weighed heaviest on my mind was health and safety, as I was responsible for this and we did have one or two nasty incidents. Sugar dust is quite explosive, and there was an incident which took place during maintenance when there was a really bad explosion caused by a spark in one of the sugar elevators. One person was quite badly hurt but fortunately it was no worse, although there was a lot of damage to the plant.

My varied life: peas, beet and Cantley

(1950s – 1970)

Bernard Sheppard
(b. 1926)

SUTTON

Bernard describes his seasonal jobs once the reed cutting finished including carting sugar beet to Cantley and working there for a year.

I think a lot of marsh work has gone by the board. In the 1950s we used to go hoeing and thinning out the sugar beet after the reed cutting season finished and after that we did pea vining for Birds Eye at Ingham and two of us used to find the labour for them as well.

They had four viners where they threshed the peas out of the pods, big machines set up on blocks with an elevator going up at one end. There were six big sieves inside the viners which squashed the pods. Then the peas were spun round in the viners and came out through lots of holes and ran down an apron. The silage or pea waste came out the other end and the farmers took that to use as fodder for the cattle. That was quite a good job and it lasted a couple of years until they put up two big stations at Filby and Upton. That's when I took up lorry driving and I started carting the peas.

I also drove the combine harvester for a contractor in Stalham all through the sugar beet harvest and then carted it to Cantley. It was piecework and I used to do two loads a day, about 18-20 tons perhaps, and I filled that lorry twice a day on my own, chucking a load on for 3s 7½d a ton. When I think of footballers today who get burnt out… We used to take a load to Cantley on a Saturday morning and go out and play football in the afternoon! The lorries were hand-filled with a fork, there were no machines to help so you just had to get on with it. When you dropped down the sides of the lorry and looked in, you had a big old hole to fill but you got used to it.

I did have one year in Cantley factory loading sugar onto railway trucks. They allowed four people to a truck and the sugar would come off the conveyor belt in two-hundredweight bags (224lb). What we used to do when there was four of us, was to have two sit out while two loaded the truck. We could do it because we got so used to getting the bags and throwing them just right. But before you got used to it that was also pretty hard work. Two-hundredweight bags of sugar! You wouldn't be allowed to lift that weight today. There was no health and safety. I think we had to use a bit of common sense and watch what we were doing.

A lot of the seasonal jobs have gone and are being done by machinery. When I was young and needed a job I'd dress the banks on a farm with a scythe or hand-hook and was paid so much a chain. It was piecework and I could earn a bit of extra money as the harder you worked the more money you got. That was what it was all about. They cut the banks with tractors now. When I drove a combine I could do 20 acres in a day; that was a good day's work but nowadays a 20-acre field is done in a couple of hours. They're out 'afore they're hardly in! You could do it with a collar and tie on.

A lot of the farms about here used to carry about 12 men, now there's only two. So that's where the jobs have gone; machinery can do the work faster and it works out cheaper. That's life and I think you've got to try to change with the times.

A Rednall in Cantley

(1960 – 2003)

Arnold 'Archie' Rednall
(b.1941)

REEDHAM

Archie followed his father and brother into Cantley and trained as a fitter. He remained there for the rest of his working life and saw the changes coming in.

My father was a first-fix carpenter and when we first moved to Reedham, he worked with a local builder installing stairs and cupboards. He used to bike to work but when it got too much for him he applied for a job as a carpenter at Cantley sugar factory. This was the first sugar factory in the country, built in 1912, and originally owned by the Anglo-Dutch Sugar Company. They had a carpenter's shop with three carpenters, their own brick company and bricklayers and a painting gang, in fact, every trade you can think of.

My dad got my brother a job at the factory and I always remember when I first went and going into the manager's office. As I was trying to think of something intelligent to say to get my apprenticeship, he just said, 'You're Bert's boy aren't you?' and I said, 'yeah'. 'Alright, you can start on Monday.' And that was it!

When my dad went to work there, one of the foremen was a Dutchman from the original Anglo-Dutch Company. His nickname was 'the farmer's boy', because he dressed like one. He was just retiring as I started my apprenticeship as a trainee fitter. I did a five-year apprenticeship with day release at Norwich City College and I used to drive there on my motorbike. In the morning I'd be in the machine shop learning how to operate machines such as turners and grinders, then in the afternoon I did Maths, English and Science and in the evening I was taught Technical Drawing by a chap from Laurence & Scott's. I got on very well with him and really enjoyed it. I learned a lot and it certainly prepared me for my job at the factory.

I became a maintenance engineer on the first shift from 6am to 2pm with three fitters, two electricians, a welder and a plumber and basically our job was to maintain the mechanical machinery. If a diesel pump went wrong, I fixed it. If an elevator went wrong, I would see to the mechanical parts and an electrician would handle the electrical side. There was also an instrument mechanic and other people to look after the coal-driven boilers in the boiler house which supplied the steam running the turbines, which in turn produced the electricity to run the plant.

The last year I was there they began a 'two-hat' system – traditionally an electrician had a black hat and an engineer had a red one so two-hat meant multi-skilled. The Engineering Department and the Electrical Department were amalgamated and I had to become a mechanical/electrical engineer and the electricians became electrical/mechanical engineers so we could work across both areas. As my brother was an electrician, I had quite a good knowledge of the work as I used to help him with some of his jobs. I learned how to wire up motors and lights although I wasn't allowed to work on high-voltage cables. I also did a course so I could operate the coal boiler. I wasn't terribly good at it but that was okay because I had more experienced workers overseeing me.

There must have been 200 people on a shift and everybody knew each other; many were related and worked together. It was like a family firm

Cantley during the campaign season

with everybody pulling together and that was good. During the sugar beet campaign a lot of casuals were brought in and doubled the crew, so we would work round them. When the campaign was over, we would strip out and overhaul all the machinery ready for the next year. However, employee numbers slowly dropped as technology came in.

I worked at Cantley until I was 62 and when I was offered voluntary redundancy, I took it although I did go back in the campaigns to do oiling and greasing and was quite happy to do it. So working at Cantley was very good, they looked after me and gave me my pension.

The sugar beet story: Cantley

(1974 – 1993)

Robert Fransham
(1930-2012)

CANTLEY

Bob worked on a farm for 30 years before starting at Cantley in 1974. He describes his work and the changes he experienced there.

When I first started at Cantley, I was in the yard gang for a fortnight but I didn't really like it out there. We had a big area to look after, cleaning up round the site, keeping the water levels right in the reservoirs and anything else that wanted doing. When a job came up in the factory, I applied and got it. I was on a flat rate in the yard but in the factory I was a grade 5 which paid several pounds more, so that worked out a treat.

I was trained on the cutting mills where the beet was sliced up before it went to the diffuser which washed the juice out. Nobody really wanted that job because the previous year a lot of seeded beet had come through and fibre had caught round the knives and blocked them. Luckily it was a fairly good year when I started so I quite enjoyed it. There were 24 blocks round a disk with three sections of knives in each which I had to clean and check for sharpness. There were six machines when I started, then after a year new cutting mills were installed which were much better and increased the slice, going from 200 tonnes an hour to 250, which made quite a difference to the throughput.

The work was very noisy and I'm suffering from it now. There was a gas pump below where we were working that made a terrific noise. After a couple of years they moved the pumps into a building of their own and you had to wear ear muffs if you went in there. I did that job for three years and then I thought that I would have a change because you could hurt your back in the mills, and I thought that I had got away with it up until then.

I got a job on the carbs which was where the juice was purified. The juice went through the diffuser and then gas and lime were added to trap the impurities. We had to balance the lime and gas to get and maintain a 'break', which meant the clear juice was on top. We'd test some juice in a glass and if the sediment didn't settle in half a minute it had to be filtered again before being sent on through the factory. It was quite an interesting job and we were right in the centre of everything.

After a year, a job on the evaporators came up so I went for that and did a year. It was on the top floor and I worked on my own with the white sugar pans at one end of the room and me at the other. I had to control the flow of juice in the evaporators, a marvellous system really, whereby the juice going through got thicker and was filtered before going into the white pans. A lot of people didn't like that job as it could suddenly shut down making a horrible noise and you'd have much more steam than you wanted, but I quite liked it.

The next year some relief jobs came up so I put in for one and got it. Relief jobs meant covering other people on their days off and were generally higher paid. You had to be trained on all the jobs such as boiling sugar and controlling driers, all that sort of thing. It was interesting to say the least.

The thing that beat me was when they brought in more computerised stuff. I could do the job manually, like boiling sugar and judging when the juice was the right thickness to add a cupful of sugar to seed it and start the sugar growing; I could manage that. But once they computerised it, it all worked to time and it never did seem so good. I'd rather do it myself but they wanted the computer to do it. That was what happened throughout the factory, they sort of 'improved' it. After I left they brought in a different computer system and that worked much better. As a result of computerisation a lot of jobs disappeared and a lot of casual workers were no longer needed.

Work was seasonal but could run from September through to March. Sometimes we would run out of beet if the roads were really bad, it didn't happen often as we usually had enough beet for a couple of days and if the roads were blocked after a blizzard, they were soon cleared. After the season we cleaned up ready for the next year. In the summer I used to work on the evaporators, cleaning them by putting a brush down each of the hundreds of tubes, and I tested the white pans and checked the pressure valve for any leaks. Then an inspector would come and check everything under pressure.

We also did some shot-blasting in the summer when we cleaned the diffusers and repainted their insides because the Peridite lining wears off over the years. We would blast it off one night and go back the next night to recoat them. But when I first started I didn't quite know what was going to happen. The foreman told me just to hold the light and he would blast the screens which were covered with dust.

The diffuser was a big drum with different bays and we had to go in and climb over a couple of 3ft weirs to reach the next door every third bay or so. The foreman and I wore hoods with an independent air supply, so we were alright for air. He began blasting and the dust just got thicker and I couldn't see the lamp; I was standing in the dark not knowing what was happening. The foreman knew the layout and went up and down the screens until he was sure they were clean. The air cleared quickly when he stopped and I was glad to see him! At first there was no communication from inside the drum, we just had a lamp and hammer and if we wanted something we would hit the wall. After a while we got little radios which meant they knew exactly what was happening. We did 12-hour night shifts, but that was good pay.

There was a canteen during the day but we mostly took our own lunch and when we got huts to keep our clothes in, things improved a lot. We had showers too which we needed, especially after shot-blasting, so we often ended up cleaner than when we started.

I worked with some good people including the foreman; he was in charge but he could see that if you were the one doing a job, you often knew how to do it more efficiently, and he'd let you carry on. I worked with one chap who lived across the river and he'd come across every day by rowing boat. It was maybe 50 yards but if there was a strong tide it wasn't easy; I don't think he ever missed a shift whilst I was there.

Most people stayed for a long time, it was looked on as a job for life. I was lucky to be able to join the pension scheme after just one year which made a big difference – before that you had to wait five years. That worked a treat.

Sugar processing

Cantley sugar beet factory

(1963 – 1996)

Keith Patterson
(1942–2018)

REEDHAM

Whilst working at Reedham Ferry, Keith also began work at Cantley. He describes both his work and his family's long association there.

In 1963 I started at the sugar beet factory in Cantley. It was very labour-intensive then with many jobs done manually. My first job was working as a shunter in the railyard. The railway was the only way to get the sugar from where it was bagged in the factory at one end, to the warehouse where it was stored at the far end. They would load covered trucks three times per shift and two engines were used.

What a performance that was! Massive stacks of sugar were created using 16-stone sacks; it was a cruel job but the chaps who did it made it look easy, and the finished stacks were absolutely perfect. You could not help but admire them. In the summer when the sugar was needed to feed the packing plant it was nearly as difficult a job to take the bags down again. If they didn't grab the right bag they were in trouble and ended up pulling and tugging against loads of weight. But they knew exactly which one to pull, it was an art. That's all gone, and now the sugar just rumbles along the elevator straight up into silos.

In those days when the beet campaign started, the workers began on the first day and finished on the last day – there were no days off. They worked the lot. Eventually they got one day off a month and others were needed to fill in, so there was a group of us who did 'six 'til two' shift all the while. We gained experience in a variety of jobs and when I finished in 1996, I was the process foreman on D Shift.

It was quite common for families to have worked at Cantley spanning many years, but we don't think anyone can beat my family's record. Our long association goes back from my son who started in 1984 in the office and is still there. He has had a blood relative at the factory every year for the last 105 years, except for four. His great-grandfather, Jack Shreeve, started there in 1912. He lost his arm in an accident at the factory on 12th December 1913 and then completed his time as a night-watchman, retiring in 1944. Then my son's grandfather, Charles Newson, worked there from 1947 until 1971 and I was there from 1963 to 96. There was a bit of a break when the factory didn't produce sugar for a few years during the First World War.

Cantley factory in 1912

Bringing power to the marshes

(1961 – 1995)

Kerry Berrisford
(b. 1945)

CROWNTHORPE

Kerry worked for Eastern Electricity and helped bring electricity to remote areas of the Broads.

My family moved to Great Yarmouth in 1954 and then to Gorleston. As a teenager I spent many happy hours watching boat builders at work in the small boatyards on the river and wildfowling for duck on my friend's punt on Breydon. At that time the herring fleet was still coming into Yarmouth, mooring ten deep alongside the quay, almost across the river. It was wonderful to watch the Scottish fisher girls processing the herring and we used to collect fish that fell out of the crans and take them home to Mum.

I signed up as a student apprentice with Eastern Electricity in 1961 to train in basic engineering skills before joining the Eastern Electricity depot in Yarmouth a year later. Then, from December 1962 I worked with the linesmen operating from the depot.

During the bad winter of 1963 I was very much in at the deep end. Lines were brought down by ice, transformers blew up as they were overloaded and the Acle marshes were inaccessible due to snow. We were called out to change a transformer which fed a cow shed and milking parlour way out on the marshes but to reach it, we had to drag the new one behind a caterpillar tractor on a homemade sledge made from curved Anderson shelter sheets and timber. We successfully replaced the faulty one!

From mid-January we had about three months of continuous deep frost which froze everything, the river was frozen over and the sea was frozen for about 200 yards out at Yarmouth. A car was driven on the frozen river all the way from Thorpe Station in Norwich to Yarmouth; there were bonfires in the middle of Oulton Broad and the roads were badly affected by rutted ice. We got about in Land Rovers and trucks but I also continued to attend Norwich Tech and rode along Acle New Road on my motorbike with no traffic at all. I never missed a day and I didn't fall off.

We were defrosting pipes in the hospital using welding equipment, repairing broken electricity cables that had frozen up and replacing water-damaged electricity meters in people's homes. All sorts of problems. We couldn't lay new cables because the cable drums were frozen and we couldn't unwind the cable. So we had to bring the drums into the stores, warm them up for two or three days and repair the faulty section with the warm cable before it froze again.

Most of the marshes were supplied by overhead 11,000 (11KV) volt lines. We did lay a few cables underground to avoid flight paths of geese and duck on Breydon, and a number were laid across parts of Acle and Haddiscoe marshes. But generally they were on poles and the main lines were all on poles. The main line from Yarmouth to Acle runs alongside the Acle New Road and there are always some poles leaning over; it's difficult to keep them upright in what is basically a peat bog. They have massive cruciform timbers bolted to the base to act as stabilisers and lots of wind stays to hold them at a right angle to the lines. In wet snow and freezing conditions, the lines build up a layer of heavy ice up to 9cm in diameter which can cause them to break.

33kV line to Long Stratton under construction 1986

When I got my first engineering job at Norwich in 1966, we were still doing some rural electrification schemes. We provided the first electricity supply into the Stratton Strawless area and we installed electricity for the first time into little hamlets and isolated farms well into the 1960s and 70s. The overhead line to Acle meant that supply could be taken off it to farmsteads on the marshes en route, *and by the 1970s most homes on the marshes were connected and many wind pumps were converted to electricity.*

People who lived and worked on the marshes were completely resilient and quite happy with oil lamps, having had them all their lives, and there are plenty of tales about electricity going to those homes for the first time. Tom, one of our foremen, put in a supply to an isolated farm in North Norfolk. They erected a long section of single-phased 11KV line with a transformer on the end to provide one light and one plug. The day the supply went live, Tom went to the farm to demonstrate it to the farmer, showed him how to switch on the light and promised to return in a week to see how he was getting on. When he did, he was met at the door by the farmer who said, 'Cor, guv'nor, that bloody electricity, that's bloody wonderful that is! God, you lit that light the other day and the bugger ain't gone out yet!' They were just so used to lighting oil lamps and dealing with wicks!

I remember one incident on the North Norfolk coast when a gale was blowing and trees were down. There was no communication and lots of people including a nursing home, were off supply. I could see the disconnected line was an 11KV line so I isolated it and against the normal safety rules, I borrowed a ladder and got up to the transformer to replace the wire. Unluckily for me, there was a lightning strike on the line further up. It knocked me off the pole and burned my leg. I was dazed on the ground and a guy who had been watching asked, 'Does that happen very often?' I said, 'No, generally only once!' I wasn't hurt, just shocked, and I managed to put the line jumper back on and went home – I still have a mark on my leg where I had a 50p in my pocket when I leant against the pole and it burned.

I was involved in building the main primary substations all over Norfolk and Suffolk, as well as laying mains 33KV cables, and when Stalham bypass was built we put in a primary substation there. We laid cable along the bypass and past Stalham Staithe where the ground is completely waterlogged. So we had to use dewatering equipment which meant putting perforated rods in the ground to suck water out and into the broad. We lowered the water table 10ft using vacuum pumps to create a dry, safe space and over Christmas 1969, I was out there every day filling the diesel tank to keep the pumps working and avoid flooding – which would have been disastrous.

Access to the Broads can be difficult. When switch gear became obsolete, we had to load replacements onto boats off quaysides like Potter Heigham, take it upriver and unload using JCBs at the other end. We got our linesmen and equipment over ditches and boggy ground using a variety of vehicles such as Argocats and caterpillar tractors to get onto a site. Once at Thurne we had to borrow the vicar's boat to get the switch gear to a substation that was

Transporting equipment 1985

inaccessible. Often we would strap the poles onto a pole bogey and tow it across by Land Rover or Bedford 4x4 when the marshes were dry enough to take the weight in summer.

Latterly we have pioneered the use of helicopters to transport men and equipment to the work site and we have commissioned 6x6 Land Rovers with flotation tyres, one of which was the longest Land Rover in the world at the time and was used by the Electricity Board for a fundraising event when we did the Beaujolais Run to pick up wine.

Faults generally occurred in the winter and I remember hiking miles at night across Haddiscoe marshes in bad conditions to inspect the lines. Despite the problems of overhead lines, at least you can see them. Underground lines are much more expensive to put in and much more difficult to repair. My current company does not install overhead lines but there are still reasons why, in areas like the Broads, they are the best solution.

Underground cables laid across a peat bog eventually sink in, particularly the old cable which was lead-coated. You lay a cable 3ft deep and it ends up 10ft deep, also loops of cable occur where the ground level is variable and that puts pressure on the cables, and joints are pulled apart. Around Wroxham, Horning and Wayford Bridge, cables have been laid in boggy conditions making repair and maintenance work very challenging.

When the supply went off, it was very difficult for farmers on the marshes as very few had standby generators to begin with. We had to work hard to keep them on supply and make it reliable. Before they had electricity, farmers were reliant on their own resources but once they were connected, they started up pig-rearing units and milking parlours, and when the wind pumps were converted to electricity and the supply failed, the farmers were in double trouble – they couldn't pump out the marshes to keep the water level down, they were unable to heat their homes or cook, there was no lighting in the cattle sheds, and they couldn't grind feed materials for the cattle. It was very difficult working on the marshes but eventually many did buy standby generators.

Some of the linesmen were amazing. They were hard as nails, out in all weathers, on top of poles in freezing conditions and in temperatures of -20° in 1963. Every piece of metal they touched, they froze to. Unsung heroes to be honest.

A farming family: barn conversions

(2005 – 2018)

Joanna Burroughs
(b. 1961)

WHEATACRE HALL

Joanna is a member of the Burroughs farming family. She has converted barns into holiday lets and invites visitors to view the dairy unit.

I was born in 1961 at my grandparents' farm in the tiny village of Hoe, near East Dereham. The reason I was born there was because it was a Saturday, Norwich livestock market day, and my father was there so he sent my mother off to have me. Our own farm was at Cawston in North Norfolk and when I was about 11 we moved to Kirstead near Brooke.

My father, Tony Key, was a livestock farmer dealing with cattle from all over the country. He came from Aylsham where my other grandparents and my great-grandparents farmed. Henry Key farmed at Plumstead near Norwich, so the Key family is quite a large farming family in Norfolk.

I met my husband, David, when we were both members of Loddon Young Farmers Club and we married in 1982. The Young Farmers Club was very big then in Norfolk and I think many farmers met their future wives and husbands through them. When we first married we lived in Aldeby and then moved here to Wheatacre Hall and our two children are now heavily involved in the family farm.

Back in 2005/2006 we looked as a family at what to do with the barns in the farmyard. They were falling rapidly into disrepair and although they were large, they were not really big enough to lend themselves to modern farming. Over the years one had been a grain dryer and some of the others housed storage and livestock. There was an old granary and a range of traditional Norfolk cart sheds. So after considering several options we decided to look at self-catering holiday lets. We are actually very well-placed here being close to the Suffolk border at the southern tip of the Broads and 20 minutes from the coast. David thought it would be a nice little sideline for me but it has turned into a full-time job!

Planning permission was gained and we started work on the barns in the summer of 2006 and converted six barns by June 2007. It was a very busy build and a huge learning curve. I spent all day every day on site with the builders, which has proved invaluable because now I know where all the services are, how things were built and how everything works. It has served me well and we later converted a further two small cart sheds.

There's lots of outdoor space and we hire out bikes to enable guests to explore the local countryside and we actively encourage them to look round the farm, especially the dairy unit where we have a viewing gallery. I'm concerned that our younger guests really have no idea about where food is produced so if we can send them home with a bit of information on why British food is the best, then hopefully, I will have done my job.

Bringing the story of the Broads alive

(2010 – 2019)

Nicola Hems

MUSEUM OF THE BROADS, STALHAM

Nicola studied Heritage Management and became Curator at the Museum of the Broads in 2010. She is interested in all aspects of Broads history.

The aim of the museum is to bring the story of the Broads alive and I am fascinated by the objects and the stories we tell of the people who lived and worked in this area over the past few centuries up to the present day. Some people worked on the land as marshmen and they and their families and especially their wives led hard, isolated lives. Other people built, sailed or worked on boats, or worked as farmers, or just lived in the villages as shopkeepers.

I'm the first curator at the museum so when I joined the role wasn't really defined. Obviously, the administrative side had to be dealt with, but my remit was also to increase the number of visitors. One way is through our annual exhibitions which cover many different topics and the whole idea is to explore stories not normally told at the museum. We have covered both world wars, beer and brewing, high streets, and in 2019 we looked at the lost railway of the Broads.

The WW1 exhibition was absolutely fascinating. We had a grant from the Heritage Lottery Fund and worked with a film-maker and students at Stalham High School to record the stories of local families during that war. These formed the basis of an exhibition we put on in 2014 and then again in 2018. It was a phenomenal project with a lot of local involvement, and it got a lot of publicity.

The Lost Railway was our special exhibition for 2019. It commemorated the 60th anniversary of the closure of the Midland and Great Northern (M&GN) line that ran from Great Yarmouth to North Walsham, Melton Constable and beyond. The railway was built in 1876 and was very important to the development of tourism in the Broads. Without it, tourism and subsequent boat hire would not have happened – boat hire became really important from the 1880s in this part of the world. The railway also opened up the seaside to people from the Midlands and London which led to the establishment of holiday camps on the coast. We worked closely with Barton House Railway and the M&GN Circle and displayed some of their loan items.

I have also introduced Heritage Open Days which have been a great success and we open for both weekends of the scheme. It's really popular and it's fantastic publicity for us because, of course, it is nationwide.

We are an accredited museum and an independent charitable trust with 80 volunteers, all of whom have skills and experiences different to mine, so it's a fascinating place to be. Before I joined, the museum was operated entirely by volunteers. We aim to be a community museum and because of our location at the northern end of the Broads a lot of our volunteers are very local and some of our stories are local to us.

The museum opened in Potter Heigham in 1996 and moved to our Stalham site in 1999. Since

Steamboat Falcon

2017 the Trust has owned the four buildings here and each building is themed and named after a different broad: Barton, Surlingham, Wroxham and Oulton.

The two brick buildings that are now Barton and Surlingham are around 200 years old and were used as dry stores for wherries and latterly for storing coal. The stores were situated on Poor's Staithe where the wherries used to load and unload. It's an historic site and the least changed staithe in the Broads. It's called Poor's Staithe because it was owned by the Poor Commissioners who raised funds to look after the poor of the parish. The other buildings, Wroxham and Oulton, were originally used as boatsheds.

Visitor services and displays telling the story of the wherry are based in Barton and outside in Friends Way, we have some large boats and other objects from wherries. Surlingham looks at the management of the landscape through the work of marshmen and marshwomen; it also looks at wildlife and houses special exhibitions. Wroxham looks at the origins of the Broads and the holiday industry while the Oulton boatshed has some of the most iconic craft that ever sailed the Broads.

Outside, we operate our steamboat Falcon three days a week so our visitors can really experience what the Broads are about and also spot some wildlife such as kingfishers and otters. We got a new electric boat in 2019 called the Marsh Harrier which is wheelchair accessible and we run her the days that Falcon isn't in service.

We have around 5,700 exhibits in the collection and every week we get donations of small items such as family holiday photos which are phenomenal through to much larger objects – two people have offered us boats recently. We get around 8,000 visitors annually and open from the Easter holidays to the end of the October half term; some visitors come on boats as we have mooring outside the museum. We publicise widely; I give talks and have been interviewed for local radio stations and TV and have also appeared in 'Great Canal Journeys' and in a Channel 5 programme called 'Walking Britain's Lost Railways'.

We are in the process of expanding the museum having purchased the Cooke's Staithe site in June 2019. It is immediately next door and will give us the opportunity to develop and display more of our collection and tell different stories, and we will be bordered on three sides by water! We are the only museum for the Broads so if people want to find out about the heritage of the Broads and what is happening, come to us! We do still remain a hidden gem; we are not on the main thoroughfare, so we have to work to get people to come and visit us.

The Norfolk potter

(1999 – 2019)

Pat Southwood
(b. 1961)

SALHOUSE

Pat wanted to be a potter from the age of 10. She has had a pottery in Salhouse since 1999 and her pots combine both Norfolk and Japanese influences using silt from the Broads in her glazes.

Studio potters will always use one type of clay and keep their choice of glazes to an absolute minimum as you need to know them inside out. When you open that kiln you want to know exactly what you are going to find. Different clay bodies will give different colours simply because of the amount of iron oxide present in the clay. It is a bit like the difference between painting on the back of a white envelope and on a buff envelope; it's going to change the result because of the background colour.

When you first start making your own glazes, you follow the glaze recipe religiously otherwise it can go horribly wrong. But with experience, you begin developing your own recipes that reflect your own voice – it's the only craft that has so much chemistry and physics in it.

I was involved in a collaboration with Creative Arts East in 2005 when they paired six local crafts-people with six people involved with traditional Norfolk crafts, and as my studio is an old thatcher's yard I was paired with some thatchers. They had me doing all sorts of exciting things, like running up roofs in February and making brotches. I then had to make a work inspired by my time with the thatchers for a touring exhibition around Norfolk. I ended up taking the thatch that had been removed from a local roof and burning it to use the ash to make a glaze. This was possible because thatching reed is very high in silica which is the glass-making part of the glaze.

When I heard that Hoveton Great Broad was being dredged, I was excited by the possibility of using the silt in my glaze – no-one else was using silt from the Broads in their work. I thought it would have very fine silt particles blown from the fields, the size of particles I use for glazing, as well as fish bones and snail shells that would give me calcium. I understood that the antifouling paint put on the bottom of cruisers was copper-based and would very likely give me green. So I arranged with a Natural England warden to go out on a boat to collect some silt and I did some experiments in my electric kiln – it looked like a dog's dinner! But then I tried the wood kiln and it magically turned into a wonderful and beautiful glaze.

The new material and the influence of its origin had an impact on what I was doing. Normally when throwing a pot, you draw up the sides with one hand on the inside and one on the outside, but I began working in a way that stretched the clay from the inside only. I would shape the pot so the rim and base were the size and shape I wanted, while the clay in between was a solid cylinder without shape. I then put a contrasting thin layer of clay on the outside and, using paint stripper, I would quickly dry the outside a little while keeping the inside wet.

As I continued the throwing process without touching the outside (as it would have spoiled the surface quality), the outside would split, with marks similar to those you see in mud on a hot

day. My work reflected the nature of the broad – the earth was cracked and dry, the fish and plants were not surviving, everything was slightly desiccated and unwell, and the water was cloudy and dark. I wanted to bring together this method of making and the concept of the restoration of the broad.

As the process of cleansing Hoveton Broad went on, I intended my work to become lighter and brighter, with lighter greens moving more into blues and the surface becoming less stretched and more whole; more cohesive. I wanted a sense of water moving and times changing.

I have long been interested in Japan and in 2009 I did a workshop in Mashiko with Hamada Tomoo, the grandson of Shoji Hamada who was perhaps Japan's most famous export potter. The ceramics produced in Japan are wood-fired. It is a long-winded process and more expensive simply because of the time involved. So for my wood kiln I have to cut the wood to fit the fire box and because it has two fire boxes, one on either side, I have to put wood in every five minutes. The object of the exercise is for the flame, ash and anything else to go up through the ware box so the flames lick around the pots and ash lands on them. When the temperature is sufficiently high for long enough, the ash landing on the pots begins to melt, flux, and turn into a very rudimentary glaze. That is how glazes were discovered by the Koreans long ago when someone noticed that with wood from a particular type of tree the pottery came out a little shinier, and they realised that some trees had more fluxing materials than others.

Through my work I am trying to combine my connection with Japan with Norfolk influences. I try to bring together the feeling I get from Japanese ceramics and the feeling that I want to convey. I can't claim Japanese culture as my own, I'm a Norfolk girl, so I'm trying to combine the two so that the forms have a resonance within Japanese culture but also have a relevance to contemporary Norfolk life.

A man of the marshes: eels

(1950s – 2018)

Wally Mason
(b. 1947)

ROCKLAND ST MARY

Wally began eeling as a child with his dad and as an adult became a part-time eel catcher.

I did a lot of fishing as a child but mostly we went out babbing for eels. My dad would get big worms from the garden at night and next day he'd get a yard of cotton wool and a big needle and thread them together like a big bunch of grapes. Then he'd get a piece of willow stick and a little lead weight.

We'd go out on the boat and he'd have a sack which he wet and tacked to make a sheet in the middle of the boat, then he'd slip one end over the other end and cut a hole in the sack and put the pail under it – eels do bite but they suck more than anything. We just kept bobbing up and down with the stick testing the line, and once we hit the mud we would keep bobbing gently up and down. When there was a real tug, we'd lift the stick over the top of the sack, give it a flick and the eels dropped off into the pail.

We mostly got one at a time. One day, when I was about 11 years old, I got a big one and grabbed it. I was excited and as I lifted it up, the tail hit the side of the boat. Plop! At the same time my weight and all the worms caught my father on the ear. He was not amused and hit my ear just as quick. 'Sit still and behave yourself', and that was all he said. He didn't take me next time as punishment but he knew I loved it.

They used to eat the eels years ago; they would skin them, gut them and fry them, or if they were jellied the outside skin was left on. Smoked eels are supposed to be a big delicacy. There's just one centre bone and if it's left in you could chop it up like a sausage, maybe in breadcrumbs, or you could cook it with your mushrooms and bacon.

Eels are marvellous when you think about it. They come from the Sargasso Sea, 2,000 miles away and they get here by the tides, just floating on the sea. When people catch a little eel here that's about four inches long they think it's about three months old but it has actually taken the eels about 18 months to get here, and that little eel could be about five or six years old, which is fascinating. Then the males go back and start it all over again, similar to salmon really.

We've got so many rules now yet there are still poachers shooting pheasant and duck, or eel fishing and putting nets where they shouldn't or don't have a licence – if there's a bit of money they're going to try and earn it. Years ago you never needed a licence but now you need a licence for each net and the nets have to be washed.

I used to go out at night to catch eels, setting off with the eel nets in the boat before it got dark, and I'd sink them down in the centre of the river. I'd chuck the first net in and then go with the tide dropping the others. I had to remember where they were because the next day I had to go back. I'd hook up the nets, empty the eels into a bin and then wash them and hide them somewhere on the riverbank in a sack or a cage – today, they have to use cages because there are so many otters about which rip off their necks and it would be a week's work for nothing.

Wally with his eel nets 2019

Eeling is hardly worth doing now. I finished up with just ten nets in the end and I was lucky if I got a pail a week. They're just not about, although you'll get some big ones in ponds and lakes. The eels mostly went to big eel companies in Holland which used to send over a tanker every six weeks to Kings Lynn, Yarmouth and Lowestoft and finish up with three or four tonnes of eel. About 80 or 100 eel-fishing people were involved and we'd get a few shillings for our catch. Now we buy them from the Dutch company, mostly smoked.

There's been a big decline in eels and there are no trawlers round the coast now, that's all finished. And there are not many people out doing whelks and cockles either. I've sold my licences and I've finished. As much as I love the water, it was a lot of hard work chucking weights onto the mud, cleaning the nets and working the tide.

There are one or two eel catchers still about but where I had 20 nets when I was doing it, they have about 300, and they might get half a pound of eels in each one. I couldn't compete with them. They just go down the river with about two miles of nets working all day. If the eels aren't there now, it isn't worth it anyway.

Now I'm retired I still go out fishing. I love rowing a boat and I love the Broads. I just like to sit in a boat, pull the oars in and let it drift from side to side. Then I row back and let it do it again, just twirling around, with the water lapping up against the boat.

Fishing and eeling

(1950s)

We used to fish on the River Waveney with an old chap called Billy Thurston who taught me a lot about wildlife and fishing.

We would row up to Geldeston or perhaps down to the old Beccles swing bridge to fish. He knew the river like the back of his hand and we fished in lovely, reedy stretches where there were weeds in fast, flowing waters which were so clear. We caught everything: bream, rudd, roach, dace, tench, perch and gudgeon.

When we babbed, we would cut a straight hazel pole off the bank, about 6ft long, and wrap it round with 8ft of line. We'd thread lobworms onto worsted wool and tie them into a big bundle to hook onto the end of the line. Then we sat in the boat and bounced the bab up and down on the gravel bottom of the river. Eels would grab it, their teeth digging right through the worm and into the worsted wool so they were well and truly caught. We would drop them into a tin bath and the process would start again. They were fantastic things, up to an inch and a half thick, and sometimes we even got them up to two inches in Fritton Lake – the eels there were massive… absolutely out of this world!

Mike Page
b. 1940

Norfolk from the air

(1978 – 2019)

Mike Page
(b. 1940)

STRUMPSHAW

Mike has been an aerial photographer for over 40 years and has built up an enormous collection showing changes in the Broads.

I got my flying licence in 1978 and just had to get my own aeroplane. I bought a Cessna 150 and kept it at Seething airfield. I later sold it and bought another Cessna G-BOIV which I've had now for 24 years. At age 79 I now share the plane and fly as a passenger but when I flew on my own, I trimmed the plane so it continued to fly while I opened the window to take a picture.

The photography all started because I like to build up a history of an area and I now have a massive library of roughly 170,000 digital images and about 40,000 film images on 35mm film. When I'm taking pictures we fly at different heights, anything from 500ft, the minimum you are allowed to fly over land, up to 5,000ft. I don't generally go much higher as I can already get everything I want in the frame.

One of my favourite subjects is coastal erosion and that started because of the land that disappeared at Benacre and Covehithe. Over a mile of coastline has gone since I was a kid when we used to go down to a bungalow called the Four Winds next to a wartime gun emplacement. It has all disappeared into the sea and is gone forever. Things change so rapidly every week and every day with coastal erosion.

I also like to photograph wind farms, particularly big wind farms. Somerton was the first to be built over 25 years ago but it's small by today's standards. There are also several massive solar farms now and thousands of solar panels on houses. I like to document development sites, especially around Brundall and in my own area – that is all history as far as I'm concerned.

The Norfolk Broads have changed a lot since I was young. The rivers that I remember fishing as a teenager were crystal clear, then the rivers and broads got into a really bad state in the late 1980s and 90s and became just shallow muddy water. Many of the broads are being mud-pumped by the Broads Authority, especially the smaller ones and they are beginning to clear and grow weed again. The top end of the Waveney and the Bure are good now although the lower reaches are still very muddy. On Barton Broad where they put the fish barriers in, you can see crystal clear water on one side and muddy water on the other and it shows that the Broads Authority is finding ways to keep areas of Broadland clear.

Fish barrier Barton Broad 2006

My family and the Broads

(1963 – 2018)

Bryan Read
(1925–2020)

NORWICH

Bryan's family includes Boardmans and Colmans who have long been involved with the Broads. He relates some of the additional work with which he has been concerned over the years.

My grandfather had a flour mill in Beccles which burnt down in 1896 so he moved to Westwick Street in Norwich and then, in the 1930s, to King Street – I took over its running in 1963. My father also had a mill at Horstead which unfortunately also burnt down in 1963. One of the reasons my grandfather moved to King Street was only wherries could get up to Westwick Street whereas larger coasters could get to the quay there. At King Street, there was also a bucket elevator which was used to discharge the grain. In 1936 there were 660 coasters coming into Norwich bringing in coal, grain and timber but the only export from Norwich was scrap metal which was loaded at Corporation Quay just above Carrow Bridge.

My father had a lot of connections with the Broads and loved sailing. We've had quite a few boats, one in particular was the Harrier, a sailing cruiser built in 1900 and bought by my uncle in 1917. He handed it on to my father in 1945 and now it's mainly used by my grandchildren and great-grandchildren. So broads and rivers have been very much part of our lives.

My father was a Port and Haven commissioner representing Norwich – commissioners had responsibility for operating and maintaining the port of Great Yarmouth. They also had responsibility for ensuring that the rivers Yare, Waveney and Bure were properly maintained for navigation. In the early days, this was for commercial traffic before the holiday traffic and hire boat industry took over during the 1900s. When my father died in 1963 I succeeded him as one of the representatives of the Port and Haven. It was important as in those days we were importing a lot of grain by coaster up to Norwich. Pre-war it would have come from Argentina to Antwerp or Rotterdam in large ships and then transferred to smaller 300-tonne coasters and come right up to Norwich.

The waterways, particularly after the war, hadn't been properly maintained, they were polluted and the banks were eroded. The problem was because different organisations each had different responsibilities. The Port and Haven had responsibility for navigation

Read's Flour Mill, Norwich, 1968

and waterways, Anglian Water Authority was responsible for maintaining the banks, and local authorities, overseen by the County Council, had responsibility for various aspects of the use of the rivers. In the 1980s there were discussions about developing a unified authority but there was considerable conflict between agriculture, tourism and other environmental interests, and particularly from the Port and Haven which didn't want to lose its navigation powers.

I was involved with the discussions as a member of the Port and Haven and as a result I lost my seat. Discussions went on over a ten-year period and in the end common sense prevailed. Against significant opposition the Broads Authority (BA) was formed with statutory powers by an Act of Parliament in 1988, and I was involved in the appointment of the Chief Executive. The BA was given very wide powers including responsibility for navigation, and it oversees what is now called the Broads National Park. For legal reasons the name cannot be used in formal documents but it can be used for promoting the Broads.

I am part of the Norfolk Windmills Trust and a lot of our responsibilities are around the maintenance and, if possible, the restoration of windmills. We have been involved in quite a few in the area. We would have liked to have maintained Stubb Mill at Hickling but Norfolk Wildlife Trust has taken over responsibility as it is in the middle of one of their special areas. We are currently restoring Stracey Arms Mill, not to working condition, but we are putting on new sails because the mill is very much a key feature of that particular area, as are many of the other mills.

The Broads Society was set up about 1960 to help promote the Broads and keep an eye on what was going on. Where necessary it made presentations to the various authorities which eventually became the BA. I became president about 2000. Aitken Clark, the first Chief Executive of the BA, reckoned that there was a place for a charitable body which could do things which the BA hadn't

Stracey Arms Mill ca. 1990

the powers to do, so I got a few people together and we set up the Norfolk and Suffolk Broads Charitable Trust or Broads Trust. We had a legacy of £10,000 left by one of our Broads Society members, a great Broads woman and a Colman, Lady Mayhew. The only condition the Broads Society made was that funds were not to be used on any project in which the BA was involved and this has worked out well.

We run an organisation called 'Love The Broads' where hotels, restaurants and companies can add perhaps an extra £1 to the bill on a voluntary basis, and that comes to the charity. We've been working closely with the Lake District which has been doing this for a long time. We have supported both fairly major and quite small projects including additional mooring in the South Walsham Broad area, a tender for the wherry Maud which is run by a trust and needed some additional help, and a wheelchair with extra wide tyres to go on soft ground at a bed and breakfast – we felt that this was a very worthwhile project. In all cases our aim is to help people enjoy the Broads more.

CHAPTER 5

Conservation & ecology

- COYPU & MINK
- NATURE RESERVES
- ISSUES & PROJECTS

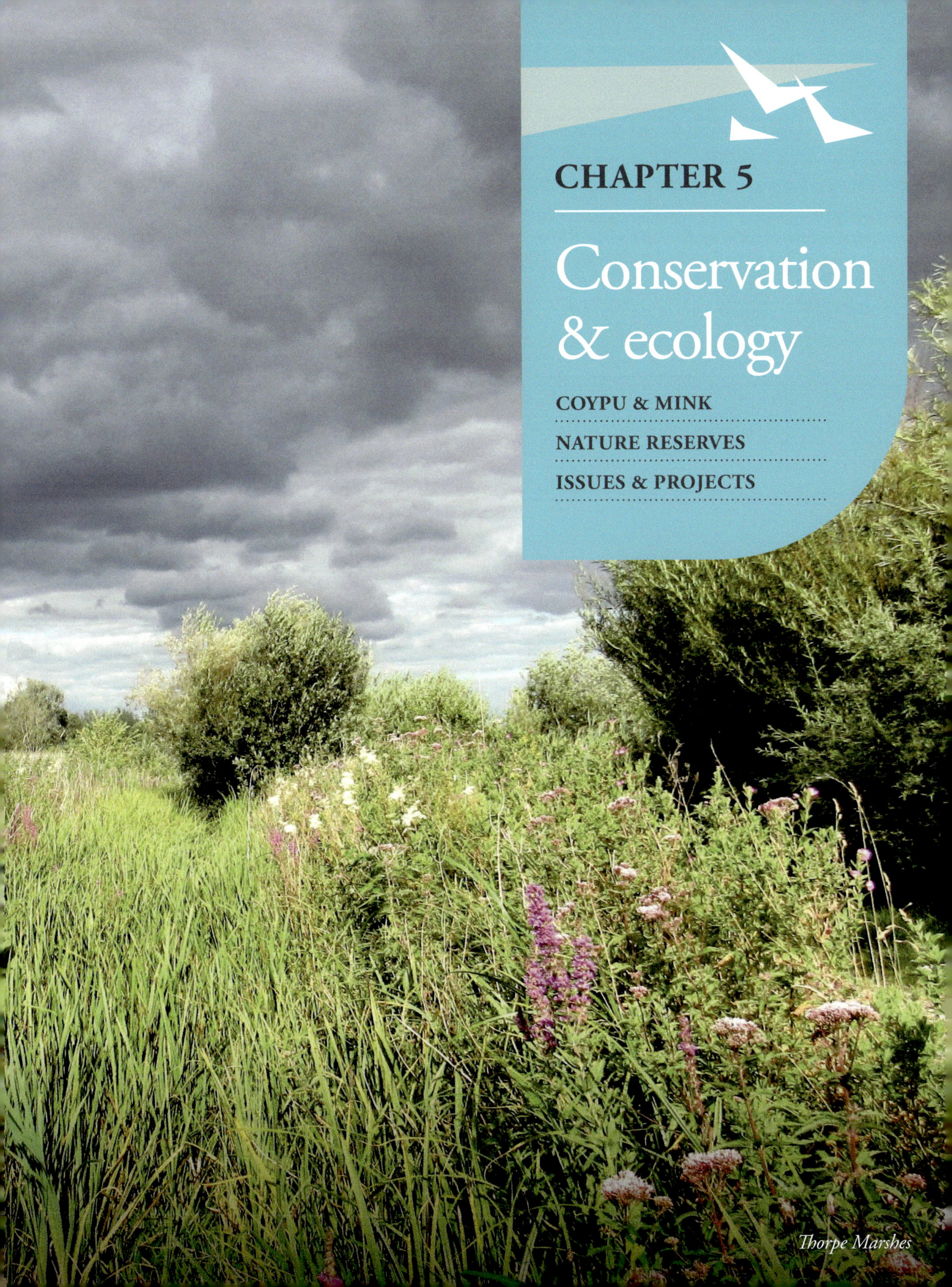

Thorpe Marshes

Wheatfen Reserve

A life with introduced animals

(1976 – 2019)

Simon Baker (b. 1951)

BROADS & MARSHES

Simon joined the Coypu Research Laboratory in Norwich (CRL) to work on the feeding ecology of coypu. Later he became involved with mink control.

My new job in 1976 meant moving to Norfolk so I bought a small 125cc motorbike to get me to Norwich with all my gear. I got as far as Oxford when it seized up and I hitchhiked to Norwich to start work. It was my first proper job and it was very interesting, except I did little work on feeding ecology. The majority of the work was on the population dynamics of coypu: how the population increases and decreases, what causes that, and what impact trapping and weather has on numbers.

Coypu were introduced into this country around 1929 for their fur. They are a semi-aquatic South American rodent weighing up to 8kg and an adult measures around a metre from nose to tail. They bred all year round with litters averaging five or six young, and the main population in Norfolk probably originated from three fur farms around Norwich. Once they escaped, the population in the Broads increased steadily until by the late 1950s and early 60s they were widespread, and people were worried about the problems they were causing. They ate crops and although they didn't live exclusively in burrows, they would tunnel and cause problems with drainage systems and dyke banks. Their feeding was also very specific and Ted Ellis, the well-known local naturalist, was one of the first to point out that many of the rarer plants were disappearing and that the nature of some broads was changing. The farmers didn't like them, the conservationists didn't like them, the water authorities didn't like them and the public didn't like them either, because they looked like a large rat with orange teeth. So they didn't have many friends.

We think there could have been 200,000 coypu in East Anglia by the early 1960s and the first eradication campaign was started in 1962. I suppose because it was relatively soon after the war, they tried a military-style eradication programme. They started trapping from the outside, somewhere in the Fens, and trapped in concentric rings moving inwards to push coypu back towards what were called the 'inner redoubts' in the Broads. In hindsight, the problem was that while coypu were being controlled in the low-density populations at the periphery, they were

Coypu traps in a small dinghy

breeding like mad in the prime habitat of the Broads, and emigrating outwards into the areas that had already been cleared. In addition, a few coypu were always left behind as the trappers moved forward.

The first campaign coincided with the very hard winter of 1962/63 and this probably killed 90% of the population. However, because of the big trapping effort happening at the same time, many people thought it had made a larger impact than it actually did. The dykes and broads were frozen and the coypu couldn't feed properly and got very nasty lesions on their tails, many starved to death and females aborted their litters. The campaign was ended after a few years with coypu numbers reduced to relatively low levels.

We then had a series of fairly mild winters and the coypu population, fairly predictably, started to rise and people saw the same problems happening all over again. In 1977, the government of the time decided to set up a Coypu Strategy Group to advise on the future control of coypu. By this time, there was quite a bit of research in place, including a number of models saying roughly how many coypu there were in the wild and what might happen in the future. For example, if 15, or 30, or 45 trappers were employed, models suggested what was likely to happen in each case given different weather scenarios.

They had one other crucial bit of information available, provided by the study area running between Norwich and Reedham, where the CRL field staff was attempting an actual eradication programme. The area had quite a difficult habitat around the Surlingham and Rockland Broads with lots of big reed beds and extensive grazing marshes that went down to Reedham itself. We could never get down to the last coypu in the study area

Cage traps

because coypu could come in from either end, but we did get them down to very low numbers and we showed, with reasonable certainty, that any coypu still there had come in from outside. In fact, CRL was able to show that the models worked and that eradication was technically possible in an area where people said you couldn't do it. This allowed the Strategy Group to recommend a new eradication programme.

There were two bodies operating in parallel at this time. As well as CRL, there was the Coypu Control Organisation which employed the trapping force and was entirely separate. It was funded 40% by Anglian Water, 50% by government and 10% by Internal Drainage Boards, whereas CRL was funded by the Ministry of Agriculture to develop the strategies to be employed by the campaign and to provide all the background advice. Following our advice, 24 trappers and three foremen were employed to carry out coypu control.

An interesting programme was established; I don't think there's ever been anything quite like it. It was set up as a 10-year scheme but a key consideration was to have an early and successful completion date. However, this meant that

Trappers crossing a long ligger

trappers would be out of a job early and we realised that this was not a great incentive. It was a non-pensionable job and not particularly well paid, so the scheme was designed in such a way that if the trappers were successful in eradicating coypu within six years, they would get a bonus of three years' pay. That would then fall off from six years to ten years on a pro-rata daily basis. So the trappers knew that the quicker they eradicated coypu, the larger the bonus they would receive.

When you're trying to eradicate something you'll only know you've achieved it in retrospect and, in the case of the coypu, it was deemed that the last viable population ceased to exist in April 1987, although three isolated old males were found after this date. Coincidentally, this was a few weeks past the six year mark so the trappers earned an almost full bonus. However, trapping continued until January 1989, to ensure there really were none left.

There had to be an independent check because a lot of money was going to be paid out to the trappers, so the field team from CRL set out small rafts filled with stock feed carrots throughout East Anglia. The rafts were 2ft square with a little ridge round the edge and if there were coypu about, there would be droppings or tooth marks. Rafts could be left for a couple of weeks whereas traps had to be checked the next day so it was possible to cover a much greater area. We knew from earlier work that coypu liked the rafts because they couldn't stay in the water all the time, and if danger threatened they were able to pop back in the water. If they had carrots to eat, it's even better.

The original modelling also suggested that as research progressed, trapping would become more efficient and the use of resources and improved techniques would become more effective. This proved correct. For example, in the Middle Yare study area we were able to show that a trap set on a baited raft was actually 50% more effective than a trap set on the land. So during the campaign increasing numbers of traps were put onto floating rafts.

Coypu were found all over East Anglia, from the Thames to South Lincolnshire and inland to near St Neots, but the most densely populated area was Broadland with its grazing marshes and broads. For the purpose of allocating trapping resources, East Anglia was divided into nine strategic regions and most effort and resources were put into those regions where most coypu were killed in the previous quarter per unit of trapper effort. This brought the population down over the whole area at a similar rate, rather than what had happened in the first eradication campaign, which was to try and sweep them into the sea.

In total 34,000 were accounted for and the last coypu was caught by CRL staff in December 1989. CRL was then closed and we all moved on to other jobs. It probably was, and is, the largest-scale eradication of an invasive alien mammal that has ever been achieved.

During the campaign we were catching the odd

mink which had escaped from fur farms and when we brought in rafts we caught a lot more. Although mink are carnivorous we caught about 370 in coypu traps baited with carrots. They are semi-aquatic and like to get out onto rafts in the same way that coypu did and they were caught when they wandered into the trap. These were humanely dispatched with a shot to the head, as were the coypu.

In the early 1960s the government began getting slightly worried about the spreading population of American mink across the country because of escapes from farms. The first wild mink killed in Norfolk was in a hen run in 1957, and in 1962, legislation was brought in to control mink farms to make them more secure. About half went out of business but the mink population in Norfolk continued to grow. I couldn't prove it but I think the intensive coypu trapping probably slowed their expansion in East Anglia. Mink can wipe out water voles even at very low densities. They are very catholic in what they take and can go after kingfishers, both wild and game birds, and fish. Although they cause a different type of environmental damage to coypu they certainly are a very big problem. I would go as far as to say, unless you control mink, you will not have water voles.

After I'd retired, in 2012, I went along to a meeting about mink and introduced species held in North Norfolk and introduced myself to the speaker who was from the County Council. I was asked if I would like to join the strategy group which was supporting the mink control going on in Norfolk, and after I did a review of what was going on, I became chair of the strategy group for my sins.

My involvement with mink had been off and on since the coypu days. When I began a regional job in the Wildlife Service, one of my tasks was to visit mink farms to check that they complied with the keeping regulations, and this included farms in Norfolk. I was also involved dealing with the aftermath when animal rights activists raided farms and let mink go. The mink that had been kept in small family groups were let out into a big enclosure and then out of the enclosure into the wild. When mink unknown to each other meet, they fight like anything, and we would go in and find injured or dead and dying mink. The damage they did to each other was horrendous, not to mention the wildlife damage caused when they got out.

The Norfolk Mink Project had its origins in 2003 trying to control mink in the Wensum Valley because of the catastrophic decline in water voles. It then expanded into the Norfolk Broads and along the River Nar. We decided that because mink can move such a long distance, with over 70% moving more than 50k from their place of birth, trying to control them in relatively small patches wouldn't solve the problem. As a result, the current Norfolk Mink Project covers the whole county.

The project is based on volunteers detecting and trapping mink using mink rafts developed by the Game Conservancy Council. These have clay pads which are kept damp by blocks of Oasis that go under the clay and into the water, so any mink around leave their footprints in the clay. The pad is near a tunnel and if footprints are found, a trap is slipped into the tunnel to hopefully catch the mink. It can then be humanely dispatched and any non-target animal released unharmed. The project has around 300 volunteers around Norfolk and information can be found on our website.

We have made extremely good progress. In the first year on the Wensum alone about 170 mink were taken, and in the last few years we are averaging around 70 in the whole of Norfolk, so numbers are very much reduced. However, although we work closely with other counties in East Anglia, there will still be mink coming into the county and with a very modest budget we are unlikely to eradicate them from Norfolk in the near future. Nevertheless, the project is allowing water voles to survive in the Broads which has always been one of the prime locations for the species in the country.

Mission impossible

(1975 – 1989)

Ivan Watts
(b. 1926)

BROADS & MARSHES

Ivan wanted a change of job and in 1975 answered an advert seeking coypu trappers. He tells about his role and working himself out of a job.

I had no practical experience of the work other than the fact that I was a country person and knew where the marshes were. Much to my surprise I got the job. Training was very basic, I followed a couple of chaps for a few days to learn the ropes and then I was on my own. Coypu Control ran on a shoestring budget in the early days, you supplied your own transport, clothing and even the gun to kill the coypu – it was four or five years before Coypu Control supplied a weapon.

We had to look for signs of coypu such as traces of reed mace that they would chop down and leave lying about and we also looked for their droppings floating in the water. They were very partial to greater reed mace, particularly the succulent inner part of the stem, and they liked carrots. Coypu had two enormous top incisors which were living teeth so as they chomped, their teeth were ground down but kept growing. I never saw it myself but they were carnivorous to an extent. I have seen quite a number of mollusc shells laid out on the bank where they had brought them up from the river bed to open. You could say they were mainly vegetarian but every now and then they would fancy something more solid.

We used specially designed traps with a flap at one end connected to a treadle. The coypu was enticed in with carrots usually and pressed the treadle as it entered which allowed the flap to drop without causing it any harm. We checked the traps regularly and dispatched any coypu cleanly. Normally we buried the corpses on the spot in mass graves as we might have 20 or so on an average day. Later on, the Coypu Research Laboratory (CRL) began asking for quite a few corpses as they were constantly looking at things.

We had a very leaky boat with no buoyancy aids and I often worked solo: managing the boat, sorting out the traps and trying to catch coypu. When I think back, I think what a mad thing it was to do! A new system came in about 1980 with a nod towards health and safety. We were issued with a buoyancy aid which was quite helpful as we wore long boots and if you fell in the water they filled up and took you straight to the bottom. We continued working solo if we were working an area of land but worked in twos if we were on the water.

It was all-weather work and it could be a bit tricky at times if we had high winds and a small open boat loaded with traps. On many occasions we had to break the ice to do our job and there were times when we had to turn back. Generally we were paddling along with an oar at the bow and stern, out of the way of holiday traffic on the river. Our initial outboard motors were well-worn little British Anzanis which weren't always practical to use. It was a brute of an engine especially when we were miles from anywhere and it wouldn't start; we often had a long row home.

We worked from 7.30am to 4pm with half an hour for lunch. It was quite a long hard day with a fair bit of physical work carrying the traps.

Initially I worked in the Halvergate marshes and the marshes nearby but gradually found myself covering the whole of Norfolk and little bits of Suffolk and Lincolnshire. When I was trapping on Halvergate, the nearest I could get to the marshes by road was Wickhampton Church although I might be working near the Berney Arms, a good 4½ miles away! When you're alone you do think that if you blundered into a dyke and couldn't get out, that would be it!

I could go all day and not see a soul. The marshes were divided into areas which were overseen by a marshman and occasionally I'd bump into them checking on the cattle or perhaps horses and sheep. Often they had to bring cattle up from the marshes to be loaded onto a lorry, a four- or five-mile journey. I bumped into one chap at Herringfleet, off the River Waveney, who kept coypu as pets. He told me his daughters never had dolls, just coypu. He showed me a picture of two coypu side by side in a little child's pram, with bonnets on. You never saw such a sight in all your life!

There was a reed cutter who really stands out in my mind, Eric at How Hill. He knew the marshes like the back of his hand, a real grafter. It wasn't unusual to see him knee-deep in water scything the reed down. It was lovely to hear the scythe going through the reed as he cut it off just about water level. He was a lovely chap to talk to.

Being a solitary person on the Halvergate marshes, I saw wonderful wildlife like crested grebes and coots. I could pass a nest of eggs, watch birds going on and off them as I approached or suddenly see chicks trailing behind the parent bird. If I wasn't watching the wildlife, there was always the cattle and flora changing with the season. Some of the cattle were quite friendly but not the bulls. I was chased by a bull, a close shave – the old feller ran faster than me!

I'm glad I never ate coypu because a chap I worked with used to take corpses home to boil up and give to his ferrets. One day it killed them

Ivan in the Coypu Control boat

all. It wasn't until later that we learned that coypu carried Weil's disease which can be fatal; they also had liver fluke. Certainly they carried diseases we knew nothing about. We would be handling coypu and then use the same unwashed hands to eat sandwiches at lunch time. Later on we were issued with protective gloves.

We operated in an area stretching from north of the Thames to Humberside, about 13,000 square miles of Eastern England covered by 24 trappers. That was over 500 square miles each, even if you say it quickly!

The eradication programme didn't start until 40-45 years after the coypu first escaped and not everyone agreed with it. I didn't experience anything personally but I was told trappers returning to their vans could find the air let out of their tyres. We had only a few cases where there were problems with an estate owner because he didn't agree with it. Although we had the mandatory right of entry onto their land, you couldn't really enforce that sort of thing.

We just caught as many as we could. We didn't monitor anything during the early stages of eradication but I do remember the day a colleague and I caught over 70 coypu, which was exceptional. Around 1978 to 1980 we were catching 10-12,000 animals a year over the whole area. Their gestation period was roughly the same as a pig, 132 days, and they had large litters. It was not uncommon to see a female coypu with a dozen young trailing behind in a line.

As things became more organised, CRL would give us an idea of what area they wanted us to survey and trap. We would start from the source of the rivers in the county and work down to the sea, dealing with adjacent lakes and ponds as we went and we gradually saw the number of females taper off. The technique worked and we knew we were getting the upper hand, when week after week we put out traps and would sometimes get nothing. It got to be repetitive, even boring.

CRL checked our daily catches and they could see 'zero' coming up day after day. I can't say they ever really accepted that there were no more coypu to catch as their model showed there were still a number of females out there. We insisted we were doing well and, of course, we were gradually working ourselves out of a job. In 1989 I was made redundant at 62 with some severance pay which had to keep me going until I received my state pension. I didn't make any money out of the job but then you can't have everything. I had a lot of wonderful experiences instead.

CRL had a little broad called Calthorpe Broad. It was fenced off and the coypu were allowed to do their own thing there. However, in a very high wind a tree was blown down and it knocked over a fence. Out went the coypu. I could never see the funny side of that until much later.

Mink farm

(1960s)

After working on a farm I went to work on a mink farm in Blofield and instead of getting £3.50 a week and giving my mum £2 a week board, I started there on £5.50.

Well, that was nearly doubling my wages at the farm so I went for it. But I wish I hadn't because of the aggravation in the mornings. I was rushing down on my bike, jumping into my dad's little old reed cutting boat and bailing it out, then chucking my bike in, shooting across to the other side of the river, riding down the railway line and then another two or three miles to Blofield. I didn't stay there too long.

The mink were in cages with big runs and my job included mixing up their feed of minced-up tripe, liver and fish in a barrow. They were breeding them and there used to be about 200 mink each side of the big long sheds. They used to kill them and sell the furs. Mink were fast and as sharp as anything, the same as ferrets. One day there was a big storm and the tree broke down the netting and they got out. There's still plenty of mink about now on the Broads.

Wally Mason
b. 1947

That gal and her dawg

(1979 – 1989)

Jennie Crohill
(b. 1958)

BROADS & MARSHES

Jennie worked with the Coypu Research Laboratory (CRL) from 1979 and describes going out with her dog in search of coypu and the issues around it.

I started work as one of three trappers, I was the only lady and I had no experience other than being a country girl brought up on a smallholding. At that time we were trying to work out whether it was feasible to eradicate coypu in a given area. I was shown the basics on how to trap coypu and kill them humanely using a .22 and initially we worked through the Upper Yare Valley from Norwich to Reedham on both sides of the bank, and up the River Chet to Loddon. After the training, my days were spent alone on the marshes in a Land Rover.

We each had a different segment of the marsh. We set traps on a Monday and checked them every day. When we caught coypu we would dispatch them and take details such as their weight and sex, and if they were female we would check if they had bred, so we could build up a picture of the population within that area. We did this work with the focus on eradication until the mid-1980s. In this time we proved that we could clear and eradicate coypu within a small given area; it was really useful information for the government, as it showed that coypu eradication campaigns were feasible and could be a success.

At this point there was some discussion about whether there was a need to completely eradicate coypu. Some conservation bodies thought that they did some good within the Broads and I can certainly understand that opinion. There is no doubt that coypu ate their way through an awful lot of vegetation which kept some waterways clear. The converse was that coypu also went through a crop of sugar beet very quickly so the farmer was no friend. In the 1970s and early 80s the coypu was still confined more or less to Norfolk and Suffolk so there was concern about them getting further afield; if they had got into the Thames catchment area, an eradication programme would no longer have been feasible. The fact that agriculture was so important to this area and had to take precedence, and that coypu was a non-native species, meant that the eradication continued.

Our role at CRL changed, we needed to research the coypu's life cycle and observe how they moved about and how they bred. So in the mid-1980s we started to use radio telemetry to track coypu. It was cutting-edge science at the time and because coypu spent considerable time underwater, the systems had to be able to cope with being submerged. We liaised with the Fisheries Laboratory in Lowestoft which was beginning to use tags on fish and we made up little collars with transmitters. When a coypu was trapped we would anaesthetise it, which could be tricky, and then attached the collar and released it. As the coypu was nocturnal, two of us working separately would follow them through the night across the marsh.

We each had a receptor to pick up the radio wave and we then used triangulation methods to pinpoint the location of the coypu. We might have five or six coypu with collars so it made for a busy night tracking them all from dusk to dawn. Each had a reference number so we got to know the ones that were being tracked regularly but when the programme ended we had to dispatch the coypu when we caught them again. There was

Coypu at CRL

Setting up a coypu cage

a female that we caught time and time again and became quite a favourite with all of us; it was a difficult day when I dispatched her.

At the laboratory in Jupiter Road we had pens where we housed about ten coypu at a time and we got to know them very well. Despite our boss not being keen that we made pets out of them, the chap who did most of the pen work would line them up and offer Mars bars which they took very nimbly in their front paws. They would then sit back on their haunches and munch away with a look of delight on their faces. I remember one female weighed about 12 kilos, which was absolutely enormous, and an awful lot of that was down to Mars bars.

When coypu fur is properly treated it is known as nutria and is absolutely beautiful. It's the reason they were originally brought here. As I knew the coypu I'd shot were incinerated once CRL had finished with them, I thought I'd have a go at making a jacket. I skinned several not very successfully – there was something in the process I didn't do properly. I kept the skins for many years and eventually they were thrown out but a friend made a big pair of gloves which looked like bear paws.

The health and safety aspect of the job was never really considered in the 1970s and early 80s. I had a .22 pistol issued to me which was kept overnight in a filing cabinet and in the morning I'd strap it on and spend the day walking round the marshes, possibly popping into the local post office in Loddon. No-one gave it a thought. Everybody used to refer to, 'that old gal and her dawg', as we went up and down the marshes; they knew who we were and what we were doing. The dog was a Jack Russell called Toby, a little star who spent every day with me and got to know coypu scent, and on occasion he did find them.

All carcasses went back to the laboratory and were logged on the computer system against our reference number. Toby had his own number as I used to put him on the kill sheets. So he was actually a member of MAFF (Ministry of Agriculture, Fisheries and Food) as it was then.

A coypu bite could be dangerous to humans as well as dogs so we had to give them a great deal of respect. Like any rodent, their front teeth grow continuously throughout their lifetime and could be an inch and a half long and very sharp. If you put your hand in their way they would take your finger off.

The UK was not the only country with a coypu problem. Three of us from CRL were seconded to France to swap ideas at their research centre and

River Yare and Reedham marshes

explain how we had managed to eradicate coypu from large areas of Norfolk and Suffolk. I was quite astonished at the French method. Whilst we had employed cage traps on floating rafts baited with carrots and were then shooting the coypu, the French used similar rafts but would bucket out poison along with the carrots. A lot must have gone into the rivers and we did see a Frenchman happily fishing just downstream. I understand they have not eradicated coypu as effectively as we did and they are still at large in some parts of France.

I think my overriding memories of working on the marshes are the wonderful characters I met. They came from a breed of old boys who grew up on the marsh and maintained the windpumps and dykes, often eel-catching, doing a lot of wildfowling and keeping cattle and sheep. They were the true men of the marsh and they told stories of their growing up in an era that we'll never see again.

I can particularly remember one character from Hardley, a gentleman in his seventies known to me as Mr Porter. He had always lived on his own and he used to ride his bicycle with his waders rolled down to his knees and his old crome for clearing weeds attached to his crossbar. I would see him every time I worked on that section of the valley. He always had about two weeks' worth of dinner down the front of his jumper and he spoke in the broadest of Norfolk with a huge amount of swear words in between, and he was a mine of local information. I remember asking whether he'd travelled very far in his lifetime and he told me very grandly, 'Yep, I have, I've travelled. I've been to Yarmouth and I've been to Lowestoft and I've been to Norwich, but I he'n't been nowhere else'. It was common for people of his generation not to have travelled much. They grew up in a particular village and were very satisfied with what they did and their style of life, and they didn't have any reason to go further afield.

I work these days for DEFRA, the Department for the Environment and Rural Affairs (formerly MAFF), as a farm inspector. I enjoy my work but I think it will soon be time for me to bow out, become an old lady and go back walking on the marshes with my dawg.

Seven years a trapper

(1982 – 1989)

Paul Frapwell
(b.1961)

BROADS AND MARSHES

Paul wanted to be a gamekeeper when he left school but there were no positions so he applied to Coypu Control and became a trapper in 1982 for seven years.

I remember standing on the corner opposite what was the Castle Pub in Wroxham on my first day, and waiting to be picked up. Seeing this fresh-faced lad, totally green behind the ears, I think he wondered why they had employed me. We met up with another trapper at Ridlington and they showed me the runs that the coypu had made when cutting across the banks, the cut reed mace where they had been eating, and the damage on the sugar beet field. They showed me what I would be doing and I knew it was something I would enjoy.

I stayed with them for two months and then I got my own van and was let loose. When the other guys saw that I was safe, they authorised for me to get a .22 pistol. There was no official training but being a country boy I'd been brought up with air rifles, nevertheless they kept a close eye on me to begin with and eventually it was just a tool to do the job.

I remember my first coypu on Acle marshes. We had found lots of trails going across from one dyke to the other and set out some cage traps and when we returned the next morning, we found it. Occasionally we saw them out on the banks if we were out early but they were mainly nocturnal, except in harder weather, when we would see them moving through the reed beds or feeding in a field of sugar beet.

We always went back first thing in the morning to check the cages, even in the worst weather, and we would dispatch them and send some to the Coypu Research Laboratory (CRL) for autopsies. I would say that CRL developed a very successful strategy because before the end of the 10-year programme we were finished! We hit the coypu really hard to start with and the numbers got fewer and fewer as we went on. Some people said that we would never do it but we persisted. We set up cages every time we saw a sign and we always followed up reports from members of the public.

I personally didn't come across any organised opposition although some people felt they should not be killed. When you explained the reasons, people would agree it had to be done. The Marsh Road from Wickhampton Church to Seven Mile House and the banks of the River Yare were sunken and potholed where coypu had burrowed through the banks and created big cavities underneath. Marshmen would sink into them along with their tractors and when high tides pushed up the rivers, the banks were not strong enough to withstand them.

We covered a vast area in Suffolk, Essex and Norfolk. I was based in Norfolk but we went everywhere including all the way through to Stoke Ferry. At one time our boundary was just the River Yare but then we had to go to Haddiscoe Island which was over-run. This meant we had to go down to Yarmouth, across the river, through St Olaves and then onto the island.

I've been on the Sandringham estate and worked the rivers all the way through there, with access to areas closed to the general public. Landowners were generally good to us and gave us every assistance and local gamekeepers also helped out as much as they could. We used to moor boats at places like Hickling Broad, particularly in the winter when there were fewer public boats around. Then from Hickling we worked through Candle Dyke, Heigham Sands, Martham and Thurne Broads, and the Bure and Ant rivers – coypu could travel a long way following the watercourses, especially the bucks.

In January 1983 I caught 32 coypu and in February I caught 32 but after that it tailed off. I went the whole of August, October, November and December without catching any. Then we seemed to find pockets and we'd go in and do our best to eradicate them.

In the culverts where the water ran underneath the roads through drainage pipes, one method was to set four cages facing either way and we would catch all manner of things: water hens, water rails, ducks, water voles, land rats, coots, rabbits, hares, pheasants... I have even got a picture of my colleague holding a bittern that flew off when we released it. The worst things we caught were cygnets in the spring because if it went in one way, it was very difficult to withdraw it the other way because its feathers would stick in the cage, and all the time there would be an angry cob or its mate hissing and flapping at you.

People did say that once we finished the coypu we should go after the mink as they do so much damage, and it's probably why we don't see so many coots and water voles around. There was never the same kind of eradication programme but when you go around the Broads now you do see mink rafts that have been put out, often by local gamekeepers. Coypu were vegetarian but mink will eat absolutely everything. If there is a family of young ducks they won't stop until they have finished them off.

Last coypu caught in Norfolk

We all had tetanus jabs and if we were bitten we had to notify the doctor. Working along watercourses, Weil's disease was always a danger but I do not know of anyone who actually got it.

While we were working on the marshes we were lucky to get to know the marshmen quite well. I remember once when I was working near Wickhampton, a cow got into the dyke and the marshman was trying to drag it out with his tractor. I thought I'd be helpful and give a hand. So we lassoed the cow round the neck and he managed to pull it out of the dyke and onto the track. Without thinking I untied the rope off the back of the tractor. 'No, don't do that', he said, 'don't do that!' And, of course, the cow took off down the track with me hanging onto it as best I could. I could run fairly fast but I couldn't keep up. That cow went through three marshes before we managed to corral it against two fences and tie it up.

I've fallen in the water many times; it was an occupational hazard. We wore big, heavy Bullseye thigh boots and many times when working beside a dyke, one foot would slip and we'd get a boot full of water; in the winter it was absolutely freezing. Once when we were working on Ormesby Broad in a boat, I leant over to grab a tree branch to pull us in. The branch was dead and I went full frontal into the water – I managed to get back in the boat before my lifejacket inflated!

A hard frost in the Broads

We were out in all weathers; we didn't have a choice. Some winters were really hard but it also depended on where you were working. I used to park the van at Wickhampton church and walk all the way down to the Yare and if there was a strong wind, it just drained the energy out of you. The good thing about snow was that you could see the coypu tracks. The giveaway was the large pads on the back of the hind legs, the five claws on the front feet and the tail drag.

The marshmen used to walk miles and miles and we would see them first thing in the morning and perhaps last thing in the afternoon. As time went on they started getting quad bikes so that made things easier, and occasionally they were kind enough to give us a hand and put the traps on their bikes as we couldn't get our vans to a lot of places.

I think I was the last Norfolk trapper to catch a coypu in Norfolk. That was in 1986. Some people say the coypu are still about, but I don't think it's possible because what is thought of as wilderness is actually very heavily monitored. There are rangers with the Broads Authority, Norfolk Naturalists and the Wildlife Trust and others, and they monitor everything, not just coypu. The only way that coypu could make a comeback in this country is if they were released from zoos.

I do miss the work, I was on my own most of the time and it could be a bit boring when nothing was being caught. But I used to pay attention to what was around and keep an eye on the wildfowl and the ducks, the flora and fauna, and thoroughly enjoyed myself. I had seven years of coypu trapping and I got to know a lot about the marshes. It was a big part of my life. After the coypu control programme finished, I became a member of the Norwich and District Wildfowlers Association and as we went around places like Halvergate and Wickhampton marshes I'd keep my eyes open but I never saw any sign of coypu after we officially finished. Despite missing trapping, I wouldn't want to be doing it now; it was a different era and time has moved on.

I have some cartoons Tony Hall used to do for the EDP. One I remember had a coypu saying, 'Ah, the glorious sound of leather against willow!' 'Wuss there a cricket match on, coypu?' 'No, a short-sighted cow just run into that there tree!'

The making of Strumpshaw Fen

(1975 – 2000)

Mike Blackburn
(1944 – 2019)

STRUMPSHAW

Mike was interested in wildlife from childhood and later studied biology and freshwater biology. He began work with the RSPB as warden at Strumpshaw reserve in 1975.

I was asked to go to Strumpshaw at very short notice when the lease with Strumpshaw Hall was imperilled. The land was considered worthless from the owner's point of view but for wildlife it had a lot of promise. To help secure the lease we had the help of Dr Martin George of Nature Conservancy as it was then, also Mr Key from Strumpshaw Hall and the RSPB. My remit was to write a management plan to enhance the wildlife and habitat, manage some very good floristic meadows and extend the reserve to good wildlife areas. I also needed to limit shooting as at that time it was rather indiscriminate.

I was completely on my own until in 1980 a pair of marsh harriers decided to nest and I was given an assistant to ensure that the birds bred successfully, which they did. I did have some volunteers but in the 1980s I also got a lot of workers due to a brilliant government-financed training scheme.

When I first arrived I lived in a little caravan exactly like the one in an episode of Father Ted. I lived in it until winter set in and it got too cold and I went into lodgings. In 1978 I moved into a cottage provided by the estate which is now an office and accommodation for volunteers. We started to open to the public once I lived on site and we had a system of hides for viewing birds and wildlife. One viewing point was developed from an old shed on the edge of Strumpshaw Broad and we built a number of hides surrounding the reed fen.

That area was very different from what it is now as the reed beds were tidal and in poor condition because of enrichment by nitrates and phosphates from the river. Some areas were cut annually but if the reed had been used on a roof it would have deteriorated very rapidly. They were also infested with great hairy willowherb, nettle and canary grass, and a huge amount of scrub had taken over the reed beds, mainly willows and alders.

The River Yare took in the whole of the Norwich sewerage works which meant that the river had a large amount of nitrate and phosphate, while the small sewerage works at Strumpshaw was pumping out far too much poorly treated effluent into a small stream called Lackford Run. The latter closed in the 1990s but the Norwich effluent will never be completely resolved as there is nowhere else to get rid of that amount of treated sewage.

I started clearing the scrub within a short time of taking on the site and it became a major operation. We learned that if the water levels were raised sufficiently, the roots of the willows and alders didn't regrow so there was no need for pesticides. The scrub was then burnt on beds of corrugated iron which we took away to limit the amount of nutrient being released into the fen system.

Strumpshaw Broad was tidal and joined to the Yare until 1978 when some friends at Anglian Water said that if they were passing by with their equipment they would put in a dam for me. The dam went in just a day or two after I married so we never had a honeymoon, the dam was vital. We moored the machinery in the entrance to the dyke mid-morning and worked all day to build a clay

Caravan on the reserve 1975

Dam 1978

dam using clay from the river bed. About three in the afternoon as we were finishing off, we heard a boat from further down the dyke and, believe it or not, we had dammed in the local police boat! They were very worried about what their chief would say but in the end we scraped a narrow channel for them to get their boat through.

Once we were closed off from the river, we were expecting a shortfall of water but it was much worse than anticipated. Subsequently we learned that two drinking water boreholes immediately adjacent to the reserve were pumping 24 hours a day and taking water from below the reserve in the chalk layers. To make that right we had to build sluices which meant that when the river had very high water or after very heavy rain, we could use the river water.

When I first saw Strumpshaw Broad in the 1970s it was almost extinct and covered with vegetation and silt but on old maps it shows as a sizeable area. Once we had the dam in place and could control water levels, we began to dream of a reclamation project and finally put a scheme together in 1980.

The surface vegetation, known as 'hover' in Norfolk, had grown over the silt and needed to be pulverised. We took a new approach to this using a gadget called a mud cat. It had a high front-mounted, high-pressure water jet which converted the hover to a pulverised mash which was then pumped into a bunded area to allow the water to be decanted off through an exit pipe. This ensured we wouldn't run out of water and we were left with a clear, pristine broad.

Waterways are amazing places, they soon start to recover and aquatic weeds reappear. Wildfowl increased at Strumpshaw, particularly tufted duck and pochard and at the same time we started to see dab chicks, great crested grebe and kingfishers. Some of the meadows had been derelict for many years so we started grazing them and as this continued we noticed that the meadows were floristically very rich, so slowly we allowed haymaking to take over from grazing. There was a viable population of birds like snipe, redshank, yellow wagtails and lapwing by this time; it was a very rich area for wildlife.

When I started, the reed quality was poor and areas which had been cut were quite often burnt by the reed cutters. Within a year or two we decided to put reed cutting on a rotation although the cutters preferred to cut annually because the reed is clean and there is hardly any waste. However, we did various experiments and proved that a reed bed does not support an optimum

Reclaimed Broad

population of birds such as reed warblers, sedge warblers, reed bunting, bearded tits and all the associated insects until the reed bed had accumulated two years of dead reed followed by a fresh growth. So we decided to put reed cutting onto a double wale or better still a triple wale. The last time I had the reed tested whilst still warden, Strumpshaw reed was the best in the Broads but places like Hickling also produce good reed.

Marsh harriers began to breed in 1980 at a time when water levels were controlled for the first time, there was much less scrub and reed beds were becoming healthier. They reared five young successfully and have bred every year since in much larger numbers and have spread out to other areas.

Other changes which followed the improved water quality and levels included the marsh pea or Lathyrus palustris. This is a rare plant in the fens and Strumpshaw was notable for being the only site in Britain where it was setting viable seed. Milk parsley, a wetland plant, also expanded as did the swallowtails. There were three adults in 1975 and when I left in 2000 the highest count was 45 in one day. Raft spiders have been introduced, water soldier in the dykes has been a success and otters started breeding on the reserve in the late 1980s as the fish population developed in the improved waterways. Mink were always there but they are continually trapped now.

Buckenham and Cantley marshes came up for sale in the early 1990s and we purchased them following an appeal, raising £1,000,000. The area was nationally important for widgeon and bean geese. The year after we bought Cantley marsh the river wall was collapsed by a surge tide and the marshes went under for a considerable time. Because the water was 47% seawater, all the invertebrates were killed. I well remember

Bearded tit

receiving a letter from one of the locals the following spring, congratulating the RSPB on having bought the marshes and getting rid of all the birds. The lack of invertebrates meant that there was no food for them to breed; however, the grassland and invertebrates did recover as did the summer and winter birdlife.

I stopped working at Strumpshaw in 2000 and I remain very proud of what we did there. We created a very good area of fen, expanding it from 300 to nearly 2,000 acres, with a complete mix of fen wildlife.

Twenty-five years at Wheatfen

(1992 – 2017)

David Nobbs
(b. 1951)

WHEATFEN

David promoted crop spraying and chemical control of insects for many years before he moved into conservation work and became the warden at Wheatfen Nature Reserve.

After working in the farming industry from the age of 15, in 1992 I took a year out and completed a one-year course at Otley College on teaching conservation. Ironically, I had spent several years promoting the use of chemicals for crop spraying, killing beetles and bugs and now I was trying to preserve them. I sort of went from one extreme to the other and doing the qualification led to my connection with the Broads.

I had a four-month placement at Wheatfen near Surlingham and helped with the winter work such as reed cutting, tree maintenance and fen management. It was a physically hard job. After Ted Ellis' death in 1986, Phyllis Ellis was very much involved in the formation of the Ted Ellis Trust in 1987 and also the Friends of the Trust. At that time there was no full-time staff apart from the warden, John Tooley, and some volunteers. I came in to help John and after four or five months the contract was extended. Very sadly John died in 1993 and as I had been there over a year, I was asked to stay on. Phyllis had a wonderful understanding of Wheatfen having lived there all those years and I was happy to accept and carry out her advice.

Wheatfen was a wonderful reserve but, as nature took its course, the broad practically silted up and we were losing water. If nothing was done, we would have lost some of Wheatfen's wonderful diversity of wildlife. The ironic thing is that Ted's philosophy was 'Let nature take its course and study that', but towards the end of his life he realised that something more had to be done.

The job of warden was 95% practical. From October to March we cleared the vegetation from the dyke edges and that included cutting and preserving the reed beds to enhance diversity. The reed wasn't suitable for commercial use so we just left it in heaps, as that was good for wildlife.

I was lucky to inherit eight or nine volunteers and over my 25 years as warden, more joined me and many stayed until I retired, including Bill who was well into his 80s. We needed to find a way to benefit Wheaten for the future; to know what

David

Wheatfen ca. 2017

should be maintained and preserved and what should be encouraged, so we started by looking at Ted's wonderful maps which showed where everything grew.

Through Ted's work, Wheatfen is one of the most recorded reserves in the country. We have books of species recording over 900 beetles, 700 or 800 moths and endless records on fungi for which Ted was renowned. Along with specialists, we surveyed the area knowing that whatever work was done was going to affect something else. There is no point cutting something down when a key species relies on it.

The dykes were the most important thing; they were the arteries of the reserve. Wheatfen is unique in that it is tidal with no water control so we wanted to get our dykes restored, and with various grants we got that done.

Wheatfen is known for being the home of the very important swallowtail butterfly. When I first arrived I didn't see one for three years but now it is one of the best sites in Broadland. We also discovered a rare beetle not found anywhere else in Britain, so we had to manage that.

Ted Ellis was really the first to discover how our waterways had declined due to chemicals in the water. There were hardly any plants and the bottom was just mud when I started. But after a major mud-pumping programme and various companies no longer dumping phosphates in the river, things greatly improved. Now there are many water lilies and water weeds with insects living on them.

The Broads are gradually sinking and salt water is coming in. Over 25 years Phyllis recorded the tides every morning and I carried on that work. When I started, we were flooded about four or five times a year and by the time I left it was 15 to 20 times a year and we had seaweed floating down the River Yare. We are lucky to be tidal as the salt comes in and goes out quickly. If the water was stopped the salt would sit for months. I suspect that over time plants do adapt and Wheatfen is an ever-changing environment; it's just a question of prioritising what you feel you are able to do.

When the reserve was initially set up there was very little access as the paths were in a poor state so people went around wearing boots. Over the years we built footpaths and bridges, had a warden's office and study centre built and the car park enlarged. Visitors could visit from dawn to dusk and we got the walks up to about 2.5 miles which is quite acceptable. We promoted Wheatfen as a quiet, peaceful, non-commercial place. We had a linkup with a university in Holland and one of the things I always enjoyed was when we invited students to come over at Christmas. They would stay locally and help me on the reserve.

I was very pleased to be involved with the appointment of my successor in 2017 and I see a bright future for Wheatfen. Ironically, funding was very tight when I first started but when I left we were probably in the best financial position ever because of some quite large legacies. I feel proud of what I achieved.

Looking back to move forward

(2017 – 2019)

Will Fitch
(b.1990)

WHEATFEN NATURE RESERVE

Will is the current warden at Wheatfen. As a child he was obsessed with fishing and then did a two year wildlife course at Easton College with work experience with the Broads Authority.

My work experience with the Broads Authority was hard work and certainly not everyone's cup of tea but we were surrounded by harriers, bittern, bearded tits and swallowtails in the summer. When I finished college, I took a role as Assistant Ranger with North Norfolk District Council and soon became the Senior Ranger responsible for half a dozen sites, including Holt Country Park. We did a lot of work opening up pathways and replanting native shrubs and trees and by the time I left, we had the biggest population of silver-washed fritillary in the county. I learned a lot and when the job at Wheatfen came up I was ready to move on.

As part of my college course I had learned about the habitat here and its 140 acres run by the Ted Ellis Trust. There is a mixture of reed bed, fen, wet woodland and a little bit of dry woodland together with tidal dykes linking two broads, Wheatfen Broad and Deepwaters. I've been here three years now but have never learned to swim although I have fallen in many times, but I float rather well.

When I first arrived I was thrilled to hear a cuckoo as it has been in serious decline for many years. I spent my first few months getting to know the site and getting ideas from the previous warden and the volunteers. Then we started to draw up a management plan which would take us forward over the next five years. The plan is based on three principles, the most important being hydrology. The site floods and the water has a lot of agricultural runoff with nitrates and phosphates which fen plants hate, so we need to get the water off site as soon as possible. This meant dredging the dykes sympathetically and doing surveys first to see what was in them. Some are dredged by hand, and I rely very much on the fantastic volunteers as we dredge the old-fashioned way using traditional dydles and cromes, simply because it works.

What we call Eleven Bridges Dyke was dredged in March 2019 and when we surveyed it in the summer, we saw dragonfly larvae, diving beetle larvae and a lot of molluscs that had drifted back in with the tide. So, the dykes really can heal up incredibly quickly. However, Ted found many ridiculously rare molluscs living in the dykes and some liked a blocked dyke! So we have to be very careful. We have to think ahead and we've always got to look back to move forward.

Scrub clearance work is the second principle. Ted had watched the willows invade the fen and now there is some phenomenal woodland with fungi, lichens and mosses. There is even one moss that doesn't have a common name and isn't found anywhere else in the UK; its Latin name is Timmia megapolitana. We have to think, 'What can we cut out, what can we remove?'

Swallowtail chrysalis

Swallowtail butterfly

The final principle of fen management is reed cutting and fen mowing. I find mowing regimes fascinating as the time of year and repeat cuts can affect plant species massively. For example, a marsh harrier wants really thick dense reed with a little bit of water underneath but rare fen flowers don't want to compete with thick heavy reed. So it is about applying the right regime, in the right area at the right time. It takes a lot of time and is all linked into the hydrology.

The reed cutting is done by hand, occasionally with traditional scythes. There is a purpose to this because a scythe cuts slowly so you can avoid areas in the reed bed where you know there might be swallowtail chrysalis or other rare species lurking. We do also use mowers but they can be incredibly difficult as they sink in the wet terrain and you wrestle with them the whole time.

Our reed is poor quality as we have fens rather than pure reed; it means that all the flowers are mixed in. We stack piles of reed once it's cut as it is a great habitat for beetles and spiders and the rest. The management plan dictates that I cut the fen areas on different rotations, but it has to be adaptable, so if swallowtails are in one area over the summer with caterpillars feeding on the milk parsley, then the chrysalis will be spending their winter on it, so the last thing we want to do is cut it.

The Trust's vision is based on Ted's legacy of wildlife conservation as a public amenity as well as for research and education. Wheatfen is unique in that it's not a commercial reserve; we don't charge people to come round, we don't have tea shops or that kind of thing. Everyone is welcome but they have to explore it in their own way. The aim is to keep it as wild as possible and it needs to be peaceful and tranquil, so we can't afford to have swarms of people where it gets to the point that paths are eroded and wildlife is disturbed; it's a fine balance.

A lot of people come to see the star wildlife: harriers, bitterns booming in spring, bearded tits, and swallowtail butterflies that are only found in the Broads in summer. There is no end to wildlife rarities at Wheatfen for as well as Timmia megapolitana there is a beetle called Galeruca laticollis that you won't see anywhere else in the UK. We are not sure why it's here but its larvae feed on meadow rue which is also rare but thankfully it not a particularly fussy fen flower. Every species has its own niche; if I were to cut an area at the wrong time and remove all the meadow rue, then I'd lose one of the rarest beetles.

We are in year three of the management plan and we are seeing swallowtail numbers increase as their food, milk parsley, is spreading. We are opening up new areas and lots of rare flowers are coming back. We are trying to work with nature because when management is done correctly it is replicating nature.

This year we've had three otter cubs which was fantastic. They are a somewhat contentious animal and were almost exterminated in the Broads in the 1950s and 60s. They have been brought back and they don't seem to be having any detrimental effect on the fish stocks at Wheatfen and people love to see them.

Because the water in our dykes flows in different ways and speeds, there is a big range of dragonfly species. The larvae live in the dyke for a year or two, and one of the interesting successes of the last ten years is the Willow emerald which, contrary to usual damselfly behaviour, lands with his wings open – there's always one! The Willow emerald lays its eggs on overhanging willow branches and on other tree species too, we've now discovered.

The Norfolk hawker is another rare dragonfly, a stunning brown dragonfly with big, green, goggly eyes which emerges in June; a lot of people come to see them. On our annual Swallowtail Day last year we were on Home Marsh when a Norfolk hawker took a swallowtail out in mid-flight and plunged down into the reed bed, probably to feast on it. We had two rare things fighting it out!

Early morning is a good time to see herons, or harnsers to give them their old Norfolk name. The heron is also the Wheatfen logo for the Ted Ellis Trust.

We have a few non-native species which we don't really want, one being mink which has been devastating for many species. We trap them humanely and dispose of them in a very quick fashion. Back in the 1960s there were a lot of coypu which, interestingly, ate the roots and tuber of cowbane, something that would kill a cow within the hour, but coypu loved it. They were also a staple part of the diet for Ted and Phyllis and visitors staying in the house enjoyed the delights of coypu casserole. We also have a lot of Chinese water deer and we have a duty to look after them.

Chinese water deer

There are still a few relics from Ted's experiments here. Behind the house on Home Marsh there are some sand leeks which Ted brought from Guernsey; they were part of controlled experiments and he knew that they wouldn't cause trouble to other species. Part of his legacy was not tidying up too much. When you walk around the woodland you can see honey fungus killing off large trees quite quickly which might seem a shame, but they are going to be a home for owls and bats.

There's a big, famous beech tree on Sluice Path. It's perhaps 300 years old and has a massive ganoderma bracket (a fungus) on its side which is rotting out the tree and killing it. Ted would have looked at that and said, 'Yes, that's a natural process. That's habitat'.

Marsh pea

Part of Ted's legacy is education and he wanted his research to continue and involve all ages. This means that a big part of my job is leading guided walks around the fen throughout the year and having lots of Easton College students on their weekly work placements, just like I did with the Broads Authority. We also have a very good relationship with the University of East Anglia and have had several students here since I started.

We also have a very successful forest school which is run by Ted Ellis' granddaughter, so it's all still very much in the family. The kids are aged three to seven years and once, when I was showing them some swallowtails, they knew more about butterflies than I did, which was absolutely fantastic.

Wheatfen is rigged up with data loggers within the dykes and peat and we are lucky to have a couple of scientists, who every 30 minutes, measure salinity and nutrient levels, tide fluctuations and even how the water flows on and off the fen through the peat. In 5-15 years we may see an increase in salinity levels and start to lose a lot of the fen flowers but at least we will have the concrete data. The Broads Authority are very much involved with this project and are keen to get the results so that they can shape their future management objectives.

In the meantime we will continue to research what we've got at the moment. The more we learn about the broads, the fens and habitats, the more we could perhaps recreate these habitats elsewhere, and perhaps we may start looking at stepping reserves back and re-introducing species to where they once were.

In our third year of the management plan the successes are tumbling in, mainly because of a fantastic group of volunteers that have been undertaking the work. A lot of rare fen flowers that were just small clumps are spreading, things like marsh pea, marsh ferns and milk parsley. I don't have a goal for individual species but rather for the habitat as a whole. If the health of the habitat improves, we will see an increase in these populations anyway.

Introducing children to wildlife

(1980s – 2019)

Rodger Goodrick
(b.1946)

WHEATFEN AND STRUMPSHAW

Rodger volunteers at Wheatfen and Strumpshaw Fen and introduces children to the wonders of nature through a variety of programmes.

I left school at 15 and worked in the motor engineering industry before being made redundant in 1991. I was getting interested in wildlife at this point and debated whether or not to go for a wildlife job. I applied for an internship with Mike Blackburn at Strumpshaw Fen, but having two children at school at the time I decided to keep wildlife as a hobby instead.

I was involved with the Young Ornithologists Club (YOC), which was part of the RSPB youth initiative – later the name was changed to Wildlife Explorers as they wanted to lose the emphasis on birds as it put off too many children. The children varied in age from six to fourteen, although a few did stay longer. In 2006 I took over the leadership of Wildlife Explorers until just after I retired.

At the YOC we did field trips and some parents would come along and enjoy it as much as the children; we visited near enough every RSPB site in Norfolk. We did lots of practical stuff like tree planting, nest box building and studying trees and meadows, which they liked. Bird-watching with 10-15 kids was hard going! We had one trip to Breydon Water when there was snow on the ground and we had to do two trips as there were too many children for the boat.

The children paid £1 if they could and we were able to keep the cost down when we were based at Whitlingham as they didn't charge us to use the facilities. The biggest problem there was that lots of people wanted to know what we were doing when we were pond dipping or walking, so we moved to Strumpshaw. Some of the children have gone on to work with or study wildlife and I am really pleased with that. My daughter also used to go and then re-joined years later as a leader and she encouraged me to go back to being a leader too.

The Wildlife Explorers did a small mammal survey at Wheatfen and we found yellow-neck mice, wood mice, short-tail voles, field voles, bank voles, and I think there were a couple of common shrews.

I first heard about Wheatfen by listening to Radio Norfolk. Keith Skipper used to have Phyllis Ellis on his programmes and she was asking for volunteers and I thought, 'I quite fancy that, I'll go over and have a look'. And I have been going there for nearly 30 years. Wheatfen was quite a jungle then; there was a lot of open fen with overgrown reed beds and no real bridges so you had to be careful where you walked, as one minute you could be on a path and up to your neck in a dyke the next.

Phyllis wanted the public to see the wilderness and we do just enough work so that people can walk around safely. Sometimes the tides are so high that the reserve has to be shut because you can't get on it. So far the tides are not affecting the wildlife in the river but we are frightened that they might and we have meters set up in the dykes to read salinity levels, height of the tides and other information.

Pond dipping

Volunteers cutting scrub

Due to the management at Wheatfen and across the river at Strumpshaw Fen, the marsh harrier has expanded its range since I first came. I would say that Wheatfen is slightly less managed than Strumpshaw but if we think that marsh harriers or bitterns are nesting, we stay well away from that area.

As volunteers we do a real variety of work. Originally the work was clearing the marsh and building bridges, and as there wasn't a lot of money around at the beginning some bridges were a bit Heath Robinson. We still cut the marsh on an annual basis because we want the flora and fauna to come through. With the nutrients from the river, if we left it, it would just be reed bed and stinging nettles. These days I still work on the conservation side once a month and we always need new volunteers as many of the original volunteers are not quite as active as we were.

A new field teaching school is being set up at Strumpshaw and I've committed to at least one or two days a week doing lots of practical stuff like pond dipping, bug hunting, meadow sweeping and talking about different habitats.

I'm also going into schools all over Norfolk. One of the first things I did was the 'Big Garden Bird Watch' as part of RSPB's wider picture and also the 'Big School Bird Watch'. Another project was 'Give Nature a Home' which meant walking around the school grounds to see how nature could be helped by putting in bird feeders, ponds, wildflower gardens and bird boxes. The children are always enthusiastic.

Finally, we did the project, 'Bio-Blitz', which covered anything that was in the natural world and biologically alive. I have also been involved with STEM outreach which is Science, Technology, Engineering and Maths. I used to go into several schools and sometimes did three classes a day, 90 kids, and we'd be dissecting owl pellets all day. It was great, the kids loved it and sent me little cards saying thank you; it was really enjoyable.

One of the most satisfying aspects of working in wildlife is seeing the children's faces when they arrive at Wheatfen and Strumpshaw, because some have never been anywhere like it. They don't know what they're going to see when they get there. Nearly all of them go home with a big smile on their face and you think, 'Well that's a job well done', and with a little bit of luck, we might have planted a bit of enthusiasm for wildlife.

Spreading the word about wildlife

(1970s – 2019)

Chris Durdin
(b. 1956)

THORPE MARSHES

Chris tells of his lifelong interest in birds, his work for the RSPB and his current interest in Thorpe Marshes which are managed by the Norfolk Wildlife Trust (NWT).

Watching and identifying birds was a hobby but I didn't think it would lead to a career so I studied Economics at the University of East Anglia and joined the Bird Club and Conservation Corps there. At weekends the Conservation Corps helped manage NWT nature reserves and I was treasurer of the Bird Club for a couple of years.

I answered an advertisement for a development officer for the RSPB at their headquarters in Bedfordshire and began at the age of 22. As a bird-watcher the idea of working for the RSPB was the Holy Grail. The job included work with volunteers, public relations and presenting RSPB films to perhaps a thousand people.

I had the chance to join John O'Sullivan at the RSPB regional office in Norwich around 1980, Norwich being one of the last regional offices to open. John was a great ambassador for the RSPB and had the knack of being a boss and a good friend. I met many conservationists and increasingly the numerous enquiries about birds came to the RSPB as I developed the Society's public profile – for many years I was the RSPB's spokesman and was often on Radio Norfolk. I was also their 'bird man' on the Dinnertime Show.

I had good contacts with the Veterinary Investigation Centre and its work on post-mortems when birds died for unexplained reasons; road casualties were monitored for pesticides, and botulism in ducks and gulls was also an issue. One winter we collected a huge number of dead auks, guillemots, razorbills and puffins. They were all emaciated and had died because of really difficult conditions at sea.

In the 1980s I was involved in ESA schemes as a conservation officer, dealing with conservation in areas not protected by nature reserves such as the Brecks, the Broads and the Suffolk river valleys. ESAs were set up to put money into wildlife and landscape-friendly farming, and the project officers worked in collaboration with the likes of the RSPB, wildlife trusts and English Nature. Much of the work was establishing policies, themes and practices. RSPB survey teams were in touch with farmers and I was involved in managing surveys of the Broads and requesting access across land so we could count birds such as breeding waders and wintering waterfowl.

Farmers were very supportive and did take up the ESA schemes, but not enough in the aspects that improved areas for wildlife in my opinion. The schemes were revolutionary at the time, putting money into nature and landscape rather than production. However, the current Environmental Stewardship schemes are more geared towards delivering outcomes for wildlife.

In 1986 I began running the RSPB's little tern project. It began when a bird-watcher reported

Little tern

several pairs of little tern nesting on the beach at North Denes, Yarmouth, and was concerned about their safety. We fenced off part of the beach to allow the birds to nest undisturbed and a warden was employed. Early in the season we had about 20 pairs but by the end we had 55 pairs which fledged around 90 young.

As ground-nesting birds, little terns are vulnerable to predators and at Yarmouth, hedgehogs could eat the eggs and kestrels take the chicks. Once we had run the protection scheme for five years, the data showed that the North Denes site was an important site for little terns, and eventually it was named as a Site of Scientific Interest, the highest conservation designation. The terns' nesting sites have moved around East Norfolk in recent years depending on coastal erosion and other changes.

When I first arrived I was told that in the autumn of 1979 cranes had turned up at Horsey and hung around during 1980 but did not attempt to nest. However, the following year they paired up and established a nest – immature birds often prospect new areas before starting re-colonisation. Cranes used to nest in small numbers in the UK more than 400 years ago but were lost because of hunting and the wetlands being drained; records show that they were eaten at medieval banquets.

The farmer who first reported the sighting telephoned the late John Buxton of Horsey Hall to say he had just seen two of the 'biggest bloody herons' he had ever seen. John guessed they were cranes. Cranes had remained reasonably common as a breeding bird in Eastern Europe and Scandinavia and in the late 1970s numbers were increasing. In autumn, some migrated to the Middle East and Africa but most flew west through Germany, France and into Spain. Happily, some migrants came to the UK and back to their former range as part of their spread further west. Since that first pair, numbers have slowly increased with around ten pairs in the Broads in recent years.

After 30 years with the RSPB, I decided to move on and I became involved with Thorpe Marshes which are under the Norfolk Wildlife Trust. The marsh lies between the tidal River Yare and the railway line that runs to Yarmouth and is owned by the Crown Point Estate. A tenant farmer, John Rushmer, was offered the grazing on Thorpe Marshes in the early 1960s and when I visited him he was in his 90s but remembered very clearly that the ungrazed marsh had been allowed to go quite rank, similar to what I first saw in the 1980s.

To farm the marsh he had the ditches dug out, installed a diesel pump to improve drainage and then ploughed the whole of the marsh. No herbicide was applied which was probably a factor in the quick recovery of the area when the farming stopped. The marsh was then sown with rye grass, cocksfoot and white clover, creating a typical sward that allowed dairy cattle to be grazed. It was a completely open landscape with just grass, some telegraph wires and cattle.

John had a milking herd of between 60 and 100 Friesians which initially did very well. However, the grazing began to deteriorate and it became difficult to manage the site. Getting cattle onto the marsh was also a challenge as the only available access was via a little crossing where he had to phone up the railway and open the gates before taking a vehicle or cattle across. There was some grazing of beef animals in the 1970s but that petered out and the marshes were effectively abandoned. Nature began re-wilding on its own. Today there are seven British Whites on the marshes which are part of the NWT's own herd of cattle. It is a traditional breed that can cope with quite rough conditions. They are quite often at Upton but are moved to other sites depending on where they are needed.

Around 1987 a planning application was made to dig gravel from the marshes at Thorpe and Whitlingham and I, along with colleagues from NWT and English Nature, commented on the after-use of the area. It was agreed that once the gravel was taken out there should be an area dedicated as a nature reserve. Gravel was taken out first on the south side of the river where Whitlingham Country Park is today but on the Thorpe side there was a bit of a gap before the nature reserve was established and taken on by NWT.

Thorpe Marshes came with a history of open access to the public and as they are located on the edge of Norwich it was an opportunity to engage people with the wildlife around them. There is an annual family fun day, monthly pond dipping in the spring and summer and I've been running monthly guided wildlife walks since 2012.

Living next to the marsh I have developed a great enthusiasm for dragonflies and damselflies and have recorded 21 species, most of which we see every year. The best known is the Norfolk hawker which can be found in most broads but are particularly numerous at Thorpe Marshes. They can be seen very easily over the ditches and alongside the paths, especially in June and early July; so water quality in the ditches is important. Occasionally you might see or hear water voles and there are otters which are rarely seen. Chinese water deer are around most of the time, usually well hidden in the vegetation.

Throughout the year there is always something of interest such as singing birds in springtime and marshland flowers, butterflies, dragonflies and damselflies in the summer. The gravel pit comes into its own during the winter, attracting wintering ducks including a good number of gadwalls, tufted ducks and pochards, and most winters a few goldeneyes join the tufted ducks.

Thorpe Marshes 1960s

Thorpe Marshes today from same viewpoint

Guided walk

Gamekeeper and conservationist

(1960s – 2015)

Joe Cullum
(b. 1945)

BUCKENHAM

Joe was a gamekeeper at Buckenham but also became very involved in conservation. He now volunteers with the Norfolk Ponds Project.

I was born in Blofield and all I wanted to do was work outside. There were three or four of us lads who were all keen fishermen and we used to go to Buckenham, Salhouse and South Walsham to catch roach, bream, pike and eels. We would fish with worms as that was all we had. I also went ferreting with my father and learned a lot about wildlife.

After various jobs I started as a part-time gamekeeper, working for Mr Key at Strumpshaw Hall estate and I got even more into wildlife. The RSPB took over in 1974 with Mike Blackburn as the first RSPB warden and I showed him around and we stayed friends. I then had the opportunity to become a full-time gamekeeper working with Bruce Giddy at Buckenham. It was such a lovely place with two beautiful broads, lots of alder, rich meadows and carr woodland. We made sure that they got better and better and Mr Giddy was really proud of the 80,000 rooks that came in to roost. We also had 15 grey herons nesting at that time but unfortunately, there are none now. He was a great conservationist as well as a shooting man.

I learned about gamekeeping from the people I mixed with. In the breeding season we would start by taking eggs and paying for them to be custom-hatched at the game farm, then taking them back as one-day-old chicks. We reared them until they were seven weeks old when they were put in release pens out in the woods. The pens had wooden posts with 10ft wire netting all around and there was a tunnel at the bottom so the birds could get in and out as they wished and we would feed them around the pen.

At that time we had roughly 3,000 pheasants and 600 partridge and we spent a lot of the day feeding them and making sure that they didn't stray. Foxes were always a problem; we were quite hard on them and went out lamping at night every week, sometimes twice a week if we were getting trouble. The other main predator was the carrion crow. We trapped a few mink in the early days but they haven't been seen lately.

We had private shoots once a fortnight and then weekly nearer the end of the season. The main season would start in September and we began with partridge and duck and then in the middle of October we were shooting pheasants. On shoot days we would organise the beaters and the picker-uppers who picked up the birds. It was important to have enough beaters and we tried to keep the same beaters doing the same job in the same part

Beaters' Day

of the wood every week, so they knew where they were going. Then at the end of the season we had what was called a 'Beaters' Day' when they would have a meal afterwards, which was really enjoyed.

There is a balance to be had between conservation and gamekeeping and the shooting funds most of the conservation. Nowadays there are grants, but in the early days the boss had to fund it himself so the two had to work together – if it wasn't for the shooting, we wouldn't have the special areas. The area is now a Site of Special Scientific Interest and a Special Protection Area.

Mr Giddy sold up around about 1990 and Mr Savory took over, and we carried on as we were and started getting a lot of help from various people including Natural England. Our projects were all to do with water in the dykes and broads. The aim was to get the water as clean as possible and stop nitrates getting in. Water was coming in through a leaky old sluice and polluting the broad from the river. The Environment Agency eventually repaired it with support from many people, and everything started to look better.

Mr Giddy had Buckenham Broad pumped out about 1980 and in 1999 the Savorys had Hassingham Broad pumped and this made a vast difference. We used diesel engine pumps on barges and winched them across the broad, backwards and forwards, taking out 6ft at a time. There was such horrible stuff in the mud that they didn't want it to pollute any more marshes so it was all put into just one marsh. As Hassingham Broad was mud pumped we started to see plants come up and with the cleaner water it became a real success story. Buckenham never had quite as many plants but it also did well.

We put grass headlands all the way around the low sides of the fields to stop nitrogen leaching into

Mud pumping, Hassingham Broad

the dykes and on into the broad. We also took out a lot of bream which were sold to Framlingham Fisheries and after that we started to see the water clearing and starting to look really nice. We put down mud traps in what we call the long meadow which helped only a bit as there was so much runoff, it just poured straight over the top, but everything does help. We also diverted some water through the meadow itself so it settled on the meadow which also helped a little. The answer is to stop soil being washed off the field in the first place. It's difficult, and you need landowners willing to do it and Natural England to fund it.

One of the successes resulting from improved water quality was the dragonflies coming back. Mike Blackburn asked if he could survey the marshes and an expert came down. As we were going around he saw a blue chaser dragonfly and got really excited as he thought of it as being rare. I told him that there were hundreds of them now. We wanted to increase the Norfolk hawkers as well and we actually put a little bit of water soldier in although we knew we shouldn't. They like clean water and they have increased tenfold and are spreading out well.

As the ecosystem improved, all sorts of plants thrived on the marshes. One of my favourites is the bog pimpernel, and there are lots of marsh

Spotted orchid

Blue chaser dragonfly

orchids, spotted orchids and ragged robin, and many other plants. We started to cut back the rough reed bed early each year and it came back well and looks really lovely. We tried to get milk parsley to grow for the swallowtail butterflies but it is really fussy. We put in hundreds of them but they stopped at six inches high when they should be four or five feet. So we have got some work to do to get them to grow properly.

One of our successes was the white admiral butterfly after we opened up areas and the sun was able to come in and the brambles started growing. Their host plant is wild honeysuckle and it's where they lay their eggs. Then the RSPB had the idea that they would like to release some great raft spiders and they laid down a bottle with an adult and babies beside the dyke. Overnight the spiders gradually went into the dyke and they have spread out all over the marsh, another success story.

For me, gamekeeping was what the job was about but I really enjoyed doing the conservation work because you can see what you are producing. I retired in 2015 and received a lifetime achievement award. I think it was because I did work hard on the water quality and we produced such varied wildlife: dragonflies, butterflies and lots of invertebrates. The RSPB has always been there for us, not that we've always agreed on things, gamekeepers and the RSPB don't always get on, but in general we had a really good setup between us.

I have worked with Dr Carl Sayer for 20-odd years and I'm now doing some work with him on the Norfolk Ponds Project which is very interesting. There is a big farm up at Heydon in North Norfolk with hundreds of little ponds overgrown with trees. We have cut down growth on the west and south sides so the sun can get in, and once the dead leaves and mud were removed we got to the clay or marl. Within a year the area was full of dragonflies and wild plants – the seeds from all those years ago were still there and they have all come back.

Ponds are important. They provide vital, clean, fresh water in the farming landscape and they can be wonderful habitats for aquatic wildlife and plants such as invertebrates, amphibians, fish, birds and mammals. Ponds provide a refuge for over two-thirds of Britain's rarest freshwater wetland invertebrates, and they provide a stepping stone allowing species to move through the landscape.

Shell man

(1940s – 2019)

Derek Howlett
(b. 1938)

ROCKLAND ST MARY

Derek collected snails and shells as a child and developed a lasting interest. Following retirement he was involved in many surveys along rivers and marshes.

When I was seven or eight I used to go down to Thorpe Marshes on the banks of the River Yare and find lots of little shells washed up on the shore. The sluice gate had a huge conglomeration of them and I used my mother's wire sieve tied onto a pole to take out sediments and sift the mud. I loved it. I saved up my pocket money to buy a copy of Edward Step's book 'Shell Life' which was illustrated with rough sketches, but I was able to identify things.

I remember having a group of river shells which I couldn't identify. It was because they were land snails that had fallen into the water and died but that did puzzle me for a considerable time. On the odd occasion that I went to the coast with my parents, I saw similar shells on the beaches, only they were much heavier and thicker than the freshwater and land snail shells I was used to. After this I started to put together a serious collection that was moth-balled for some years until the interest came to the fore again and I started acquiring shells from all over the world. They are all gone now except for a collection of Spondylus which I have hung onto because of their great beauty.

I would say shells were my top interest but I was interested in everything else, especially birds and butterflies. I used to breed butterflies: peacock, tortoiseshell and red admirals. I would find caterpillars, take them home and keep them in big bottles on my windowsill. Mother would go berserk when they got out. The caterpillars were about as thick as my finger, huge lovely things, and they were found mainly on nettles. I bred them right through and would then let 20 or 30 butterflies go. By doing this I was expanding the population as I was taking them away from predators that normally devour about 80% of them.

The number of butterflies is going down and down and what I was doing back then ought to be done by somebody now. I'm just too old to get involved anymore but if it could be done we would be able to release more of these creatures for people to enjoy.

Not very much used to happen on the marshes; cattle grazed and the old boys would check daily to see that none had fallen in the dykes. Nowadays if something stands at twelve inches high, the machinery is out to cut it down! I say, leave it alone! If you go to Rockland marsh now it has been cut to extinction and doesn't support any life. It looks like parkland and many species of butterfly that used to breed there 50 years ago are gone. They can't breed when the grass is cut and caterpillars are exposed to bad winter weather and killed.

When I finished work around 1993, I went down to Wheatfen just to help build bridges and the like – it's the best nature reserve in Norfolk without any shadow of a doubt; they may mow footpaths or cut trees if they grow into reed beds, but basically it is management through neglect. I met Roy Baker and Keith Clark there. Roy was an academic and Keith was a manager of one of the water authorities and an expert on diatoms (single-celled algae) and algae. We talked and I told them that I'd done some snail surveys for the likes of the RSPB as a volunteer.

A year later, Roy told me that they were setting up a Wheatfen Partnership to survey marshes and other places, in return for a pie and pint at lunchtime. Keith would do the diatoms, Roy the freshwater invertebrates and the writing up, and I was asked if I would do the snails. It took off and we've done surveys for every river system in Norfolk. Roy found the customers such as the former English Nature, the Environment Agency and Norfolk Wildlife Trust and the surveys were just one-offs unless we were asked to do a follow-up.

We did a five-year study of Haddiscoe Island, an island within the Norfolk Broads. We were asked to survey the salt dykes and a peripheral dyke as they were going to be re-profiled and enlarged; this was to ensure that nothing would be damaged. It was an interesting area to study as it was grazing marsh and nothing else, and there are only three or four houses. We did everything: moths, butterflies, snails, algae, invertebrates, aquatics and we also saw some unusual migrant birds and butterflies coming in. Roy has written it up and this one is our final farewell.

Spondylus

We found a very rare species of snail, Anisus vorticulus, which caused some controversy with the proposed dualling of the Acle Straight. It is one of the rarest freshwater snails in the UK but with this find, they wouldn't do the road works. We had various meetings and spoke to someone in the higher echelons to explain that as the snails were in the dykes on one side and the other side was meadow, the road could go through the meadow. We were told it couldn't be done but were never given the reason!

We have found Segmentina nitida, another very rare freshwater snail and also Corbicula fluminalis, an Asian clam, in the River Chet. We got to a point whereby, if we found a new site, we just didn't tell anyone. In doing so, we protected it. I don't know for sure but I have a feeling that when landowners find out that there is a rare snail on their land, they think it will be made a Site of Special Scientific Interest with restrictions. They don't want that so they slub out the dykes and destroy the species.

I was doing a bit of work by myself on some beaches and found another new clam called Ensis americana; it's a little razor clam that was new to this country. Everyone gets over-excited when a new species is found and they think it will take over. The American clam is semi-tolerant of slightly salty water and could be a pest if it blanketed everywhere, but it hasn't. There was also a big controversy over Himalayan balsam, a beautiful plant that is obviously alien to this country, but it has its place in my book. It flowers in September when everything else has died back, and bees like it – we do have to look after the bees.

However, people are pulling it out and destroying the nectar. I've even had someone tell me that the bees won't use it because it is poisonous for them. We've seen people tramp across everything

Anisus vorticulus

Himalayan balsam

to pull the stuff out. Not only are they destroying the nectar source but also rare snails living on the surface of the mud in between the reeds. Half the trees in this country are alien but we don't cut them down!

Thinking about what will happen in the future is a problem we're always talking about. Some youngsters are getting involved and breeding caterpillars and so on like I did and they need to be encouraged. They need to continue and really get involved. Will it happen? Every organisation is having problems attracting youngsters.

Of course things can happen when you are out in the marshes, but the main thing is to be careful and keep an eye out for what is around you, and to make sure that there is a pub nearby.

Wildlife conservation in the Broads

(1950s – 2019)

Rodney Aldis
(b. 1948)

YARE VALLEY

Rodney grew up in Brooke and discovered the River Yare at an early age. He was involved with conservation issues in Australia and today volunteers with Chet B-line and the Wild Patch project.

My brother and I were fortunate as our mother was quite prepared to let us cycle for miles; she had been free to roam around Brooke as a child and she thought it was important to let children explore their neighbourhoods. By age of seven I had found Surlingham Ferry. At the time there was a rowboat ferry there, where you could row yourself across the Yare but you had to leave a boat on either side. So you would row over, pick up a boat and tow it back before rowing over again. There was an honesty box in which to put the tuppence fare. They had the same type of ferry at Coldham Hall and I remember crossing at Surlingham and cycling to Brundall and then re-crossing at Coldham Hall. There were still freighters coming up to Norwich so you had to be watchful before you cast off.

One person I knew reasonably well was Archie Taylor. He was around 70 years old in the early 1960s and one of my uncles told me that back in the 1920s Archie was a British cycling champion. He lived by the staithe at Rockland and made his living partly by cutting reed and selling it to local thatchers, and partly by owning a number of rowboats which we used to hire as children for the sum of ten shillings. He was a really good fly-fisherman and I remember rowing down the Fleet Dyke and coming across Archie on his boat catching perch with a fly rod. Another story I heard about Archie was that when the Broads froze over, which they did frequently back in the 1930s and 40s, he could actually shoot a flying duck whilst skating on the ice!

A group of us would get a boat from Archie and row out to where the old wherries had been sunk. We'd anchor up against one of them, climb onto the hull and bob for eels inside. In the 1970s there was an unfortunate pollution spill from the May & Baker factory in Norwich and this probably made eating eels more dangerous because of the mercury in the water.

I taught for 12 years in Australia, living for a time in the Macquarie Marshes of New South Wales which had some resemblance to the Broads, in that there were large areas of open floodplain grassland grazed by cattle. Environmental change was being caused by upstream dams and the diversion of water to irrigate cotton resulting in less flow downstream and across the floodplain. This was about the same time that marshes in the Broads were being ploughed because of high wheat prices.

In both places there were big battles which eventually led to solutions to reduce environmental damage. In the Macquarie Marshes, an increase of water allocation for wildlife and a restriction on water extraction by irrigators allowed water birds to breed. On the Broads, environmental stewardship schemes were introduced with payment to farmers to keep the marshes under grass.

My recent involvement with the Norfolk Broads has been mostly through bird and breeding bird surveys as well as helping with the British Trust for Ornithology's national bird atlas. Coming back after many years away, some changes are very noticeable. One is the variety and number of birds of prey now. The marsh harrier was rare when I was a child with perhaps no more than one or two pairs around, buzzards were non-existent. I had only read about bitterns but had never actually seen or heard one.

Another change is the number of greylags and Canada geese. It was quite a novelty to see a wild goose back in the 1950s. When I was ten, I remember finding a flock of about 50 greylags near Surlingham Pistol Club on a cold, snowy day and being quite awed. I never saw otters but I have seen quite a few recently. In the 1960s we sometimes rowed down the Fleet Dyke to the river and then upstream to what is now Strumpshaw Nature Reserve and saw mostly mallards we flushed out from the dykes and reed beds.

Now that I am retired, I carry out some voluntary conservation work mainly with the South Yare Wildlife Group and the Bergh Apton Conservation Trust. Our project at the moment is to establish a pollinator corridor, or B-line, from Poringland at the head of the River Chet to its confluence with the Yare. B-lines come under Buglife, a national organisation seeking to connect habitat along river valleys and the wider landscape. The plan is to have as much pollinator-friendly habitat as possible along the Chet as insect populations are declining. Bees and hoverflies are recognised more and more as being essential for our ecosystems. So we really have got to tackle it.

My other project is also with the South Yare Wildlife Group on their Wild Patch project. In a way it led to the development of the Chet B-line. The idea behind Wild Patch is to change the mind-set of tidying the landscape, and to encourage people to let areas go a bit wild to provide more habitat for a multitude of different creatures such as beetles, bees and butterflies – most are small but they are an important part of food webs. Gardens have been a major focus for the project because that is where most people can have a direct effect. Community areas and road verges play a role too and wild patches can be part of B-lines.

As individuals we can all make a contribution but there is little point if the majority don't. Most of us can be part of making pollinator corridors a useful way to help biodiversity and help secure our food supply.

Marsh harrier

Bittern

A better future for people and wildlife

(2004 – 2019)

David North
(b. 1954)

NORFOLK WILDLIFE TRUST

David was a keen bird-watcher as a child and his skill in finding nests was highly valued by his Naturalists Club. He studied Ecology and now works with the Norfolk Wildlife Trust (NWT).

My role for the past 15 years was as Head of People and Wildlife at the NWT, an interesting role as it combines the management of both the education and engagement team and the conservation team. They both require a passion and enthusiasm for nature and the protection of Norfolk's wildlife.

The educational team delivers events during the school term and takes up to 5,000 children a year to sites like Cley Marshes, Hickling and Ranworth Broads, and Holme Dunes. We try to develop a passion, knowledge and understanding of nature in children to set them up for adulthood. During school holidays we attend big events like the Norfolk Show and small pond and dyke dipping events, and we take people rock pooling at West Runton.

Much of the work is about inspiring individuals and communities to take action for Norfolk's wildlife and we do this by taking them to wonderful places and showing them fantastic things. I have learned that people are inspired by face to face contact with people who are really enthusiastic about what they do.

I'm privileged to have been involved with two projects connected to the NWT Cley Marshes site. The first was the creation of a visitors centre around 2005/6 which has a window looking across the marshes to the sea, and from 30,000 visitors a year we now get over 100,000. Then in 2012/13 we had a project to build the Simon Aspinall Wildlife Education Centre for school events, and we also bought some land on the coast which very excitingly joined Cley Marshes with our Salthouse Marshes reserve. Both projects have been very successful.

We will carry on buying nature reserves because we need more protected sites but we need them to be bigger and preferably adjacent to existing sites because it makes them more resilient to climate change and easier to manage. NWT was the first wildlife trust to be formed in the UK and started with the purchase of Cley Marshes by the Norfolk Naturalists Trust back in 1926. There are now more nature reserves than McDonalds in the UK!

Our current project involves individual volunteer groups managing commons, village greens or

Little egrets, mallards and a heron

small sites right in the heart of a community. This is a sustainable approach to conservation and depends on us all taking small actions within our communities. The thing which unifies the projects is that they are not on reserves, they are trying to inspire communities to love sites in their own area, to visit them and look after them better. I've always been interested in how people relate to nature and I think most nature conservation problems are ultimately solved by changing human behaviour, not by sorting out the wildlife.

I think everyone realises that nature globally is in trouble. The main factors are habitat loss, climate change, pollution, non-native invasive species and over-exploitation. In terms of habitat we have lost 98% of all the original wild flower meadows that were here in Norfolk before the Second World War; agriculture has changed so meadows may look green but they are deserts for wildlife. We have also lost a lot of our heathland and common land through enclosures and that habitat loss has caused huge damage to wildlife.

Climate change is having its impact along the coast as we see more storm surges and rising sea levels causing more saline intrusions into the Broads where invasive non-native species are also a real issue. North American mink is a top predator but now control programmes are in place. A more historic example is the grey squirrel which brought in squirrel pox, so we lost our red squirrels entirely from Norfolk by the early 1970s. Also the American signal crayfish introduced crayfish plague to white-clawed crayfish, a very rare native species.

Not all non-native species are bad however, and today some are valued as almost conservation allies. It's now thought that rabbits were first introduced by the Romans rather than the Normans but, because they are good heathland browsers, they have become important to the ecology of the reserves in the Brecks. Non-native species can also adapt to climate change in some cases; breeding spoonbills are back on the North Norfolk coast and they feed on Hickling Broad and the Potter Heigham marshes. Little egrets are everywhere now not just along the coast and the Broads – when I was a teenager I had to travel to the Camargue in the south of France to see my first little egret. Mediterranean gulls have sites on the North Norfolk coast and I think Titchwell has over a 100 breeding pairs. So, given half a chance, wildlife is very adaptable and very resilient.

Hummingbird hawk moth taking nectar from red valerian

During the last Ice Age as the climate cooled, species were able to move south. Then, as the climate warmed 12,000 years ago, habitats re-established themselves and species were able to move back north. They could do it because they could move through a connected countryside. When we have isolated nature reserves, the rare species that require a specialist habitat die out if conditions change or there's a bad winter or a disease. There is no chance for that habitat to be recolonised.

NWT works in conjunction with farmers to help improve the long-term outlook of nature and we have a national project called 'Living Landscapes' through which we can offer advice. We need farmers to create more special, semi-natural habitats and we are keen to work with them through some of the environment farm payments schemes. We also need to find a balance whereby farmers still make money whilst creating a benevolent environment for wildlife. The NWT project with farmers can be seen as a win-win situation as most small farmers have diversified these days and are not just producing food.

Farmers have always been the guardians of the countryside in many ways but nevertheless we have lost wildlife. About 80% of Norfolk has intensive arable farmland with wheat, barley, sugar beet and rape, so we need to create field margins for pollinators and look after our ponds which are often scrubbed over and dried out. We need to restore some balance in those habitats because, if we are not careful, broads could become ghettos for wildlife surrounded by intensive farmland, developed land, towns or roads. Wildlife needs to be able to move through the countryside which means that connectivity between areas is important, particularly as a response to climate change.

We also need a balance between tourism and wildlife. People want to come to the Norfolk Broads and the North Norfolk coast because of their wonderful natural beauty and it brings huge benefits to the local economy. It is important to work with the tourist industry and I believe they have a responsibility to help protect the environment. Ultimately we all depend on the health of natural systems for clean air, for our well-being and our health. Nature is part of our fundamental quality of life, so I say that we all have a responsibility to do our bit to work in harmony with nature and help look after the planet, because that is our life-support system.

In many of our intensive arable fields there are virtually no earthworms because of pesticides and herbicides. Wild flowers are mostly confined to our roadside verges, protected sites and nature reserves. When we start losing wild flowers, we lose insects and then our birds. Globally, there has been a huge loss of insect life, perhaps 50% in 50 years. Lose pollinators and we lose our food supply. So these are serious issues and I believe we can all take action as individuals but equally we need governments to make the right policy decisions to protect the wildlife.

We are the first generation in human history to be aware of the scale of impact that humanity is having on global natural systems and we are the last generation in human history that can really get things right. We really need to change the way we do things so that we are living more sustainable lifestyles. I think there is still time to do it but it is urgent, and it's important for the future of not just the Norfolk Broads but for the future of our children and their children.

Humanity has gone through two massive revolutions that have changed the way everyone lives on this planet. The first was an agricultural revolution 10-12,000 years ago when we started farming and it led on to the growth of cities and specialisation. The second was the industrial revolution led by Britain in the 18th and 19th centuries which eventually changed the way everyone lives on the planet. Now we need a third revolution – a sustainability revolution.

I believe we need to keep optimistic because it's only when we believe change and a better future are possible for both wildlife and people that we will make it happen. So I'm a great believer in optimism, even though I struggle with it sometimes.

Preserving the fish stock

(1990 – 2019)

Steve 'Budgie' Burgess
(b. 1960)

HORNING

Steve was a fisheries manager in Kent and visited the Broads to pursue his love of pike fishing. He now works in Horning and campaigns for the preservation of pike stocks.

Angling has been a lifetime interest for me and as Norfolk is renowned as a great area for pike fishing, I came most winters for 30 years. Even when I lived in France I would come back and live on my boat for the winter period. In about 2013 we decided to settle in Horning where we run a tackle shop and we are lucky to have two seasons – casual anglers and general coarse fishermen come in the summer and in winter we are at our busiest as we specialise in predator fishing.

Fishing in the Broads has always had a troubled history. Back in the 1960s, fishing was almost wiped out by a Prymnesium parvum outbreak which is algae that becomes toxic as it decays. Luckily, the fish gradually came back thanks to people like John Curry from the Pike Anglers Club working with organisations such as the John Innes Centre to find a way to combat the problem. The algae thrive on higher saline levels but researchers found that using hydrogen peroxide counteracts the effect, and they liaised with organisations including the Broads Authority (BA) to remedy the situation. The BA's involvement is primarily because when they dredge, it can stir up the spores and cause another outbreak, so they carry hydrogen peroxide now.

Over the years the Broads have been sinking and become more susceptible to salt incursions. This is because the three main rivers on the Northern Broads, the Thurne, the Bure and the Ant are semi-tidal, and in the past five or six years, there has been an increase in the regularity and extremes of these salt surges resulting in salt water being pushed further up the rivers.

Many people will say that we have always had these sorts of surges and that is true, but this is a tidal system not an estuarine system, it is not meant to be salt water. The normal extent of the surges is around Acle where we regularly experience high fish deaths. But in recent years, salt levels have reached lethal limits as far up as here in Horning. It has become a regular 'freak occurrence'. Any increase results in fish deaths but only if the fish can't escape as fish will try and move ahead of any surge. This is changing the behaviour and location of the fish and it is also affects fishing.

I understand that something like 60 different types of small invertebrates and crustaceans have been lost because saline levels are now too high for them. Because they are at the bottom of the food chain there is a knock-on effect as we go up the chain, so the whole ecosystem of the Broads is changing. It is now believed that the way to combat it is by installing a device known as a slipper dam down at Yarmouth, basically a barrier to stop the tide surges pushing up the Bure. There were concerns that this could impede navigation but it is like an inflatable tube that boats can just go over, so it should not be a problem.

A few decades ago it was decided to reintroduce the European otter which had become almost extinct mostly because of ecological change and hunting. It seemed a great idea at first but, in my opinion, the process was rushed as instant success was needed to help secure future funding; it has been acknowledged by the Otter Trust

Dawn on the River Bure

that perhaps they didn't get it right. Areas which never had otters suddenly had 30 or 40 pairs and that has had an impact on the system. Otters are voracious predators not only of fish but have been filmed taking swans and ducklings, especially in the Wroxham area. This is nature but there has to be a balance.

Otters have a reputation that they kill for fun, but they don't. They undoubtedly do eat pike; I have seen them with pike between 8-12lb which is obviously far more than they need, but it's believed that they take that size because it is easier to catch. The good thing is that otters kill mink which are the real villains of the Broads.

Coarse fish has never been part of the UK diet. It is a tradition amongst English anglers that even though we are allowed to kill fish, we don't; it is a sport and we return them to the water. Over the last few years there have been changes to fishing as East European anglers have brought their tradition of having coarse fish as part of their diet. It causes friction amongst the communities which is a shame. There are three types of fishermen in the Broads: those who fish for sport; those who fish more for the pot; and a third element which is the real problem, the criminal element who want to take as much as they can to sell. Again this is having an effect on fish stocks as pike is the preferred fish.

For me though, as an angler, the most frustrating reason why predators such as pike are in decline is, quite simply, angling pressure. No matter how responsible we are with the way we catch, handle and then return them, it is pressure. And like a lot of creatures they thrive on neglect, they want to be left alone. Pike have a reputation based mostly on their rather fearsome looks but they are very delicate and are affected by ecological change. I suppose in a way anglers could be considered to be selfish wanting to protect the pike because of our desire to catch it. It is the need for balance again.

Pike is the apex predator serving an important role in removing sick and weak fish. Breeding levels are dictated by the apex predator and without them all the prey fish will get out of balance and there would be too many non-predators such as bream, roach and rudd. Indeed we are seeing this already; people catch nets full of these fish and think the Broads must be healthy. They also claim to see pike all the time, forgetting that what they are seeing and catching are small pike because there is a shortage of bigger breeding fish. No-one really knows at this stage whether this is due to otters, salt surges or something else, but having mainly small pike is a sign of an unhealthy and unbalanced system. We have seen a big decline especially over the last five or six years.

When I first started campaigning, a lot of the old boys didn't believe there was a problem but now they are agreeing that there is. The only reason I saw it first is because I'm out on the river most days whereas they are fishing once every couple of weeks. Now, even the most diehard say that if we have to stop pike fishing for three or four years to let stocks recover, then so be it. However, there are worries from the commercial side who are concerned that people won't want to come if they can't fish for pike.

Pike

In the summer the broads are shallow and the water warms up very quickly; the higher the temperature the less dissolved oxygen there is in the water. Normally this is not a problem as fish will stay inactive and feed as needed. But when an angler catches a fish it could be on the end of the line for 20 minutes, exerting itself and reaching a different level of exhaustion. When the fish is unhooked and returned, it is put back into the margins where there is not enough oxygen for it to recover properly. Anglers don't realise this, they will hold them, nurse them and think that they are recovered, but they are not, and many will die some 12 to 15 hours later.

On an average 100m stretch of the Bure there will be many thousands of roach but only one or two pike so it only takes a few pike to be caught and die to see the effect. It is very difficult to persuade holiday-makers that what they are doing is detrimental. There is no law in place in the Broads; it is not controlled by fishing clubs and there are no restrictions other than the normal close season. Practically everywhere else in the country that is run by fishing clubs, summer pike fishing is not allowed. This ban is something that people have been trying to bring in here for some time and now that all the research has been done, we are close to it being accepted.

Convincing local business owners that it won't affect their businesses is something that I have been involved with. Having a business based on pike fishing has helped people relate to me as I can say, 'Guys, all you're doing is killing the golden goose. Let people fish pike in the summer for the next couple of years and there won't be any pike fishing here for the next 20 years'.

We have to look to the long-term future. The people who take a chalet in the summer could go bream and roach fishing and the guy who wants to fish for pike can be advised to come in November and December. By actually accepting and supporting the summer ban, businesses will give themselves an extra season and that's what happens here at the tackle shop. All summer long I have customers buying half a pint of maggots for catching roach. Then as soon as October comes I am selling to guys coming down for pike fishing, hiring boats or coming out with us for a day's instruction.

It is not a good picture for the Broads at the moment, be it for water birds, pike, fish, crustaceans and invertebrates because of changes in salinity. Every year we have massive salt surges and we get away with it, one day we won't. And then it'll all be over. My background in fisheries management does tell me one worrying thing… normally by the time the problem is so great that people notice it, it is often too late to do anything about it.

I certainly don't want to see the end of fishing, boating or sailing. In my view the BA is there to do one thing, look after the Broads, and the way they fund that is by things like boat tolls, so I have no issue with that. If it means that we have to have certain bans brought in to restrict pike fishing, then so be it. If I can only go fishing once a month but it means my great-great-grandchildren can go once a month as well, I'll have that – rather than me going every day, and they lose out.

Looking backward from forward

(1973 – 2050)

Tim O'Riordan
(b. 1942)

NORWICH

Tim is Emeritus Professor of Environmental Sciences at UEA and has been interested in ecological issues facing the Broads since the 1960s. He gives an historical perspective and also looks ahead.

Things started to change in the Broads after we joined the European Common Market in 1973. Farming subsidies associated with drainage and increased production were introduced and a number of farmers in the Broads area switched from grazing marsh, with a high water table, to a much lower water table for arable farming. Once pumps were subsidised, big electric pumps dramatically increased drainage compared to the old coal and diesel systems.

At the same time we began to realise that wildlife, and particularly the plant life of dykes in the Broads, was very varied, and that some species, especially the stonewort, were of international importance. It was clear that because farmers needed to keep the dyke systems open in the 1960s, they had safeguarded the rich diversity of plant life and consolidated what was already a very rich ecological treasure trove.

Then water companies began building larger sewage treatment works in places such as North Walsham and Stalham. Their main pollutant was a phosphate which underwent a secondary rather than a tertiary treatment which would have removed it, but in those days this was seen as too expensive. Also, the link between phosphate addition and loss of plant life, the so-called eutrophication transition, was not fully known. A huge transformation took place between 1972 and 1978 when virtually all the plant life died in the main broads – it was that quick.

My late colleague at UEA, Brian Moss, did a huge amount of work and showed the direct link between sewage treatment works, phosphate build-up and loss of plant life, and he proved it by creating exclusion zones. Essentially, big rubber cylindrical exclusion mats were placed on some broads to keep phosphate out of the protected areas and allow natural regeneration. Patches of wonderful plant life were re-created, while the rest of the broads were an ecological desert full of algae, which are microphytes.

When tertiary treatment plants were put in at Barton Broad and Stalham, phosphate levels dropped significantly, and it was hoped that Barton Broad areas would return to something like a wildlife paradise. In fact, it did not. We discovered it was because phosphates had got into the sediment from the decaying algae and were being recycled by boat and tidal movement stirring up the mud.

The decision was taken to dredge out the excess sediment and put it in big holding areas beside the broad – an extremely expensive process. Then exclusion zones were put around the dredged areas to see whether that would aid the return of the desired plant life. The answer was yes it did, partially, but not completely.

Between 1972 and 1987 three things became clear. Firstly, broads could from time to time restore themselves given the right degree of phosphate control, dredging and exclusion. Secondly, to do

Cockshoot Broad

this would require constant maintenance and would be very expensive and the returns, quite frankly, were really not worth it from the point of view of the ecology of the nation. Thirdly, once you have a rich and varied ecology system that has broken down, getting it back to anything like its natural state is virtually impossible and requires a huge amount of effort over a long period of time – it is not practical to do.

We concluded there were only three things that we could do. One was to treat some smaller broads through dredging and exclusion zones, and Cockshoot Broad, just off the River Yare, was one of the test cases. Despite all the work it has not restored itself, and it proved that ecological restoration is a mug's game and takes too long, with uncertain outcomes. That being said there are still schemes for the restoration of essentially private or non-navigable broads to see if they can be brought back to life; Hoveton Great Broad is an example of where a lot of work is being done.

Tactic two was to safeguard plant life in drainage ditches, particularly in the margins where pure water from the fields came through springs rather than runoff from the surface. At the margins of these areas there was a large amount of natural regeneration of extremely varied and famous plant life like Potamageton and water soldier. As a result it was seen that we ought to have sites of special scientific interest imposed on those dykes that had the greatest chance of staying in their rich natural state. This still required maintenance.

This led to the third stage and was known as the Halvergate Marsh debate. Should we be paying farmers to restore nature and maintain an already highly resilient system, or pay them to destroy it with drainage and conversion to agriculture, and essentially removing anything remotely resembling interesting plant life? A big battle took place between 1981 and 1985.

In 1981 the Wildlife and Countryside Act was passed which ruled that if a farmer wanted to drain

Water soldier

A marsh dyke

land and was impeded from doing so because of wildlife interest, then the Nature Conservancy Council, later to become English Nature, was required to pay the farmer the equivalent of what was lost in revenue. In effect, farmers were to be paid not to plant wheat, when the wheat was not necessary and was an unreliable crop, as these are not naturally fertile areas. Farmers were to receive huge amounts of money for doing nothing. By definition, it was only the wealthy farmers with the resources, technology, tractors and drainage systems that would benefit and could use the system to their advantage, whereas the most deserving landscape farmers got nothing.

So in 1983 a group of us went to the government and argued that we should not be paying farmers not to produce with huge subsidies from the conservation purse – that was an outrage! Rather, we should have the agricultural purse investing in better management of the dykes and elsewhere for the enhancement of nature, the landscape, and the traditions of the open marshes.

That led, in 1985, to a trial scheme called The Broads Marsh Conservation Scheme, which was a joint investment between the Countryside Commission and the Ministry of Agriculture, Fisheries and Food (MAFF). It was brokered by the Nature Conservancy Council and was a very successful programme, largely because it was run by field officers who knew and understood farmers and could bring them into the system. Farmers were given a flat payment per hectare, per year, for maintaining the dykes – for as long as they maintained them.

Most of the farmers were tenants of land often owned by distant landowners. The tenants were regulars who came back every year and the landowners were, by and large, in favour of the scheme as they were not interested in making lots of money, they just liked the marshes. The deal was a good one at the time – it guaranteed extra income that farmers referred to as 'back pocket payment'. From this came an important piece of legislation and the introduction of Environmentally Sensitive Areas (ESAs), which were areas protected by MAFF, Nature Conservancy and the landowning authority.

The Broads grazing marshes became part of the Broads ESA in 1986 and it ran very successfully until 2006. There was also a lot of investment in conservation enhancement in the 1980s and 90s funded by the EU, the UK and the Broads Authority (BA). Aitken Clark, the BA chief executive at the time, felt that the Broads would be better protected if it was recognised as part of an international wetland complex, and I think that he singlehandedly created an unstoppable commitment to the Broads and the enhancement of its natural world. In an area that was primarily boating, he managed to find a way to keep the boating and conservation interests closely allied.

These approaches worked well until 1999, when a test case came about because of the Sandford Clause in the National Parks Act of 1995. This had laid down how far conservation should trump any other aspect of use, particularly public enjoyment and economic activity. A lot of control over public use resulted from that legislation. The battle between conservation and boating interests came to a head in the Hickling Broad area in 1999 with the unexplained appearance of vast quantities of the stonewort species, Chara intermedia, an internationally-recognised endemic species. These outbreaks are a sign of benign ecological conditions and do not last for too long unless protected in some way.

The outbreak led English Nature to stop boating on Hickling Broad as the chara was taking over the area. There was an outcry from the boating interests which included people who sailed in big races and had big clubs. Aitken Clark set up the Upper Thurne Working Group to see how this could be best managed with selective cutting. About 6% was removed which was about a tenth of what the boating interest wanted but twice what should have been done from the conservation point of view.

The group managed, slowly, to build a coalition between boating, the parishes, the BA, conservation bodies and the Norfolk Wildlife Trust who owned Hickling Broad. I was asked to be the chair and I did that from 1999 until 2015. Over time it has become a very constructive body for bringing together the interests around the whole of the Upper Thurne catchment area. Chara has re-emerged three or four times since 1999 but we have always found a way around it, helped by excellent consultation and monitoring processes undertaken by the BA, Natural England and the Environment Agency. We have also done a lot of dredging and re-management so the area is now much better for both boating and conservation.

Chara intermedia

I think our biggest success was our involvement with the parishes and holding meetings in the parishes with local people, as they are behind the economic activity that makes a small village tick, like the restaurants and bed and breakfasts. The working group now has a website and it has led to a greater recognition that with good consultation and well-monitored scientific activity, we can manage plant life even when it is highly sensitive, internationally important and highly connected to boating.

The issue of drainage, which is still ongoing, is much less manageable, as is the increase of nitrogen emissions from overly intensive farming. With grazing marshes you get very little runoff but when marshes are drained, as in much of the Upper Thurne area, you have two side-effects – one is nutrient-rich water from the fertilisers and the other is that these soils have ochre. Ochre is a ferric hydroxide iron product that is a bright orange sediment that colours the ditches and has a negative effect on wildlife, particularly damsel- and dragonflies. It also clogs up the drainage systems. It is a real problem and one which we haven't completely resolved.

However, there has been positive change in the last ten years and water management boards have become much more environmentally sensitive and supportive. They are more consultative and are really careful with the management of water drainage. They have better protection now for areas likely to suffer from too-deep drainage, nitrogen emission and, above all, ochre emissions. We are not there yet but at least we have a better arrangement, with more experimentation and a huge improvement in consultation and research.

The final bit of the story is the threat of climate change causing rising sea levels, and changes to the Norfolk coastline. The Norfolk coast is eroding at the far north-eastern tip around Happisburgh but if you go west from there, towards Scolt Head Island in Kings Lynn, Brancaster and Blakeney, it is accreting, because the sediment is moving west. Going south towards Great Yarmouth and Lowestoft it is also accreting, but much more variably, as the east side is more susceptible to storms.

In some parts of Norfolk, just north of Great Yarmouth and Hemsby, there has been loss of property with houses falling onto the beach. Storms can take sand and sediment out but this natural movement is suffocated by sea walls or off-shore reefs as in the case of Sea Palling, and this has led to a reconsideration of what we could do with the Norfolk coast and the Norfolk Broads.

The big challenge is that some areas will be protected simply because they are too important to lose, and the most important is the gasworks at Bacton: a huge national asset. It will be safeguarded but Shell will actually pay for much of it. The proposal is to put sediment-rich new sand in front of the Bacton plant and to do it on a five-yearly basis forever, a process known as seascaping. There will also be a lot of investment in coastal protection where there is significant or high-value coastal property and particularly where there are high numbers of people and housing such as around Great Yarmouth and Lowestoft.

More sparsely populated areas have a much less certain future. For the time being it is thought that areas which are Broads-related, such as around Winterton and Horsey, will continue to get sand. The Environment Agency has said that it plans to keep up the sand/sediment combination for at least another 25 years and probably 50. It will cost about £2,000,000 a year and raises the question of what the cost benefit will be and whether it can be done forever? This is relevant especially if the tides start to rise when we get strong storms.

Storm surge is the number one problem, not sea level rise. This is when you get a huge volume of water building up in the southern North Sea, up to three or four metres high, and in extreme cases it absolutely hammers anything in its way. All existing walls, defences and banks are knocked about. It doesn't matter how much you invest in coastal protection, a big storm will take them out and then the question is whether you rebuild or not. The last big storm was December 2013; it thrashed the north and east coasts and it took Yarmouth to within a few centimetres of being flooded. If the wall had been overtopped 4,500 homes would have been under water.

This shows how vulnerable the system is, and the chances of a recurrence in the next ten years are very high; we could very likely have a couple of them. This raises the question of how long we can maintain the Broads, which are artificially protected, and how much we should use a more flexible approach, which would carry huge risks for the ecology and the coastal scene.

The line right now is to stay as we are because (a) there is no public appetite for a sudden change; (b) the country does not have the resources for it right now; and (c) it is too early for a really combined public commitment. Specialist interests,

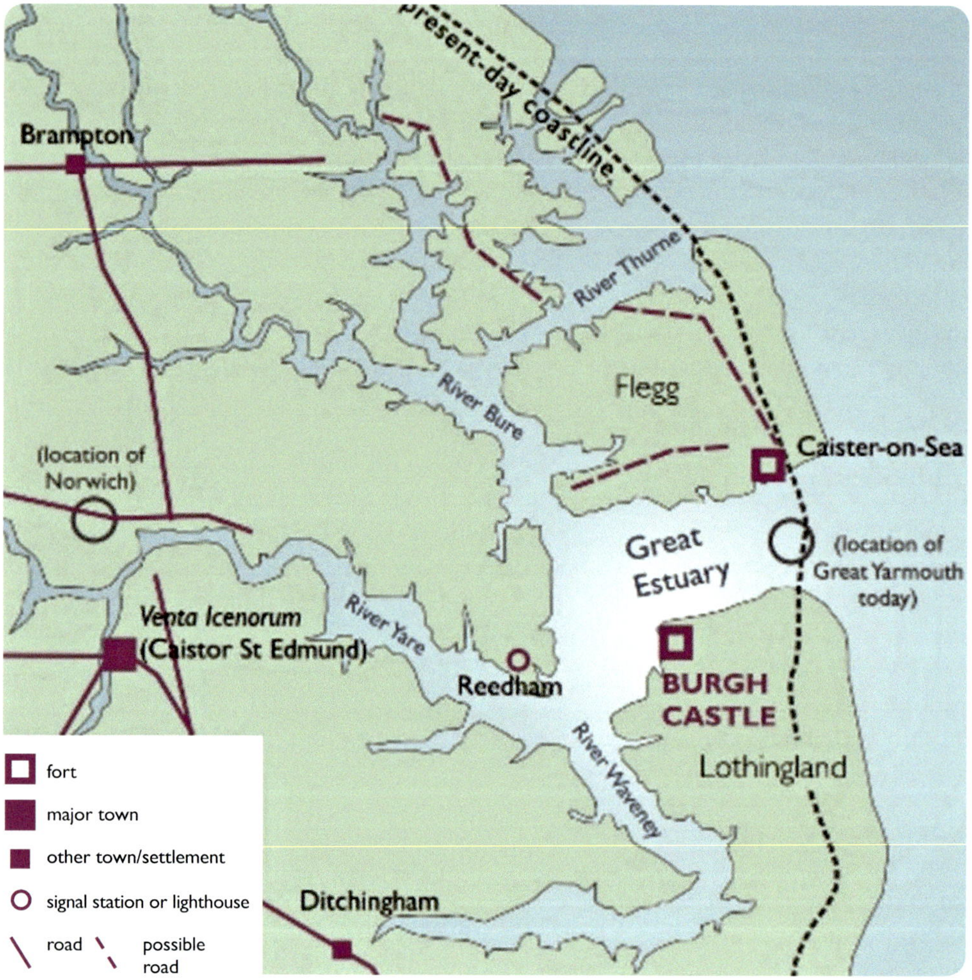

The Great Estuary 3rd to 4th centuries AD

researchers and coastal managers might say that we will have to let things go over a period of time, but when it comes to restaurateurs, holiday accommodation and communities like Walcott and Sea Palling, the idea of losing them is still politically very difficult, even though they are very small in terms of the economy.

So we are in limbo. For at least another 10–15 years we will restore, unless there is a massive storm on the scale of half as much again as the 1953 flood, which was 20–30% more than what we had in the 2013 storm. It is a possibility, and it would mean a major reconsideration of the Norfolk coast. It is one of the quirks of human nature that we actually have to wait for an event to happen, as nothing is done based on prediction. Then we say, 'I told you so'.

There is a slow recognition that the sea is beginning to rise into the water table on the east coast of Norfolk which brings the problem of salt intrusion. This, along with plant life protection and better drainage is a concern for the Hickling area. The coastal drains are becoming saltier and over time it is going to be almost impossible to stop. We then only have two options. The first is to start building a Roman-type edge to some of the broads with much more salt marsh – it could involve some very sophisticated pumping and the potential for big carbon sequestration. I think this is most likely over the next 10–15 years with the new water management body overseeing four or five trial schemes on the east Norfolk coast. A longer-term possibility would be some kind of tidal protection barrier at the mouth of the Yare – not necessarily at the sea edge as that would take out the whole of Yarmouth's harbour. It could be in the river corridor but this option has three big questions which have not been resolved as yet.

Firstly, exactly where should it be, what should it be protecting against and what do you do about the downstream area when the barrier is up against a very high tide with strong winds? Secondly, if the barrier goes down what do you do about the ecosystems which depend on flushing? We already have the problem of nitrogen build-up. I don't think we have got our heads around what would happen if ecosystems were polluted or important riverside developments such as Horning or Brundall became significantly flooded as a result of a Yare barrier.

The third issue is that a barrier might cause the end of anything called the Norfolk Broads, and by 2075 and beyond, the Broads could become a wetland again. It would mean that the cities and bigger communities would stay but a lot of the smaller ones would progressively have to be abandoned by 2100 – we do have to think in the longer-term. So there is an issue that the Broads could turn full circle in the lifetime of people being born today with a return to a version of the Roman scene – some protected areas, a new ecology and considerably more wetland than now.

That is likely to be the long-term prospect but we're not designing for it right now. Instead we are designing an expensive, utterly futile half-way house. We are creating more wetland and investing more in its management to keep the macrophytes going. We are pumping like crazy to keep the sea down but all of this is increasingly expensive and increasingly futile. It is almost a case of, 'This is what we have to do because that is what the public expects'. But somewhere down the line we will have to give way. It would take just one massive catastrophic event which may well occur between now and 2050, and possibly by 2025, to make us reconsider what to do about the Broads.

Personally, I think we need more genuinely constructed debate amongst people, and we should start to design our coastal and riverside systems so we don't feel that we are doing nothing. A much more innovative, integrated and progressive approach to the whole concept of land and water management and the enhancement of nature is needed.

There will be big changes in the agricultural financial system as the farming community from 2020 will get less of a guaranteed payment. Many studies have found that by 2025 to 2027 around a third of farming communities in Norfolk will be significantly affected and will lose around a third of farm income, meaning that farmers will either have to produce more or earn less.

What will happen to these farms? One possibility is some form of 'nature endowment farming' requiring much more focus upon water management and conservation. We are a very dry area and over the course of time we will suffer greatly from drought and heat. The winter of 2018-2019 was one of the driest on record and with hot dry summers there is a chance that we will run out of water for agricultural use on a regular basis. Along with water resource planning and reservoirs in farming areas, the public will be encouraged to use less water and utilise more waste water in their homes. All this is likely to become commonplace by 2030 and houses will be built with this in mind – they should already have been built like this!

Another exciting idea is an economy based on some variant of 'nature's endowment and services'. For example, we might recreate peat areas and create more wetland and reed beds for carbon sequestration. There is also the possibility of having a more localised agricultural economy, with farmland being rented out to communities like Stalham or North Walsham for community allotments based on organic systems. From an economic point of view the farmers gain a lot, and from an agricultural and food point of view, the community gains.

I can't imagine a world where we won't have much more localised food production by 2050, or even 2025. This is partly because food will not be moved around in the same way as before and partly because of the push to get away from livestock production.

In the next 20 years, I foresee a shift of agriculture within Norfolk and elsewhere, towards organic grass-fed livestock as a specialist and high-end product, with more people utilising vegetable-based food which is locally produced. I think that the outcomes of Brexit together with climate change and the need to recreate some kind of natural system, will require us to enhance these opportunities. If we don't, we are going to be in deep trouble.

I do think that a very relevant part of oral history is to view history from the future, a reflection of how we perceive ourselves in, say, 30 years, in 2050. Won't they be saying, 'Why did you wait so long?' I think this will be spelt out by our own children and their children. 'Why did you take so long to get your head around this world, because it has gone to pieces? You knew all this and you did nothing about it...'

Image credits

Some images have been supplied by WISEArchive and the contributors to this book. Licensed Shutterstock images have been used. All other images are credited below.

CONSERVATION & ECOLOGY

Glossary

AI Centre Artificial Insemination Centre

Allen scythe a petrol-powered mower

Anderson shelter used to protect from bomb blasts during the war

Archimedes screw pump machine to transfer water from one level to another and into ditches

Argocats semi-amphibious, all-terrain vehicles

Babbing fishing for eels using bait and no hook

Baulk of timber beam of roughly-squared timber

BEM British Empire Medal

Binder used to cut and bind cereals

Bittern (1) small Norfolk dinghy (2) bird belonging to heron family

Bob a shilling in old currency (slang)

Bowsprit a large spar projecting forward from the prow of a ship

Brotch 2ft-long wooden staple used in thatching

CAD computer-aided design

Caen stone French limestone used after the Norman Conquest in 1066 for major buildings

Carvel-built hull planks laid edge to edge and fastened to a frame to form a smooth surface

Catamaran boat with two similar parallel hulls

Chain unit of measurement equal to 66ft or 20.1168m

Clinker-built hull planks edges overlapped and fixed to a frame; traditional method

CNC computer numerical control used to convert CAD design into numbers

Coaster shallow-hulled ships used to carry goods along the coast

Copper large vessel for heating water

Covering board curved plank around the deck edge; painted white on wherries for visibility

Coypu large South American herbivorous, semi-aquatic rodent

Cran a measure used for herring – 37½ gallons or 28 stone (Cran Measures Act 1908)

Crome a rake with strong curved tines

Crotch wood where a trunk/branch splits to form a Y

Cuddy cabin

Cut canal e.g. Haddiscoe Cut between Reedham and St Olaves

Deek an alternative word for dyke

Didal triangular spade used to clear ditches

Dinghy small sailing boat

Drosstone machine used in the early method of spraying on fibreglass

Dydle scoop for clearing mud from a ditch

EDP Eastern Daily Press

ESA Environmentally Sensitive Area

Fathom of reed six bundles of reed, 6ft long

FHDS Farm & Horticulture Development Scheme

Foot drain 1ft-wide drain used on marshes

Ft/foot/feet 1ft = 30cm or 12 inches/12"

Foul-foot/foul-in-the-foot an acute, highly infectious foot rot in cattle

Gaia Theory hypothesis which views the earth as a single organism

GPO General Post Office

GRP glass reinforced plastic

Grup mud/muck in the bottom of the ditch

Half decker open day boat

Harnser heron (Norfolk)

Herringbone parlour milking parlour with milking machines down the middle and two aisles

HLS Higher Level Stewardship

Hydrological modelling a system to monitor water flow and quality

Inch 1" or in – see also ft/foot/feet

In stick sticks or splines between planks to enable them to air-dry

Iroko teak substitute

Jolly boat small sail boat used for sheltered waters

Keel early Broads trading vessel; Middle Ages

kV kilovolt or 1000 volts

Leat mill dyke supplying water to a mill or its mill pond

Level area of marshland drained by a mill

Ligger plank of wood across a dyke (Norfolk)

Lighters flat-bottomed barges, often old wherries

Linnaean System system of classifying and naming organisms; after Carolus Linnaeus

Lofting drafting technique where curved lines are drawn for use in plans for boats

Lug sail a four-cornered sail suspended from a spar

Macrophytes a general term for aquatic plants

Microphytes single-cell organisms found in fresh and salt water; algae

Meg/Meag long pole with a scythe on the end

Mendelism the theory of genetic inheritance formulated by Gregor Mendel

Mill race/mill run current of water turning a water wheel or the channel of water to or from the wheel

MTB motor torpedo boat

Mud pumping process of dredging waterways

Mycology study of fungi

Ocarina ancient wind musical instrument

One Design a class that consists of just one model or design

Poor Trusts charities established after the 1811 Enclosure Act to aid parishioners in need

Post mill earliest English mill, 12-19th centuries; mill's body is mounted on a single post which is turned to bring the sails into the wind

Post mill with roundhouse protects the exposed trestle supporting the post and provides storage space

Quant long pole used to move a wherry

RCD Recreational Craft Directive

Rond area of low lying land between the river and floodbank, reeds grow and help protect against erosion (Norfolk)

RPM revolutions per minute

Shilling 1 shilling or 1s = 12 pence or 12d; £1 = 20s; old currency

Soke dyke ditch running parallel to a river to take any water seeping through

Slub out clear out the ditches (Norfolk)

Smock mill Herringfleet Mill (Suffolk) is the last full-height example in the Broads and has a typical wooden, octagonal body; the name derives from the smock worn by farmers in earlier times

SPA Special Protection Area

Spline piece of wood placed between planks to allow air-drying

SSSI Site of Special Scientific Interest

Staithe wharf where wherries loaded and unloaded; now used for mooring boats

Swathe cutting reed to lie evenly in one direction

Tilley light versatile paraffin pressure lamp

Tower mill brick built; 19th century; requires only the cap to rotate

YBOD Yare and Bure One-Design boat

Wale single/double reed beds cut every year or every two years

Weavers Way 61-mile walk between Cromer and Great Yarmouth

Wherry traditional cargo boat on the Broads

Wherryman's Way 35 miles of walks between Norwich and Great Yarmouth

Whiteclawed crayfish Britain's only native crayfish species and largest freshwater invertebrate

Wildfowling shooting ducks, geese, or other waterfowl for food and sport

Yard 1 yd = 0.9144m, 3ft or 36"

Zoonosis disease that can be transmitted to humans from animals

Index

G

H

I

K

L

M

N